RELIGION, REVOLUTION,

AND REGIONAL CULTURE IN

EIGHTEENTH-CENTURY FRANCE

The Ecclesiastical Oath of 1791

TIMOTHY TACKETT

PRINCETON UNIVERSITY PRESS

Copyright © 1986 by Princeton University Press
Published by Princeton University Press,
41 William Street, Princeton, New Jersey 08540
In the United Kingdom: Princeton University Press,
Guildford, Surrey

ALL RIGHTS RESERVED
Library of Congress Cataloging in Publication Data will be found
on the last printed page of this book

ISBN 0-691-05470-3

This book has been composed in Linotron Granjon

Clothbound editions of Princeton University Press books
are printed on acid-free paper, and binding materials
are chosen for strength and durability

Printed in the United States of America
by Princeton University Press
Princeton, New Jersey

Pour Grégory et Nicolas

Table of Contents

PART THREE
FRENCHMEN CONFRONT THE OATH

List of Tables

List of Figures

Preface

The central concern of the present study is a single "event" of sorts: the loyalty oath to the French constitution imposed on all parish clergymen during a few brief weeks at the beginning of 1791. As such, it is a contribution to the rehabilitation of the event—or, at any rate, of a certain variety of event—as a legitimate subject of historical inquiry.[1] For the oath of 1791 was undoubtedly a critical turning point not only in the French Revolution but in modern French history as well. It was one of those very particular kinds of historical happenings, with the potential for sharply jolting the whole historical landscape, for thrusting into prominence long-developing features of a new political and mental topography, and perhaps also for creating new fissures of its own across that landscape. A study of the antecedents and circumstances surrounding this occurrence can help us reflect on the extent to which the *political* and *social* revolutions which swept over France at the end of the eighteenth century may also have marked a *cultural* revolution.

The problem of a cultural revolution after 1789 is not new. But insofar as the question has been posed, it has usually led to considerations concerning France as a whole and the extent to which entire social groups may have been affected by cultural continuity or discontinuity.[2] The present study, however, can lend itself to a somewhat different approach. As the reader will soon discover, one of the key areas of focus is the *region*: the proportion of clergymen accepting or rejecting the oath in the various districts or departments or provinces of the country. It is evident that there was nothing ephemeral about these regional patterns of oath-taking. In fact, the map of clerical reactions in 1791 was remarkably similar to the map of religious practice in the middle of the twentieth

---

[1] See, for example, Michel Vovelle, "L'événement dans l'histoire des mentalités," in *Idéologies et mentalités* (Paris, 1982), 321-24.

[2] See, notably, Philippe Goujard and Claude Mazauric, "Dans quel sens peut-on dire que la Révolution française fut une révolution culturelle?" *Europa. Revue d'études interdisciplinaires*, 2 (1978), 35-65. Also Emmet Kennedy, "Toward a Cultural History of the French Revolution," paper presented at the meeting of the American Historical Association, Washington, D.C., December 1980.

century.[3] It was also similar, in many respects, to the political geography of the nineteenth and twentieth centuries as measured by election results and predominant political affiliations.[4] An important objective of the present inquiry will be to determine, insofar as possible, whether these regional patterns actually predated the Revolution, or were created out of the Revolutionary cauldron itself.

A number of historians have been fascinated by the striking correspondence between the oath of 1791 and the patterns of twentieth-century "religiosity." For John McManners, such parallels represent one of the "most mysterious" aspects of the whole oath experience.[5] For Charles Ledré, there could be no doubt that the proportion of jurors in a given region was directly related to the "degree of faith."[6] It will be argued here that the oath was a community experience as well as an ecclesiastical crisis and that the regional reactions of clergymen in 1791 can be revealing of the attitudes and religious options of the lay population with which the clergymen lived. Thus, the study of the oath takes on added significance. An exploration of the origins and meaning of the oath geography may throw light not only on a critical event in the development of the Revolution, but also on the inception of the "Two Frances"—the clerical France and the anticlerical France—of modern times.[7]

There is, to be sure, no shortage of studies on the religious history of the Revolution, studies in which the oath is commonly a central motif. A great many of these works, published near the turn of the present century, directly participated in a lengthy and obsessive debate over the proportion of "refractories" and "constitutionals" in the country as a whole, a debate closely tied to the political struggles between clericals and anticlericals. Yet there was little effort at numerical precision. Aside

[3] A comparison, department by department, of the percentage of priests refusing the oath and the proportion of the population attending mass or performing their "Easter duties" in the 1950's yields a correlation coefficient of 0.7. See Claude Langlois, "Le serment de 1791 et la pratique religieuse des Catholiques aux dix-neuvième et vingtième siècles," in *Proceedings of the Eleventh Annual Meeting of the Western Society for French History*, John F. Sweet, ed. (Lawrence, Kansas, 1984), 166-75.

[4] See Emmanuel Todd and Hervé Le Bras, *L'invention de la France* (Paris, 1981), 138 and *passim*; also Lynn Hunt, "The Political Geography of Revolutionary France," *Journal of Interdisciplinary History*, 14 (1984), 535-59.

[5] John McManners, *The French Revolution and the Church* (London, 1969), 49.

[6] Charles Ledré, *La réorganisation d'un diocèse français au lendemain de la Révolution. Le Cardinal Cambracérès, archevêque de Rouen* (Paris, 1943), 2.

[7] Theodore Zeldin has argued that the religious question was "the most fundamental cause of division among Frenchmen" from the mid-nineteenth to the mid-twentieth centuries: *France, 1848-1945: Anxiety and Hypocrisy* (Oxford, 1981), 230.

from a recent sketch by Michel Vovelle, the only general statistical synthesis on the oath is found in an article published by Philippe Sagnac in 1906, an article which was based on a single source and which covered only 43 of the 83 departments of the Revolution.[8] Despite the appeal of Bernard Plongeron in 1969 for a new attack on the problem,[9] the sheer dimensions of the task—the need to determine the options of some 60,000 clergymen throughout the country—has probably frightened away most scholars. If I ultimately decided to take up the challenge, it was after having discovered that much of the basic spadework had already been accomplished. Over the last hundred years, a collection of obscure but patient local historians (many of them priests) has been busily occupied establishing lists and catalogues of the Revolutionary clergy. A number of these studies and compilations are in print, but others are preserved in manuscript only in local archives and libraries. Verified and standardized—and complemented by additional statistics gathered in some fifty archives—the data from these studies form the foundation on which the present work is constructed.

Given the nature of the subject and the need to make reasoned judgments about the behavior of large numbers of individuals, a substantial measure of quantification has been unavoidable. At an earlier stage of research, experiments were made with a number of more sophisticated modes of quantitative treatment (regression analysis, discriminant analysis, etc.). But the application of such methods proved less than satisfactory for a number of reasons. First, many of the key variables were so heterogeneous, incomplete, and of uncertain reliability that the significance of the statistical results could be seriously put into question. The problem is particularly in evidence when one attempts to deal with the country as a whole and to interrelate the wide variety of conflicting and often overlapping geographical units of the Old Regime. Second, in so culturally and historically diverse an entity as France, different variables might have different effects in different regions of the country. The dangers of the so-called "ecological fallacy" are ever present.[10] Indeed, in the few cases where data could be broken down accurately to the level of the districts, correlations among variables might differ markedly for the various quad-

[8] Michel Vovelle, *Religion et Révolution: la déchristianisation de l'an II* (Paris, 1977), 61-71; Philippe Sagnac, "Étude statistique sur le clergé constitutionnel et le clergé réfractaire en 1791," *RHMC*, 8 (1906), 97-115.

[9] Bernard Plongeron, *Conscience religieuse en révolution. Regards sur l'historiographie religieuse de la Révolution française* (Paris, 1969), 17-36.

[10] See, notably, Todd and Le Bras, 403-14.

rants of the kingdom.[11] Third, it soon became evident that some of the variables in question were related, if related at all, in a non-linear fashion. The kinds of mathematical approaches required to deal with such a state of affairs became extremely complex and abstract and generated output that was all but impossible to interpret in a meaningful historical sense. In this predicament, I found it necessary, first, to target about a dozen departments or regions of France for much more intensive local studies; and, second, to confine myself to such elementary forms of quantitative generalization as percentage comparisons and correlation coefficients. Frequently, I have fallen back on older forms of historical epistemology like the use of examples and counter-examples or of gestalt impressions based on the examination of maps. One cannot discount the possibility that future historians, armed with more complete series of information, may be able to refine and correct many of the conclusions and hypotheses presented here.

In its development, the study is divided into four parts. Part One seeks to set the ecclesiastical oath in its broader context within the Revolution and to outline the overall patterns of oath-taking as they have been identified from the statistical survey. In Part Two, I seek to move from the identification to the analysis of oath-taking trends by exploring the problem of clerical motivation. After first allowing the individuals in question to present their own explanations, I have initiated a prosopography of their careers and family backgrounds and an examination of the ecclesiastical relations and political movements which might have affected their options. In Part Three, the emphasis is shifted from the clergy to the laity and to the symbiotic interaction which existed between the two. A series of essays take up the question from several perspectives in an attempt to understand popular reactions to the oath in diverse sections of the country. Among the more important issues addressed are the strength of regional integration into the central state, the presence and attitude of local Protestant populations, the degree of "clericalism" predating the Revolution, and the pattern of cultural relationships between urban elites and rural masses. Inevitably, given the present state of historical research, many of the arguments of Part Three are more speculative and tentative than those in Part Two. A final section, Part Four, attempts to bring together the principal conclusions of the study and to offer reflections on the importance of the oath for the later regional religious history of France.

[11] Note, for example, the correlation between the oath and the number of vicaires per parish. See chp. 5.

Acknowledgments

By its very nature, the present study has been heavily dependent on the assistance and collaboration of a whole group of colleagues and friends. At various points in its conceptualization and research I greatly benefitted from conversations with Michel Vovelle, Dominique Julia, Marie-Madeleine Compère, Claude Langlois, Jack Censer, Jane Turner Censer, Donald Sutherland, Peter Jones, Louis Pérouas, Robert Forster, Alan Forrest, Emmet Kennedy, and Roger Dupuy. Many of these individuals also generously shared with me their unpublished data and manuscripts. Other manuscript material was graciously shared with me by Colin Lucas, T.J.A. Le Goff, Alex Poyer, Frank Tallet, Lynn Hunt, Paul Mandon, Adrien Loche, Paul d'Hollender, Michel Vernus, Gaston Bordet, Jean Godel, Jean Girardot, Jean Meyer, Alison Patrick, Abbé Valéot, Robert McIntyre, and Stephen Clay. Of particular importance were the data bank and content analysis of the *cahiers de doléances* made available to me by Gilbert Shapiro and John Markoff. As an outsider to religion, I also benefitted from the insights of many of my Catholic colleagues and students at Marquette University and the Catholic University of America.

My research assistants, Rosine Schmidt, Carol Miller, and William Moore contributed valuable service in the organization and analysis of data, and Bill Moore performed extra labor typing parts of the manuscript and assisting in the preparation of the maps. The map of oath-taking by district was drawn by Jean Paquette in the Marquette University Media Center. Several additional maps, generated by computer, were programmed by Robert McIntyre, who offered enormous assistance in a number of computer-related projects. Additional help in computer analysis came from Bruce Meier and Tom Faden at Marquette University and Juan Gallegos and Ardoth Hassler at Catholic University. I received financial support for research trips to France and free time in the United States from the American Council of Learned Societies, the American Philosophical Society, Marquette University, and the Catholic University of America.

The completed manuscript was read in its entirety by Jack Censer,

Isser Woloch, and Donald Sutherland. Although I did not agree with all of their criticisms, I deeply appreciate their advice and assistance. I also benefitted from the comments and criticisms of the Washington/ Baltimore Old-Regime study group. Various chapters and versions of chapters were discussed among faculty and students at George Washington University, the Johns Hopkins University, Cornell University, and the Universities of Reading, Manchester, Norwich, Lampeter, Paris XII, and Lublin.

For various forms of hospitality and logistical support during the research period may I also thank Dominique Julia and Marie-Madeleine Compère, Claude and Anne Langlois, Adeline and Gustave Aubert, Earl and Jean Tackett, and Jeff and Marilee Jaquess. And, finally, a very special word of appreciation to Catherine Aubert-Tackett and Gregory and Nicolas Tackett, who assisted me over the years in so many ways.

Abbreviations

A.A.E.   Archives des affaires étrangères, Mémoires et Docu-
                 ments, France

A.C.   Archives communales de . . .

A.D.   Archives départementales de . . .

A.E.   Archives épiscopales du diocèse de . . .

A.M.   Archives municipales de . . .

A.N.   Archives nationales

B.M.   Bibliothèque municipale de . . .

ACSS   *Actes du . . . Congrès national des Sociétés savantes. Section
                 d'histoire moderne et contemporaine*

AHRF   *Annales historiques de la Révolution française*

Annales, E.S.C. *Annales. Economies. Sociétés. Civilisations*

AP   *Archives parlementaires de 1787 à 1860, recueil complet
                 des débats législatifs et politiques des chambres françaises.
                 Première série*

Barruel   Abbé Barruel, *Collection ecclésiastique ou recueil complet
                 des ouvrages faits depuis l'ouverture des Etats-Généraux
                 relativement au clergé et sa Constitution civile, décrétée
                 par l'Assemblée nationale, sanctionnée par le roi*

CHR   *Catholic Historical Review*

DDC   *Dictionnaire de droit canonique*

DTC   *Dictionnaire de théologie catholique*

FHS   *French Historical Studies*

JMH   *Journal of Modern History*

RH   *Revue historique*

RHMC   *Revue d'histoire moderne et contemporaine*

PART ONE

INTRODUCTION AND BACKGROUND

ONE

The Oath and the French Revolution

O N any of several chilly Sunday mornings in the winter of 1791, parish clergymen throughout France were asked to stand in their churches before their congregations and swear a solemn oath of allegiance to the nation, the law, the king, and the new Revolutionary constitution. In many respects, the oath ceremony in question was a signal occurrence among the great and tumultuous events which had been unrolling in France over the previous two years. Like the election of the Estates General in 1789 or the Festival of Federation in 1790, it was an event which was directly witnessed by even the smallest and most isolated villages of the country, an event which thrust the experience of the Revolution clearly and unambiguously into the lives of common men and women everywhere. But while the first electoral assemblies and the Federation ceremonies had generally been marked by a buoyant sense of optimism and unity, the ceremony of the oath of 1791 was often overladen with tension and uncertainty. Far from the earlier ritual communions of patriotic affirmation, the ecclesiastical oath staked out a real and deadly serious obligation, wherein a failure to conform entailed a clergyman's ejection from his functions and his ostracism from the community of the Revolutionary nation. For, as everyone knew, it was primarily directed at establishing acceptance of one critical aspect of the new constitution: the sweeping reorganization of the French Church, a reorganization which had begun on the night of August 4 and which had culminated in the Civil Constitution of the Clergy. And it was precisely over this issue that the Revolution would experience the first great parting of the ways, a major schism within the French Church and clergy, but also a great and lasting schism across the political allegiance of the entire population.

To believe the accounts of contemporaries, the issue of the oath soon became a veritable obsession, unleashing emotional reactions and factional strife in parishes everywhere. There were villages in which a clergyman's acceptance of the new legislation could elicit an extraordinary outpouring of enthusiasm, with vigorous applause, bell ringing, parades, and pomp in endless variations. Elsewhere, the same action might incite storms of popular outrage, leading on occasion to open riots and physical attacks

3

against the priest himself.[1] Intimate friendships were shattered over the crisis of the oath. Wives, it was said, were being turned against their husbands, children against their parents, servants against their masters—to the extent that some observers voiced fears for the continued stability of the French family.[2] In the towns, one could read poetry about the oath,[3] attend plays about the oath,[4] hear public lectures on the subject by eminent specialists, or buy engravings depicting the event to put on one's wall.[5] By the spring, the whole issue had so permeated popular consciousness that even young children might be seen reenacting the oath ceremony as they played in the streets.[6]

Soon, moreover, the enforcement of the oath and the dismissal of thousands of clergymen from the officially sanctioned Church would set in motion a chain of events which embittered whole segments of the rural population. In some areas the non-jurors represented such a large proportion of all local priests that it was all but impossible to find replacements, and the "anticonstitutional" clergymen had to be left for up to a year and a half with little effective supervision over their preaching activities.[7] Rapidly appreciating the problem, the legislators in Paris abruptly revoked one of the more important reform measures of their Civil Constitution, allowing priests with only minimal previous experience to move into vacant posts.[8] This legislation, rushed through in

[1] See below, chp. 7.

[2] Yves-François Besnard, *Souvenirs d'un nonagénaire*, 2 vols. (Paris, 1880), 2:37-39; *arrêté* by the directory of Haut-Rhin, November 2, 1791: A.N., F[19] 465; Charles Jolivet, *La Révolution en Ardèche* (Largentière, 1930), 281; A. Sicard, *Le clergé de France pendant la Révolution*, 3 vols. (Paris, 1912-27), 2:153-54. See also below, chp. 7.

[3] Emile Sévestre, *L'acceptation de la Constitution civile du clergé en Normandie* (Paris, 1922), 327.

[4] There were at least 8 performances of a play called "Le serment du vicaire" playing at the Théâtre de Variétés Amusantes in Paris in 1791: information kindly shared by Emmet Kennedy.

[5] Jean-Claude Meyer, *La vie religieuse en Haute-Garonne sous la Révolution* (Toulouse, 1982), 70.

[6] Hervé Pommeret, *L'esprit public dans le département des Côtes-du-Nord pendant la Révolution* (Saint-Brieuc, 1921), 129.

[7] To cite only a few examples: in July 1791, the department of Pyrénées-Orientales complained of the numerous refractories left in parishes near the Spanish border for lack of replacements: A.N., D XXIX 85; nearly two-thirds of refractory curés and vicaires in Vendée were still serving in October: A.N., F[19] 1255-56; the district of Sévérac still had 30 to replace in November: A.D. Aveyron, L 1937; Haute-Saône, Vienne, and undoubtedly a great many others had unreplaced refractories as late as August 1792: Jean Girardot, "Clergé réfractaire et clergé constitutionnel en Haute-Saône pendant la Révolution," *Mémoires de la Société pour l'histoire du droit et des institutions des anciens pays bourguignons, comtois, et romands*, 24e fasc. (1963), 129; and Marquis de Roux, *La Révolution à Poitiers et dans la Vienne* (Paris, 1911), 396-99.

[8] Motion introduced by Mirabeau on January 7, 1791: *AP*, 22: 66-69.

January 1791, opened the floodgates to an enormous flow of priests throughout the kingdom, as young clergymen looking for rapid careers and newly released regulars searching for employment streamed into openings around the country. Many villagers discovered not only that their accustomed priests had been ousted but that they had been replaced by unknown outsiders. To further confuse the issue, the National Assembly—much to the ire of the new Constitutional Church—steadfastly maintained its earlier pronouncements on religious toleration and allowed the continued presence of the refractory clergymen and their participation in a parallel, non-official cult. Henceforth, two competing churches would each claim sole powers for administering the sacraments efficaciously. The state of religious chaos was gradually clarified after numerous departments began cracking down unilaterally to banish the local refractories and after the provisional government itself issued its decree of August 1792, leading to the blanket deportation of all non-jurors. But the residue of the crisis was lasting and profoundly unsettling. Where people's eternal souls were at stake and where people were still genuinely concerned over the fate of those souls, the potential for unrest and anxiety was substantial.

But if it was a capital event in the history of the French village, so too the oath of 1791 marked a major crisis in the political life of the nation. In both Paris and the provinces it was probably the central public event, the single most discussed problem during the first six months of that year. Virtually all newspapers, at every point on the political spectrum, wrote at length on the issue, covering their pages with enumerations of priests who had or had not fulfilled their obligations and recounting the debates, theological and political, surrounding this "Battle of the Oath."[9] For weeks, the National Assembly began most every session with the reading of testimonies on the reception of the oath in the members' constituent districts. Buoyed up by the inflation of rhetoric, which was rapidly taking on a life of its own, deputies and journalists on both sides predicted the most dire outcome. There were endless references by Right and Left to an impending civil war. It would be a return to the sixteenth century and to the Holy League and the Wars of Religion.[10] "In the midst of the effervescence which presently excites the capital," wrote the *Révolutions de Paris*, "the slightest spark would be enough to ignite a civil

[9] Emile Sévestre, *L'acceptation*, 163-65. Also Maurice Giraud, *Essai sur l'histoire religieuse de la Sarthe* (Paris, 1920), 367-68, 395.

[10] Thus Voidel in his speech of Nov. 25 and Barnave on the following Jan. 25: *AP*, 21:7-8; and 22:491-92; also the *Courrier de Paris dans les 83 départements*, issue of Jan. 7, 1791.

war.... Malcontents, long divided, have now rallied together in the sinister glimmer of the torches of fanaticism."[11]

In fact, open civil war would not come so soon. But a kind of internal cold war was breaking out in full intensity. It was the question of the religious legislation and the oath which, as much as any other single issue, stripped away the veneer of concord and harmony which had been maintained for the most part since the summer of 1789. By forcing the separation of the sheep and the goats among the French clergy, by imposing an absolute, unambiguous stance for or against the new constitution, the oath would come to reinforce and solidify the Manichaean universe of revolutionary politics and give visible substance to the underlying paranoia which had gripped the National Assembly and much of the population since the inception of the Revolution. And the issue was also of the greatest importance in the growing division between the king and his kingdom—a king who could never reconcile himself to the Civil Constitution and the juring clergy and who could never escape his remorse for having sanctioned the legislation in the first place. As he fled toward Varennes in June of 1791, one of the key items on his agenda for a restoration was the reinstatement of the Church of the Old Regime. It is little surprising, then, that many historians have seen the oath of 1791 as one of the pivotal events in the French Revolution.[12]

The Background

The origins and antecedents of these controversial reforms can be traced to a number of sources well back into the eighteenth century.[13] Indeed, many of the National Assembly's ecclesiastical policies had been prefigured by proposals emanating from the clergy itself. In the heat of its epic struggles with the Jesuits and the orthodox episcopacy, the Jansenist

---

[11] *Révolutions de Paris*, no. 81 (Jan. 22-29, 1791), 113-14.

[12] See, for example, John McManners, *The French Revolution and the Church* (London, 1969), 38; Bernard Plongeron, "Le fait religieux dans l'histoire de la Révolution française," *AHRF*, 47 (1975), 113; François Furet and Denis Richet, *La Révolution française* (Paris, 1973), 127-28, 130-34; Albert Mathiez, *Rome et le clergé français sous la Constituante* (Paris, 1911), 1.

[13] A detailed discussion of the origins of the Civil Constitution is beyond the scope of the present study. In any case, an immense literature on the subject already exists. Among the more important studies, see Mathiez and McManners, cited above; Ludovic Sciout, *Histoire de la Constitution civile du clergé (1790-1801)*, 4 vols. (Paris, 1872-81); Pierre de la Gorce, *Histoire religieuse de la Révolution française*, 5 vols. (Paris, 1909-23); C. Constantin, "Constitution civile du clergé" in *DTC* , vol. 3, pt. 2 (Paris, 1938), cols. 1537-1604; André Latreille, *L'Eglise catholique et la Révolution*, 2 vols. (Paris, 1946-50).

movement had not only put into question the power of the papacy and lambasted the abuses of the bishops, but had also leveled searching indictments against a wide range of ecclesiastical practices and institutions. Some of the "Gallicano-Jansenists" seem even to have exceeded the *philosophes* in their anticlerical harangues and calls for radical reform, going so far, for example, as to demand the suppression of all Church property.[14] While the contingent of avowed Jansenists or Jansenist sympathizers in the National Assembly was certainly small, several—of whom Grégoire, Camus, and Lanjuinais were the most notable—would hold key committee positions and would exercise leadership in ecclesiastical debates out of proportion to their numbers.[15]

Perhaps even more influential during the last decades of the Old Regime, however, had been a movement gaining ground and loosely described as "curé syndicalism" or "Richerism." The well-publicized campaign by the curé of Vienne, Henri Reymond, for the augmentation of both the revenues and the political power of the parish clergy within the Church would be frequently echoed in the pamphlet literature and the *cahiers de doléances* of the Clergy and the Third Estate on the eve of the Revolution.[16] Though he based his indictment on the very special and atypical ecclesiastical situation in his own province of Dauphiné, Reymond had, nevertheless, elevated his demands to encompass a vast program of reform for the economic, educational, and career structures of the Church, a program that would anticipate some of the revolutionary reforms. Numerous of the curé deputies to the Estates General were undoubtedly familiar with Reymond's program, and several of Reymond's writings are known to have circulated within the Ecclesiastical Committee which would draft the Civil Constitution.[17]

Nor had the French bishops themselves been altogether isolated from the winds of change. In the years after mid-century, finding themselves increasingly under attack from the *philosophes*, from the *parlementaires*, and from their own curés, the prelates sensed the need for a searching

---

[14] Dale Van Kley, *The Jansenists and the Expulsion of the Jesuits from France, 1757-65* (New Haven, 1975); and "Church, State, and the Ideological Origins of the French Revolution: the Debate over the General Assembly of the Gallican Clergy in 1765," *JMH*, 51 (1979), 629-66.

[15] See, above all, Edmond Préclin, *Les Jansénistes du XVIIIe siècle et la Constitution civile du clergé* (Paris, 1929).

[16] Maurice Hutt, "The Curés and the Third Estate: the Ideas of Reform in the pamphlets of the French Lower Clergy in the Period 1781-1789," *Journal of Ecclesiastical History*, 8 (1957), 74-92; Charles-Louis Chassin, *Les cahiers des curés* (Paris, 1882); and the author's *Priest and Parish in Eighteenth-Century France* (Princeton, 1977), chps. 9 and 10.

[17] Thus, for example, the *Cahier des curés de Dauphiné*: Tackett, 261.

reevaluation of the Church's situation. Led by archbishops Loménie de Brienne, Le Franc de Pompignan, Du Lau, and Boisgelin, the bishops had made proposals in the General Assembly of the Clergy for the reform of clerical taxes, the improvement of the revenues of the lower clergy, and the modification of the benefice system—including recommendations for the appointment of curés by competitive examinations, an enforced apprenticeship period as vicaire before taking charge of pastoral functions, and a reform of clerical education. There had even been talk of changing diocesan boundaries in order to suppress the minuscule "diocèses crottés" of southern France.[18] Perhaps the bishops' most heralded success had been the creation of the Commission on the Regular Clergy which reformed some aspects of monastic life and reduced the number of religious houses. In 1790 these measures would be cited by the National Assembly as a precedent for the suppression of all monastic vows. Yet, all in all, the bishops' efforts were probably less a manifestation of the desire for Enlightened transformation than an effort to rationalize and centralize their administrations and thereby curb the threat to traditional discipline posed by elements of the lower clergy.[19] And when the final General Assembly of the Old Regime met in 1788 most of the reforms proposed ten to twenty years earlier were still no closer to execution. The same kinds of vested interests and privileges which had undermined the royal government's attempts at transformation from above ultimately paralyzed the efforts of the clergy. Yet the bishops' very failure to effect such changes would go far in publicizing the need for extensive reform.

Nevertheless, the push for clerical reform had not come solely from within the Church. In the second half of the eighteenth century, armed with their particular version of "Parlementary" Gallicanism—stressing not only the relative independence of the French Church from Rome, but also the general domination of the state over the Church—several of the Parlements had pushed the long-standing rivalry of authority between themselves and the clergy to a new level of intensity. In the 1740's and 1750's, in the affair of the *billets de confession*, the Parlements

[18] See the *Collection des procès-verbaux des Assemblées générales du Clergé de France depuis l'année 1560*, 8 vols. (Paris, 1767-80), especially the speech by Loménie de Brienne in 1775: vol. 8, pt. 2, cols. 2527-37; the report by archbishop Du Lau in the *Procès-verbaux de l'Assemblée générale du Clergé ... en l'année 1780* (Paris, 1782), 864-66, 888-90; the *Procès-verbaux de l'Assemblée générale du Clergé ... en l'année 1785* (Paris, 1789), 890-933; and the ms. *procès-verbaux* of the Assembly of 1788, especially the report by archbishop Boisgelin: A.N., G⁸ 706.

[19] See the report of Loménie de Brienne in 1775, cited above, and the speech by De Lau in 1780: *Procès-verbaux, 1780*, 218-19.

had even claimed powers of supervision over the distribution of sacraments; and their dominant role in the destruction of the Society of Jesus in the 1760's is well known. In the last decades of the century, through a careful cultivation of the *appel comme d'abus*, certain of the Sovereign Courts were interposing themselves in the name of justice and reform into a wide range of ecclesiastical affairs: granting benefices, naming curés, or creating new parish annexes despite the objections of the bishops; and establishing fundamental changes in the mode of tithe collection, much to the disadvantage of the ecclesiastical tithe owners.[20] A few of the courts were also actively encouraging the "revolt of the curés" against the bishops on the eve of the Revolution.[21] There can be little doubt that numerous deputies of the Third Estate, trained in the law and often in the service of the royal courts, were well versed in the theory and practice of Parlementary Gallicanism, and that the Gallican lawyers—Durand de Maillane, Treilhard, and Martineau—even more than the Jansenists or Richerists, were among the most influential contributors to the Civil Constitution.

Far more difficult to disentangle is the influence of the Enlightenment on the thinking and actions of the generation of 1789. Much of the problem stems from the very complexity, the inherent contradictions of the Enlightenment itself as it was actually experienced by eighteenth-century Frenchmen. It was a generation which had by no means abandoned Catholicism, at least at the superficial level of a social context for the rites of passage. Christianity was the predominant, usually the sole, frame of reference whenever a need was perceived to solemnify or consecrate an event. The near millenarian enthusiasm of the early days of the Revolution was commonly expressed in a religious idiom drawing heavily on Catholic language and ritual. And, nevertheless, two generations of attacks on the established Church and on revealed religion invariably left an effect on elements of the social elite—even though many members of that elite had probably never fully articulated to themselves their precise beliefs, had never fully understood the inconsistencies be-

[20] Jean Egret, *Louis XV et l'opposition parlementaire* (Paris, 1970), 50-67; Louis S. Greenbaum, *Talleyrand, Statesman Priest* (Washington, 1970), chps. 4 and 5; *Procès-verbaux, 1785*, 128-39; Henri Marion, *La dîme ecclésiastique en France au XVIIIe siècle* (Bordeaux, 1912), 187; Georges Frêches, *Toulouse et la région Midi-Pyrénées au siècle des Lumières*, 536-43; Tackett, *Priest and Parish*, 106, 109-110, 187, 233-34, 246-47; Norman Ravitch, *Sword and Mitre* (The Hague, 1966), 24-50; Van Kley, *The Jansenists, passim*.
[21] Tackett, *Priest and Parish*, esp. 240.

tween their formal adherence to Catholicism and their predilection for the "new ideas."

For most of the *philosophes*, as for many of the leaders of the Revolution, there was a curious tension between religion viewed in the metaphysical sense and religion viewed as a social reality. Regardless of their personal positions on the ultimate truth of the religious world view, they returned repeatedly to the social utility of religion for the masses. It was for this very reason that few public figures would be more praised and lionized by the *philosophes* and by the early revolutionaries than the village parish priest: precisely because of his perceived role of instilling a sense of civil obedience and religion among the uneducated, hopelessly unenlightened, and potentially dangerous lower classes. Yet the esteem shown for the humble lower clergy would soon prove but a thin overlay to an even more powerful and deep-seated sentiment of anticlericalism. Indeed, anticlericalism emerges as one of the most powerful legacies of the Enlightenment's position on religion—all the more influential in that it reactivated and reinforced a visceral institutional anticlericalism long present in French society. If the leaders on the Left of the National Assembly ultimately provoked a crisis over the oath in 1791, it was partly because an underlying irritation and impatience with priests—particularly with priests who seemed to be slowing the progress of the Revolution—got the better of their efforts toward benevolent tolerance for the "consolations of religion" among the masses.[22]

Yet, a certain strand, a certain conception of Enlightenment had also exercised a powerful influence over clergymen themselves. Wide groups of ecclesiastics at all levels of the hierarchy had come to share many of the basic assumptions of the movement: a belief in the powers of human reason (limited, to be sure, by revealed truth), a heady confidence and excitement over the discoveries of science, a faith in the possibility of progress within substantial areas of human endeavor.[23] A whole generation of amateur curé scientists, botanizing, stargazing, or prospecting for geological finds had appeared on the scene, few of whom saw contradictions between the free exploration of the scientific world and the truths of revealed religion. A certain kind of "Enlightenment" was also reflected in the rhetoric with which the curés did battle against the upper clergy. In the writings of Henri Reymond and others, a new discourse

---

[22] Many of these points will be further developed in chp. 11 below.

[23] See especially the works by Bernard Plongeron, "Recherches sur l'Aufklärung catholique en Europe occidentale (1770-1830)," *RHMC*, 16 (1969), 555-605; and *Théologie et politique au siècle des Lumières, 1770-1820* (Geneva, 1973).

had been evolving, appealing to reason and utility as the norms by which the clergy should be structured. How unreasonable, how unjust, that such basically inactive elements as monks and priors and abbots *in commendam* should control so much of the clergy's patrimony, while the curés, the most useful members of Church and society, should be largely excluded from wealth and influence. There were appeals for the natural right of no taxation without representation (on the diocesan tax boards), and for government (of the diocese) with the consent of the governed (the parish clergy). One could even find hopes expressed for the "progress of religion" toward a Church purified of all of its abuses.[24] A substantial segment of the clergy confronting the oath of 1791 had not only been reading the same books as the Third Estate, but had come to write and think in a similar vocabulary. It was the events of that year which would prompt a rapid reevaluation of the distinction between words and things.

The Civil Constitution

But whatever the heritage of attempted and proposed ecclesiastical reform witnessed and experienced by the generation of 1789, it would be a mistake to underestimate the creative character of the revolutionary process itself and the degree to which the total package of Church legislation surpassed the expectations of almost everyone. Although the revolutionary legislators liked to fancy themselves as new Solons giving rational laws in their detached wisdom, it is impossible to separate the ecclesiastical legislation of the National Assembly from the rapidly evolving political situation and the ever-present need to adapt and improvise in reaction to specific developments. In this sense, the events leading to the creation of the Civil Constitution and to the crisis of the oath moved forward with a kind of tragic inevitability.

It was the initial and largely unpremeditated acts of August 4, 1789, suppressing both the tithes and the *casuel* fees and initiating the eventual disappearance of clerically owned seigneurial rights, which first necessitated a vast reorganization of the economic structures of the Church. The continuing fiscal crisis, which had already destroyed the Old Regime and which now threatened the Revolution, served to push the deputies toward ever-more-comprehensive reforms. Once they had expropriated the Church's last remaining source of economic independence, its vast property holdings, the revolutionaries had little choice but to treat the

[24] Tackett, *Priest and Parish*, 260-68.

11

clergy as state paid and state regulated functionaries. And this decision, in turn, threw open the gate to a far greater "rationalization" of the clergy: the eventual elimination from state payrolls of all those ecclesiastics who served no particularly "useful" purpose in state and society—where utility was defined under specific Enlightenment categories. It was this logic which led to the interdiction of religious vows and the ultimate suppression of chapters and canons. But the final ecclesiastical reform package was made even more radical by the intensifying political struggles in the National Assembly. An initial set of relatively moderate proposals within the Ecclesiastical Committee—established to draw up the clerical constitution—was blocked by the two bishops who sat on the committee. The consequent doubling of the committee's membership in order to strengthen the Left and end the deadlock had the effect of radicalizing both the committee and the legislation which it eventually sent to the floor of the Assembly. It was during this later stage of the process, for example, that the committee added the radical provision for the popular election of all curés and vicaires. The great debates in the Assembly itself, which climaxed in the passage of the Civil Constitution on July 12, 1790, contributed in further exacerbating divisions between a clerical Right and an anticlerical Left and confirming the conviction on the part of the Left that the episcopal deputies were using religion as a mere pretext for "counterrevolution."

It would be difficult to underestimate the stunning impression of innovation and transformation which the new legislation left on clerics and laymen alike. Even if a great many of the individual measures now being instituted had already been suggested in the course of the eighteenth century, the entire set of transformations, taken as a whole, appeared amazingly radical. One way of evaluating the extent of the shock is to pass in review the principal elements of the new legislation and compare them with the views of French laymen in the *cahiers de doléances* of 1789. Though it would be impossible to examine all of the *cahiers* (some 40,000) produced by the laity, the two hundred odd "general cahiers" of the Third Estate—those written to be taken directly to the king in Versailles—provide a good sampling of the stated desires of what were probably the realm's most influential commoners. (See Table 1.)[25]

To judge by the cahiers, it was probably in the area of clerical discipline

[25] The descriptions in the text and the material in Table 1 are based on data kindly shared with me by Gilbert Shapiro and John Markoff from their massive content analysis of all of the general cahiers of the Third Estate. For the details of this analysis and the problem of the groups who wrote and are represented in these cahiers, see below, chp. 11.

Table i

Anticipation of the Ecclesiastical Legislation of the Revolution
in the General Cahiers of the Third Estate

Grievance	Number of Occurrences	Percentage of All Cahiers
Abolish regular clergy	8	4
Abolish all tithes	20	10
Abolish some kinds of tithes	75	37
Sell all Church land	5	2
Sell some Church land	50	25
Abolish chapters	3	1
Lay election of curés and bishops	5	2
Abolish *casuel*	95	47
Abolish present Concordat	28	14
Abolish some or all clerical privileges	26	13
Modify diocesan boundaries	4	2
Open clerical posts to talent	88	44
Abolish all simple benefices	24	12
Require episcopal residence	80	40
Reduce wealth of bishops	22	11
Provide pensions for sick or old priests	29	14
Give curés greater voice in diocesan affairs	6	3
Number of cahiers analyzed: 202		

and conduct that the new decrees were most responsive to the expressed sentiments of the population. A whole section of the Civil Constitution was devoted to enforcing the residence of bishops and parish clergymen, a demand that had appeared in some 40 percent of the grievance lists. Even more popular (in 47 percent of all cahiers) had been the demand to forbid the collecting of *casuel* fees, a practice that would be abolished outright on the night of August 4. Other provisions of the laws instituted requisite training periods at lower positions in the hierarchy before attaining the positions of curé or bishop, a measure that would, in fact, open up the episcopacy to all men of talent and merit, regardless of birth. Such a change had been requested, in one form or another, in 44 percent of the cahiers.

More central to the ecclesiastical reforms, however, were the very substantial modifications of the economic structures of the Church: the suppression of the tithes, the nationalization of Church lands, the conversion of all clergymen into functionaries or pensioners of the state, and a sweeping redistribution of clerical incomes. Henceforth, the bishops would see their incomes slashed from an average of perhaps 40,000 to 50,000 *livres* per year (with many ranging well over 100,000, if additional benefices held in plurality were considered) to a mere 12,000 *livres* per year in most of the new dioceses. At the same time, the lowest paid of the parish clergy would experience a net gain, as the Old-Regime minimum "portion congrue" of 700 *livres* was converted into a base salary of 1200 *livres*.[26] Finally, all clergymen would be given some measure of security in sickness and old age through the benefit of guaranteed pensions. Yet few Frenchmen had anticipated these economic changes in 1789. If numerous cahiers throughout the kingdom had pleaded for an augmentation of the *portion congrue*, only about one in ten had specifically mentioned lowering episcopal incomes. Approximately the same proportion had asked for the suppression of the tithes, and scarcely one in fifty had suggested the sale of all Church land. To be sure, a significant proportion of the population had envisioned some tampering with ecclesiastical revenues to assist in paying Church or state debts or to provide for added social or educational services. Almost one-forth of the cahiers asked for the alienation of a portion of Church property, and over one-third requested a partial suppression of certain types of tithes.[27] During the last decades of the Old Regime, not only the Parlements, but the General Assembly of the Clergy and, especially, the curé syndicalists in the Reymond mold, had all proposed certain modifications in the economic structures of the Church in order to achieve various specific goals. But if the revolutionary settlement was, in a sense, the logical extension and completion of such Old-Regime proposals, there had been little to prefigure transformations which would place the clergy in such a position of total economic dependence on the state.

Equally radical and even more controversial was the massive simplification and rationalization of Church organization. Thousands of Old-Regime positions—canonries, chapels, simple benefices (i.e., those where no functions were required) and almost the entire corps of regular clergy—were abolished outright or programmed for suppression with the death of the incumbents. Also erased were the bishops' assistants, the

---

[26] Under the Old Regime, some curés actually collected much less than 700 *livres*. Now, all would have a minimum of 1200. But many of those curés formerly making over 1200 *livres* would actually experience a net decline in income under the Revolution. See below, chp. 4.

[27] For example, that the tithes on some items such as hay or fish or garden vegetables be abolished.

vicars-general, young noblemen for the most part, waiting for promotion to an episcopal see, who now found their careers abruptly shattered. Judged "useless" for society, all such clergymen were retired with relatively modest lifetime pensions—unless they agreed to purposeful employment as teachers or parish clergymen. In all, close to three-fifths of the entire religious corps of 1789, including the women religious, found themselves suddenly removed from their former positions, the majority with substantially reduced incomes.[28] If the suppression of the Jesuits and the activities of the Commission on Regulars seemed to serve as a kind of precedent, there was little that could have prepared French citizens for such a radical definitive solution. As we shall see, the sudden reduction in the number of clergymen active in religious life would have a profound effect on the reception of the Civil Constitution in certain regions.[29] Of those writing *cahiers de doléances*, only 12 percent asked for the suppression of all simple benefices, 4 percent for the suppression of all regulars, 1 percent for the suppression of the chapters.

In a similar vein, the Civil Constitution organized a "rationalization" of the dioceses of the kingdom and a reduction of the number of parishes. Extraordinarily diverse in their range of sizes under the Old Regime (varying from about 20 to over 1200 parishes), the dioceses were now made coterminous with the newly established administrative districts, the departments. In the process, over fifty bishoprics and all archbishoprics were abolished, along with perhaps several hundred parishes.[30] Only four demands in 202 cahiers could be even vaguely construed as calling for this kind of reshuffling in the Church's organizational structure. Moreover, in what was perhaps the single most dramatic change of all, the National Assembly instituted the selection of new curés and bishops through lay elections in the departmental (for bishops) and district (for curés) assemblies. Although there was considerable justification for rationalizing the Old Regime's inequitable system for the bestowing of benefices, the lay election of clergymen probably took most Frenchmen utterly by surprise. Indeed, if elections there were to be, the Revolutionaries would probably have garnered greater support by placing the choice

[28] The numbers and categories of the clergy alive in France in 1789 have been calculated by the author and Claude Langlois, "Ecclesiastical Structures and Clerical Geography on the Eve of the French Revolution," *FHS*, 11 (1980), 352-70.

[29] See below, chp. 10.

[30] Though, in general, the enormous local opposition disallowed the suppression of many parishes outside the larger towns.

in the hands of either the corps of curés or the parishes themselves.[31] In any case, no more than 2 percent of the Third Estate cahiers made any references to lay elections of clergymen, and even these in no way anticipated the selection process that was ultimately chosen.

Finally, a number of measures were adopted by the Revolutionaries which would redefine the relation between the French Church and Rome. By unilaterally abrogating the Concordat of 1516, the legislators abolished the *annates*, the tax which the pontiff had formerly collected from the Gallican clergy. But far more important was the position taken on the lines of authority linking the pope and the French clergy. Whenever a new bishop was named, he was not to seek confirmation from Rome, but he was only to write to the pontiff, informing him of his election "en témoignage de l'unité de foi, et de la communion qu'il doit entretenir avec lui."[32] While 28 of the general cahiers of the Third Estate (14 percent) asked either for the suppression of the Concordat or the return of the Pragmatic Sanction of 1438, none went so far as to exclude the pope from the confirmation of new bishops. Here, too, the Parlementary Gallicanism of the Ecclesiastical Committee had pushed the National Assembly vastly beyond the expressed opinions of the French population in 1789.

The Oath

Yet ultimately it was not the Civil Constitution itself which provoked the crisis of 1791, but the requirement of a formal oath in favor of that constitution. The oath ceremony had long played an important role in the political and social relations of the Old Regime. When Louis XVI was consecrated at the altar of Reims Cathedral in 1774, swearing an oath to faithfully serve the kingdom and carry out his duties as king, it was the perpetuation of a millenarian tradition closely related to the feudal practice of oaths of personal fealty and obedience. But clergymen too were accustomed to participation in such rituals, taking oaths not only to perform their pastoral duties faithfully but to maintain allegiance to the civil state. At least since the period of Louis XIV each newly consecrated bishop was required to appear at the chapel of Versailles in

---

[31] Suggested, in fact, by several authors. For example, the "Projet de décret" for the new constitution of the Church by a "curé de campagne," July 1790: A.N., D XIX 45; also, the proposal of Abbé Suarde, *La France ecclésiastique telle qu'elle peut être avant quinze ans* (Paris, 1790).

[32] *AP*, 17:58 (title II, art. 19).

the presence of the monarch and pronounce an oath of loyalty to the king's person.[33] In Alsace, as part of the government's effort to Frenchify the clergy after the annexation of the province in the seventeenth century, each new benefice holder took a similar oath of fidelity to the king and to the Sovereign Council of Alsace.[34]

For most people an oath was still thought to have a distinctly religious character. According to Durand de Maillane, specialist in canon law— and member of the Ecclesiastical Committee—"The oath is an act of religion whereby he who is swearing takes God as his witness for his sincerity and truthfulness." Thus, to break one's oath or to swear falsely was nothing less than the sin of blasphemy.[35] By all evidence, the act of oath-taking was taken extremely seriously. Several of the Third-Estate cahiers specifically asked that the number of oaths used in public life be limited, notably those required during criminal court proceedings. "Nothing is more sacred than an oath," wrote the cahier of Riom, "but nothing is more common than the abuse of oath-taking [in the courts]."[36] In their explanations of the oath clergymen would often emphasize the religious nature of the act requested of them, citing the canonists as authority.[37] And many were deeply tormented that their souls might be in danger if the new oath asked of them should contradict their earlier oaths to their bishops pronounced at the time of their ordinations.[38] But the masses too could view oath-taking with a kind of religious awe. The extreme Left newspaper, the *Révolutions de Paris*, recognized this fact, despite its general distaste for the "fanatical"—i.e., religious—character of oaths. "The common people," it warned, "do not make light of the sacred bond [of an oath]."[39]

[33] Pierre-Toussaint Durand de Maillane, *Dictionnaire de droit canonique* (Lyon, 1770), article "serment."

[34] André Schaer, "La francisation du clergé alsacien," *Bulletin ecclésiastique de Strasbourg*, 84 (1965), 471, 477.

[35] Durand de Maillane, article "serment"; Claude-Joseph de Ferrière, *Dictionnaire de droit et de pratique*, 2 vols. (Toulouse, 1779), 2:241-42.

[36] *AP*, 5:561. Similar complaints are found in the Third-Estate cahiers of Artois, Moulins, Villers-Cotterets, Toul, and Verdun.

[37] For example, Louis-Marie Robiche, curé of Saint-Pierre-de-Brégy, in a speech on Jan. 30, 1791: A.D. Oise, Series L, District of Crépy (unnumbered).

[38] For example, the statement by Guillaume Le Clancher, curé of Montgommery, Jan. 26, 1791: Emile Sévestre, *Liste critique des ecclésiastiques fonctionnaires publics insermentés et assermentés en Normandie* (Paris, 1922), 380; and by the parish clergy of the diocese of Boulogne: Augustin Deramecourt, *Le clergé du diocèse d'Arras, Boulogne et Saint-Omer pendant la Révolution*, 4 vols. (Arras, 1884-86), 2:133.

[39] *Révolutions de Paris*, no. 78 (Jan. 1-8, 1791), 673.

This longstanding tradition and the quasi-religious aura surrounding oath-taking may help us understand the exceptional predilection manifested for such ceremonies by almost everyone at the beginning of the Revolution. Indeed, perhaps not since the days of the Holy League in the late sixteenth century had so many oaths been pronounced, and with such fervor.[40] Nor should one overlook the enthusiasm in the France of the 1780's for the Roman republican tradition of rhetoric and oath-taking. It was in this context that Jacques-Louis David's famous painting, the "Oath of the Horatii," had achieved such acclaim. As Lynn Hunt has suggested, the fascination with oaths was perhaps part and parcel of the extraordinary importance lent by the Revolutionaries to the spoken word. In the very newness, the rootlessness, of their enterprise, the patriots relied on the ritualistic quality of loyalty oaths to help stay their resolution and affirm the creation of a new national community. The oath played a key symbolic role in the transference of sovereignty from the person of the king to the community as a whole and helped confirm the new ties of citizenship which bound individuals to that community.[41]

The oath of January 1791 was by no means the first such act in which clergymen might have participated during the Revolution. A curé who had involved himself in politics, participating in elections or serving in office, might easily have sworn half a dozen oaths or more.[42] But even those ecclesiastics—the majority—who eschewed political activities, would probably have taken part in two if not three earlier ceremonies of this sort. In addition to certain spontaneous oaths at various critical points during the year 1789,[43] all clergymen and laymen in the National Assembly, as well as many in towns and villages throughout the kingdom, had already sworn oaths on or about February 4, 1790 in response to a personal appearance by the king before the national body and the monarch's appeal for unity in the face of widespread popular unrest.[44] Every

[40] Ibid. On the general question of Revolutionary oaths, see J. C. Colfavru, "Le serment. De son importance politique pendant la Révolution," *Révolution française*, 2 (1882), 970-82.

[41] Lynn Hunt, *Politics, Culture and Class in the French Revolution* (Berkeley, 1984), 20-21, 27, 45. See also Jean Starobinski, *1789. Les emblèmes de la raison* (Paris, 1979), 65-67.

[42] *E.g.* Nicolas-Daniel Sénéchal, curé and mayor of Dizy (Marne), had already taken seven oaths in Jan. 1791: Emile Bouchez, *Le clergé du pays rémois pendant la Révolution* (Reims, 1913), 211.

[43] See, for example, the oath of loyalty to the National Assembly taken in July 1789 by the curé and vicaire of Upaix in the Hautes-Alpes: A.C. Upaix, BB 2.

[44] *AP*, 11:431-34. In the following days, the same oath was taken by the members of the Châtelet, by the *corps de marchands* of Paris, and by the officers of the admiralty. Following the decree of February 28, it was required of all troops each year on January 14: *AP*, 11:455, 553,

deputy who wished to continue sitting with the Assembly had to pronounce words that were to be the direct model of the ecclesiastical oath
of the following year: "I swear to be faithful to the nation, the law, and
the king, and to maintain with all my power the Constitution determined
by the National Assembly and accepted by the king." While a few deputies
from the nobility attempted to place restrictions on their oaths, indicating
their dissatisfaction with the new laws as they had thus far been elabo-
rated, all ecclesiastics apparently followed suit without difficulty.[45] And
though the evidence is somewhat sparse, there is no indication that clergymen in the kingdom had any difficulties with this first oath.[46]

But by the spring of 1790 the atmosphere within the National Assembly
was evolving rapidly. Heated debates over the definitive nationalization
of Church property and the end of religious vows were polarizing the
Assembly around the religious issue. Deputies on the Right became increasingly suspicious that their opponents were attacking the Catholic
religion itself, while those on the Left were convinced that religion was
being used merely as a pretext to thwart necessary reforms. On April 12
the Jacobin-sympathizing Carthusian monk, Dom Gerle, abruptly introduced a resolution that Catholicism be declared the state religion, with
sole rights to public religious celebration.[47] Gerle hoped that such a
resolution would fend off allegations that the Ecclesiastical Committee
was attempting to "destroy religion." But the proposal ignited what was
surely the most acrimonious confrontation between the clergy and the
Left since the beginning of the Revolution, with Mirabeau invoking
visions of a new Saint-Bartholomew and one ecclesiastic predicting God's
imminent malediction on the whole of France. The leadership on the
Left finally succeeded in tabling the proposal and passing, on April 13,
a compromise "deliberation," declaring that so majestic a matter as religious belief could never be the subject of legislation. The opposition,
however, refused such a compromise and abstained on the vote. On April
19, for the first time since the triumph of the National Assembly the

---

740. In his oath in January 1791, Curé Gaspar Gaudry of Pontcarré, near Paris, recalled his
previous oath of March 7, 1790: A.D. Seine-et-Marne, L 282.

[45] The bishop of Perpignan initially added an apparent restriction: "espérant que la Constitution sera perfectionnée dans les législatures à venir." But when criticized for this, he announced
that no restriction was involved, just a comment: *AP*, 11:431-34, 518.

[46] No centralized records were kept for this oath. I have found only one case of a refusal by
a parish clergyman: the curé of Terny (district Soissons): A.N., D XXIX bis 22, dos. 235,
no. 14.

[47] *AP*, 12:702-703, 714-19. Similar resolutions had already been introduced on Aug. 28, 1789
and Feb. 13, 1790, but had been tabled as being out of order: *AP*, 8:505 and 11:589-90.

previous summer, a substantial minority of delegates—over 300 in all—convened in a separate assembly and formally published a dissenting opinion in favor of Dom Gerle's original motion.[48] These events in Paris would have far-reaching effects, particularly in the Protestant regions of the kingdom, as hundreds of towns and villages felt obliged to take stands in supporting or opposing the deliberation of April 13.[49]

Thus, as the National Assembly initiated its general debate on the Civil Constitution in May 1790, opinion in both Paris and the provinces was already sharply polarized. When a new call for a solemn oath of allegiance was issued in July 1790—an oath virtually identical to that of February and designed to commemorate the fall of the Bastille one year earlier—the context had been sharply altered. The bishop of Clermont, one of the more articulate spokesmen of the Right among the clergy, and the leading opponent of the Civil Constitution within the Ecclesiastical Committee, announced that his oath would now have to be restrictive: "Here, in recalling what I must render unto Caesar, I cannot forget what I must render unto God. . . . I make an exception in my oath for everything which concerns spiritual questions." The words were ominous for the future and would serve as a model for numerous restrictive oaths in 1791. But, while an unspecified number of clergymen in the Assembly stood up at the end of the bishop's speech as a sign of adhesion, the Assembly chose to ignore his remarks because of the festival of unity which was about to take place. Throughout the kingdom, in village churches and town squares, clergymen generally followed the majority of the deputies, only rarely indicating reservations or restrictions.[50]

The law of the Civil Constitution of the Clergy itself contained no oath-taking requirements for clergymen presently in office. Its only provision concerned an oath formula—the same as that of February 4, with the additional promise "to look carefully after the welfare of my parish-

---

[48] *Déclaration d'une partie de l'Assemblée nationale sur le décret rendu le 13 avril 1790 concernant la religion* (Paris, April 19, 1790).

[49] The full reverberations of this event throughout the kingdom have not always been appreciated. See below, chp. 9.

[50] *AP*, 17:12-17. A. D. Millard writes that "presque tous les ecclésiastiques" of the department of Marne took the oath of July 14, with only a few rare cases of restrictions: *Le clergé du diocèse de Châlons-sur-Marne* (Châlons, 1903), 5-7. Everywhere in the Sarthe, curés are said to have enthusiastically taken part in the July 14 festival: Giraud, 172-73. There were, nevertheless, a few exceptions: *e.g.*, the refusal of the curé of Villers-devant-Mézières (Ardennes): municipal minutes, July 14, 1790: A.N., D IV 18 (Ardennes). The rector of Ploulech would formally retract his civic oath on Nov. 17, 1790: A.N., F¹⁹ 418 (Côtes-du-Nord).

ioners"—to be applied in the future to all newly elected curés and bishops. The direct legal basis for the general oath of 1791 was another decree, passed on July 24 with far less fanfare and controversy, which regulated clerical salaries and which expanded the oath requirement to all incumbent curés and bishops before they could receive payments from the state.[51] Unfortunately, there is almost no evidence as to how many clergymen actually followed the provisions of this law or whether departmental administrations were even making any efforts to carry it out. To judge by the number of complaints from ecclesiastics that they had received no pay at all for 1790, it may be that most local authorities had not yet been forced to confront the problem in November 1790. Indeed, the application of the Civil Constitution was extremely slow in many departments—as the new departmental administrations were inundated with decrees of all kinds—and the new law was usually not even published before September or October.[52] Yet there were some notable exceptions. Already in early October, the department of Aisne was moving vigorously to enforce the oath, threatening all clergymen—and especially the bishop of Soissons—with the loss of their positions if they failed to cooperate. Similar measures were apparently taken in November in the city of Lyon, the district of Noyon (Oise), and the department of Var, and were being proposed in Bouches-du-Rhône. Though no specific deadline seems to have been given by the Aisne administrators, those of Lyon and Var leveled fifteen-day ultimatums on the clergy within their jurisdictions.[53]

In the meantime, the National Assembly was closely following the unilateral actions of these local administrations as well as the growing opposition encountered by other departments in their attempts to enforce specific articles of the Civil Constitution. In retrospect, it seems clear that

---

[51] *AP*, 17:733 (article 39). The oath requirement is in title II, articles 21 and 38, of the Civil Constitution of the Clergy: *AP*, 17:58. Some priests in their oath explanation in 1791 would specifically refer to the law of July 24 rather than to the oath decree of Nov. 27. For example, Gendresse, curé of Berchère in Seine-et-Marne: A.D. Seine-et-Marne, L 282.

[52] On the inability of clergymen to collect salaries in 1790, see the comments by Abbé Gassendi: *AP*, 20:276. On the time lag for the publication of the Civil Constitution in Normandy, see Emile Sévestre, *Les problèmes religieux de la Révolution et de l'Empire en Normandie* (Paris, 1924), 106-107.

[53] In general, see La Gorce, 1:320. On the situation in Aisne, see A.N., D IV 15, no. 280, and Louis-Victor Pécheur, *Annales du diocèse de Soissons. Vol. VIII. La Révolution* (Soissons, 1891), 49, 53, 58; on Noyon: A.D. Oise, L[v] (District Noyon) "Cultes"; on Bouches-du-Rhône: letter from the department directory, Nov. 16, 1790: A.N., D XIX 80, dos. 604, no. 8; on Lyon: Maurice Wahl, *Les premières années de la Révolution à Lyon* (Paris, 1894), 240, 251-54.

many of the bishops and the overwhelming majority of the parish clergy were doing everything possible to cooperate with the Revolution. In their "Exposition of Principles" of October 30, most of the bishops within the National Assembly took a cautious position, critical of certain aspects of the new law, but announcing their intention of awaiting a judgment from the pope. Many expressed confidence that the pontiff would ultimately demur on the question.[54] But the dominant "patriot" faction within the Assembly was becoming restive over this policy of procrastination. In November several letters were read before the national body indicating the adamant opposition to all ecclesiastical reforms on the part of some bishops and canons, and a delegation from Loire-Inférieure appeared in person to present an impassioned accusation against the bishop of Nantes.[55] The delegates were particularly irritated by the bishops' opposition to the election of Abbé Expilly as replacement for the deceased prelate of Quimper—the first such bishop chosen through the provisions of the Civil Constitution. There was also evidence that some clergymen— a small minority, no doubt—were refusing to read the Assembly's decrees and were dragging their feet in the preparations for the sale of Church property.[56]

It was in this mood of growing suspicion and impatience that the National Assembly passed its decree of November 27, 1790, a decree which required an oath of allegiance to the constitution from all bishops, parish clergymen, and clerical teachers. Those who refused to comply within one week from the time the decree was published locally would be removed from their posts and replaced. Those who protested this or any other law would be liable to prosecution. Ostensibly, the decree was drawn up in a joint session of the Committee for Research, the Committee for Reports, the Committee for Land Transfer, and the Ecclesiastical Committee. But Durand de Maillane would later argue that he and the majority of his colleagues on the Ecclesiastical Committee had been opposed to the idea, fearing the consequences and preferring rather to make use of existing laws and to prosecute only those who openly defied the constitution. The decree of November 27 would, in fact, be the work of the more radical Committees for Research and for Reports, the organs of investigation and repression sometimes described as the distant pred-

---

[54] *Exposition des principes sur la Constitution civile du clergé* (Paris, Oct. 30, 1790): see *AP*, 20:153-65. See also below, chp. 5.

[55] *AP*, 21:1-2.

[56] Sciout, 1:304-17; Mathiez, 370-77; La Gorce, 1:304-306.

ecessors of the Committee of Public Safety.[57] Viewing the question of the acceptance of the Civil Constitution as exclusively a political issue, the members of the two committees seem never to have grasped the religious ramifications of the measure.

The debates over the proposed decree—impassioned, unruly, and extremely acrimonious—are revealing of the complexity of motives involved in the decision to require the oath. First and foremost, there was the exasperation, almost rage, against the blatant refusal on the part of the bishops and of certain other priests fully to obey the law, a law duly determined by popular sovereignty and the general will as embodied in the National Assembly. According to Voidel, rapporteur of the Committee on Research, an insidious faction, a "league," had formed among a portion of the clergy against the law, against the popular will. And in the eyes of the deputies of the majority, nothing was more heinous than such a faction, an intermediary interest group foisting itself between the people and the sovereign.[58] They were all the more impatient in that they were being asked to await the decision of a "foreign power," the papacy. Negotiations were currently under way concerning the status of the papal territories in and around Avignon, and the patriot purists were indignant at the very suggestion of trading away the liberty of a French-speaking population in order to garner favor with a foreign potentate. To admit such a situation, argued Voidel, would be to "admit the existence of two states, two sovereignties, a perpetual opposition of opinions and interests, an ultramontane veto and the virtual impotency of national power...."[59] An oath by the clergy was necessary in order to "stabilize public opinion." It was essential to take an unambiguous stand, to put a stop to the anarchical breaking of laws, and to disprove the rumor circulating in some regions that the National Assembly was attempting to change or destroy religion.[60] Ironically—given the future course of events—one deputy argued that an oath would help prevent a possible schism, since it would indicate to all concerned, laity and clergy alike, that violations of the law would not be countenanced.[61] Both in his speech of November 26 and in a later debate on January 21, Voidel would argue

[57] For the decree of Nov. 27, see *AP*, 21:80-81. Pierre-Toussaint Durand de Maillane, *Histoire apologétique du Comité ecclésiastique de l'Assemblée nationale* (Paris, 1791), 123-25 (note).

[58] Speech by Voidel, Nov. 26: *AP*, 21:7.

[59] Ibid.

[60] See the reports sent to the National Assembly by the department of Aisne in October: A.N., D IV 15, no. 280.

[61] Speech by Camus on Nov. 27: *AP*, 21:78-79.

23

that the oath was ultimately a "measure of indulgence." The Assembly was willing to drop all prosecution of past law breakers of the Civil Constitution in return for the repentance embodied in the act of oath-taking: the deputies would thus "gloss over earlier errors, give a warning to all those who had strayed from their duties, and punish those who remained obstinately refractory to the law."[62]

Underlying all of the justifications for the oath was the assumption that the bishops were simply using religion as a pretext to promote their own selfish class interests; to preserve their wealth, privilege, and prestige; and to oppose the Revolution generally. "Ministers of religion!" entoned Voidel. "Put an end to your pretexts; admit your weakness; you long for the return of your former opulence; you long for your privileges, your supposed marks of distinction and superiority...."[63] Whatever the truth of this warning in the case of certain bishops, it seems clear that the growing polarization of the political process was leading to a dangerous oversimplification, a lack of comprehension for the complexity of the situation. The Left's irritation against the bishops was only compounded by the fact that, during the preceding eighteen months, many of the prelates had unambiguously supported the Right, dragging their feet and attempting to slow the Revolution at every opportunity. When Abbé Maury or the Bishop of Clermont attempted to argue the canonical or theological problems involved in the Civil Constitution, the Left could only reply impatiently that theology was irrelevant, that it only obscured the issue. "Theology," sneered Pétion, "is to religion what pettifoggery is to justice."[64]

If it was inconceivable that the prelates could be motivated by anything but self-interest, it also seemed evident that it was the bishops alone who were at the core of the problem. Hardly a word was said about the rest of the clerical corps. The pensioned ecclesiastical "retirees"—the former canons, chaplains, priors, and members of the regular clergy—were thought to be out of the public eye and could thus be safely left alone. As for the 60,000 other "ecclesiastical public functionaries"—the curés, vicaires, and teachers—the oath seems to have been imposed almost as an afterthought, with little or no debate. It is revealing that in his initial analysis of the debates of November 26-27, the usually more astute editor of the *Courrier de Paris* mistakenly described the legislation as

[62] Speech on Jan. 21: *AP*, 22:364-66.
[63] Speech on Nov. 26: *AP*, 21:7-8.
[64] Speech on Nov. 27: *AP*, 21:74-75.

affecting only the bishops and archbishops.[65] Neither the bishops, nor the Ecclesiastical Committee, nor the king's ministers, nor the king himself seem ever to have anticipated any major resistance on the part of the curés and vicaires. It was simply assumed that parish clergymen would continue to back the Revolution as they had from the beginning, and that they would have no difficulty reiterating their oaths of February 4 and July 14.[66]

The most dramatic debate in the whole controversy came on January 3 and 4, after the king had finally signed the oath decree, and as the deadline drew near for the clerical members of the Assembly to take their oaths. It was a *dialogues de sourds*, prefiguring much of the agony and misunderstanding of the oath experience throughout the country, with the two sides viewing the situation from altogether different optics and speaking with different vocabularies. Cazales, nobleman from Languedoc and the longstanding spokesman of the Right, argued that those opposing the oath would only be following their consciences and that the government must maintain freedom of conscience; Lameth responded that everyone must obey the law and that all the talk of conscience was merely a ploy. Cazales asked for a declaration that the National Assembly had no desire to touch the spiritual authority of the Church. Mirabeau returned, cutting to the heart of the matter: "It is quite obvious that this is not the real issue. The problem is that the dissidents call 'spiritual' what the Assembly calls 'temporal.' "[67] When a few deputies tried to take restrictive oaths—following the example set by the bishop of Clermont and the suggestion of the *Exposition des principes*—they were shouted down by the majority: "Yes or no! No explanations." And in the process the Assembly quickly passed an amendment which, in some respects, was even more significant for the final schism: all oaths would have to be "pure and simple," without restrictions, explanations, or preambles. Henceforth there was to be no middle ground, no room for compromise or ambiguity, or the maneuvering of consciences. You could only be for or against, a patriot or a counterrevolutionary.[68]

In retrospect, it seems likely that some kind of schism was inevitable in any case. Despite the conciliatory efforts of certain French bishops,

---

[65] Issue of Nov. 28, 1790.

[66] La Gorce, 1:337; Marcel Reinhard, *Religion, Révolution et Contre-Révolution* (Paris, 1960), 71-72; Rodolphe Reuss, *L'Alsace pendant la Révolution française*, 2 vols. (Paris, 1881-84), 2:115-16. See also the speech by Cahier de Gerville, Minister of the Interior, Feb. 18, 1792: *AP* 38:622.

[67] Debates on Jan. 4: *AP*, 22:16-18.

[68] Debates on Jan. 4: *AP*, 22:8.

the pope would soon issue a blanket condemnation of the whole Civil Constitution. In fact he had already reached this decision several months earlier, though it was long kept secret for political and diplomatic reasons. At some point, clergymen would invariably have been forced to make a choice. But by thrusting the issue directly into a religious oath—and the decree specified that it must be pronounced after Sunday mass before the assembled congregation—by demanding the assent of the conscience and soul as well as the political reason, the Assembly had succeeded in enormously aggravating and polarizing religious differences within the country at an altogether inopportune time, throwing into total disarray a highly influential segment of the elite which had long backed the Revolution. Such a point of view was also supported by the *Révolutions de Paris*. It would have been preferable, the editors argued, to have asked the priests to give only their *tacit* approval of the Constitution and to have requested resignations only when clergymen felt that they could not do so. But "far from adding to their tacit acceptance, a solemn oath will only pique the clergy's scruples and put into question the very legitimacy of the government."[69]

Enforcement of the Oath

In the weeks following January 4, 1791 the generally intransigent position taken by the National Assembly on the issue of the Civil Constitution was gradually modified and softened somewhat. In part, it was a question of the relatively more moderate Ecclesiastical Committee taking charge once again through its control of the day-to-day implementation of clerical policy. But, in addition, there was the rapid realization, on the part of many deputies, that acceptance of the oath would be far from unanimous, and that the enforcement of the new law was creating a schism of major proportions in the midst of the Church and the society.

A sign of the new temper of moderation was the "Instruction" of January 21, in which the Constituent attempted to explain and rationalize its recent decisions. Indeed, the very act of justification represented a major shift from the position of early January in which the will of popular sovereignty had been seen as reason enough. Central to this declaration was the statement that the National Assembly had neither the intention nor the power to meddle in spiritual matters and that its sole aim was to effect needed reforms in the "external" questions of Church organi-

[69] No. 78 (Jan. 1-8, 1791), 676-78.

zation. It all but apologized for the necessity of requiring an oath—to confound the "enemies of the Revolution"—and it beseeched clergymen to take up their traditional role as peacemakers and teachers of civil discipline by obeying the law.[70] Even Abbé Maury acknowledged the conciliatory tone of the statement, though he was quick to counter by adding that merely saying that the "spiritual" had been left untouched did not make it so.[71] Nevertheless, to believe the oath statements of ecclesiastics themselves, the "Instruction" had a considerable effect in allaying the doubts of wavering clergymen.[72]

In late January the Assembly lifted some of the pressure off the refractories by guaranteeing them a small but significant pension after they had been replaced, and on February 23 they were granted the right of remaining in their parishes until they could be replaced.[73] One month later, on March 18, the deputies effectively jettisoned their earlier one-week time limit for subscribing to the law, permitting individuals to take their oaths up until the very moment they were replaced.[74] The wave of conciliation reached its peak on May 7, 1791 when the Assembly adopted a policy recently established in Paris and passed the so-called "toleration decree." Refractory priests were now given permission to say mass within constitutional churches and even to buy or rent churches of their own to practice their beliefs as they saw fit. The only proviso was that they refrain from saying anything in public against the Civil Constitution or the constitutional clergy.[75]

But if it is possible to follow the evolution of the oath policy of the National Assembly on nearly a day-to-day basis, the information available on the regional execution of this policy is far less complete. There can be no doubt that during the early weeks of 1791 there was a great deal of uncertainty on the part of local administrations. The new institutional framework of the departments, districts, and municipalities had only just

[70] *AP*, 22:364-66.

[71] Ibid.

[72] Thus, for example, in Somme: Michel Destombes, *Le clergé du diocèse d'Amiens et le serment à la Constitution civile* (Amiens, 1971), 353-54; in the district of Mur-de-Barrez (Aveyron): A.D. Aveyron, L 1937; and in Moselle: Lesprand, vols. 3 and 4, *passim*. But there were also a number of examples of priests refusing even to publish the "Instruction" of Jan. 21, notably in the department of Nord: A.N., D XXIX bis 21, dos. 232, nos. 4-12, 19-20.

[73] *AP*, 23:42-45. Joseph Lacouture, *La politique religieuse de la Révolution* (Paris, 1940), 46. The decree allowing unreplaced refractories to stay on temporarily simply confirmed a policy already practiced by the Ecclesiastical Committee: Reuss, 2:114-16.

[74] *AP*, 24:152-53, 180.

[75] La Gorce, 1:432-33; Lacouture, 52-53.

been created, and many administrators were still feeling their way into the workings of this novel experiment in self-government. The problem of implementing the religious legislation was increased by the string of successive decrees concerning the oath. The original law promulgated on December 26 was followed only later by the decree forbidding restrictions (signed by the king toward mid-January) and by the various decrees specifying which priests were actually to be held to the oath.[76] Initially, authority for enforcing the oath was primarily in the hands of the municipalities, bodies which, at this stage in the Revolution, held considerable independence from central control.[77] It was the law of March 12 which thrust the departmental administrations directly into the fray, requiring them to draw up formal lists by name and position of all priests taking or refusing the oath within their jurisdictions. Given the inevitable time lag for the communication and distribution of legislation downward to the level of the municipalities, further lengthened by the transportation difficulties of mid-winter, it was sometimes well into February or even March before the essential laws had come through. If the oath process in the Parisian Basin had been completed by the first weeks of January—and a number of patriot priests had fulfilled the requirement in December, even before the king had signed the law—it was apparently well into February before all districts of Bas-Rhin, Nièvre, and Moselle had published the decrees.[78] In Marne, the first requirement was quickly enacted, but the interdiction on restrictions was officially announced only on February 17 and reached many villages in early March, long after the oath ceremonies had been completed.[79] There were additional complications in some of the non-French-speaking regions like eastern Lorraine, where even many clergymen did not know French and where municipalities were hard-pressed to unravel the intricacies of the decrees in a language they scarcely understood.[80] It is not surprising that the Ecclesiastical Committee found itself inundated with requests and inquiries

[76] The decrees of Feb. 5, Mar. 28, and Apr. 15-17 would expand the oath to include special preachers and confessors or chaplains in prisons, hospitals, and convents: Plongeron, *Conscience religieuse*, 25.

[77] *AP*, 24:52.

[78] Villages near Paris were publishing the law in early or mid-January: see the minutes of the village of Stains: A.N., D XIX 81, dos. 621. On Bas-Rhin, see Reuss, 1:97; on Nièvre, see the letter from the directory, Feb. 4, 1791: A.N., D XXIX bis 21, dos. 224, no. 4; on Moselle, see P. Lesprand, *Le clergé de la Moselle pendant la Révolution*, 4 vols. (Montguy-lès-Metz, 1934-39), vols. 3 and 4, *passim*.

[79] Millard, 5-7.

[80] See, for example, the village of Gandren: Lesprand, 3:270, 348.

of all kinds as officials at various levels attempted to determine their duties and obligations.[81]

Nevertheless, despite all the complications, most of the initial ceremonies themselves seem to have been clustered in January or early February, even in the more remote areas of the country. Already on January 9 the Parisian clergy was being subjected to the oath. By the following Sunday, curés and vicaires in Marne, Orne, Poitiers, and Rennes were beginning to fulfill their obligations. On January 23 the ceremony was being organized in Aisne, Moselle, Vosges, and Doubs; and by January 30 in Ain, Landes, and parts of Alsace.[82] When the ceremony dragged into February—as it did in Morbihan and Tarn, for example—it was probably an indication of massive opposition by the local clergy and of hesitancy, on the part of the department leaders, to face the general turmoil which they knew the oath would likely engender.[83]

But if the initial oath procedures were organized and implemented throughout the kingdom in relatively short order, the evaluation of the oaths actually sworn was a far more difficult and time-consuming enterprise. A particularly difficult problem which local administrators had to face was the interpretation of oaths taken with various kinds of restrictions or observations. Perhaps the most common restrictions were those patterned after the oath of the bishop of Clermont or the prescriptions of the *Exposition des principes*. A clause was inserted directly into the body of the oath, excluding from one's affirmation of allegiance anything which touched on the "spiritual" aspects of religion, or asserting one's allegiance to the "catholic, apostolic, and Roman" Church. But there was a myriad of other possibilities and variations, some inspired by local advice from superiors, some improvised by individuals as the spirit moved them. One might, for example, simply add a reference to the instruction of January 21 or a relatively innocuous statement about one's attachment to the Christian religion in general. Or one might swear precisely the oath stipulated but add a preamble or a postscript or a comment in an adjoining sermon. An even more intractable difficulty arose when restrictive oaths were taken but were not reported as such by municipalities

[81] Many of these were passed on by the Ecclesiastical Committee to the Committee for Research and are contained in A.N., D XXIX bis, 20-23.

[82] On Paris, La Gorce, 1:363; for the other regions, information comes primarily from diverse dossiers in A.N., D XXIX bis 20-21.

[83] Augustin Cariou, "La Constitution civile du clergé dans le département du Morbihan," *Mémoires de la Société d'histoire et d'archéologie de la Bretagne*, 45 (1965), 66; and E. A. Rossignol, *Histoire de l'arrondissement de Gaillac pendant la Révolution* (Toulouse, 1890), 176.

anxious to maintain their curés.[84] Some of these restrictions were removed immediately when clergymen were advised of the decree of January 4.[85] But a great many others were not, and the Ecclesiastical Committee became increasingly involved with complex exercises in semantic interpretation. In point of fact, despite the explicit interdiction of the National Assembly's decree, the Committee would often reveal itself as remarkably flexible in the acceptance of certain kinds of restrictions. In February, for example, one of its members, Abbé Expilly, recommended ignoring an apparent restriction by a curé in Haute-Saône, because it was contained in a postscript and not in the body of the oath.[86] On another occasion, a respondent for the Committee seemed to indicate that almost any kind of restriction might be ignored as long as an individual adhered in his actions to the Civil Constitution: it was not what you said, but what you did. But, in this case, as in many of the Committee's letters, the local authorities were counseled to rely, above all, on their own good judgment: "votre patriotisme et lumières."[87]

The problem, of course, was that the patriotism and enlightenment of individual administrators might lead to widely differing interpretations. Within the five Norman departments, Emile Sévestre discovered an enormous range of reactions among district administrators. The *procureur syndic* of Rouen rejected as dangerous all variations from the formula specifically prescribed by the National Assembly. His colleague in Caen, by contrast, was ready to pass all kinds of restrictions as long as they did not transgress the "spirit of the oath."[88] In Maine-et-Loire, in Sarthe, and in Seine-et-Marne, the local political leadership would frequently invalidate oaths for the slightest variations from the norm, even when it was only a question of including the National Assembly's own words and decrees.[89] The officials in one village even tried to throw out an oath because the curé had raised his left hand rather than his right.[90] But in

---

[84] See the numerous examples in Côte-d'Or: B.M. Dijon, fichier Reinert; also in Ardèche: Jolivet, 277; and in Sarthe: Giraud, 253.

[85] For example, in Sarthe: Giraud, 237; and in Ardennes: Jean Leflon, "Le clergé des Ardennes et la Constitution civile," *Présence ardennaise*, no. 13 (1952), 11.

[86] Jean Girardot, *Le département de la Haute-Saône pendant la Révolution*, 3 vols. (Vesoul, 1973), 2:62.

[87] Letter to the district of Nogent-le-Rotrou, Mar. 7, 1791: A.N., D XIX 82, dos. 646, no. 2.

[88] *L'acceptation*, 292, 301-304.

[89] Alison Patrick, "How to Make a Counter-Revolution: Departmental Policy in the Maine-et-Loire, 1790-1793," paper given at the meeting of French Historical Studies, Pittsburgh, 1979; A.D. Seine-et-Marne, L 282-83.

[90] Sévestre, *L'acceptation*, 316.

Somme a number of priests were apparently allowed to slip in the "minor" modification "to maintain the purely civil and political [aspects of the] Constitution";[91] and in the district of Saint-Hippolyte (Gard) administrators encouraged preambles of various types as a means of reassuring the local population.[92] On other occasions, a patently invalid oath might be accepted because a curé framed it with a rousing patriotic address.[93] A particularly curious illustration of local variations in policy is the case of the curé of Vatimont. In 1791 Vatimont was being disputed by two different departments, Moselle and Meurthe. While the former listed the curé as a refractory, the latter judged him a legitimate juror. Only when the priest himself protested the classification did Meurthe declare him to be a non-juror.[94]

Indeed, taking note of such differences in the interpretations of individual districts and departments, some historians have suggested that regional administrative policy could be critical in the ultimate outcome of the oath locally.[95] In a later chapter it will be necessary to explore such a possibility in greater depth. But it is clear that, as the spring wore to a close and the summer began, the situation was progressively clarified for both the priests taking their oaths and the administrators evaluating them. By summer the "battle of the oath" had been raging for several months. Old-Regime bishops or their agents were inundating the countryside with pastoral letters and brochures arguing their position,[96] and patriot officials were countering with massive propaganda barrages of their own.[97] Before the end of spring, moreover, the pope's long-awaited decision had finally been made public, and his bulls were being distributed throughout the realm.[98] As far as the local political leadership was concerned, pressure from the patriotic clubs was becoming an ever-more-powerful factor. Jacobin groups in the towns, large and small, of every

[91] Destombes, *passim*.

[92] Albert Durand, *Histoire religieuse du département du Gard pendant la Révolution française. Tome I (1788-92)* (Nîmes, 1918), 202.

[93] Thus the cases of François Landel, curé of Beaume-la-Roche and Philibert Lardet, curé of Puligny, both in Côte-d'Or: B.M. Dijon, *fichier* Reinert.

[94] Lesprand, 4:147-48.

[95] Bernard Plongeron, *Conscience religieuse en Révolution* (Paris, 1969), 30-31.

[96] See below, chp. 5.

[97] Numerous examples could be given. Note, for example, the departments of Vienne: Roux, 380; of Sarthe: Giraud, 232; of Calvados: letter from the *procureur-général-syndic*, Feb. 19: A.N., F[19] 410; and of Haute-Garonne: report by directory, Mar. 8: A.N., D XXIX bis 21, dos. 229, no. 15.

[98] The most important of the two bulls, entitled *Charitas*, was published April 13, 1791.

department set themselves up as self-appointed watchdogs over the orthodox interpretation of oath legislation, systematically scrutinizing oath statements and continually prodding the directors to follow up on denunciations of closet refractories.[99] Moreover, and perhaps most important, by the end of the spring all the constitutional bishops had been elected and were beginning to take charge of their new dioceses. Soon the acid test distinguishing the constitutionals from the refractories was less one's oath per se than one's willingness to accept the new bishop and read his pastoral letters during holy services. The Ecclesiastical Committee made this clear in numerous advisory letters to the districts and departments. However flexible one might be with restrictive formulas, it was essential that a clergyman "communicate" with the juring bishop if he were to remain a legitimate juror himself.[100] Numerous departments were now forced to reevaluate entirely their lists of constitutionals and refractories.[101]

Thus, by the summer of 1791, when the position of the pope had been clarified, as the scrutiny of clubs and administrators became ever more intense, as clergymen found themselves forced to come to grips with their own consciences and were confronted with the ultimate test of the acceptance of and cooperation with the newly elected bishops, there were few clerical "public functionaries" who could avoid taking a clear and unambiguous stand. By July or August virtually all clergymen were in the process of being replaced or had been marked for replacement when suitable substitutes could be located. There were undoubtedly isolated cases of secretly "refractory" clergymen—usually, in fact, those having taken restrictive oaths—who remained unknown to the central authorities because of false statements furnished by municipal leaders. Yet it can be argued that, for all practical purposes, these clergymen were actually

[99] Michael L. Kennedy, *The Jacobin Clubs in the French Revolution. The First Years* (Princeton, 1982), 164-67, has argued that the oath crisis was of central importance in the revival and growth of the clubs in 1791. There were numerous examples of their activities concerning the oath: in Normandy: Sévestre, *L'acceptation*, 340-43; in Toulouse: Meyer, 65; in Berry: M. Bruneau, *Les débuts de la Révolution dans les départements du Cher et de l'Indre* (Paris, 1902), 169-70.

[100] See, for example, the Committee's letter to the district of Nogent-le-Rotrou, Mar. 7, 1791: A.N., D XIX 82, dos. 646, no. 2; and to the department of Drôme, Mar. 29, 1791: A.N., D XIX 85, dos. 671.

[101] Such was the case in Haute-Saône, where an especially liberal policy on restrictions had initially allowed the great majority of priests to be categorized as jurors, but where over half the "jurors" in question became refractories when they were forced to accept or reject the new bishop: Girardot, "Clergé réfractaire et clergé constitutionnel," 126-27.

cooperating with the Revolution and that in the context of a political and social analysis they can be considered as constitutionals. The inner sentiments of an individual soul may well be of interest to the theologian or the Catholic apologist. But such distinctions are of marginal relevance here before the fact that the individual tacitly acknowledged the new legislation by remaining in his parish and at least passively accepting the constitutional prelate.

It is the hypothesis of the present study that with patience one can determine the positions of the overwhelming majority of vicaires and curés in the spring and summer of 1791. But to determine the patterns of reactions is one question. To explain and understand those reactions is another proposition altogether.

The Statistical Approach to the Oath:
An Overview

Historiography of the Oath and Problems of Methodology

How many clergymen actually took and maintained the oath of allegiance to the Constitution in 1791? From the beginning, the question has intrigued and perplexed historians of the period. And, as with so many other problems of central importance for understanding the Revolution, the debate over the oath has reverberated through later French history, continually acquiring new resonances, echoing the contemporary struggles and preoccupations of later generations.[1] The historical tug-of-war over the numbers taking and rejecting the formula of allegiance had already begun in the winter of 1791, as the National Assembly itself attempted to demonstrate that the constitutionals represented "la très grande majorité."[2] The pope, on the other hand, was convinced by his entourage and by the French ambassador, Bernis, that the overwhelming majority had gone in the opposite direction—an interpretation that may have helped propel his general condemnation of the oath and the Civil Constitution. In the meantime, throughout the winter and spring of 1791, the debate raged in rival French newspapers of the Left and the Right.[3]

In the course of the nineteenth century, the episode of the oath continued to fascinate successive generations of historians. Research was pursued with particular vigor by local clergymen whose natural interest in the Revolutionary experiences of their own dioceses was strongly encouraged by Rome, eager for both religious and political reasons to identify the French "martyrs" and "confessors of the faith." Some bishops even mobilized their entire dioceses for systematic parish-by-parish his-

---

[1] See the comments in this regard by the Catholic historian, Paul Pisani, "Le serment de 1791," *Revue du clergé français*, 91 (1917), 481.

[2] *AP*, 24:52.

[3] Emile Sévestre, *Le personnel de l'Eglise constitutionnelle en Normandie, 1791-1795* (Paris, 1925), 2-3. In his bull of April 13, 1791, the pope maintained that very few *(perpauci)* priests had accepted the oath.

tory projects into Revolutionary traditions.[4] Inclined toward hagiography and untrained, for the most part, in the techniques of historical research, the clergy of the mid-nineteenth century nevertheless performed a valuable function in recording the popular recollections of events still present in many of the parishes. Toward the end of the century, this clerical research into the "religious persecution" of the Revolutionary era drew additional inspiration from the contemporary struggle between Church and state which marked the early Third Republic. The trials and tribulations of late-eighteenth-century clergymen were directly compared to the difficulties confronted by priests in the era before and after the Separation of 1906. Local clerical history became a veritable vocation, and rare was the department in which there was not at least one curé devoting years of his life compiling lengthy catalogues on the activities of his predecessors in the midst of the great upheaval—often with the explicit objective of fortifying contemporaries in their own struggles against the Republican anticlericals.[5] Invariably, in all such catalogues, the enumeration of clerical reactions to the oath was one of the central areas of focus.

A major turning point in this historical tradition came in 1906 with the publication of an article by the lay historian Philippe Sagnac, offering the first statistical analysis of oath options throughout the kingdom.[6] Making systematic use of the incomplete survey ordered by the National Assembly on March 12, 1791 Sagnac attempted several generalizations about the clergy as a whole and reached the notable conclusion that a clear majority of ecclesiastics—57.6 percent was his precise figure—had accepted the oath. Not surprisingly, the article incited a spate of rejoinders by clerical historians, critical not only of Sagnac's methodology, but also of the reliability of his source. He was quickly taken to task for the general incompleteness of his documents (with extensive data on only 43

---

[4] See the introduction to the study by Louis Bauzon, Paul Muguet, and Louis Chaumont, *Recherches historiques sur la persécution religieuse dans le département de Saône-et-Loire pendant la Révolution*, 4 vols. (Chalon-sur-Saône, 1889-1903), vol. 1, "Introduction." A similar inquiry was organized in Manche in 1866: Sévestre, 26-27.

[5] See, for example, the introduction to the work by R. de Boysson, *Le clergé périgourdin pendant la persécution révolutionnaire* (Paris, 1907), vii-viii: "La Franc-Maçonnerie, qui décréta la Terreur, règne encore aujourd'hui; elle excite contre vous les mêmes lois d'exception; elle essaie, comme autrefois, de vous mettre en révolte contre vos chefs et de vous faire trahir vos serments." Ludovic Sciout, *Histoire de la Constitution civile du clergé(1790-1801)*, 4 vols. (Paris, 1872-81), 1:2, takes a similar position.

[6] Philippe Sagnac, "Etude statistique sur le clergé constitutionnel et le clergé réfractaire en 1791," *RHMC*, 8 (1906), 97-115.

of the 83 departments); for the inclusion in the figures of numerous non-parish clergymen exempted from the oath; for overlooking the wide span of time during which the documents were drawn up (as early as March and as late as September 1791); and for failing to make distinctions between simple oaths and oaths taken with restrictions. Other critics argued that all such figures were, in any case, irrelevant, since so many clergymen had retracted their oaths in response to the papal condemnation.[7] But the debate over the Sagnac article was salutary insofar as it led to the realization that no reliable conclusions were possible without a refined and standardized statistical approach. Indeed, many of the most carefully crafted studies on the oath written by ecclesiastics—notably those by Sévestre on Normandy, Lesprand on Moselle, Constantin on Meurthe, Sabarthès on Aude, Prévost on Aube, and Giraud on Sarthe—were published precisely in the two or three decades following the Sagnac article.[8]

The majority of such studies were not only more scrupulous in their methodology, but also more comprehensive of the complexities of clerical motivation in the quandary posed by the oath—reflecting in part the mitigation of French religious conflict in the aftermath of World War I. For Abbé Giraud, writing in 1920, the "heroes" of the drama were no longer those ecclesiastics who had totally rejected the oath, but rather those who had taken a restrictive oath and who had struggled desperately to reconcile allegiance to Church with allegiance to country.[9] This trend would continue and even accelerate after World War II, particularly in the years following the Second Vatican Council, as clerical historians demonstrated increasing objectivity and even sympathy for the plight of the constitutional clergy. Of particular importance, in this regard, are the writings of Bernard Plongeron.[10]

[7] For example, Paul Pisani, L'église de Paris et la Révolution, 4 vols. (Paris, 1908), 1:184-89; Pierre de La Gorce, Histoire religieuse de la Révolution, 5 vols. (Paris, 1909-24), 1:399; Sévestre, 3-9; also, some years later, Joseph Camelin, "Pourquoi et comment dresser par diocèse une liste exacte et quasi officielle du clergé constitutionnel," RHEF, 23 (1937), 326-32; and Jean Leflon, La crise révolutionnaire, 1789-1846 (Paris, 1949), 71-73. See also Albert Mathiez, Rome et le clergé français sous la Constituante. La Constitution civile du clergé. L'affaire d'Avignon (Paris, 1911), 465-68.

[8] See bibliography for references.

[9] Maurice Giraud, Essai sur l'histoire religieuse de la Sarthe de 1789 à l'an IV (Paris, 1920).

[10] Bernard Plongeron, Les réguliers de Paris devant le serment constitutionnel (Paris, 1964) and Conscience religieuse en révolution. Regards sur l'historiographie religieuse de la Révolution française (Paris, 1969). See also Jean Godel, La reconstruction concordataire dans le diocèse de Grenoble après la Révolution (Grenoble, 1968); Michel Destombes Le clergé du diocèse d'Amiens et le serment à la Constitution civile, 1790-91 (Amiens, 1971); Adrien Loche, Les prêtres de la Drôme devant la

Yet, despite the numerous local studies of the clergy and the oath published in the twentieth century, the investigation first attempted by Sagnac for the country as a whole has remained largely in abeyance. A preliminary goal of the present undertaking has been to relaunch the 1906 inquiry for each of the eighty-three French departments in existence at the beginning of the Revolution. Initially, this entailed a critical assessment of the original documents from the March 12 survey—both those preserved in the National Archives and those held only in departmental archives which Sagnac never examined.[11] But this incomplete set of contemporary reports had to be supplemented by a wide variety of archival materials and by the information in numerous printed and manuscript local studies assembled by whole teams of clergymen since the middle of the nineteenth century.[12] Though a few of the latter were inspired as much by hagiography as by history, most have been found surprisingly reliable in their information on the oath. More than is sometimes realized, the generation of clerical historians of the turn of the twentieth century was powerfully influenced by historical positivism. The majority, moreover, seems to have approached the task in a spirit of near piety. After all, they were engaged in separating the wheat from the chaff (i.e., the refractories from the jurors); they were weighing men's souls. And with this kind of responsibility, it was important to be accurate; it was essential not to err.[13]

One of the principal reasons for the long disputes and contradictions over the question of the oath has been the failure to bring together comparable figures. For this reason, the task of standardizing the data, derived from so many different sources, has been particularly important. Insofar as possible, the figures presented here refer only to those diocesan priests holding positions at the beginning of January 1791, positions which

---

Révolution (Saint-Vallier, n.d.); and Léon Gruart, *Le diocèse de Senlis et son clergé pendant la Révolution* (Senlis, 1979).

[11] Among the reports found to be near useless were those of Dordogne, Pyrénées-Orientales, and Haute-Saône. But most have been found to represent serious and conscientious efforts on the part of local administrators, and many have been only slightly modified even after the most extensive independent research by local scholars. Thus, *e.g.*, the report sent by the Aude has been verified for its high accuracy by A. Sabarthès, "La Constitution civile du clergé dans le département de l'Aude," *Bulletin de littérature ecclésiastique*, 60 (1959), 38-56, 135-49, 141.

[12] For a detailed account of the sources and methodology, and a justification of these, see Appendix I.

[13] Among the more hagiographically oriented is A. Lecler, *Martyrs et confesseurs de la foi du diocèse de Limoges pendant la Révolution française*, 4 vols. (Limoges, 1897-1904). Nor should one only be wary of clerical historians. The study of Joseph Roman, *Le clergé des Hautes-Alpes pendant la Révolution* (Paris, 1899), is filled with errors and virtually unusable.

specifically bound them to the oath: parish clergymen, ecclesiastical teachers, and chaplains (aumôniers) assigned to such public institutions as
prisons, hospitals, and military installations. To be sure, regular clergymen, chapter clergymen, and other miscellaneous benefice holders sometimes voluntarily participated in the oath ceremonies, and in a few instances they were virtually forced by public opinion to take the oath.[14]
But the overwhelming majority of non-parish clergymen would remain
outside the public eye, free from such political options until August 1792.
Also excluded are those miscellaneous priests—former monks or canons
or chaplains, for the most part—who flooded into the parish clergy after
the spring of 1791 to take up posts vacated by the refractories. But all
such exclusions, dictated by the nature of the law itself, can also be justified
historically. For the vast majority of the population, it was the parish
clergy already established in office at the beginning of the Revolution
which constituted the most influential representative—and often the only
representative—of the Church locally. In their day-to-day lives, most
eighteenth-century Frenchmen rarely if ever encountered the primarily
urban-based canons and regulars.

An additional difficulty concerns the evolution of the oath over time.
In every department there was always a fraction of the clergy which was
in flux on the whole issue: unable to make up its mind, changing its
mind under the influence of various secular or ecclesiastical pressures, or
taking up restrictive positions on the question subject to modification in
one direction or another. Wherever possible, restrictive oaths have been
judged, not in terms of the precise words pronounced, but in terms of
the clergymen's ultimate decision in the autumn of 1792 to remain at
their posts or to emigrate—a methodological solution persuasively defended by Emile Sévestre. But, obviously, it is not always feasible to
follow each individual through 1792, and one must sometimes resort to
estimations and to a certain amount of guesswork.[15] As for those ecclesiastics who accepted the oath but refused to accept the constitutional
bishop, those whom Mathiez described as "non-schismatic jurors," all
have been counted here as retracting their oaths—for this is exactly how
they were classified by departmental administrators.[16] In order to follow

[14] Plongeron, 76-81.

[15] Emile Sévestre, *Liste critique des ecclésiastiques fonctionnaires publics insermentés et assermentés en Normandie (Janvier-Mai 1791)* (Paris, 1922), 15. Note that no figures are available for Sarthe in 1791, but Giraud, 226-48, argues that the overall figures changed very little from 1791 to 1792 and so the latter figures have been used here.

[16] Mathiez, 467.

up on the restrictions and to trace the movement of retractions, oath-taking percentages have been calculated for three different periods: first, for the spring of 1791, at the time of the official government survey; second, for the summer of 1791, after the position of the pope had become widely known and as clergymen were being required to prove their allegiance to the constitutional bishops; third, for the autumn of 1792, following the August decree which ordered all refractories to leave the country. In point of fact, the history of the oath did not end with the beginning of the Republic. There would be several later oath requirements and several waves of retractions—especially in the months following the Terror and the de-Christianization of the Year II. But the sources for tracing clerical opinion during this later period are usually far less satisfactory, particularly for the period of the first Separation (1795-1801), when government record-keeping on the clergy became much more meager. In any case, the principal objective here is to assess the *initial* reactions of clergy and laity to the transformation of religious structures. With the onset of official and club-inspired anticlericalism, already emerging in 1792, the whole context and meaning of oath decisions would be dramatically altered.

Despite the considerable care taken in obtaining and standardizing figures on the oath, the statistics are inevitably far from perfect. If something is known about every department, there are about ten in which data are incomplete for portions of the department and a dozen for which the reliability of the sources used is not altogether certain.[17] Elsewhere, information is available only for the parish clergy and sometimes only for the curés. And, unfortunately, the evolution of the oath through 1792 can be followed in only about half of the departments. Though future research in local archives—especially in municipal and parish archives—may substantially improve the accuracy, there are half a dozen cases in which the physical destruction of documents through war or fire may render such refinement forever unattainable. Nevertheless, it is still possible to obtain a relatively dependable picture of the positions of close to 50,000 parish clergymen, representing an estimated 83 percent of the curés and 72 percent of the vicaires holding posts in 1790.[18] Even if one excludes those departments for which the reliability of the data is some-

---

[17] The "reliability factor" must be taken into account when making use of the tables in Appendix II.

[18] See Table 2. In 1790 there were an estimated total of 39,000 curés and 20,500 vicaires in the kingdom: Timothy Tackett and Claude Langlois, "Ecclesiastical Structures and Clerical Geography on the Eve of the French Revolution," *FHS*, 11 (1980), 357.

what uncertain, the figures still touch on three-fourths of the total contingent[19]—though, unfortunately, in both cases information is probably less complete for the ecclesiastical teachers and chaplains.[20]

The information from this quantitative survey on the oath will serve as the basis of the analysis throughout much of the present study. But, in the remainder of the chapter, it will be useful to present a preliminary overview on the oath over time, by clerical position and by geographic region.

The Oath over Time

To the question which has so haunted historians of the Church and the French Revolution, it now seems possible to respond with a large measure of certainty. To be sure, the diversity of sources and the very fluidity of opinion among some of the clergymen prevent the compilation of an overall summation of oath adherence at a single point in time. Yet if one brings together data ranging for given departments from the early spring through the summer of 1791—and, as we shall see below, the percentage change during this period was relatively slight—one arrives at what is certainly a closely defined order of magnitude for the first half of the year. (See Table 2.) From these calculations it is clear that the initial phase of the "battle of the oath" was won by the constitutionals. Yet the margin of victory was remarkably close and precarious. Between 52 and 55 percent—probably closer to 55 percent—of the parish clergy would initially throw in their lot with the Revolution and the Civil Constitution.[21] Even when one excludes those departments for which information is less certain, the proportion of jurors remains virtually unchanged. Although the non-parish clergy required to swear the oath was decidedly more refractory, their total numbers were relatively small. Including this group would probably lower the overall proportion very slightly. Thus,

[19] I.e., 45,763 of about 59,500, or 77 percent.

[20] The circular letter of Mar. 17 from the Ecclesiastical Committee requesting a list of jurors and non-jurors in each department left some ambiguity as to which categories of clergymen were to be noted by the local administrators. It mentioned the decree calling for a survey of all "fonctionnaires publics ecclésiastiques" but then specified that distinctions were to be made between "bishops, curés, and vicaires" only: See Sévestre, L'acceptation, 175-76.

[21] The figures in Table 2 for "Total Parish Clergy," actually include, in the case of several departments, a certain number of non-parish clergymen who could not be removed. This may explain the difference between the proportions calculated from these totals (52.2-52.3 percent) and those calculated from the total for parish clergymen broken down by category (54.5 percent). The reality was undoubtedly closer to the latter percentage.

TABLE 2
Total Oath-takers by Category
(Spring-Summer 1791) (1)

	Oath-takers	Total Clergy	%
Total parish clergy (2)	26,542	50,876	52.2
Total parish clergy (2) (excluding "uncertain" departments) (3)	24,114	46,088	52.3
By category:			
Curés	18,639	32,516	57.3
Vicaires	6,534	13,661	47.8
Desservants	542	997	54.4
Total	25,715	47,174	54.5
Regular curés (sample) (4)	70	123	57
Non-parish clergy:			
Collège professors			
Seculars	243	653	37.2
Regulars and Congreganists	391	535	73.1
(Uncertain)	(204)	(337)	(60.5)
Total	838	1,525	55.0
Seminary professors	24	327	7.3
University professors	8	37	22
Aumôniers	211	504	41.9

(1) Figures are for the summer of 1791, if known; otherwise, they are for the spring of 1791. See Appendices II and III for details.

(2) Included are a few departments in which non-parish clergymen subjected to the oath were mixed with curés and vicaires (*i.e.*, Loir-et-Cher, Nièvre, Nord, etc.).

(3) Aisne, Bouches-du-Rhône, Corrèze, Corse, Gers, Jura, Lozère, Oise, Deux-Sèvres.

(4) See text for explanation.

in terms of the preliminary question of overall totals, the data presented here would confirm the approximate validity of Sagnac's estimation.

On the other hand, it is now evident that many historians have overestimated the number of oath retractions occurring during the early years of the Revolution. For about half of the departments one can follow the evolution of oath-taking ratios over specific intervals of time. (See Table 3.) Thus, in the thirty-five departments for which such calculations are feasible, only about six percent of the constitutionals are found to have retracted between the spring and the summer of 1791. Based on the records of another set of thirty-six departments—not altogether the same set—an additional six percent would seem to have retracted between the summer of 1791 and the autumn of 1792. By the latter date the proportion of jurors in the country may have dipped just under the fifty percent mark. There were, to be sure, exceptions to this pattern, areas in which

TABLE 3

Oath Retractions: All Parish Clergy

(Spring 1791 to Autumn 1792)

	Oath-takers	Total Clergy	%	% Decline
For 22 departments (1):				
Spring 1791	9,096	15,741	57.8	—
Summer 1791	8,689	"	55.2	4.5
Autumn 1792	8,126	"	51.6	6.5
For 35 departments (2):				
Spring 1791	13,950	23,563	59.2	—
Summer 1791	13,114	"	55.7	6.0
For 27 departments (3):				
Summer 1791	9,953	17,355	57.3	—
Autumn 1792	9,324	"	53.7	6.3
For 36 departments (4):				
Spring 1791	12,904	23,233	55.5	—
Autumn 1792	11,374	"	49.0	11.9

(1) Departments of Basses-Alpes, Ariège (diocese of Couserans), Aude, Calvados, Cantal, Charente, Drôme, Eure, Indre, Isère, Manche, Mayenne, Morbihan, Moselle, Orne, Haut-Rhin, Seine-Inférieure, Somme, Var, Vienne, Vosges, and Yonne.

(2) Departments in note 1, plus Ain, Aube, Bouches-du-Rhône, Côtes-du-Nord, Doubs, Gard, Haute-Garonne, Gironde, Marne (except district of Reims), Puy-de-Dôme, Basses-Pyrénées (diocese of Lescar), Seine-et-Marne, and Seine-et-Oise.

(3) Departments in note 1, plus Hautes-Alpes (except districts of Embrun and Briançon), Cher, Creuse, Indre-et-Loire, Maine-et-Loire.

(4) Departments in note 1, plus Aveyron, Côte-d'Or, Dordogne, Doubs, Eure-et-Loir, Finistère, Landes, Loir-et-Cher, Lot, Lot-et-Garonne (diocese of Agen), Lozère, Rhône-et-Loire (districts of Montbrison, Roanne, and St.-Etienne only), Vendée, and Haute-Vienne.

the pope's condemnation and pressure from local clerical leaders would seem to have influenced far greater numbers to repudiate their initial decisions.[22] But, however the calculations are made, the overall effect was to reduce the proportion of oath-takers by only about six percentage points during this period of a year and a half. For the overwhelming majority—nearly 90 percent—the initial decision seems to have been steadfastly maintained, at least through the early months of the Republic. The relative firmness in oath commitments throughout this period should not be overlooked. It is perhaps an additional indication of the serious reflection on which clergymen had based their initial reactions.[23]

The myth of large-scale early retractions can be traced in part to the confusion between retractions occurring in 1791 and those—much more numerous—announced after the interval of the Terror. It was often perpetuated by the ecclesiastical administrators of the early Concordat period, eager to substantiate a massively non-juring clergy, and by Catholic apologists of the later nineteenth century.[24] But a second source of error has been the failure to distinguish between true renunciations of legitimate oaths and the public recognition of originally restrictive oaths. In a few departments, such as Haute-Saône, the invalidation of large numbers of oaths in the summer of 1791—as administrators first began enforcing the interdiction on restrictions—produced a flood of "new" refractories that impressed many contemporaries as a wave of retractions. The impression was only reinforced by the actions of those individual clergymen who, harassed by their consciences, formally "retracted" oaths that were actually restrictive and invalid to begin with.[25]

In point of fact, a substantial number of all "refractories" had probably

---

[22] Among the departments revealing large declines in the proportion of oath-takers in early 1791 were Aude (70 to 58 percent) and Bouches-du-Rhône (70 to 50 percent). But note that in the case of Aude, there is some doubt as to the exact date of retractions. See Appendix II.

[23] It is to be noted that a movement in the opposite direction, from refractory to juror, also occurred. But this was much more rare and usually insignificant statistically. See, however, Giraud, 225-26.

[24] Among the studies which lump together retractions occurring at any time between 1791 and 1801 are Antoine Durengues, *L'église d'Agen pendant la Révolution. Le diocèse de Lot-et-Garonne* (Agen, 1903), and Joseph Beauhaire, *Chronologie des évêques, des curés, des vicaires et des autres prêtres de ce diocèse [de Chartres]* (Paris, 1892). For this very reason, both works are difficult to use.

[25] Jean Girardot, "La Constitution civile du clergé et son application en Haute-Saône," *Bulletin de la Société d'agriculture, lettres, sciences et arts du département de la Haute-Saône* (1933), 27-28. Also Marquis Marie de Roux, *La Révolution à Poitiers et dans la Vienne* (Paris, 1911), 385; and Rodolphe Reuss, *La Constitution civile du clergé et la crise religieuse en Alsace (1790-1795)*, 2 vols. (Strasbourg, 1922), 1:85.

sworn restrictive oaths, following in this the specific recommendation of the bishops in their *Exposition des principes*. Unfortunately, the number of restrictive oaths, as opposed to outright refusals, is extremely difficult to estimate. Many administrators made no distinction between the two types of reactions, listing restrictions and total rejections under the blanket category of "refusals." And some clergymen, knowing that restrictive oaths were unacceptable, never even bothered to present themselves.[26] In twenty-seven departments where the distinction was made in a relatively consistent manner, fully one-third of the refractories are found to have taken restrictive oaths.[27]

The Oath by Clerical Position

If the changes in oath-taking status over time were relatively minor, the differences registered between the various categories of clergymen were considerable. Inevitably, the most dramatic contrast separated the "upper" clergy from the "lower" clergy. At a time when more than fifty percent of the parish clergy were opting for the Revolutionary settlement, only seven of 160 bishops and episcopal coadjutors of the Old Regime and only four of the prelates in the newly created dioceses would ultimately join the ranks of the constitutionals.[28] But, even within the lower clergy, there were significant variations, variations which provide preliminary evidence of the motivation involved in the oath decision. (See Table 2.)

Within the corps of parish clergymen it was the curés who registered

[26] The National Assembly officially rejected the distinction between restrictions and refusals in the lists which they requested from the departments on Mar. 12, 1791: *AP*, 24:52; and many, though not all, administrators respected this wish. See, for example, the district of Lavaur, cover letter to oath lists, A.D. Tarn, L 1056. The town council of Strasbourg refused even to attend oaths which were to be restrictive: A.N., D XIX 82, dos. 641, no 5. There are several examples of priests not even bothering to take restrictive oaths: e.g., in Calvados: Sévestre, *L'acceptation*, 343-44; in Moselle: P. Lesprand, *Le clergé de la Moselle pendant la Révolution. Les débuts de la Révolution et la suppression des ordres religieux*, 4 vols. (Montguy-lès-Metz, 1934-39), 4:36-37.

[27] Of 8,474 invalid oaths for which such data exist, 2,876 were restrictive. But among individual departments, the proportions varied from 3 percent to 100 percent restrictive oaths. Included in these statistics are all or part of the departments of Ain, Allier, Basses-Alpes, Aube, Aude, Calvados, Cher, Côtes-du-Nord, Doubs, Eure, Gers, Indre, Isère, Loire-Inférieure, Lot, Manche, Marne, Haute-Marne, Mayenne, Morbihan, Moselle, Orne, Pas-de-Calais, Seine-Inférieure, Seine-et-Marne, Somme, and Yonne. See Appendix II for sources.

[28] John McManners, *The French Revolution and the Church* (London, 1969), 48. This is not, however, to minimize the range of nuances in the positions of individual bishops. See below, chp. 5.

the highest oath-taking rates for the country as a whole. Close to three-fifths of the parish priests (57.3 percent) had declared their willingness to accept the Civil Constitution by the summer of 1791 and, in all likelihood, the jurors still constituted over one-half of the total during the early years of the Republic and the Terror. The same overall proportion seems to have held not only for the secular curés—the vast majority in most areas of the kingdom—but also for the small contingent of curés who were members of regular orders.[29] Although it was clearly not the massive backing which many in the National Assembly had hoped for and expected, the numbers of curé patriots were substantial and significant, nevertheless. The backing of so many of these influential parish leaders was an important if limited victory for the Constituent and helps to explain the undeniable vitality of the Constitutional Church in large areas of the country through 1793.

Among the assistant priests, the vicaires, however, the situation was somewhat different. Curiously, many contemporaries were convinced that this category of clergymen had backed the Revolution even more strongly than the curés. One deputy, Pierre-Louis Prieur, extolled their praises before the Assembly itself in March 1791: "There is no one among us who does not know how much the vicaires everywhere in France have given proof of their patriotism since the beginning of the Revolution. . . . It is they, before all others, who have given the example in accepting the oath."[30] Other more cynical analysts have cited the examples of vicaires who took the oath so they could assume the posts of their own refractory curés.[31] But, in actuality, almost everywhere in the kingdom a larger proportion of vicaires than of curés rejected the oath. For France as a whole, the percentage of oath-taking vicaires was a full ten points lower (47.8 percent), and in certain departments the difference was as great as 20 points.[32] In only fifteen of the seventy-four departments for which distinctions can be made did the vicaires attain higher percentages than the parish priests—and in most cases it was a difference of only a few percentage points.[33] The reasons for the divergence of reactions between

[29] The sample included Aude (4 out of 5 regulars were jurors); Cher (13 of 18); Marne (7 of 9); Moselle (5 of 25); Haut-Rhin (7 of 18); Sarthe (13 of 25), and Somme (21 of 23). See Appendix II for sources.

[30] *AP*, 24:88.

[31] See Charles Jolivet, *La Révolution en Ardèche* (Largentière, 1930), 265; and Sévestre, *Liste critique*, 310.

[32] The greatest differences were in Doubs (23 points lower), Ardèche (20 points), Landes (19 points), and Moselle (18 points): see Appendix II.

[33] The greatest differences were in Lot (8 points higher), Indre-et-Loire (8 points), Cher (6

these two groups of parish clergymen will have to be taken up with some care at a later point. But it is clear from the outset that the vicaires differed from the curés in numerous ways. Not only were they younger, on the average, than the curés, but they were almost always serving in the presence of other priests, and a substantially greater proportion inhabited towns rather than villages. The position of vicaire was also, by its very nature, distinctly more transient and less rooted in the parish.[34] Yet the variation in the relative oath-taking rates of vicaires and curés from region to region would also suggest that different sets of forces may have been at work in different sectors of the kingdom.

It was undoubtedly some combination of these same forces which explains the curious difference in oath percentages between the vicaires in general and that special category of assistant priest known most commonly as "desservants."[35] In fact, the latter group accepted the oath in a proportion only slightly less than that of the curés: between 54 and 55 percent for the kingdom as a whole. There were actually two types of desservants under the Old Regime, one named to annexes in outlying settlements within larger parishes, the other assigned to assume the direction of parishes in which the curé was too disabled or aged to perform his normal tasks. But, in either case, the desservants had substantially greater authority than the vicaires. More importantly, they had already accomplished a significant upward step in their careers, one that usually assured them nomination to full curial status within a relatively short span of time. Undoubtedly, it was the desservant's far greater permanence and integration into the local society, coupled with the expectation of an imminent promotion to a cure, which put him in a situation closer to that of the parish priest.

Although the evidence for the non-parish clergy held to the oath is far less complete, it seems clear that this group was substantially more refractory than the curés, vicaires, or desservants. Of the *aumôniers* or chaplains, only about two-fifths would pass to the constitutional clergy. Yet it is difficult to generalize about the motivation of this heterogeneous group. Some aumôniers were seculars; others were members of religious orders. A certain number regularly participated in pastoral functions, ministering to the poor and sick in hospitals and holding religious services in chapels which served as annex parish churches. Others ministered

---

points), and Var (6 points). Nowhere else were the vicaires' juring rates greater than 4 points higher than those of the curés.

[34] See the author's *Priest and Parish in Eighteenth-Century France* (Princeton, 1977), 98-99.

[35] Also called "vicaires en chef" in the north and east, and "pro-curés" in the southeast.

primarily to prisons or military barracks or to women religious in convents, and thus had very little association with the general population. The great majority, however, were serving in large and middle-sized towns, a milieu in which—as we shall see—most clergymen tended to refuse the oath.

Within the teaching corps, still essentially dominated by the clergy, the elite corps of university and seminary professors generally took even stronger stances against the oath and the new organization of the Church. Only a little over one-fifth of the university teachers would seem to have taken the oath, though the data on this group are particularly incomplete. The most striking and massive refusal, however, emerged among the corps of instructors in the major seminaries. Of those for which information could be gathered, only 7 percent, twenty-four of 327, were willing to cooperate with the new Church. A fourth of the jurors were in the single diocese of Sens, whose bishop, Loménie de Brienne, had thrown in his lot with the Revolution. In most local histories, the overwhelming refusal by the seminary instructors is attributed to the superior theological understanding of this group. But that greater learning did not necessarily lead to a rejection of the oath is well illustrated by the case of the ecclesiastical secondary teachers. Taken together, the *professeurs de collège* would appear to have backed the Civil Constitution in much the same proportions as the curés (55 percent jurors). Nevertheless, some striking differences were visible between the various elements of the teaching corps. By and large, there was a substantial cohesiveness among the teachers of a given school, with the great majority, if not the totality, opting *en bloc* for or against the oath. A very loose correspondence was clearly in evidence between the decision of the professors and that of the parish clergy in the same departments.[36] Yet the key factor was probably the order or congregation to which the teachers belonged. Close to 90 percent of the Oratorians and Doctrinaires and 70 percent of the Benedictines enthusiastically embraced the Revolutionary legislation, while professors belonging to the Carmelites, the Barnabites, the Eudists, and the Cordeliers were generally refractory. Even more remarkable, only 37

---

[36] Much of the information on oath-taking among the *professeurs de collège* was very kindly shared with me by Marie-Madeleine Compère and Dominique Julia. See the first volume of their *Les collèges français, 16e-18e siècles. Répertoire 1. France du Midi* (Paris, 1984). Their research will eventually give us a far more detailed picture of the professors' reactions to the Revolution. The correlation coefficient between the percentage of teachers taking the oath per department in the summer or spring of 1791 and the percentage of parish clergy taking the oath in the same departments was 0.34 for a total of 74 departments: a weak but significant correlation.

percent of the teachers belonging to the secular clergy took the oath, as compared to 73 percent of the regulars and the *congréganistes*.[37] One can presume that the secular clergy teaching in the secondary schools were more tightly disciplined and controlled by the episcopacy than were the teaching congregations, many of whose members were simple tonsured clerics. In any case, the relatively strong overall backing which the teachers lent to the National Assembly would greatly enhance the continuity of education during the early years of the Revolution and facilitate the indoctrination of the youth. In terms of their functions and influence in society, the curés and *collège* teachers were figures whose significance to the Revolution was far greater than that of the chaplains, the seminary professors, or the university professors.

The National Assembly would be much less successful, however, in winning over another category of ecclesiastics with perhaps an even greater visibility and importance for national public opinion: the clergy sitting in the Constituent itself. In fact, the influence of the ecclesiastical deputies had been deemed of such import that they were asked to swear the oath directly in front of the Assembly itself. The results were starkly disappointing, even astonishing to the members of the Left who now controlled the Constituent. By best count, only 81 of 263—less than a third—of the clerical deputies present in Paris actually subscribed to the oath and did not retract in the following weeks: significantly below the national rate.[38] In truth, the clerical representation in the assembly was anything but a microcosm of the corps held to the oath throughout France. About a sixth of the deputies were prelates, and another eighth held

[37] Preliminary statistics for oath-taking among the *professeurs de collège*: Oratorians: 144 oath-takers out of 165; Doctrinaires: 142 of 160; chanoines de Notre Sauveur: 34 of 45; Benedictines: 18 of 26; Barnabites: 9 of 22; Sacramentaires: 10 of 26; Josephists: 10 of 15; Cordeliers: 1 of 8; Lazarists: 0 of 4; Carmelites: 2 of 6; Eudists 1 of 15; seculars: 243 of 653; unknown affiliation: 215 of 311.

[38] For the identification of clerical deputies sitting in early 1791, see Armand Brette, ed., *Recueil de documents relatifs à la convocation des Etats-Généraux de 1789*, 4 vols. (Paris, 1894-1915), vol. 2. Those deputies taking the oath can be found in *AP*, 21:678-79 and 22:1-2. Some of these retracted immediately or claimed they had taken restrictive oaths: see *Liste de MM. les archevêques, évêques, curés et autre membres ecclésiastiques de l'Assemblée nationale, qui croyant ne pouvoir, par devoir de conscience, prêter le serment dans la formule qu'exigeait l'Assemblée, ont adopté le 4 janvier celle qui avait été proposée par M. l'évêque de Clermont* (Paris, 1791). But an unspecified additional number were absent from Paris in early January—perhaps because of Christmas duties—and their options are not generally known. Thus, for example, Poupard, curé de Sancerre and deputy from Bourges, took the oath in Bourges on Jan. 16, 1791, but is not mentioned in the *AP*: see notes by Chanoine Laugardière, A.D. Cher, J 828.

posts, which under different circumstances would have left them immune to the requirement altogether.[39] Among this non-parish clergy in the Assembly, only 12 percent took the oath.[40] As for the curés, fully one-fourth came from towns (compared to perhaps two percent of the curés generally), and several held positions or distinctions besides their cures which were quite atypical of the average priest.[41] Yet, even among the simple rural curés in the Assembly, only two-fifths (42 percent) accepted and maintained the oath.[42] Without putting into question the theological considerations which undoubtedly weighed in the minds of the deputies,[43] one suspects the powerful effects of politics, of political perceptions and alignments forged through the intense experience of the previous months in Versailles and Paris. Invariably, the deputies had been forced to confront the blossoming anticlericalism among sectors of the Parisian population and among some segments of the National Assembly itself, and a number of deputies had become personally convinced of the ill-will of some of their colleagues in regard to the Catholic religion.[44] The situation of the clerical deputies can alert us to the potential importance of purely political considerations and to the general social ambiance in which ecclesiastical options were made.

The Oath in Town and Country

Indeed, there is ample evidence, even from this preliminary overview, that the milieu in which priests lived weighed heavily on their reactions in 1791. A particularly revealing distinction concerns the size and nature

[39] Of 301 clerical deputies, 210 were curés; 3 were professors; 50 were bishops, archbishops, and coadjutants; 38 held positions for which they would not have been held to the oath if they had not been deputies.

[40] Eleven of 95 for which the options are known.

[41] Six curés held positions as canons conjointly; there was also a curé-*officiel*, a curé-*conseiller au Parlement*, and a curé-vicar-general. At least two of the curés are known to have been nobles.

[42] Sixty-two of the 147 for which the options are known.

[43] Grégoire describes a special meeting which was held among many of the ecclesiastical deputies just before they presented themselves for the oath ceremonies, a meeting during which there was apparently a good deal of discussion and soul searching: Henri Grégoire, *Mémoires*, 2 vols., H. Carnot, ed. (Paris, 1840), 1:15.

[44] See, for example, the letter to a friend by curé Fournier of the bailliage of Amiens. The curé argued that he did not believe the Civil Constitution was bad in itself. His greatest doubts concerned the use which certain deputies—"égarés du côté de la religion"—might make of it: Michel Destombes *Le clergé du diocèse d'Amiens et le serment à la Constitution civile, 1790-91* (Amiens, 1971), 326-28.

of the communities in which individual clergymen served. The vast majority of parishes in Old-Regime France were relatively small and primarily rural and agricultural in character. But perhaps 2 percent of the municipalities with some 18 or 19 percent of the French population contained 2,000 or more inhabitants living in a central agglomeration— the definition of a "town" used by the Napoleonic administration, which will serve for present purposes as well as any other.[45] Within these towns the parish clergy subscribed to the oath at a somewhat lower rate than in the kingdom generally: just over 43 percent by the summer of 1791. (See Table 4.)[46] The overall trend seems to have held, moreover, in four out of five of the individual departments.[47] If the non-parish clergymen held to the oath are included—as a rule much more numerous in the towns than in the country—the proportion drops to 41 percent.[48] But, even more significant, the proportion of oath-takers seemed to drop proportionately as the towns became larger. In the smallest of the towns, those with under 8,000 inhabitants, the jurors among the parish clergy were actually in the majority—with 52 percent oath-taking, only slightly below the kingdom-wide rate for all constitutionals. Whatever it was that made the perception of the oath different in the urban milieu seems to have been scarcely present in this class of towns. But in the group with populations between 8,000 and 20,000, the proportion of jurors fell to 41 percent; in those between 20,000 and 50,000, it dipped to 32 percent; and in the largest provincial capitals of the realm, with over 50,000 inhabitants, only 25 percent of the parish clergy adopted the Civil Constitution. Only Paris, with its huge conglomeration of upward of 600,000 persons and its unique social and political conditions, did not seem to fit the general pattern.

The origins of this curious correlation between oath-taking and the urban setting remain to be explored. Yet the significance of the phenom-

[45] René Le Mée, "Population agglomérée, population éparse au début du XIXe siècle," *Annales de démographie historique, 1971* (Paris, 1972), 467-93. The Napoleonic definition is preferable to the legal formula of the Old Regime itself which had often been designated during the Middle Ages and was no longer related to reality. Le Mée has also been used for the population of the towns in question. These figures are for 1806 and are obviously not the same as in 1791. But the proportionate differences between towns had probably not changed very much.

[46] Figures are for 640 of the 728 "towns" listed by Le Mée, 88 percent of the total.

[47] The departments in which the juring rates of the town clergy were higher than those in the surrounding rural areas are as follows: Creuse, Dordogne, Indre-et-Loire, Isère, Lot, Lozère, Morbihan, Puy-de-Dôme, Pyrénées-Orientales, Haute-Saône, Var, and Yonne.

[48] Among *fonctionnaires publics* held to the oath in the towns, for which figures are known, 1,480 of 3,593 appear to have taken the oath.

TABLE 4

Percentage of Jurors in Towns

Parish Clergy Only

(Spring-Summer 1791)

	Total Oath-takers	*Total Clergy*	*Percent*	*No. of Towns*
Small towns (2-8,000 population)	627	1,199	52.3	541
Medium towns (8-20,000 population)	235	577	40.7	68
Large towns (1) (20-50,000 population)	159	495	32.1	22
Largest towns (2) (over 50,000 population)	62	248	25.0	8
City of Paris	57	119	47.9	1
Total for which data available	1,140	2,638	43.2	640

(1) Orléans, Caen, Dijon, Besançon, Montpellier, Tours, Grenoble, Angers, Reims, Nancy, Clermont-Ferrand, Amiens, Toulon, Poitiers, Limoges, Troyes, Brest, Nîmes, Lorient, Metz, Dunkerque, Saint-Omer.

(2) Marseille, Toulouse, Bordeaux, Nantes, Lille, Strasbourg, Lyon, Rouen.

enon is apparent from the outset. For France as a whole, the contingent of town clergymen would lower the oath rate by only about one percentage point.[49] Yet the strength of the Constitutional Church would be greatly reduced by the defection of this influential and highly visible segment of the parish clergy. It was precisely these urban clergymen who would most frequently and directly confront the departmental and district administrators, and the concerted opposition of such priests would have an adverse effect, out of all proportion to their numbers, on the tone of relationships between Church and state. For the Revolutionaries and the Revolution, the loss of so large a segment of the town clergy was to present a particularly unfortunate turn of events.

[49] Removing the urban parish clergymen would raise the oath rate from 54.6 to about 55.8 percent.

The Geography of the Oath

For contemporaries themselves, however, the most obvious and unsettling pattern to the oath-taking experience was not the town and country split but the broader regional polarizations. The unequal geographic distribution of oath-takers was readily apparent to the National Assembly in the letters from constituents pouring into Paris in January and February 1791. While clergymen in whole blocks of departments were overwhelmingly enthusiastic in their response, elsewhere they were massively refusing the oath. Indeed, one of the Assembly's chief rationales for its March survey of oath-takers was to enable departmental administrators in predominantly refractory areas to identify regions from which replacement clergymen might hopefully be recruited.[50] While the broad contours of this distribution were known to the Revolutionaries themselves and were outlined more carefully by Sagnac, the statistics presented here, almost complete for the entire kingdom and broken down by district rather than by department, permit a much finer resolution of the oath landscape. Inevitably, given the nature of the sources, a photographic representation of the phenomenon at a given moment is impossible. But the composite map for the spring and summer of 1791 is a close approximation of a reality which, in any case, changed by only a few percentage points during the period. (See Figure A.)[51]

Far more than the traditional representation by department, the breakdown by district provides trenchant testimony of the extraordinary range in clerical reactions. If aggregate departmental rates extended from below ten to above ninety percent, the district-level proportions stretched out across almost every possible percentage increment, from zero to one hundred percent jurors, with a median value at fifty-nine percent and with six or seven distinct nodal points scattered across the entire spectrum.[52] But, despite the motley appearance of the map, an overarching

[50] *AP*, 24:52.

[51] When data for both the spring and the summer of 1791 were available, the summer data were used by preference. In the case of Sarthe, data were taken from August 1792, but these figures were apparently little changed from 1791: see above, note 15. The map represents parish clergy or curés only, except in those cases where it was not possible to distinguish parish clergy from all *fonctionnaires publics*. In a few departments for which data by district were not available, alternate sub-departmental units have been used (*e.g.*, nineteenth-century *arrondissements* or Old-Régime ecclesiastical divisions). Those departments for which data were considered "uncertain" have been indicated by thicker boundary lines on the map.

[52] The maximum distribution was at 60 percent oath-takers per district. Other nodal areas

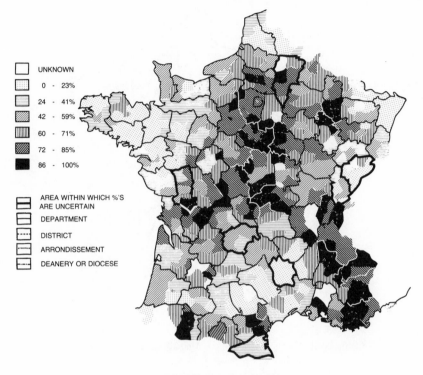

FIGURE A
Percentage of Jurors by District, Spring-Summer 1791.

regional coherence in oath-taking patterns remains striking—a coherence that emerges all the more clearly if one projects a single dichotomy separating the districts above and below the median. (See Figure B.) Of the predominantly refractory zones, the largest and most cohesive marked off the whole northwestern corner of the French hexagon: the "West" of Normandy, Brittany, Maine, Anjou, and Lower Poitou. A second major center of non-jurors was concentrated in the core of the Massif-Central—in Velay, Auvergne, Gévaudan, and Rouergue—but with a southwesterly extension across much of Languedoc through the middle Garonne valley as far west as the Landes. Smaller, but equally refractory, zones could be found at other peripheral points on the French map: in the northern region of Flanders, Artois, and Hainaut; at the eastern frontier from northern Lorraine and Alsace to the southern limits of Franche-Comté;

were in the vicinity of 8-14 percent, 35-39 percent, 67-69 percent, 75-78 percent, and 98-100 percent.

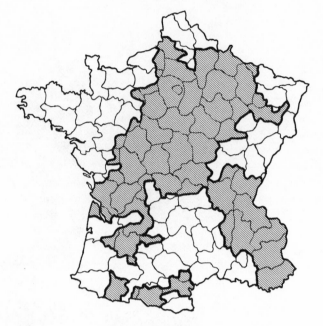

FIGURE B
Oath-taking Above and Below the Median. (Shading marks areas
within which most districts were above
the median oath-taking rate.)

in the far south of Roussillon; and the far southwest of the Basque
country. In all of these regions, district juring rates often dipped into
the lowest sextile: below twenty-four percent.

The zones of strong support for the Civil Constitution were, in some
respects, more widely scattered and diffuse. The "darkest" districts of
the upper sextile, with over eighty-five percent oath-takers, were to be
found in the Parisian Basin—particularly in the south, toward Orléanais—as well as in eastern Champagne, in Berry-Bourbonnais, in parts
of Poitou, in portions of the Pyrenees and Mediterranean Languedoc,
and along the southeastern frontier from Bresse and Bugey to Provence.
But if one focuses more generally on all those districts above the median,
two major zones emerge in which the substantial majority of the parish
clergy embraced the Revolution: first, the Alpine sector, from Lyon to
Nice, and including most of Dauphiné and Provence; and, second, a large
central wedge of provinces, bounded approximately by Picardy, Champagne, and central Lorraine in the north, and by Guyenne and the
Gironde at the "point" in the south.

Given the paucity of information on the evolution of the oath after 1791, it is much more difficult to trace the later geography. A fragmentary picture is suggested by mapping the percentage decrease in oath-takers through the autumn of 1792. (See Figure C.) By and large, the departments registering the most retractions seem to have been those which were already predominantly refractory themselves or which adjoined refractory zones. This was notably the case in portions of the west and the Midi. By contrast, the heavily constitutional departments in the region around Paris seem to have changed only very slightly in the months following the initial oath. Thus, the movements of retractions through late 1792 had the primary effect of further polarizing the country. As the Convention took power and the Republic was created, the two Frances of the oath were becoming even more distinct and at odds with one another.

In the following chapters, as we attempt to sort through the circumstances and motivations surrounding the reactions of priests and laity to the oath of 1791, we must continually refer back to these overall patterns for the nation as a whole. From this preliminary analysis it is evident

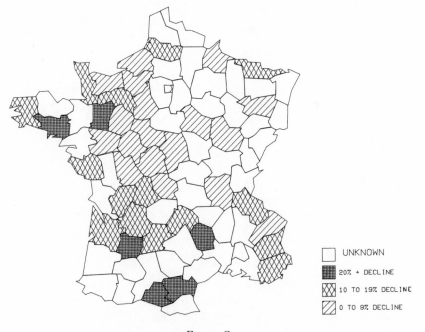

UNKNOWN

20% + DECLINE

10 TO 19% DECLINE

0 TO 9% DECLINE

Figure C
Extent of Oath Retractions, Spring-Summer 1791 to Fall 1792.

that attitudes toward the Civil Constitution were conditioned not only by the personal backgrounds and ecclesiastical experience of clergymen, but also by influence from the secular society in which they lived and worked. No explanatory scheme which fails to come to grips with the remarkable patterns of regional variation and town-and-country diversity can hope to be viable beyond the local microcosm.

PART TWO

THE CLERGY CONFRONTS THE OATH

THREE

Clergymen Explain Their Oaths

FOR the clergyman confronting the oath of allegiance in the winter of 1791, there was no shortage of advice on the meaning and legitimacy of that option. Not since the spring of 1789 and the initial debate over the powers and composition of the Estates General had a single issue given rise to such a flurry of debate and discussion everywhere in the country. At the highest level of authority, the bishops in the National Assembly had taken up the challenge as early as October 30, 1790 in their widely circulated discourse, *L'exposition des principes*. Several of their more combative and articulate colleagues—among whom the bishop of Boulogne was no doubt the most influential—would sustain the struggle in various published tracts against the ecclesiastical reforms and the oath. On the constitutional side, the deputies Grégoire, Camus, Treilhard, and Martineau all wrote learned treatises explaining and justifying the new laws.[1] These, too, would be circulated throughout the kingdom, along with the National Assembly's official statement of January 21. Soon the "battle of the oath" was joined by clergymen and laymen alike in virtually every department. Old-Regime bishops distributed pastoral letters, written by themselves or by others; patriot priests countered with defenses of the constitution; departmental administrations passed out reprints of appropriate speeches and articles; and local popular societies entered the fray—in spite, or perhaps because of the obvious limits to their theological backgrounds.[2]

But if a great deal is known of the intellectual positions of the political and ecclesiastical leadership, the motives and attitudes of the simple parish clergy are immensely more difficult to ascertain. The number of such

---

[1] *L'exposition des principes sur la Constitution civile du clergé* and, by the bishop of Boulogne, *Instruction pastorale sur l'autorité spirituelle de l'Eglise* (1790). On the constitutional side: Armand-Gaston Camus, *Développement de l'opinion de M. Camus, député de l'Assemblée nationale dans la séance du 27 novembre* (1790); Louis Martineau, *Rapport imprimé par ordre de l'Assemblée nationale* (1790); Jean-Baptiste Treilhard, *Discours imprimé par ordre de l'Assemblée nationale* (1790); Henri Grégoire, *La légitimité du serment civique exigé des fonctionnaires ecclésiastiques* (1791).

[2] A good summary of the debate as it appeared in printed brochures, pamphlets, etc. is in C. Constantin, "Constitution civile du clergé," *DTC*, vol. 3, pt. 2, cols. 1537-1604. See also Augustin Sicard, *Le clergé de France pendant la Révolution*, 3 vols. (Paris, 1912-27), vol. 2, livre 2, chap. 1. Many of the more important writings themselves are in Barruel, *passim*.

clergymen who actually delivered public explanations of their decisions will, of course, never be known. By law, the oath ceremony was to take place after the mass on Sunday, and contemporary descriptions suggest that many curés either devoted an entire sermon to the subject or delivered summary comments before or following their oaths. Given the enormous publicity surrounding the event, the vast majority of clergymen probably felt some obligation to interpret their actions to their parishioners. Unfortunately, however, the written accounts of such ceremonies are not usually preserved in any systematic fashion. And even where the minutes of village officials can be found, they often give no indication of the local clergyman's justifications—other than vague comments on the "edifying" or "dangerous and disruptive" speeches accompanying the oath.[3]

Nevertheless, through the use of certain "series" of documents in the National Archives and in selected local collections, it has been possible to assemble original or summary oath explanations for approximately 200 parish clergymen.[4] Under the circumstances, any attempt at a statistical analysis could only be specious. Though the cases examined represent virtually every region of the kingdom, there is no way that the "sample" as such can be easily controlled. While many of the documents used are actual transcriptions of speeches or sermons, others are only summaries, written by the clergymen themselves or, in some instances, by outside observers. Perhaps it was precisely the most articulate, carefully reasoned, and—ultimately—the most atypical explanations which struck observers as being worthy of inscription in the official documents. But, limited though it may be, the collection of oath explanations can help to illuminate the differences in outlook between the refractory clergy, on the one hand, and the constitutional clergy, on the other. There will be ample occasion

---

[3] I have examined only those minutes preserved as copies in the national or departmental archives. More information may eventually be culled from the original deliberations in the municipal archives.

[4] The principal "series," as it were, for such oath explanations are drawn from three collections of documents in the A.N.: D XIX 80-88, D XXIX bis 20-23, and F¹⁹ 398-481. Oath documentation for four departments have also been scrutinized with some care, namely Calvados, Seine-et-Marne, Moselle, and Côte-d'Or: Emile Sévestre, *Liste critique des insermentés et assermentés (janvier-mai 1791)* (Paris, 1922), 303-414; A.D. Seine-et-Marne, L 282-83; P. Lesprand, *Le clergé de la Moselle pendant la Révolution*, 4 vols. (Montguy-lès-Metz, 1934-1939), vols. 3 and 4; B.M. Dijon, ms. Reinert. But numerous other sources have been drawn upon when appropriate. On the rarity of explanations inscribed in municipal deliberations, see Michel Destombes, *Le clergé du diocèse d'Amiens et le serment à la Constitution civile, 1790-1791* (Amiens, 1971), 325-26. Of the approximately 200 explanations examined, 94 have been retained here as examples. These 94 represent 40 different departments, with an inevitable concentration among the 4 departments listed above.

to take up the more abstract analysis of the social historian. It is not unfitting that we first allow the clergymen to speak for themselves.

The Refractory Clergy

In their explanations justifying refractory positions, few clergymen developed single-sided rationales. Typically, a clergyman might enumerate four or five objections, with little indication of their ranking within the individual's hierarchy of values. Among the justifications listed, a certain number of ecclesiastics made no effort to hide their unhappiness over the effects of the Civil Constitution on their own vested interests. The curé of Aubenton (Aisne), for example, was obviously upset over proposals to abolish his parish. He could never approve a policy, he said, which would lead to the suppression of his own benefice.[5] And a few, like the desservant of Poyans (Haute-Saône), unabashedly linked their refusals of the oath to the National Assembly's seizure of Church property.[6] Yet public statements in this vein were generally rare. Patriots on the Left had been badgering the Old-Regime bishops for months, asserting that their opposition to the Civil Constitution was motivated primarily by the loss of their wealth, and clergymen everywhere seemed anxious to affirm their indifference to questions of revenues. The rector of Port-Louis (Morbihan) specifically proclaimed that monetary concerns were of no importance to him and that, if the reforms were accepted by the Church, he would willingly accept whatever salary was decided for him. In Bridoré, near Loches (Indre-et-Loire), the curé even offered to stay on at a greatly reduced salary—700 *livres* instead of the 1,200 which he would normally have received—if only officials would accept his restrictive oath.[7]

In fact, the vast majority of refractory oath explanations concentrated on questions of religion and theology. To be sure, references of this kind were frequently somewhat vague and imprecise. The Civil Constitution was filled with errors; it would touch "the spiritual"; it was against religion. It is difficult to know whether comments of this kind represented theological limitations on the part of the clergymen or efforts to simplify issues for lay consumption. But, whenever they chose to be more specific, most refractories made it clear that they had been closely following and pondering the published debates. Central to the thinking of the majority was the argument by authority. For some clergymen, the authority in

[5] A.N., D XXIX bis 20, dos. 220, no. 21.
[6] A.N., D XXIX bis 20, dos. 212, no. 4.
[7] A.N., D XXIX bis 20, dos. 215, no. 12; and D XIX 83, dos. 656, no. 18.

question resided essentially with the pontiff in Rome and, until he had announced his decision, it was impossible to take an unrestrictive oath. "All depends on the Pope," as the curé of Luc in Normandy (Calvados) put it. "Until the holy father in Rome has pronounced," wrote the curé of Merville (Nord), "one must abstain from taking a position." In numerous parishes that January there were commentaries on the passage from the New Testament traditionally mobilized to buttress the theories of papal supremacy: "Thou art Peter, and upon this rock I will build my Church."[8] Yet the strict ultramontane position was probably less common than appeals to hierarchical authority in general, to that of the bishops alone, or to that of the bishops and the pope together. Whatever his patriotic attachment to the Revolution, the curé of Brûlon (Sarthe) had no choice, as he explained it, but to follow his bishop. For Grandin, curé of Ernée (Mayenne), only the bishops had the right to judge in matters of religion, and it was clear that they had virtually all rejected the Civil Constitution. "In the midst of so many pitfalls," wrote a curé of Nonant (Calvados), it seemed best to follow the advice of "one of the greatest members of the Gallican Church," the bishop of Clermont.[9]

Yet, as many priests were quick to explain, it was not just a question of deference to a respected leader. A great many refractories viewed their predicament through the optic of a rigidly disciplined and hierarchical Church, particularly as that Church had been reordered and restructured after the Council of Trent and the Catholic Reformation. The refractory parish clergy in Brittany and Normandy were especially adamant that hierarchical authority was integral and essential to the Catholic religion itself. "There is a link between discipline and faith," announced the curé of Arromanches in Calvados. For the rector of Port-Louis (Morbihan), faith in the "catholic, apostolic, and Roman Church" implied "a perfect submission to ecclesiastical superiors." Without authority, said the rector of Saint-Pol-de-Léon (Finistère), there can be no Church. And the authority of that Church can pass only through the bishops.[10] In this respect, the National Assembly had clearly stepped beyond its sphere of authority. In a petition signed by several dozen rectors in Côtes-du-Nord, the primary complaint against the whole Civil Constitution was that it had

[8] Sévestre, 321-24; J. Peter and Charles Poulet, *Histoire religieuse du département du Nord pendant la Révolution*, 2 vols. (Lille, 1930), 2:120-21; and, as an example of the use of this biblical passage, the statement by Le Breton, curé of Ducy-Sainte-Marguerite: Sévestre, 333-38.

[9] H. Roquet, *Observation de Me. Beucher, curé de Brûlon* (Le Mans, 1929), 48-49; A.N., D XXIX bis 21, dos. 228, no. 25; Sévestre, 317.

[10] Sévestre, 306; A.N., D XXIX bis 20, dos. 215, no. 12 and dos. 212, no. 2.

destroyed the principle of authority and hierarchy: through the lay election of pastors, through the unilateral rearrangement of dioceses, through the provision that dioceses be administered by bishops in consultation with a conclave of "episcopal vicars." Only the pope and the councils were empowered to deal with spiritual matters, never the civil government.[11]

The National Assembly had erred fundamentally in ascribing a mere "spiritual primacy" to the pope in Rome. The "sovereign pontiff," as the curé of Quesques (Pas-de-Calais) argued, held both a spiritual primacy and a primacy of jurisdiction, with real powers as the central voice of authority within the Church.[12] Perhaps never had so many parishes throughout the country listened to so many sermons based on the same biblical text: "Render therefore unto Caesar the things which are Caesar's; and unto God the things that are God's."[13] The problem, of course, was to decide what things actually belonged to Caesar and what things belonged to God. But, in the eyes of many refractories, there could be no doubt that the state was encroaching on religious terrain, "overturning the gates of the sanctuary," as the stock phrase would have it.[14]

For some of the refractories, however, there was much more involved than a jurisdictional struggle between Church and state. In the eyes of these clergyman, the real issue was nothing less than an attack by the forces of philosophy against both the clergy and religion itself. The curé of Giéville (Manche) described the whole crisis as an ideological confrontation between the beliefs of the Church and of Scripture, on the one hand, and "the new philosophy practiced and preached by Voltaire and Jean-Jacques Rousseau," on the other. Farther south, in the department of Orne, the curé of Mantilly was convinced that statues of Rousseau were now being placed in all the churches of Paris and that the Catholic religion would soon be abolished.[15] "I see clearly," wrote the influential Guilbert, curé of Nancy and onetime leader of the local curés in their

[11] Hervé Pommeret, *L'esprit public dans le département des Côtes-du-Nord pendant la Révolution* (Saint-Brieuc, 1921), 121-22; also, the description of the oath of the curé of Remiremont (Vosges): D XIX 82, dos. 645, no. 11.

[12] Louis Trénard, "Eglise et Etat: le clergé face à la Révolution dans les diocèses du Nord de la France, 1788-92" in *Christianisme et pouvoirs politiques* (Lille, 1973), 84-85.

[13] See, for example, the curé of Balleroy (Calvados): Sévestre, 309-10; and the curé of Solers (Seine-et-Marne): A.D. Seine-et-Marne, L 283.

[14] *E.g.*, the statement by the priests of the *doyenné* of Campigny (Calvados): Sévestre, 311-14.

[15] A.N., D XXIX bis 21, dos. 226, no. 4, and dos. 225, no. 23. The curé of Forbach (Moselle) was also said to have made snide remarks about the National Assembly's reverence toward Rousseau: A.N., D XXIX bis 21, dos. 225, no. 11.

struggles against the bishop, "that the plan is to annihilate the clergy. . . . Your philosopher legislators at first dared not attack the clergy directly. . . . Today we are in an abyss and it will take a miracle to extricate us."[16] The Civil Constitution was nothing but the "persecution of the Church" by the National Assembly (curé of Champigny-le-Sec, Vienne); it was the "certain ruin of the Church" (curé of Luc, Calvados); it had been perpetrated by "Protestants, Jansenists, and unbelievers" (vicaire of Châteauneuf, Cher); by "apostates, Jews, Protestants, and all around scoundrels" (curé of Fayl, Haute-Marne).[17] At least two clergymen also saw far-reaching political ramifications to the Civil Constitution. For the rector of Plaintel (Côtes-du-Nord), the new legislation had "broken the sacred bond which had united the French monarchy to the see of Saint Peter since the time of Clovis." And curé Julien Haye in Sarthe was openly preaching the refusal of "any oath contrary to the well-being of the Capetian and Bourbon monarchs, our legitimate kings and masters."[18]

Yet statements such as this, linking religious orthodoxy and monarchical legitimacy—and anticipating a future credo of counterrevolutionary ideology—were extremely rare. Indeed, to judge by the oath explanations examined, far more refractories harbored a continuing sympathy for many of the Revolution's accomplishments and were deeply distressed by the choice which had been thrust upon them. The parish priest in Les Allemands (Doubs) sadly recounted how he had long preached submission to the law and devotion to the nation, but was now compelled to a restrictive oath to avoid eternal damnation. In Nesle-l'Hôpital (Somme) the refractory curé had never ceased extolling the patriotism "which flows like blood in our veins"; while the non-juror of Graulhet continued to pray daily for the protection of the National Assembly, desiring only that the Church itself be allowed to consecrate the reforms, "to baptize the Constitution." Le Breton, curé near Château-Gontier (Mayenne), took pains to emphasize that, though he could never betray his conscience by becoming a juror, neither could he betray the nation, the law, and the king in all of his other duties as a citizen.[19]

It was particularly among these patriot refractories that every con-

[16] Eugène Martin, *Histoire des diocèses de Toul, de Nancy, et de Saint-Dié*, 3 vols. (Nancy, 1903), 3:83-84.

[17] A.N., D XXIX bis 22, dos. 233, no. 17; Sévestre, 321-24; A.N., D XXIX bis 21, dos. 225, no. 13, and dos. 232, no. 4.

[18] Pommeret, 117-19; Maurice Giraud, *Essai sur l'histoire religieuse dans la Sarthe de 1789 à l'an IV* (Paris, 1920), 250-51.

[19] A.D. Doubs, L 445; Sicard, 2:156-57; A.N., D XXIX bis 21, dos. 229, nos. 1 and 2.

ceivable stratagem was devised to negotiate a compromise, to find the means of formulating limitations or restrictions which could be acceptable to both Church and state. Several, like Gislot of Villiers-en-Bière (Seine-et-Marne) or the curé of Brettnach (Moselle), argued that their restrictive oaths had been given before the National Assembly's interdiction on these had been published and that the Declaration of the Rights of Man expressly forbade retroactive laws.[20] Others, such as the curé of Pré-d'Auge (Calvados) or the curé-mayor of Luttange (Moselle), pointed to the earlier oaths which they had already sworn on July 14 or at the time they had taken office as public officials.[21] Acts such as these should surely suffice, especially since superfluous oaths were forbidden by canon law and would scandalize their parishioners. They used restrictions which, it was argued, were only reiterations of the National Assembly's own language in the decree of January 21. Or they tried "hypothetical" restrictions, which would have application only if the National Assembly were not true to its promise—an unlikely event, it was argued.[22] One ingenious clergyman came up with the perfect restrictive phrase: "as long as it was agreeable to God." Who, after all, could possibly disagree with the will of God?[23]

The descriptions of oath-taking and the explanations themselves provide ample evidence of the deep personal crises which the oath sometimes engendered. When Curé Claude Jacqueau stood up in a village near Dijon to take his oath, it was obvious to all present that he was overwhelmed with emotion and anxiety. He began to pronounce the words, but he soon broke down, choked with tears, and was ultimately forced to ask the schoolmaster to read the notes of his proposed oath. Likewise, the vicaire of Aubenas (Ardèche) attempted to read the oath legislation "in a pitiful voice, interrupted with sobs," and soon found himself unable to continue.[24] For the parish priest of Bonnétable (Sarthe), the quandary of the oath "gnaws away at me day and night; all sleep has left my eyes; my health is breaking down; I may soon succumb." There were even reports of priests whose hair had turned white overnight in the torment

---

[20] A.D. Seine-et-Marne, L 283; and Lesprand, 4:37-38. See also the oath of the curé of Veaugues (Cher): A.N., D XIX 45.

[21] Lesprand, 3:381; and Sévestre, 366.

[22] *E.g.*, the oath by the curé of Attilly (Seine-et-Marne): A.D. Seine-et-Marne, L 283.

[23] Sermon by a canon of Nevers: A.N., D IV 45.

[24] B.M. Dijon, ms. Reinert; and Charles Jolivet, *La Révolution en Ardèche* (Largentière, 1930), 280.

of the oath.[25] Several ecclesiastics used the image of trying to navigate between two reefs, "both equally dangerous." They wrote in language that might have been culled from a Racinian tragedy, of being torn "between one duty which commands me and another duty which forbids me." It was fine to render unto Caesar and unto God, but what do you do when the "two powers" directly contradict and confront one another?[26] You were damned if you did and damned if you didn't—and unfortunately, in this case, the adage could be taken literally as well as figuratively. If only he might have two souls, said the curé of Saint-Cyr (Loiret), so that he might give one to God and the other to his parishioners.[27] Many dwelt at length on the soul-searching, the consultations with friends, the readings of tracts, of Scripture, of the Church Fathers, of the acts of the councils.[28] In Cambrai (Nord), the curés and vicaires of the city came together for an all-night prayer vigil to seek illumination on the question.[29] Almost everywhere there were requests for more time to think the matter over, to seek advice, to study the question. The curé of Brûlon, who had long fervently backed the Revolution, inscribed his feelings in his parish register: "One trembles at the present state of crisis of the French clergy. We await with dread the outcome of this catastrophe."[30] For Louis Pérouas, historian of Limousin, it was no more, no less, than the "greatest drama of the conscience among the clergy in more than ten centuries."[31]

In the midst of such a dilemma, immobilized by doubts of all kinds, a number of clergymen ultimately reduced the decision, as they described it, to an interrogation of their consciences. "My conscience is my compass," wrote the curé of Nonant (Calvados). Or, for the curé of Saint-Privat (Moselle), "My conscience, which I was accustomed to consult and take as a guide for my conduct, forbade me to take the oath."[32] While the conscience was hardly new to theological discourse—and one clergymen specifically cited the writings of Saint Augustine in this regard[33]—it is tempting to associate appeals such as this with the ethical precepts of

[25] Giraud, 222-25; and Sicard, 2:153.

[26] E.g., the curés of Sailly and of Ville-sur-Yron (both in Moselle): Lesprand, 4:160 and 3:192-94; and the curé of Luc (Calvados): Sévestre, 322.

[27] A.N., D XXIX bis 21.

[28] E.g., the curé of Anguerny: Sévestre, 325-26.

[29] Peter and Poulet, 1:118.

[30] Roquet, 48.

[31] "Le clergé creusois durant la période révolutionnaire," *Mémoires de la Société des sciences naturelles et archéologiques de la Creuse*, 39 (1976), 565.

[32] Sévestre, 315-16; Lesprand, 3:152.

[33] Curé Delcher of Brioude: Ernest Gonnet, *Essai sur l'histoire du diocèse du Puy-en-Velay (1789-1802)* (Paris, 1907), 111.

Rousseau, precepts which seem to have made strong inroads among the clergy in the last decade of the Old Regime.[34] In these rational explanations for their decisions, the "instinct divin" was sometimes given greater weight than either the authority of the Church or the perceived purity of the orthodox faith.

The Constitutional Clergy

In some respects, the explanatory statements given by the constitutional clergy seemed to develop an even wider range of justifications than those given by the non-jurors. This group, no less than the refractory clergy, occasionally indulged in justifications that were not really justifications at all, with vague references to the purity of their motives and their desire to follow the "true principles." Once again, there were ample appeals to the conscience; only, in this instance, the divine instinct, the "light of his conscience, the movement of his heart," led individuals directly to the opposite conclusion.[35] There was also an occasional seconding of the curious distinction made by the curé-deputy, Grégoire: the oath was not a religious act at all, but rather an external, civil commitment, which could easily be taken even if one did not agree with everything the National Assembly had done. And, in a few rare instances, priests seemed to justify their oaths primarily in terms of the material benefits which the Civil Constitution had brought them.[36]

But most jurors for whom oath explanations are preserved seem to have taken the attacks of the refractories in earnest and to have made at least some effort to counter those attacks. Thus, the curé of Epineuil (Cher), Petitjean, delivered a lengthy speech/sermon, enumerating the principal objections against the Civil Constitution and developing rebuttals point by point. The new laws, he concluded, did *not* threaten the position of the clergy, did *not* violate dogma or sacraments or evangelical morality.[37] To those who would follow the authority and example of the

[34] Daniel Mornet, *Les origines intellectuelles de la Révolution française, 1715-1787* (Paris, 1933), 208-209.

[35] *E.g.*, the vicaire of Pont-Saint-Esprit (Gard): F[19] 426; the curé and vicaire of Lenault (Calvados): Sévestre, 412-14; the curé of Brioude: Gonnet, 111.

[36] Granger, curé of Janville (Eure-et-Loir) specifically mentioned Grégoire: A.N., F[19] 424; see also the curé of Lisores: Sévestre, 372-76. Grégoire's oath speech is in *AP*, 22:14-18. The vicaire of Tassé (Sarthe) alluded to his economic gain from the Civil Constitution, as did the *congruiste* curé of Chaillol (Hautes-Alpes): Giraud, 249-50; and the author's *Priest and Parish in Eighteenth-Century France* (Princeton, 1977), 273.

[37] A.N., F[19] 414.

bishops, the jurors responded with cynicism and derision. The bishops, wrote the curé of Roissy (Seine-et-Oise), were all hypocrites whose lives were "a tissue of scandals," who were more interested in "vain pretensions" than in regular residence in their own dioceses. Their ambition and avarice had been a disaster for the whole Church, tarnishing the image of all clergymen, as the curé of Le Coudray (Seine-et-Oise) put it. Bécu, curé in one of the parishes of Lille, echoed the stinging condemnation of so many others, indicting these "ambitious prelates, desperate because they might lose their temporal possessions [and who were thus] cloaking themselves in the veil of religion."[38] Like the curé of Chaumont-en-Vexin (Oise), Bécu speculated ironically on the sudden disappearance of the "Gallican Liberties" which the bishops had previously promoted so vigorously among the clergy. In France, according to the curé of Chaumont, the ultramontane argument had always been considered "contrary to the spirit of the Gospels."[39] There were also references to the virtual class struggle within the Church, the theme so frequently emphasized by parish clergymen during their struggles with bishops at the end of the Old Regime: to the situation in which "the lazy possessed the wealth of the Church and the laborious were left with nothing" (curé of Vanchy, Ain).[40]

But, if they commonly scorned and condemned the episcopacy, the jurors reiterated their deference toward the National Assembly. In many respects, the attitude of the constitutional clergy represented the triumph of Gallicanism—and of the most extreme form of "Parlementary" Gallicanism, at that. On the question of whether or not the new laws would have an effect on "the spiritual," it was ultimately the word of the bishops against the word of the Assembly, and the jurors proclaimed their trust in the latter. "I would see myself as insulting the National Assembly and libeling the purity of its views," announced the curé of Perthes (Seine-et-Marne), "if I were to suppose it had the least intention of encroaching on spiritual authority." And, like many others, he specifically referred to the assurances of the "Instruction" of January 21.[41] In the end, the duty to obey the law and the civil power was placed above the obedience owed to ecclesiastical superiors. Had not Jesus Christ himself—asked the curé of Martragny (Calvados)—given the example of obedience to civil au-

---

[38] A.N., D XIX 82, dos. 646, no. 13 and F¹⁹ 474; Peter and Poulet, 1:125-26.

[39] Peter and Poulet, *ibid.*; and A.N., F¹⁹ 457.

[40] Eugène Dubois, *Histoire de la Révolution dans le département de l'Ain*, 6 vols. (Bourg, 1931-35), 2:156.

[41] A.D. Seine-et-Marne, L 282. See also the curé of Villers (Calvados): Sévestre, 362.

thority? "It is my religion which commands me to obey the law," as the oft-repeated phrase put it. Such obedience was all the more important, as the curé of Kirsch (Moselle) observed, in that the curés were the first and most important public functionaries and must thus give an example for others to follow.[42] Ironically, some of the language used might have been taken directly from the practical morality lessons taught in the seminary or from the published sermons of the ever-popular curé Réguis. The parish clergy of the Old Regime had long prided itself in its role as the teacher of civic discipline, as the right arm of the government in defusing movements of public disobedience. It was a role which had been continually reinforced through clerical training and the pastoral letters of the bishops themselves.[43] Indeed, several of the refractories also announced their intention of dutifully obeying the laws—though, in this case, the law which required them to retire peacefully from their positions—and of encouraging their parishioners to do likewise.[44]

But, in the eyes of most juring clergymen, the Civil Constitution was not just a law which they were bound to follow; it was an essential and positive good. Like a national refrain, like a litany, came the series of stock phrases which summarized, for a majority of oath-takers, the ultimate justification of the ecclesiastical legislation: the reforms had returned to the spirit of the religion of Jesus; they had brought back the primitive purity of the Church, so long debased by time and by acts of avarice. "The National Assembly has consummated reforms that ten centuries of Church councils had been unable to effect" (curé of Epineuil, Cher). The Civil Constitution was "all the more respectable in that it was founded on the principles of the primitive Church, on the maxims of Saint Paul, on the wisest decisions of the councils" (vicaire of Saint-Sulpice-le-Guérétois, Creuse). It was "altogether in conformity with the former discipline of the Church, with the maxims and lessons of the Gospels as given by Jesus Christ to the ministers of his religion" (curé of Saint-Saturnin, Somme). In this sense, the constitutionals enthusiastically embraced the nationalization of clerical wealth, an act which would rejuvenate and respiritualize the mission of the clergy.[45] Again and again, these near millenarian ideals were placed in pendant with their attacks on the bishops and the regular clergy, who represented all that was evil

---

[42] Sévestre, 328-333; and Lesprand, 3:361-62. See also, for example, the curé of Livry (Seine-et-Marne): A.D. Seine-et-Marne, L 282.

[43] Tackett, *Priest and Parish*, 164-66.

[44] *E.g.*, the curé of Brûlon: Roquet, 48.

[45] A.N., F¹⁹ 414; Pérouas, 567; A.N., F¹⁹ 476.

and corrupt in the Church: "Beware of the false prophets [the bishops and opponents of the Constitution] as if they were ravenous wolves."[46]

For a curé near Toul (Meurthe), the deputies in Paris were not only the "fathers of the country," but the "protectors of religion." It was obvious, thought the parish priest of Condécourt (Seine-et-Oise), that "God, the Conserver of the Universe, has chosen to send us our Revolution." And more than one priest gave sermons on the verse from Exodus: "Here is the finger of God."[47] A curé in Bourg (Gironde) compared the whole Constitution to the "dogmas of religion." Another, in Landes, called it a "miracle" operated by God through the National Assembly. For a third, in Seine-et-Oise, it was "a Second Religion."[48] In the speech of the curé of Puéchabon (Hérault), it was the work not simply of "God," but of "the God of the French, the God of the Fatherland." Romain Pichonnier, curé of Andrezel (Seine-et-Marne), used a similar phrase: "The God of the French will no longer be the God of superstitious priests and of haughty pontiffs. He will be the God of the Gospels, the protector of the weak, the consolation of the feeble, ... the avenger of despots and of the leaches on the people."[49] Not surprisingly, a few of the constitutionals seized upon the old Roman saying: "the voice of the people is the voice of God."[50]

For a great many of those accepting the oath and the Civil Constitution seemed clearly to have adopted a new conception of the priest and of his role in society, a conception that clashed sharply with the clerical image inculcated by the Church leadership since the Council of Trent and the Catholic Reformation. The emphasis was less on the priest's position within the ecclesiastical hierarchy than on his position in the midst of the lay community and on the allegiance which he owed to the National Assembly. The image was that of the "citizen priest," a phrase that had been stimulated both by certain Enlightenment writers and by the tracts of Henri Reymond and other leaders of the "revolt of the curé" in the

[46] Le Turc, Recollet in Cassel (Nord): Peter and Poulet, 1:127.

[47] A.N., D XXIX bis 20, dos. 213, no. 29; and F¹⁹ 474. On "the finger of God" see, for example, the oath of Claude Passerat, curé of La Rochepot (Côte-d'Or): B.M. Dijon, ms. Reinert.

[48] A.N., F¹⁹ 429; the *archiprêtre* of Léon (Landes): Joseph Légé, *Les diocèses d'Aire et de Dax ou le département des Landes sous la Révolution française, 1789-1803,* 2 vols. (Aire, 1875), 1:93; and the curé of Crosne (Seine-et-Oise): A.N., F¹⁹ 474.

[49] F. Saurel, *Histoire du département de l'Hérault pendant la Révolution,* 2 vols. (Paris, 1894-95), 2:59; and A.N., D XIX 81, dos. 628.

[50] *E.g.,* the curé of Avensan (Gironde): Albert Gaillard, "A travers le schisme constitutionnel en Gironde," *Revue historique de Bordeaux,* 5 (1912), 28. See also Marcel Reinhard, *Religion, révolution, et contre-révolution* (Paris, 1960), 78.

decades since 1760.[51] The curés of Ravigny (Mayenne) and of Triel-sur-Seine (Seine-et-Oise) readily described themselves as both "priest and citizen." The parish clergyman of Evry (Seine-et-Oise) even signed his oath "curé-citoyen."[52] In the face of the post-Tridentine efforts to separate the clergy from the laity, the citizen priest stressed the similarities, the affinities of the two. All Christians, said the curé of Bourbon-Lancy (Saône-et-Loire), were but part of a single family. As in the days of the primitive Church, the only distinction between the clergy and the others was the priest's specific function of bringing spiritual and temporal aid.[53]

Far more than their refractory colleagues, the jurors emphasized the morality and ethics of Christianity over its theology and dogma. The curé of Lorry (Moselle), for example, attributed his decision to take the oath to "having found nothing in the Constitution . . . which was contrary to the sublime morality of the Gospels."[54] Though keenly aware of the attacks on the Church by Enlightenment writers, the jurors were convinced that the reforms wrought by the National Assembly would remove all justification for such attacks.[55] Indeed, unlike the refractories, the constitutionals readily adopted certain of the Enlightenment's key words and ethical categories. Several priests made reference to the Enlightenment goals of "happiness" and "utility." The new constitution was the "code of national happiness" (curés of Montesson in Seine-et-Oise, and of Inglange in Moselle). It would bring "happiness to all future generations" (curé of Gondrecourt, Meuse); to "all Frenchmen" (desservant of Airaines, Somme).[56] Bécu, in Lille, raged against the parasites in the Church who must be removed for the greater "utility of religion." The curé of Coupesarte (Calvados) approved of the Civil Constitution for its "general usefulness" to society and religion; while a neighboring curé in La Trinité reiterated his desire to be both faithful to religion and "useful to his country."[57] To their own patriotic citizenship, the constitutionals contrasted the "fanaticism" of their non-juring rivals—a word with the connotations of an intolerant, "superstitious," unenlightened religion. A curé near Chartres was incensed by the "sacrilege" and "fanaticism" of

[51] See the author's "The Citizen Priests: Politics and Ideology among the Parish Clergy of Eighteenth-Century Dauphiné," *Studies in Eighteenth-Century Culture,* 7 (1978), 307-328.

[52] A.N., F[19] 449 and 474.

[53] A.N., F[19] 468.

[54] Jean Eich, *Histoire religieuse du département de la Moselle pendant la Révolution* (Metz, 1964), 170-71.

[55] *E.g.,* the curé of Saint-Martin-en-Bière (Seine-et-Marne): A.D. Seine-et-Marne, L 282.

[56] A.N., F[19] 474; Eich, 171; A.N., F[19] 451; Destombes, 70-71. See also Pérouas, 566.

[57] Peter and Poulet, 1:125-26; Sévestre, 398-99 and 401.

the local refractories; the parish priest in Ravigny took aim at the "rage of fanaticism"; and others spoke contemptuously of the "dévots" who opposed the Civil Constitution.[58] A small but significant number were so intent on explaining the importance of their role in lay society that they scarcely made reference to religious issues at all. In these cases, the oath became a fundamentally secular statement, a profession of faith in the Revolution and the lay state. The lengthy speech of François Voyant, curé of Combs-la-Ville (Seine-et-Marne), focused entirely on the political and social benefits of the new constitution, while that of curé Léonard Saugères in nearby Blandy (Seine-et-Oise) hardly touched on Church questions and mentioned the word "God" only twice in passing, dwelling primarily on his own acts of "citizenship" during the previous months.[59]

It was in parishes served by "citizen clergymen" that the oath-taking ceremony often unrolled in a festive and fraternal atmosphere, symbolizing the acceptance and integration of the priest into the lay society. There were patriotic songs and speeches, and the local national guardsmen in their best uniforms paraded, saluted, and accompanied the priest to the church door and even to the pulpit. In Hesse (Meurthe) the oath initiated a day-long celebration, during which the curé invited the village officials to dinner, and the officials invited the clergyman and the whole population to a "feux-de-joie" bonfire.[60] After the oath-taking ceremony in Courménil (Orne), all of the parishioners accompanied the clergy back to the rectory in procession. The curé offered a "frugal meal" to one and all, during which everyone, laity and clergy alike, swore "friendship, fidelity, and fraternity" to one another.[61] Other ecclesiastics took the occasion to donate special alms to the poor, as they had often done on the great religious feast days of the year.[62] In Fontainebleau, and in a number of other parishes, the assembled laity seems to have joined in with the clergy in a joint pronouncement of the oath.[63] In Samois (Seine-et-Marne), the curé and the community officials profited from the spirit of fraternity and good will surrounding the oath to patch up a series of differences over religious practice in the village which had recently di-

[58] Curé of Gellainville (Eure-et-Loir): A.N., D XXIX bis 22, dos. 233, no. 7; curé of Ravigny (Mayenne): A.N., F¹⁹ 440; Barret de Pélisseau, canon in Vabre (Aveyron): A.N., D XXIX bis 21, dos. 231, no 2.

[59] A.D. Seine-et-Marne, L 282. See also the oath of the curé of Gondrecourt (Meuse): A.N., F¹⁹ 451.

[60] A.N., F¹⁹ 450.

[61] A.N., D XXIX bis 20, dos. 216, no. 23.

[62] E.g., the curé of Valence-en-Brie (Seine-et-Marne): A.D. Seine-et-Marne, L 282.

[63] Ibid.

vided the parish. "And if we are to take an oath," spoke the curé of Vert-Saint-Denis (also Seine-et-Marne), "let us also swear to love one another, to be mutually charitable, . . . and to love God with all our hearts."[64]

The Confrontation

It would be dangerous to advance too far on the basis of these clerical justifications alone. Above and beyond the methodological problems posed by the sources, one must take careful note of the context in which the oath explanations were given. In many respects, they were essentially public postures, intended for popular consumption. And one should not overlook the warnings of the social psychologists on the inherent difficulties of "telling more than we can know." Even in the present century, far more self-conscious and sensitive to the complexities of human motivation, most people, when they give reasons for their actions, seem not to interrogate their memories at all, but to rely on *a priori* theories about responses, theories grounded in personal and cultural assumptions as to what are "logical," "acceptable," "believable" explanations.[65]

Yet it is perhaps precisely in the realm of assumptions, assumptions of the acceptable and the ideal, that the explanations of an articulate minority can provide useful insights. Despite their considerable diversity, the commentaries of the jurors and the refractories suggest two strikingly different perspectives among clergymen as to the role of the priest in society. One of those roles was linked more closely to an orthodox model forged at the time of the Catholic Reformation; the other evoked the influence of a certain strand of the Enlightenment, typified by the writings of Rousseau and, in particular, by his Vicaire Savoyard. If the refractory attached the priest primarily to the ecclesiastical hierarchy, the juror would insert him first and foremost within the whole lay community. If the first saw him as a servant of God, the second saw him as the servant of mankind. While the first conceived of his option as an individual decision taken in the midst of a brotherhood of fellow clergymen, the second saw it as a community celebration through which the priest's oath was integrated into the patriotic stance of the whole society. In the very language that they spoke—the refractory's emphasis on salvation and truth, the constitutional's stress on happiness and utility—the two sides

[64] *Ibid.*

[65] Richard E. Nisbett and Timothy D. Wilson, "Telling More Than We Can Know: Verbal Reports on Mental Processes," *Psychological Review*, 84 (1977), 231-59.

revealed a fundamental confrontation of world views, of mental universes.[66] More than an intellectual decision, the oath involved a personal and almost emotional choice between two self-images, two identity structures. Where one or the other of these images dominated in an individual, the decision may have seemed relatively easy. But, among those attracted to both clerical roles—as was surely the case of a substantial number— the oath of 1791 may have posed not only a dilemma for the intellect but a tearing psychological experience as well. It was this veritable identity crisis, one suspects, that might lead to the near mental breakdown of clergymen like Claude Jacqueau and the vicaire of Aubenas.

But if the examination of oath statements is revealing of certain patterns of thought, it also gives rise to numerous questions. What link existed, for example, between the clergymen's image of themselves and the laity's image of the clergy? And to what extent were the contrasting conceptions of the sacerdotal profession related to the geographical diversity of the oath? As we have seen, the collection of statements examined can hardly be viewed as a "sample" in the statistical sense of the word. Yet it is worth noting that, among those cases considered here, clergymen defending a more traditional "Tridentine" role of the priest were well represented in Brittany and in others of the western provinces; while the model of the "citizen priest" seems to have been particularly enunciated in a large central segment of the country from Picardy to Bourbonnais and Berry, from eastern Normandy to western Lorraine, and above all in the area around Paris (in the departments of Seine-et-Oise and Seine-et-Marne, Eure-et-Loir, and Somme, for example). We will return to many of these themes and perspectives in a later chapter. But first it will be necessary to examine more carefully the collective biographies and experiences of the jurors and the refractories.

[66] Pérouas, 564, gives some additional striking examples of this clash of world views among jurors and refractories in Creuse.

FOUR

Collective Portraits

THE theological arguments justifying the positions of the juring and non-juring clergy can be readily grasped from the oath explanations of an articulate minority. Yet the forces and motives which impelled those individuals to opt for one position or another are still far from clear. Whatever the importance of intellectual considerations, the oath decision could never be altogether disassociated from the priests' social and career experiences, from their political perceptions and affinities, from their personal inclinations. As a first approach to the problem of motivation it will be necessary to probe the possible differences in the biographic profiles of the two clergies. Are there, in fact, any significant differences in the backgrounds, careers, or personalities of the jurors and non-jurors? Is it possible to trace the portrait of the "typical" constitutional or the "typical" refractory?

To be sure, these or similar questions have often been posed in the past. For an older generation of clerical scholars, anxious to separate the sheep from the goats and to provide moral exemplars for ecclesiastics confronting the anticlericalism of the Third Republic, the answer was axiomatic. The difference between the two clergies was ultimately related to the moral and religious character of individual "souls": the weak and the self-serving, on the one side, and the courageous and morally upright, on the other. A few of the local historians and compilers of clerical biographies attempted to push their research a step farther and discover if one group of priests was not richer or poorer, older or younger, more or less educated, than the other. Yet, until recently, most such generalizations were essentially impressionistic and were of little use for comparisons between regions.[1]

In order to attack the problem in a more systematic fashion, sample local studies have been assembled for the clergy confronting the oath in ten different provinces. Chosen primarily on the basis of the sources available, the sample includes, nevertheless, a relatively broad geographic distribution. (See Table 5.) In two of the regions sampled—the depart-

[1] Among the recent exceptions are Michel Destombes, *Le clergé du diocèse d'Amiens et le serment à la Constitution civile, 1790-91* (Amiens, 1971), 363-85; and Jean-Claude Meyer, *La vie religieuse en Haute-Garonne sous la Révolution (1789-1801)* (Toulouse, 1982), 85-104.

ment of Cher in the province of Berry and the Old-Regime diocese of Gap in Upper Dauphiné[2]—the clergy tended massively to accept the oath. Oath-taking proportions for the two areas were between 75 and 90 percent, and rates in individual districts rose as high as 100 percent. By contrast, the departments of Moselle in northern Lorraine, of Haut-Rhin in Upper Alsace, and of Vendée in Lower Poitou were all characterized by decidedly refractory clerical corps. While each of the three contained regions of distinctly higher oath-taking, the means ranged between 25 and 40 percent jurors.[3] The five remaining provinces represented in the sample all exhibited juring ratios close to or slightly above 50 percent— the mean for the kingdom as a whole. These included the department of Somme in Picardy; the department of Aude in central and coastal Languedoc; three departments of coastal Normandy; a section of the Old-Regime diocese of Le Mans in the province of Maine (within the department of Sarthe); and those portions of the Burgundian diocese of Autun situated in the departments of Côte-d'Or and Saône-et-Loire. Among this final group of regions Picardy, central Languedoc, coastal Normandy, and Burgundy were all relatively homogeneous in oath-taking, but Upper Maine was cut by a particularly sharp division between a refractory area to the west and a juring area to the east. Including any one of the three Norman departments—for only one has been used at a time in the considerations that follow—there were over 6,200 parish clergymen living and working in the sample regions. Controlling for population—treating all of the regions as if they had equal numbers of priests—the "weighted" mean juring rate for the entire sample in the summer of 1791 was between 53 and 54 percent: almost precisely the average for France as a whole. There are, of course, certain limitations to the sample. Of the major sectors of the country, the Massif-Central and the extreme southwest are significantly unrepresented.[4] Even among the areas examined, not all information is available for all provinces. Normandy stands as a particularly complex case, insofar as different departments had to be used for different kinds of data.[5] But, despite such

[2] A fourth of the diocese also lapped into Upper Provence and the Comtat-Venaissin.

[3] The southern sections of Vendée and Bas-Rhin and the extreme western portion of Moselle had much higher juring rates.

[4] Relatively complete and accessible sources for these two sectors have not been located. Significantly, both regions are underrepresented in many other areas of Old-Regime and Revolutionary scholarship.

[5] This procedure is justified, first, because the three departments in question are broadly homogeneous in their economic and religious character (similar economic activities, population distributions, political traditions, clerical recruitment patterns, clerical economic structures, etc.),

TABLE 5
Ten-Province Sample of Oath-takers

Province Sampled	Description of Sample	No. of Cases	% Oath-takers (June 1791)
Alsace (Upper)	Dept. of Haut-Rhin (1)	445	40
Berry	Dept. of Cher (2)	331	77
Burgundy	Old-Regime Diocese of Autun within depts. of Côte-d'Or and Saône-et-Loire (3)	492	57
Dauphiné (Upper)	Old-Regime Diocese of Gap (4)	274	88
Languedoc (Upper)	Dept. of Aude (5)	598	58
Lorraine (Northern)	Dept. of Moselle (6)	416	32
Maine (Upper)	Old-Regime Diocese of Le Mans within Dept. of Sarthe (7)	703	49
Normandy (Coastal)	Depts. of Calvados, Manche, and Seine-Inférieure (8)	4,515*	40-50
Picardy	Dept. of Somme (9)	1,076	59
Poitou (Lower)	Dept. of Vendée (10)	469	33
Total		9,319	
Weighted Average			53-54
Total (minus Normandy)		4,804	
Weighted Average (minus Normandy)			55

*Calvados: 1407; Manche: 1437; Seine-Inférieure: 1621

(1) Ms. notes by Jules Joachim: B.M. Colmar, ms. 972.

(2) Ms. notes by Chanoine Laugardière: A.D. Cher, J 828.

(3) Numerous different sources, including, for oath status and length of service: Louis Bauzon et al., Recherches historiques sur la persécution religieuse dans le département de Saône-et-Loire pendant la Révolution, 4 vols. (Chalon-sur-Saône, 1889-1903) and ms. notes by Eugène Reinert: B.M. Dijon, ms. (non-coté); for approximate age, and social and geographic origins: registers of ordinations and of insinuations ecclésiastiques: A.D. Saône-et-Loire, G 835-36 and 2 G 330-40; for Old-Regime revenues: A.D. Saône-et-Loire, 1 L 8/107, 110, 112, 113, 116. Included in the sample are only those clergymen born within the Old-Regime diocese of Autun.

(4) Primarily ms. notes by Paul Guillaume: A.D. Hautes-Alpes, ms. 399; for revenues: A.D. Hautes-Alpes, I Q I 108 and 137; A.D. Drôme, L 87-89; A.D. Isère, L 604-24; on social origins, primarily, A.D. Hautes-Alpes, G 877-80 and G 906-908.

(5) A. Sabarthès, Histoire du clergé de l'Aube de 1789 à 1803. Répertoire onomastique (Carcassone, 1939).

(TABLE 5 cont.)

(6) P. Lesprand, *Le clergé de la Moselle pendant la Révolution*, 4 vols. (Montigny-lès-Metz, 1934-39), and Jean Eich, *Les prêtres mosellans pendant la Révolution*, 2 vols. (Metz, 1959-64); and, for revenues, Eich, "La situation matérielle de l'Eglise de Metz à la fin de l'Ancien régime," *Annuaire de la Société d'histoire et d'archéologie de la Lorraine*, 18 (1958), 45-65.

(7) Ms. notes by Charles Girault on the oath: A.D. Sarthe, 2 J 40-41; supplemented for social and geographic origins and for careers by personal research notes of Alex Poyer, kindly put at my disposal by the author; and, for revenues: A.D. Sarthe, L 339-50, 353, 568.

(8) Emile Sévestre, *Le personnel de l'Eglise constitutionnelle en Normandie. Livre 1er. Liste critique des insermentés et assermentés* (Paris, 1925); and, for revenues, Emile Bridrey, *Cahiers de doléances du bailliage de Cotentin pour les Etats-Généraux de 1789*, 3 vols. (Paris, 1907-12).

(9) Michel Destombes, *Le clergé du diocèse d'Amiens et le serment à la Constitution civile* (Amiens, 1971); and, for revenues, F. I. Darsy, *Le clergé et l'Eglise d'Amiens en 1789* (Paris, 1892), 59-130, 179-94.

(10) Yves Chaille, "Livre d'or du clergé vendéen," *Archives du diocèse de Luçon, n.s.*, 32-36 (1960-64), *passim*.

imperfections, it seems unlikely that local studies will substantially modify the overall collective portraits presented here.

Age

In studies of both the French Revolution and of revolution in general, associations have sometimes been made between political perceptions and receptivity, on the one hand, and age categories, on the other.[6] But a "generation effect" might be operative in history for sharply differing reasons. In some instances, the unique and specific experience of a given generation during the formative years of its youth and education might set the ethos and orientation of that group throughout its lifetime. Given the particularly intense ideological fermentation among the clergy in the second half of the eighteenth century—the Jansenist-Jesuit struggles, the popularization of the Enlightenment, the emergence of a "Second Enlightenment" after 1770[7]—one might well anticipate differing clerical perceptions by generation. But generations can also be defined by the recurring experiences of the career cycle or the life cycle. In this sense,

---

and, secondly, because the principal source of information, the works of Abbé Sévestre, is of unusually high quality and reliability.

[6] See, for example, Richard Cobb, "A Mentality Shaped by Circumstances," in *The French Revolution: Conflicting Interpretations*, Frank Kafker and James M. Laux, eds. (New York, 1968), 246.

[7] Bernard Plongeron, "Théologie et politique au siècle des Lumières (1770-1820)," *AHRF*, 45 (1973), 437-53. Plongeron specifies, however, that the "generation" of the Second Enlightenment was not necessarily defined by age.

the effects of age would be partly social-psychological, partly physiological in nature: hence the exuberance, openness to innovation, and self-confidence of youth—characteristics sometimes associated with the leadership generation of the Jacobin circle—or the more cautious conservatism of middle-aged groups in control of the establishment.

For the country as a whole, the overall age contours of the parish clergy probably did not differ markedly from region to region. Despite substantial variations in recruitment rates in the diverse sectors of the country, the geographic mobility of the clergy, the long-standing patterns of migration from areas of excess ecclesiastical vocations to areas of clerical shortage, undoubtedly helped standardize the local age distributions.[8] In only two of the ten sample regions—Picardy and Lower Poitou—did the average age of parish clergymen differ by more than one year from the overall norm. (See Table 6.) To be sure, the case of the clergy of Vendée is particularly striking. Among these western clerics, who would so massively reject the Civil Constitution and who would find themselves deeply implicated in a counterrevolution, some 48 percent were under the age of 40 in 1790.[9] Yet, whatever relationship may have existed in the Vendée between youth and a non-juring status—and, as we shall see, the chain of causation is by no means simple—there is no evident correspondence elsewhere between average age and oath tendencies. Indeed, among the remaining provinces both the overall mean ages and the age-contours of the diocesan clergy were remarkably similar.

For the ten regions as a whole, the average age of the refractory curés—weighted as if all regions had equal populations—was slightly greater than that of the jurors, while the average age of the refractory vicaires was slightly less. More complex and puzzling still is the curious oscillation in age-specific oath-taking rates. Even though the differences are relatively small, they are probably significant, given the number of priests studied. The lowest oath rates were registered among the youngest age group, those between 25 and 29 years of age; this tendency has already been noted by historians and has often been attributed to the younger

[8] See the author's "L'histoire sociale du clergé diocésain dans la France du XVIIIe siècle," *RHMC*, 26 (1979), esp. 200.

[9] The lower age of the Vendée clergy may reflect, in part, a major recent increase in the rate of clerical recruitment: see below, chp. 10. It may also be attributed to higher mortality rates. Differing clerical mortality is known to have existed in the early nineteenth century: see the author's article written with Claude Langlois, "Ecclesiastical Structures and Clerical Geography on the Eve of the French Revolution," *FHS*, 11 (1980), 362.

TABLE 6

Oath-takers by Age

Province Sampled	% Un-known	Percentage Oath-takers by Age											Total Known	Average Age				
		25-29	30-34	35-39	40-44	45-49	50-54	55-59	60-64	65+	<55	55+		Curés		Vicaires		All
														Jur.	Rfr.	Jur.	Rfr.	
Alsace	21	33	27	26	47	35	28	44	48	50	33	47	36	49.6	46.6	38.3	33.8	43.9
Berry	18	82	69	85	79	78	75	83	79	73	78	78	78	47.8	49.1	28.9	28.8	44.4
Burgundy	43	43	66	58	45	50	68	46	37	33	55	41	53	45.9	48.5	34.4	30.8	44.4
Dauphiné	16	96	87	89	95	95	97	85	80	73	93	79	89	50.3	58.3	31.4	32.0	45.6
Languedoc	15	65	52	77	48	59	44	48	66	63	58	59	58	48.5	48.0	35.7	35.1	44.7
Lorraine	13	28	30	40	36	32	46	53	54	45	35	51	39	51.7	51.6	37.3	34.2	45.4
Maine	22	44	56	48	51	48	45	45	52	54	49	50	50	50.1	50.3	39.4	38.9	45.3
Picardy	60	54	58	60	61	63	49	61	70	72	58	66	60	50.5	54.9	35.3	33.5	47.5
Poitou	31	18	37	44	31	32	37	35	32	34	34	33	34	47.7	49.2	33.9	30.6	42.9
Normandy (Calvados)	53	52	54	54	49	45	54	44	59	59	51	53	51	49.4	49.9	35.2	37.7	45.3
Weighted average	52	52	54	58	54	54	54	54	58	56	54	56	55	49.2	50.6	35.0	33.5	44.9

Number of cases in sample: 3,983

clerics' more recent exposure to seminary training.[10] Yet oath rates rose for those still relatively young clergymen in their thirties, reaching a maximum at ages 35 to 39. For priests in their forties and fifties the proportion fell again, before swinging back up among those over sixty.

These composite averages also conceal differing regional patterns. In Berry, in Languedoc, and in the two western provinces of Maine and Normandy, age would seem to have had relatively little bearing on individual clerical options on the oath. Not only were the differences in the average age of refractory and constitutional curés small or almost nil, but no broad generational splits were to be found between young and old—between those younger or older than 55, for example. As for the clergy of Vendée, it now appears that the most remarkable anomaly was the large proportion of priests who refused the oath within the single cohort of 25 to 29. Among the five remaining provinces, the age factor seems to have been even more important, but the patterns were not consistent. Focusing only on the cohorts older than 55 in 1790, one finds markedly higher oath-taking rates in Alsace, Lorraine and Picardy, but markedly lower rates in Burgundy and Dauphiné.

In the case of Upper Dauphiné, such trends might be linked to certain local political movements among the parish clergy and to the striking transformations in the origins of the diocesan corps. During the years prior to the Revolution, the parish priests of this region experienced an unusually intense politicization—far greater, no doubt, than in any of the other regions sampled—a politicization that would form a natural ideological link between the end of the Old Regime and the Civil Constitution of the Clergy. In this particular case, then, an ideological position seems to have affected older and younger generations differently—generations that were also unusually distinct and differentiated by their geographic and social origins.[11] But the case of Dauphiné was apparently unusual in this respect. So far as can be determined, no such movements of politicization, no such shifts in recruitment patterns, divided young and old in Burgundy, Lorraine, Alsace, or Picardy. In order to understand the much more complicated oscillations in oath-taking among age cohorts for the overall sample, we must turn to the question of career patterns.

[10] See, for example, A. Sicard, *Le clergé de France pendant la Révolution*, 3 vols. (Paris, 1912-27), 2:141-42; and Jean Leflon, "Le clergé des Ardennes et la Constitution civile," *Présence ardennaise*, 13 (1952), 6.

[11] See the author's *Priest and Parish in Eighteenth-Century France* (Princeton, 1977), esp. chps. 2 and 9. See also below, chp. 6.

Length of Service

For the curés of the Old Regime, career mobility was normally at a minimum. Most parish priests seem to have remained in the same villages throughout their lifetimes—not infrequently for forty or fifty years or more. Indeed, of all the categories of clergymen constrained to the oath, the curé was undoubtedly the most entrenched in his environment, the most enmeshed in the local networks of personal relationships. This well established *situation acquise* of the typical curé stood in sharp contrast to the precarious and insecure status of the vicaires. The majority of vicaires lived transient lives, transferred at the will of the bishops and the curés to perhaps half a dozen different posts, lodged in various kinds of temporary quarters, and paid only small salaries.[12] The status of the vicaires was in fact so impermanent and indeterminate that it has been impossible to include them in the adjoining tables.

To judge from the nine provinces for which information is available, the refractory curés would seem to have been present in their parishes only slightly longer than their constitutional colleagues, with an average of about one year's difference between jurors and non-jurors. (See Table 7.) A more detailed examination reveals, nevertheless, some interesting patterns of variation. It was the curés most recently arrived at their posts— those named within the five previous years—who took the oath at the highest rates. Both in the weighted average for the sample as a whole and in seven of the nine individual provinces, the percentage of jurors in this first category was well above the mean. Among clergymen who had served over four years, the oath rates declined progressively to a nadir in the 15- to 19-year category. The proportion of jurors rose once again, however, for priests in the highest seniority bracket, those with twenty years' service or more.

It is through the confrontation of these observations for both age and length of service that a more plausible explanation of oath reactions by generation seems to emerge, an explanation based above all on the psychological effects of the clerical career cycle itself. Almost everywhere in France, as we have already seen, the vicaires refused the oath in larger proportions than the curés. This trend was apparently most in evidence among the youngest vicaires, those who were least rooted or attached to

[12] Tackett, *Priest and Parish*, 98-99, 110-17. Also, Jean-Luc Normand, "Un essai d'utilisation des registres des insinuations ecclésiastiques: étude sur les bénéfices ecclésiastiques du diocèse de Bayeux (1740-1790)," *Annales de Normandie*, 27 (1977), 307-309.

TABLE 7
Oath-takers by Length of Service
(Curés Only)

Province Sampled	% Unknown	Percentage Oath-takers (by Years of Service in 1791)						Total Known	Average Years of Service		
		0-4	5-9	10-14	15-19	20-24	25+		Jur.	Rfr.	All Curés
Alsace	26	51	36	26	24	29	42	39	12.7	14.3	13.7
Burgundy	65	57	61	50	50	70	54	58	10.9	11.1	11.0
Dauphiné	4	96	90	94	77	85	92	91	13.6	16.2	14.8
Languedoc	32	69	49	56	61	73	56	58	12.6	15.9	14.8
Lorraine	6	35	47	45	44	53	44	44	15.9	14.9	15.4
Maine	7	61	55	47	45	53	54	54	14.5	15.1	14.8
Normandy (Seine-Inf.)	14	53	50	39	53	38	58	49	16.6	15.3	15.9
Picardy (1)	50	62	47	67	64	63	51	58	14.5	15.4	14.9
Poitou	0	41	36	46	29	27	22	35	11.7	14.3	13.4
Weighted average		58	52	52	50	55	53	54	13.7	14.7	14.3

Number of cases in sample: 3,043

(1) Sample includes the districts of Amiens, Montdidier, and Péronne only.

any particular parish and who ultimately had the least to lose by refusing the oath and being ejected from their posts. But the chances of opting for the Revolution rose among those in their thirties, many of whom were now obtaining the more stable and secure posts of desservant or were setting themselves in positions to receive a cure through the assistance of an elderly mentor. It was precisely in the period of the late thirties, as clergymen obtained their first rectories that the propensity to take the oath was greatest of all.[13] This generation had been caught by the Revolution after having only just achieved the long-coveted status and security of the parish priest. The taste of this newly attained prize could only have accentuated the difficulty of refusing the oath and of thus effectively renouncing one's entire career. When an individual had been settled

[13] In the diocese of Gap most priests received their first cures between about eight and fifteen years after their ordination to the priesthood at age 24 or 25. Since the average age and average years in service for curés in Gap were almost the same as in the other sample regions, a similar waiting period for the first parish was probably to be found most everywhere. See Tackett, *Priest and Parish*, 102.

somewhat longer—after the honeymoon with his parishioners had ended, after he had accumulated a certain economic comfort independent of his benefice—his readiness to consider the possibility of abandoning everything seemed to rise markedly. But tendencies were reversed once again for clergymen moving into their sixties and seventies. Here, most likely, a new factor came into play: the physical decrepitude of old age and, even more important, the fear of such decrepitude. Age itself made the priest somewhat more vulnerable to the threat of losing his post, his income, and his social *raison d'être*. Indeed, in the *cahiers de doléances* of individual curés, no single issue concerning the clergy arose more frequently than the problem of retirement and security in old age.[14]

Social and Geographic Origins

Whatever the efforts of the Catholic Reformation to separate and disengage the clergyman from his past, most priests probably maintained the same kind of close family ties which characterized the society of the Old Regime in general.[15] Unfortunately, a careful assessment of the effects of family experiences on later political opinions would require a depth of analysis scarcely feasible in anything but a local study.[16] In the present context, we can do no more than explore the possible statistical relations between oath options and social and geographic milieu.

An initial distinction, known to be of considerable significance in the analysis of clerical recruitment, is between those born in towns and those born in rural areas. In fact, there were whole regions of France where the overwhelming majority of young clergymen originated in villages and hamlets, while in other zones they came predominantly from the towns.[17] But, ultimately, the size and character of the parish of birth would seem little related to the patterns of oath-taking. Among the eight sample provinces for which such distinctions can be made, three reveal higher oath rates among town-born clergymen, four others had higher

[14] Charles Porée, *Cahiers des curés et des communautés ecclésiastiques du bailliage d'Auxerre pour les Etats-généraux de 1789* (Auxerre, 1927). See also below, chp. 6.

[15] Tackett, *Priest and Parish*, 145.

[16] Louis Pérouas has speculated on the ties of family between the clergy of Creuse and the local Revolutionary administrators. But he has insufficient evidence to arrive at any clear conclusions: "Le clergé creusois durant la période révolutionnaire," *Mémoires de la Société des sciences naturelles et archéologiques de la Creuse*, 39 (1976), 557-58.

[17] For our definitions of "town" or "urban," on the one hand, and "non-town" or "rural," on the other, see above, chp. 2, note 45. On general recruitment patterns, see Tackett and Langlois, 366-67, and below, chps. 10 and 11.

rates for rural-born priests, and in the eighth there was no difference at all. (See Table 8.) In only one of the sample regions, the department of Vendée, was the difference between the two groups greater than nine percentage points. And in this case the split can probably be explained by the sharp ecological division which cut the department—the dichotomy between the somewhat more "urbanized" southern and coastal zones and the profoundly rural bocages in the north roughly separating the regions of predominantly juring and predominantly non-juring clergy. When the weighted average is calculated for all of the eight sample regions, the proportion of jurors is precisely the same, regardless of the nature of the parish of birth.

But what of the actual occupational milieus of the clergymen's families? Recent research, laboriously assembled from widely dispersed sources, permits some fairly reliable generalizations about the backgrounds of clergymen in France as a whole.[18] But to trace the genealogies of specific individuals confronting the oath is an imposing and substantially more difficult task. In all, the family situation has been determined for some 1,100 men in six of the sample provinces, though in only three of these—Burgundy, Maine, and Dauphiné—are the numbers sufficiently large to inspire a full measure of confidence. (See Table 9.) Within this sample,

TABLE 8
Oath-takers by Milieu of Birth
(Urban vs. Rural)

Province Sampled	% Un-known	Percentage Oath-takers		
		Born in Towns	Born in Non-Towns	Total Known
Alsace	30	29	38	36
Berry	10	74	80	78
Burgundy	21	56	54	55
Dauphiné	34	88	88	88
Languedoc	72	74	66	68
Lorraine	28	28	37	32
Maine	42	41	47	45
Poitou	61	47	31	34
Weighted average		55	55	55
Total cases known: 2,237				

[18] Tackett, "Histoire sociale," esp. 209-216.

the overall distribution of social origins appears relatively typical of the parish clergy in the kingdom generally, with smaller contingents from peasant and artisan families, a tiny group from the nobility, and the bulk originating in the commercial, professional, and office-holding classes.[19] But the results would suggest that a priest's family background was only marginally related to his perspectives on the Civil Constitution. For three of the largest categories of clergymen—those from agricultural, commercial, and "notable" families—no clear tendencies can be detected. The weighted averages for each of these categories differed by only a few percentage points from the overall average within the sample of 60-percent oath-taking. If in Burgundy and Maine the juring clergy was above the local mean among "notable" sons and below the mean among sons of merchant families, the relationships were precisely reversed in Berry, Lorraine, and Dauphiné.

More important differences can be observed, nevertheless, among two of the social groupings: the priestly progeny of artisans, on the one hand, and of the nobility, on the other. In the case of the nobility, one must exercise caution, for the percentages represent a mere handful of cases.[20] Yet similar conclusions have been suggested for the region of Lisieux in

TABLE 9
Oath-takers by Family Profession

Province Sampled	% Un-known	Percentage of Oath-takers					
		Noble	Nota-ble (1)	Mer-chant	Arti-san	Culti-vator	Total known
Berry	75	33	79	88	85	70	80
Burgundy	30	50	61	53	70	70	57
Dauphiné	50	0	83	98	100	90	90
Lorraine	80	0	44	75	56	53	51
Maine	48	44	52	38	58	50	46
Poitou	89	—	32	25	46	33	35
Weighted average		25	59	63	69	61	60
Total cases known: 1,120							

(1) Includes all liberal professions, office-holding professions and families describing themselves as "bourgeois."

[19] The distribution in family origins for the sample (weighted means) was as follows: 1 percent nobility; 39 percent "notable"; 32 percent merchant; 16 percent artisan; 12 percent agricultural.
[20] There was a total of only 14 noblemen's sons in three of the six sample regions.

Normandy.[21] It is reasonable to suppose that an aristocratic ethos among the noble curés and vicaires influenced their massive rejection of the Civil Constitution. More significant, perhaps, is the sample of some 144 priests from artisan backgrounds, a group which revealed oath rates above average in all of the sample regions and an overall weighted mean almost ten percentage points higher than the norm.[22] It would be tempting to suppose a kind of *sans-culotte* connection, following family lines into the clergy. But the principal reason for this trend may have been more prosaic. Among all individuals entering the clergy, the young men from artisan backgrounds represented the most humble socio-economic strata. A vocation from this level in society often signified a major financial sacrifice on the part of a whole family. In their confrontation with the oath, the individual clergymen involved must have felt themselves under substantial pressure to avoid the destruction of their family's investment—the inevitable outcome of a decision to reject the Civil Constitution and abandon their careers.[23]

There was another important segment of the parish clergy which has necessarily been excluded from the above discussion: those originating from outside the diocese or department in which they were serving. Though in most regions these migrant priests arriving as "outsiders" represented only a tiny minority of the diocesan clergy, there were certain zones, notably in the center of France and the Parisian basin, in which they constituted well over one-third or even one-half of the total clerical corps.[24] In the eight provinces for which data are available, the migrant clergymen reveal a certain propensity to embrace the Civil Constitution, especially by comparison with their native-born colleagues. (See Table 10.) But a more careful examination of the individual regions reveals an

[21] Winifred Edington, "An Administrative Study of the Implementation of the Civil Constitution of the Clergy in the Diocese of Lisieux," Ph.D. dissertation, University of London, 1958, 142.

[22] There was a total of 144 known artisan sons in the six sample regions. Edington, ibid., found a similar pattern in Normandy.

[23] A study was made—conjointly with Dominique Julia—of the marriage contracts of 52 sets of parents who sent 62 sons into the priesthood in the diocese of Autun during the last decades of the Old Regime. For the artisan families, the median of the combined male and female dowries was between 1,200 and 1,600 *livres*; for *laboureur* families, it was about 1,400 to 2,000; for merchant families, between 3,500 and 5,000; for "notable" families, between 6,000 and 6,500. Sources: alphabetical tables of marriage contracts for 15 *bureaux d'enregistrement*: A.D. Saône-et-Loire, Series C and C Supplement (1928); and A.D. Côte-d'Or, Series C. Edington, 142, found that those priests who had been the recipients of pious benefactors for their clerical titles—presumably, from the humblest family origins—almost all took the oath.

[24] Tackett and Langlois, 363-64; and Tackett, "L'histoire sociale," 199-201.

even more complex and interesting picture. In four of the five provinces where the clergy opted solidly either for or against the oath, the status as a migrant actually had little bearing on the oath decision. In Burgundy, Maine, and Languedoc, however, where clergymen split quite closely on the issue, the "outsider" priests tended to accept the oath in proportions substantially greater than the means. In the absence of other imperious motives pushing the clergy strongly in opposition or in favor of the oath—motives which we have yet to discover—the position of the outsider may have been similar to that of the elderly priest. In both cases, the clergymen in question were placed in a more vulnerable situation before the demands of the Revolutionary government. It was undoubtedly more difficult for a man far from his home, with family ties that were inevitably weakened by distance and time, to abandon his only position of status and security.

Nevertheless, viewed from the perspective of the kingdom as a whole, the family backgrounds of clergymen seem to have had relatively little bearing on their decisions to accept or reject the Civil Constitution. The few apparent exceptions—the "artisan priests," the "noble priests," and

TABLE 10

Oath-takers among "Outsiders"

Province Sampled	No. of Known "Outsiders"	Percentage Oath-takers	
		Born Outside Sample Region	All Parish Clergy
Alsace	66	39	39
Berry	31	72	73
Burgundy	32	72	58
Dauphiné	62	88	88
Languedoc	84	67	58
Lorraine	62	48	32
Maine	85	62	46
Poitou	70	34	33
Total	492		
Weighted average		60	53
Burgundy, Maine, and Languedoc		67	54
Alsace, Berry, Poitou, and Dauphiné		58	58

a certain number of the migrant clergy—represented only a tiny proportion of the total ecclesiastical corps. While milieu of *residence* was
clearly important in oath options—witness the strong regional cohesion
in oath-taking patterns and the correlations between oath-taking rates
and town populations—the milieu of *origin* was generally of only marginal significance.

Ecclesiastical Revenues

There has long been something of a minor debate over the effects of
ecclesiastical revenues on clerical perspectives toward the Civil Constitution. For most historians, an unequal distribution of clerical wealth
between upper and lower clergy was a critical factor crystallizing opposition among the parish clergy against the Old Regime of the Church.
According to Abbé Pisani, economic considerations were the principal
reason for the large number of clergymen accepting the oath: "the Church
of France was very rich, but the curés were very poor."[25] More recently,
Gérard Cholvy has suggested that the largest contingents of jurors in
Hérault were in regions where the parish clergy was most impoverished.[26]
But, for other historians, curé poverty helped detach priests from material
interests, reinforcing and necessitating a more strictly religious self-image.
In his careful exploration of the clergy of Normandy, Abbé Sévestre
concluded that in regions of relative penury parish clergymen tended to
refuse the oath, "having always maintained, through the ages, an intense
preoccupation with religious concerns." The prosperous priests, by contrast, were said to have been "complacent in their facile comfort, ...
rarely rising above earthly interests," and thus attracted to the constitutional side.[27]

In fact, many of these generalizations are based on misconceptions
about curé revenues before and during the Revolution. The parish clergy
cannot be so simply characterized as "very poor" under the Old Regime.
We now know that the notorious "portion congrue," the fixed salary
paid to parish priests by non-resident "gros-décimateurs," was charac-

[25] Paul Pisani, "Le serment de 1791," *Revue du clergé français*, 91 (1917), 490.

[26] Gérard Cholvy, *Religion et société au XIXe siècle. Le diocèse de Montpellier*, 2 vols. (Lille,
1973), 1:77-78. For similar arguments, see also Fernand Bridoux, *Histoire religieuse du département
de Seine-et-Marne pendant la Révolution*, 2 vols. (Melun, 1953), 1:41-44; and Sicard, 2:143.

[27] Emile Sévestre, *L'acceptation de la Constitution civile du clergé en Normandie* (Paris, 1922),
187-88.

teristic primarily of the southeastern quadrant of France.[28] Elsewhere in the kingdom, this mode of income was received by a minority, often only a tiny minority of the diocesan clergy. Throughout most dioceses there was an enormous range of curé incomes, from the wealthy or near wealthy—well over 3,000 *livres* per year—to the decidedly mediocre— even below the 700 *livres congrue* of 1790. In purely economic terms the divisions within the parish clergy were as great as those between that corps and such wealthy ecclesiastical dignitaries as canons or priors *in commendam*. But there were also certain broad regional patterns in curé revenues. Based on the declarations of revenue of 1790, the most reliable existent source for Old-Regime benefices, the lowest net incomes seem to have been collected by the curés of the southeast—particularly by those in the Alps of Provence and Dauphiné—most of whom received only slightly more than the *portion congrue*. More common, no doubt, and characteristic of much of northern and central France from Lorraine, Champagne, and Picardy to Burgundy, Berry, and Poitou, were the parish priests who averaged between 900 and 1200 *livres* per year: hardly a level of great wealth, but enough to rank an individual among the most prosperous members of the village society.[29] In two other sectors of the country, however, the curés appear to have been particularly favored: first, in portions of the southwest (where tithe rates were, significantly, the highest in France); and, second, in the "west" of Normandy, Maine, Anjou, and portions of Brittany. In the western provinces, in particular, revenues were commonly double or even triple the apparent French average. Whenever the laity in this zone pictured the "typical" country curé, the image they held was invariably that of a wealthy ecclesiastical gentleman with a large farmhouse, substantial land holdings, and a se- cured income in kind from the tithes.[30] Within a society where wealth

[28] For this and what follows in the paragraph, see the author's "Les revenus des curés à la fin de l'Ancien régime: esquisse d'une géographie," in *La France d'Ancien régime. Etudes réunies en l'honneur de Pierre Goubert*, Alain Croix, Jean Jacquart, and François Lebrun, eds. (Toulouse, 1984), 665-71.

[29] The comparison of revenues under the Old Regime is extremely complex. Obviously, the curés differed from their parishioners in having no family to support and less taxes to pay, and in being provided with a free house and garden. It has been estimated that in Languedoc only 18 percent of the population in one village earned over 1,000 *livres* per year: Georges Frêche, *Toulouse et la région Midi-Pyrénées au siècle des Lumières* (Toulouse, 1974), 369.

[30] On the high standard of living and comfortable life style of the curés of the West, see Charles Girault, *Les biens d'église dans la Sarthe à la fin du XVIIIe siècle* (Laval, 1953), 372-91; M. E. Viviers, "La condition du clergé séculier dans le diocèse de Coutances au XVIIIe siècle," *Annales de Normandie*, 2 (1952), 3-27; Donald Sutherland, *The Chouans: The Social Origins of Popular Counterrevolution in Upper Brittany, 1770-1796* (Oxford, 1982), 201-204.

was inevitably an important element of status, the particular economic structure of the Church in these provinces greatly enhanced the prestige, the "notability," of the resident parish clergy—an observation to which we must return in a later chapter.[31]

With the implementation of the Civil Constitution, economic inequality among the curés would be attenuated but by no means erased. While setting a base minimum of 1,200 *livres* a year, the legislators gave more to clergymen serving in towns with populations over 1,000, and granted the wealthier curés salaries of 1,200 plus one-half of their Old-Regime incomes in excess of 1,200 *livres*. Thus, depending on whether an individual had formerly received 500, 4,500, or 1,200 *livres* per year, the new legislation might substantially raise, substantially lower, or have no effect whatsoever on his income. But even after having raised the economic position of the poorest and lowered that of the wealthiest, the National Assembly had effectively maintained an economic hierarchy within the parish clergy.[32]

Within the seven provinces for which such calculations are feasible, the relation between revenues and oath-taking seems rather complex. (See Table 11.) Statistically it was the group of jurors in the sample who had possessed the highest average salaries under the Old Regime. This was true not only for the overall weighted average but for the means in five of the seven individual regions as well. Yet a more careful study reveals that it was above all the curés in the higher income brackets, and especially those earning upward of 2,500 *livres* per year, who pulled up the average of the constitutional clergy in general. Among the wealthiest curés, a few of whose net incomes reached 6,000 *livres* or more, close to three-quarters affirmed the Civil Constitution, some eleven percentage points higher than the proportion for all parish priests sampled.[33] While Abbé Sévestre's indictment of the "facile comfort" enjoyed by these wealthy curés should not be altogether discounted, one suspects that the principal explanation lay elsewhere. In the first place, there may have been a kind of personality selection among those holding such lucrative posts, with the real plums in the benefice hunt going precisely to the clergymen who were most career-oriented, most "opportunistic" in their outlook. The competition for the truly wealthy benefices was often ferocious. Among priests who had invested the time and money and weath-

---

[31] See below, chp. 10.

[32] See the deliberations of the National Assembly, June 17, 1790: *AP*, 16:239-41.

[33] See also Charles Tilly, *The Vendée: A Sociological Analysis of the Counterrevolution of 1793* (Cambridge, Mass., 1964), 242n.

TABLE 11

Oath-takers by Old-Regime Ecclesiastical Revenues (Curés Only)
(In *livres* per Year)

Province Sampled	% Un-Known	Percentage Oath-takers						Average Revenues	
		Under 700	P.C. (1)	701- 1499	1500- 2499	2500+	Total Known	Jur.	Rfr.
Berry	35	62	74	71	86	100	73	1,147	1,059
Burgundy	73	47	—	58	47	100	55	1,166	1,155
Dauphiné	21	88	92	78	100	—	89	699	720
Lorraine	15	49	59	37	52	43	44	986	1,006
Maine	29	64	62	35	53	62	53	1,936	1,820
Normandy (Manche) (2)	86	100	75	59	71	68	67	2,235	2,162
Picardy (3)	69	50	45	48	74	67	50	1,001	927
Weighted average		66	68	55	69	73	62	1,310	1,264
Total cases known: 1,952									

(1) *Portion congrue.*
(2) Districts of Cherbourg and Coutances only.
(3) Parishes beginning with the letters A to L only.

ered the litigation commonly required to nail down a choice rectory, it was not only economically unsound but out of character to refuse the oath and abandon everything they had struggled for. But, in the second place, despite an absolute decrease in the value of their revenues, this group of priests still maintained an economic position decisively above that of the mass of their colleagues, who were clustered near the 1,200 *livres* minimum. For men accustomed to the status that superior income undoubtedly conferred, there was perhaps a certain satisfaction in the fact that the Revolution had maintained them in their rank.

But there was also a somewhat greater tendency to take the oath among those at the lowest end of the revenue scale, the disinherited of the Old-Regime parish corps. To be sure, the variation from the mean was not so great as for the wealthiest ecclesiastics. Yet, significantly, the curés who had received the *portion congrue* were particularly vigorous in their acceptance of the Civil Constitution, with a weighted average of 68 percent jurors and oath-taking rates higher than the local means in all but one of the sample provinces. One is thus led to believe that the economic gain brought by the Revolution to the poorest of the Old-Regime curés did exercise a certain influence over the oath decisions of this group. But if there was indeed a "logic of the cooking pot"[34] operative in 1791, it was a logic more complicated than previously suspected, structured on a non-linear relationship between oath-taking and revenues. It was neither the poorest nor the wealthiest who were the most likely to be refractory, but the middling clergymen, precisely that group for whom the Revolution had ultimately made very little difference in the economic prospects of serving one's flock.

Personality Traits

Beyond the more obvious and easily quantifiable factors like age, social origins, or income is it possible to go a step farther and make generalizations about the personal character or behavior traits of the two clergies? It has already been suggested that a form of a personality selection may have been at work among the wealthiest benefice holders—a phenomenon which would help to explain the oath options of that group. In fact, the element of individual personality has not been altogether ignored by historians. Based on his reading of one local study, John McManners suggested that in massively refractory zones the isolated jurors were often of "doubtful character," while in predominantly constitutional areas the jurors appeared as an essentially average sample.[35] One might quibble over the precise definition of "doubtful" in this context, but it would not be surprising if the rare priests to resist the general consensus of their colleagues—and perhaps of their parishioners as well—were individualists, "loners," perhaps even misfits, who differed from the norm in a variety of ways.

Sylvestre Agussol, the constitutional curé of La Cavalerie, in the overwhelmingly refractory highlands of southern Rouergue, can serve as one such example. Son of a wealthy peasant, Agussol was unusual among local ecclesiastics in that he had spent some ten years of studies in Toulouse. According to his biographer, he returned to Rouergue possessed of a "modern and strongly democratic turn of mind." But he was also characterized by contemporaries as "autocratic, unyielding, domineering, self-assured, stubborn" and as possessed of an "overweening self-confidence"—hardly the qualities encouraged in the diocesan seminaries. When the Revolution broke out, he was quick to enter into various

[34] See John McManners, *French Ecclesiastical Society under the Ancien Régime. A Study of Angers in the Eighteenth Century* (Manchester, 1960), 267-68.
[35] John McManners, *The French Revolution and the Church* (London, 1969), 58.

political activities and was chosen president of the popular society and elector to the district. Though he came under enormous pressure to retract his oath, he steadfastly refused, sleeping for years with a gun at his side for protection against the anonymous threats of his neighbors.[36]

Aside from the insights of isolated anecdotes of this kind, the difficulties of venturing systematic statements about the character and personality of jurors and non-jurors may seem all but insurmountable. Nevertheless, Emile Sévestre made one such attempt for the clergy of Normandy. Unlike Rouergue, Normandy was a province in which the clergy had split into two relatively equal groups. Based on the individual portraits of the two clergies drawn up by ecclesiastical officials or prefects at the beginning of the nineteenth century, Sévestre concluded that, with a certain number of notable exceptions, the oath-takers were more "incapable" and "unworthy" than the refractories. Over twice as many constitutionals as refractories were classed as "ignorant"; and some four times as many were cited for various moral failings.[37] The problem with such statistics is that many of the clerical dignitaries making the evaluations during the post-Concordat period were probably prejudiced against the constitutional clergy, and that they may have judged the latter "unworthy" by the very fact that they had taken the oath.

Fortunately, for another of the ten sample provinces one can make use of clerical evaluations made *before* the Revolution. In 1784 the bishop of Le Mans, Jouffroy-Gonssans, attempted to institute a procedure for providing those cures in his nomination through a competitive merit system. For this purpose, a register was opened with entries for all new vicaires, taking note of each individual's qualities and talents as determined by the seminary directors and by the older clergymen with whom the new recruits were serving.[38] Thus, personal appraisals are available for some 180 of the vicaires and curés confronting the oath—a small sample to be sure, but one which includes virtually the whole younger generation under the age of 36 or 37 years in 1791.[39] Unfortunately, not all types of evaluations were given for all clergymen, and some of the

[36] André Maury, "Sylvestre Agussol, curé de la Cavalerie, prêtre constitutionnel," *Revue du Rouergue*, 24 (1970), 27-54.

[37] Sévestre, *L'acceptation*, 247-59.

[38] A.D. Sarthe, G 908 ("Registre des vicaires") and G 909 ("Registre des prêtres du diocèse, commencé en 1785"). On the bishop's efforts to establish the *concours*, see Maurice Giraud, *Essai sur l'histoire religieuse de la Sarthe de 1789 à l'an IV* (Paris, 1920), 73-74.

[39] About 49 percent of the clergy of Sarthe as a whole took the oath. Among the age cohorts for which character evaluations are preserved, the rate was 51 percent oath-takers.

descriptive adjectives used were patently vague and ambiguous. Nevertheless, these confidential comments, inscribed from one to twelve years before the crisis of the oath, suggest important differences between jurors and refractories, differences which generally tend to confirm Sévestre.[40] In the first place, many of the refractories seem to have performed somewhat better in their seminary studies. Among those designated as "good" or "excellent" students, only 42 percent would later take the oath; while 52 percent of the "poor," "very poor," and "lazy" students would be oath-takers.[41] To be sure, the seminary was much less a center of learning than an institution for imposing discipline and an "ecclesiastical character." It is thus noteworthy that of those young men specifically cited for their "piety," only about a fourth would take the oath. Among those said to possess such eminently clerical qualities as "gentleness," "prudence," and "virtue," only a third would opt for the constitutional position.[42] On the other hand, some two thirds of the young priests described with the relatively neutral adjective "honnête," or criticized for their "haughtiness" or "quick temper," would ultimately emerge as oath-takers. And over 70 percent of those cited for assorted varieties of misconduct during or after the seminary—quarrelsomeness, drunkenness, indulgence in hunting, sexual misconduct, etc.—would later take up the constitutional position.[43] This is not to say, of course, that all oath-takers were of dubious morals. In actuality, the great majority of all the younger generation received favorable mention in this regard.[44] But there was apparently a tendency for those least amenable to ecclesiastical discipline to later accept the Civil Constitution. And there was a corresponding tendency to reject the oath among those judged to be most in the mold of the Catholic Reformation ideal, most possessed of the cardinal post-Tridentine virtues of piety, humility, and self-effacement before authority. Thus, despite the relatively small size of the sample, the conclusions would seem to reinforce and be reinforced by the arguments in the

[40] Unfortunately, the single most common type of evaluation was too unspecific to use. It seems to have been a question of an overall appraisal of all the "qualities" of an individual, making use of words like "bon," "médiocre," etc. Of those receiving generally favorable evaluations of this kind, 68 of 142 (48 percent) were oath-takers. Of those receiving unfavorable evaluations, 15 of 27 (56 percent) were oath-takers.

[41] Of those receiving "good" or "excellent" ratings, 49 of 116 took the oath; of those receiving unfavorable ratings, 34 of 65 took the oath.

[42] Of those noted for "piety," 10 of 36 (28 percent) took the oath; of those called "gentle," "prudent," or "virtuous," 10 of 29 (34 percent) would be jurors.

[43] Of those accused of such diverse misconduct, 35 of 49 (71 percent) would be jurors.

[44] Of the 180 individuals evaluated, only 49 (27 percent) received unfavorable mentions.

previous chapter.[45] At least in the case of the diocese of Le Mans, a substantial proportion of the refractories exhibited personality traits that were particularly suited to the intellectual and theological arguments proposed by many of these same refractories, arguments stipulating a clerical model based on deference and submission to hierarchical authority.

To say that a certain percentage of the constitutionals was less amenable to discipline and less successful in their studies is not to say that they were necessarily more attracted to the alternate role model of the "citizen priest." Yet an additional clue may be particularly revealing in this regard: the participation of clergymen in village politics. Under the Old Regime, such participation was certainly not uncommon, but it is usually difficult to document.[46] In fact, prior to 1787, the law and the custom of most provinces prevented priests from officially mixing in the political affairs of the village Third Estate—and from thus commonly appearing in the official documents generated by such meetings. But, during the brief period from the beginning of the Revolution to the implementation of the Civil Constitution of the clergy, the whole situation changed and ecclesiastics were to be found openly participating as mayors, *procureurs*, and other village officials.[47] Though the election of a curé or a vicaire to one of these posts was obviously contingent on local support from the population, it was also indicative of an interest, a willingness, on the part of the clergyman to involve himself in functions more directly related to the responsibilities of a citizen than to those of a priest per se. And, in point of fact, in every department for which such information has been determined, the priest-mayors and priest-*procureurs* would support the Civil Constitution in proportions greater, and often substantially greater, than the local averages. Of a total of 164 priest-mayors in ten different departments, 118 or 72 percent were oath-takers, compared to a weighted average of 53 percent for all the parish clergy in these departments.[48]

[45] An attempt was also made to use seminary reports of priests in the diocese of Metz. But the individuals identified were too few—especially among the future jurors—to allow meaningful conclusions.

[46] See, for example, Tackett, *Priest and Parish*, 156-57.

[47] Ibid., 277-78.

[48] In Calvados, 8 of 19 known curé-mayors (42 percent) took the oath; in Cher the proportion was 10 out of 10 (100 percent); in Côte-d'Or, 7 of 7 (100 percent); in Eure, 6 of 8 (75 percent); in Meurthe, 8 of 14 (57 percent); in Meuse, 7 of 7 (100 percent); in Morbihan, 19 of 23 (83 percent); in Moselle, 3 of 6 (50 percent); in Sarthe, 22 of 32 (69 percent); in Vienne, 28 of 38 (74 percent). Unfortunately, the curé-mayors are often difficult to identify and the above figures are almost certainly incomplete. Sources: Emile Sévestre, *Liste critique des ecclésiastiques fon-*

The Limits of Prosopography

In the final analysis, the biographic profiles of the clergy developed here offer only limited insights into the ultimate patterns of motivation for priests facing the oath of 1791. To be sure, our examination of the ten-province sample has revealed a certain number of interesting associations. While a few of these are related to family origins—the strongly juring priests from artisan backgrounds, for example, or the refractory priests of the nobility—a clergyman's origins were apparently far less important than his residence. In terms of the individual's political options, it was not where he came from but where he lived and worked that seemed to make the greatest difference. A more significant set of factors was related to the clerical career cycle. While there was a greater tendency for the vicaires—particularly the youngest, unestablished, and unattached vicaires—to refuse the oath, the clergymen newly named to rectories and the oldest priests, facing the uncertainties of the end of their careers, both tended almost everywhere to accept the Constitution. The same could be said of those who had possessed the poorest and, paradoxically, the wealthiest cures, and of the "outsiders" who had come to their benefices from other dioceses and other provinces.

And, nevertheless, all such findings must be kept in perspective. The very oldest, the very youngest, the richest, the poorest, the artisans' sons, the outsiders—all represent relatively restrained minorities within the ecclesiastical corps as a whole. In most cases, the percentage differences involved are of only a few points, significant, to be sure, within the sample of several thousand individuals but of limited value for understanding the major patterns of oath-taking throughout the kingdom, particularly the extraordinary geographic trends between regions. Unfortunately, collective biographies divulge very little about the mass of parish priests in the middle: middle-aged, of middle-class backgrounds, or of middling revenues.

Yet, as is often the case in social history, the most important factors

---

ctionnaires publics insermentés et assermentés en Normandie (Paris, 1922), *passim.*; A.D. Cher, J 828; O. Guilliot, "Les curés-maires des districts de Grandpré et de Vouziers pendant la Révolution," *Nouvelle revue de Champagne et de Brie*, 8 (1930), 31-45; Augustin Cariou, "La Constitution civile du Clergé dans le département du Morbihan," *Mémoire de la Société d'histoire et d'archéologie de la Bretagne*, 45 (1965), 85-86; P. Lesprand, *Le clergé de la Moselle pendant la Révolution. Les débuts de la Révolution et la suppression des ordres religieux*, 4 vols. (Montguy-lès-Metz, 1934-39), 3:10-11; A.D. Sarthe, L 198 bis; Marquis Marie de Roux, *La Révolution à Poitiers et dans la Vienne* (Paris, 1911), 267n.

can prove particularly recalcitrant to quantification. One such factor has been glimpsed through our cursory efforts to sketch a typology of personal characteristics and inclinations. In one small sample, in a single region, some remarkable parallels have emerged between theological-ecclesiological positions in 1791 and personality traits before the Revolution. Other factors of this kind, more intangible and difficult to measure, will have to be explored in the following chapters.

FIVE

The Ecclesiastical Milieu

I N the previous chapter the oath of 1791 was examined primarily from the perspective of the personal characteristics and past experiences of the individuals involved. But now it is necessary to begin exploring the broader context in which such decisions were made. Every clergyman, by virtue of his special training and functions, was keenly aware of his membership in a distinct ecclesiastical society with a separate code of dress and behavior, and a well-defined attachment to a hierarchy of authority. But what effects, if any, did this clerical milieu have on the options toward the oath? Two factors, in particular, internal to this clerical world have often been isolated for their influence, negative or positive: the local seminary through which the diocesan clergy had passed and the specific bishops at the head of each diocese. Both factors hold considerable interest for present purposes because of their potential for explaining regional variations in oath patterns. Indeed, it has sometimes been argued that the Old-Regime dioceses themselves are a key element for understanding the geographic distribution of the jurors and the refractories.[1] But an additional dimension of the ecclesiastical milieu must also be explored: the possibility of peer influence at the local level.

Clerical Training and the Oath

For many historians the link between a clerical corps's options on the oath and its seminary training would seem self-evident. The seminary, after all, was the key institution by which the Church might hope to put its stamp on future clergymen, forming and shaping them into a preconceived mold. Particularly within those departments cut by two or more Old-Regime dioceses, the role of specific diocesan seminaries has frequently been cited as an explanation for regional variation in the reception of the Civil Constitution. In the department of Meuse, for example, the priests of the former diocese of Toul, to the east, were said

---

[1] Gérard Cholvy, *Religion et société au XIXe siècle. Le diocèse de Montpellier*, 2 vols. (Lille, 1973), 1:73-78; Fernand Bridoux, *Histoire religieuse du département de Seine-et-Marne pendant la Révolution*, 2 vols. (Melun, 1953), 1:37, 44-59; Jean Castex, "La Révolution," in *Le diocèse de Tarbes et de Lourdes*, Jean-Baptiste Laffon, ed. (Paris, 1971), 111-12.

to have been predominantly jurors because of the supposedly "lax" diocesan seminary controlled by the Lazarists; while those from the Old-Regime diocese of Reims, in the west, were far more refractory, due to their training with the rigorous and orthodox congregation of Saint-Sulpice.[2] Others have described the Sulpician seminaries as rallying points for non-jurors throughout the kingdom.[3]

Yet on closer examination, a relation of this kind, between the presence of particular seminary directors and the local proportion of oath-takers, seems difficult to support. On the eve of the Revolution, the 140-odd seminaries were directed by five major congregations, a handful of minor orders or congregations, and some 42 corps of secular priests organized locally.[4] Through a careful matching of diocesan and district boundaries, it is possible to estimate the approximate oath-taking rates for most of the Old-Regime dioceses (see Appendix IV),[5] and then calculate the juring rates for clergies whose seminary training was supervised by specific congregations. In this way, clergymen trained by the Lazarists are found to be a kingdom-wide cross section of oath-takers, with juring rates ranging from below 10 percent to above 90 percent, depending on the diocese, and with a mean at almost precisely the national average.[6] But very much the same can be said of the Sulpician dioceses, in which the proportion of jurors spread out from 22 to 88 percent. In fact, the overall average was actually slightly higher for the Sulpician-trained clergies than for those prepared by the Lazarists.[7] Only in the Eudist dioceses

[2] Charles Aimond, *Histoire religieuse de la Révolution dans le département de la Meuse et le diocèse de Verdun (1789-1802)* (Paris, 1949), 15-16; also Jean Leflon, "Le clergé des Ardennes et la Constitution civile," *Présence ardennaise*, 13 (1952), 9.

[3] John McManners, *The French Revolution and the Church* (London, 1969), 56.

[4] In 1789 the Congregation of the Mission (Lazarists) would appear to have administered 46 seminaries; the Sulpicians, 15; the Oratorians, 5; the Eudists, 12; the Barnabites, 1; the Doctrinaires, 8; the Congregation of the Blessed Sacrament, 3; the Spiritins, 1; and groups of diocesan priests, 42. But a more careful study remains to be completed. Sources: Antoine Dégert, *Histoire des séminaires français jusqu'à la Révolution*, 2 vols. (Paris, 1912), vol. 1, and *La France ecclésiastique* (Paris, 1789), complemented by an assortment of local studies.

[5] An overlay comparison has been made of diocese and district boundaries by means of the diocesan map published by Dom Dubois in *Annales E.S.C.*, 20 (1965), 680-91; and the district maps taken from *La République française en 84 départements* (Paris, 1793). A district was counted as being "part" of a diocese whenever an estimated minimum of 70 percent of the district was contained within the diocese. For a number of tiny dioceses in southern France, it was impossible to derive any clear oath percentages.

[6] Included here are only those dioceses with a single major seminary. The average oath-taking rate for dioceses in which the Lazarists directed the seminary was 52.5 percent.

[7] The average for the dioceses with Sulpician seminaries was 56.9 percent jurors. The king-

was the mean oath-taking rate substantially lower than the overall average. Yet no other order was so regionally localized as the Eudists, serving, as they did, primarily in Brittany and Normandy. If the two Breton dioceses of Rennes and Dol are excluded, the average for the remaining Eudist dioceses was essentially the same as for France as a whole.[8] Even in the rare instances where seminary professors themselves accepted the oath, there was no apparent effect on the local parish clergy. Thus, rates in those dioceses trained by the Oratorians or the Doctrinaires—the two congregations most commonly supporting the Civil Constitution—differed little from the oath rates in other dioceses.[9] In this respect, the situation in the diocese of Mende provides an interesting example. Of the eight Doctrinaire directors of the diocesan seminary and *collège*, at least six, and perhaps all eight, took the oath, yet both the local parish clergy and the young seminarians of the diocese overwhelmingly refused it. In fact, the position taken by the teachers of Mende caused a near riot in the seminary. One teacher was so mistreated and abused by his students that he was forced to flee for his life, and the school itself was soon closed down. Whatever may have caused the massive opposition of the clergy of Gévaudan, it was clearly unrelated to the position of the local seminary professors.[10]

The apparent weakness of the link between seminaries and the oath is less surprising when one examines the nature and emphasis of these institutions as they existed in the eighteenth century.[11] In the first place, the length of formal seminary studies was often considerably less than is sometimes imagined. One must take care not to equate the seminaries of the Old Regime with those which would develop in the century after the Revolution. The lengthy monastic internment experienced by Julien Sorel in Stendhal's famous novel was generally atypical of the eighteenth century. In fact, the very word "seminary" might signify three rather different institutional realities: an establishment organizing brief retreats

---

dom-wide weighted mean for all Old-Regime dioceses for which such calculations can be made is 53.0 percent jurors.

[8] Excluding the two Breton dioceses causes the average to rise from 44 to 51 percent oath-takers.

[9] The weighted mean oath-taking rate in the dioceses with Oratorian and Doctrinaire seminaries, taken together, was 50.8 percent.

[10] Pierre Pourcher, *L'épiscopat français et constitutionnel et le clergé de la Lozère durant la Révolution*, 3 vols. (St. Martin de Bourbaux, 1896-1900), 3:31-33, 42-43, 48-49.

[11] The best work on the French seminaries remains the study by Dégert, cited above. Unfortunately, Dégert focuses, above all, on the foundation and early rules of the seminaries and gives little attention to their eighteenth-century development.

of a period of days for devotional exercises before ordination; one requiring longer-term residence of several weeks or months before ordinations (the so-called *séminaires des ordinands*); or one basing residence not on the ordination cycle as such, but on the academic year, and enforcing stays of one or more terms of eight to ten months each.[12] If few or any French seminaries were still in the first stage of evolution by the eve of the Revolution, many were probably somewhere between the second and the third. Thus, even in the late eighteenth century the Doctrinaire establishments in Nîmes and Mende, the Lazarist seminaries of Amiens and Albi, and all of the Eudist seminaries continued to require only occasional and intermittent sojourns of a few months each before individuals received their various orders.[13] Elsewhere, in the Lazarist seminaries of Toulouse, Boulogne, and Saint-Brieuc, and in the independently run establishment of Auch, the standard course consisted of a single academic year, plus a few brief retreats.[14] Perhaps it was only in a minority of institutions that the specified training period had evolved into two or more academic years—as seems to have been the case in Tarbes, Gap, Périgueux, Embrun, and Metz.[15] As late as 1775, according to Loménie de Brienne, the total seminary experience in most dioceses was still relatively short and was interspersed with several periods of absence.[16] When one also considers that in many dioceses clerics were

[12] Dégert, 2:3-22; Charles Berthelot du Chesnay, "Les prêtres séculiers en Haute-Bretagne au XVIIIe siècle," Thèse d'état, Université de Rennes II, 1974, 206.

[13] Albert Durand, *Etat religieux des trois diocèses de Nîmes, d'Uzès, et d'Alès à la fin de l'Ancien régime* (Nîmes, 1909), 209-229; Frédéric Izard, "Le clergé paroissial gévaudanais à la fin du XVIIIe siècle," Mémoire de maîtrise, Université de Montpellier III, 1978, 34; Stafford Poole, *A History of the Congregation of the Mission* (N.p., 1973), 87-88; Louis de Lagger, "L'église dans le Tarn: l'Ancien régime à son déclin," *Revue du Tarn*, 3e sér., 7 (1957), 4; Jean Bindet, "Le diocèse d'Avranches sous l'épiscopat de Mgr. Godart de Belboeuf, dernier évêque d'Avranches," *Revue de l'Avranchin*, 87 (1969), 70; G. Bonnenfant, *Les séminaires normands du XVIe au XVIIIe siècles* (Paris, 1915), 131-35, 199, 367-75.

[14] *Actes du synode de 1782* (Toulouse, 1782), 171-77; Arlette Playoust, *La vie religieuse dans le diocèse de Boulogne au XVIIIe siècle (1725-1790)* (Arras, 1976), 163-64; Berthelot du Chesnay, 174-75; J. Bénac, "Le séminaire d'Auch," *Revue de Gascogne*, nouv. sér., 7 (1907), 217.

[15] Edmond Lafforgue, *Le clergé du diocèse de Tarbes sous l'Ancien régime* (Tarbes, 1929), 17-23; the author's *Priest and Parish in Eighteenth-Century France* (Princeton, 1977), 78-79; Guy Mandon, "Les curés en Périgord au XVIIIe siècle," Thèse de 3e cycle, Université de Bordeaux III, 1979, 106-109; Antoine Albert, *Histoire géographique, naturelle, ecclésiastique, et civile du diocèse d'Embrun*, 2 vols. (1783-86), 2:362-64; F.-Y. Le Moigne, chapter on the Revolution in *Le diocèse de Metz*, Henri de Morembert, ed. (Paris, 1970), 150.

[16] *Collection des procès-verbaux des assemblées générales du Clergé de France depuis l'année 1560 jusqu'à présent*, 9 vols. (Paris, 1767-80), vol. 8, pt. 2, col. 2530. Bernard Plongeron, *La vie quotidienne du clergé français au XVIIIe siècle* (Paris, 1974), p. 55, estimates that the average period of stay in the seminary of 1789 was 16 months.

allowed to travel to other dioceses to attend seminary, it is little surprising to find bishops complaining of the difficulty of controlling the preparation of the local clergies.[17]

In the second place, whatever the period of seminary preparation, the theology studied was usually quite minimal.[18] Intellectual training focused, for the most part, on the practical skills necessary for the "governing of souls": how to preach, hear confession, or judge the legality of marriage alliances. In Upper Brittany, for example, young seminarians spent their time practicing singing, preaching, and giving catechism, as well as in lengthy devotional exercises. They rehearsed the baptism ceremony on small wooden dolls and took turns confessing fellow students who impersonated the various cases which they were likely to encounter.[19] In fact, a number of seminaries taught only such rudiments of theology as might be developed from reading the *Sessions* of the Council of Trent or one of the brief theological manuals.[20] There was a "strong touch of anti-intellectualism"[21] in the thinking of seminary founders like Olier and Vincent de Paul, a trend that would be reinforced by the eighteenth-century bishops in their synodal ordinances and pastoral letters. For the archbishop of Auch, writing in 1770, the seminary was the place for "the study, above all, of the eminent science of the saints, of that science which teaches us how to talk to God and to meditate: the study of the moral conduct . . . of a worthy priest."[22] And in 1784 Bishop Jouffroy-Gonssans of Le Mans wrote that it was "more important to form [the seminarians'] morals and early inspire them with the sentiments of a solid and enlightened piety than to decorate their minds with the elements of the more agreeable and useful sciences. . . ."[23]

[17] In the seminaries of Paris many clerics are said to have attended for only short periods before ordinations, despite the existence of regular nine-month terms: Jacques Staes, "La vie religieuse dans l'archidiaconé de Josas à la fin de l'Ancien régime," Thèse, Ecole des chartes, 1969, 304-305. In Gap, despite the general rule of two ten-month terms, priests were allowed to attend other seminaries for other periods of time: letters from curé Dominique Chaix of Les Baux to Dominique Villar, Sept. 4 1782 and Feb. 12, 1783: B.M. Grenoble, R 10073. In Mende only about 65 percent of the priests were attending the local seminary at the time of their subdeaconate: Izard, 36-37.

[18] On the limited teaching of theology, see Dégert, 2:168-208.

[19] Berthelot du Chesnay, 217-19.

[20] Dégert, 2:187-89, 216; Berthelot du Chesnay, 204; anonymous, *Le séminaire de Gap* (Gap, 1924), 26-29; Charles Payrard, "Notes pour servir à l'histoire du grand séminaire de Nevers," *Bulletin de la Société nivernaise des lettres, des sciences et des arts*, 21 (1906), 45; Bénac, 217-18.

[21] Poole, 96.

[22] Dégert, 2:15-16.

[23] *Mandement* of Jouffroy-Gonssans: A.D. Sarthe, 2 J 104.

But even among those clergymen who pursued their studies at greater length and who took theological degrees in a university, there would seem to have been no particular propensity to reject the Civil Constitution. At the end of the Old Regime, the proportion of parish clergymen who obtained either the *bachelier* degree or the *quinquennium* certificate of five-years' university attendance would seem to have varied substantially from region to region—from as high as one-third or even one-half to below one-fifth of all curés.[24] In three of the regions of the ten-province sample of the previous chapter and in a portion of the diocese of Reims in Champagne, it has been possible to link university studies and oath options. (See Table 12.) From this information, it would appear that degree holders in Burgundy were somewhat more refractory than their less educated colleagues. But in Maine, Dauphiné, and Champagne, there was apparently no relationship whatsoever. Moreover, a closer scrutiny suggests that it may have been primarily the sizable group of graduates serving in the larger towns—of whom a greater proportion is known to have refused the oath everywhere in France—which weighted the sample on the side of the non-jurors. If one includes only those graduates holding benefices in rural areas, the balance in two of the regions, Maine and Champagne, actually swings in favor of the constitutionals.[25]

Ultramontanism and the "Concours"

For most areas of the kingdom, it is difficult to isolate any important regional patterns in seminary curricula. On the one hand, the content of the relatively meager theological training would seem to have become progressively more homogeneous and standardized. After mid-century,

[24] Degrees can be determined since the *bachelier* and the *quinquennium* conferred certain benefice privileges and, in consequence, the degrees were formally inscribed in certain diocesan registers. University degrees did not confer all benefice privileges, however, in the provinces of Franche-Comté, Lorraine, Alsace, Roussillon, and Brittany. See Marie-Madeleine Compère, Roger Chartier, Dominique Julia, *L'éducation en France du XVIe au XVIIIe siècle* (Paris, 1976), 261-67; Marcel Marion, *Dictionnaire des institutions de la France aux XVIIe et XVIIIe siècles* (Paris, 1923), 263-65. For specific figures, see Bindet, 67; Staes, 317; Dominique Julia, "La réforme posttridentine en France d'après les procès-verbaux de visites pastorales: ordre et résistances" in *La società religiosa nell'età moderna. Atti del convegno studi di storia sociale e religiosa. Cupaccio-Paestum, 18-21 maggio 1972* (Naples, 1973), 349; Jean Roy, "Le prêtre paroissial dans deux diocèses provençaux: Aix et Arles au XVIIIe siècle," Thèse de 3e cycle, Université d'Aix-Marseille, 1975, 65, 68.

[25] Unfortunately, the file which would permit a count of the graduates living in villages in Burgundy has been lost.

TABLE 12

Oath-takers Among University Degree Holders

| Province Sampled | Known Degree Holders | | Percentage Oath-takers | | |
	No.	%	All Degree Holders	Degree Holders Residing Outside Towns	All Curés
Burgundy (1)	37	8	46	?	57
Champagne (2)	64	37	53	62	53
Dauphiné (3)	29	11	86	84	88
Maine (4)	111	16	48	57	49
Total	241				
Weighted average			58		62

(1) Registers of *insinuations*, diocese of Autun: A.D. Saône-et-Loire, 2 G 340-41, and archives of the Universities of Paris and Dijon.

(2) Department of Marne, arrondissement of Reims: Emile Bouchez, *Le clergé du pays rémois pendant la Révolution et la suppression de l'archevêché de Reims (1789-1821)* (Reims, 1913).

(3) A.D. Hautes-Alpes, G 814-28, 877-80, 896, 1810; A.D. Drôme, D 41-44.

(4) Personal research notes of Alex Poyer kindly loaned to me by the author.

after the waning of the great Jansenist-Molinist controversies,[26] most bishops came to adopt such staunchly orthodox theology manuals as the ever-popular *Théologie de Poitiers*—said to have been accepted in "most French seminaries" by 1763.[27] But, on the other hand, as seen above, there remained an extraordinary particularism in the *structures* of clerical education, a particularism which reigned from diocese to diocese and even from individual to individual. Nevertheless, two other factors closely related to the mode and nature of the intellectual preparation do help differentiate a certain number of peripheral regions of the kingdom and throw light on oath reactions: first, the relative weakness of the Gallican tradition; second, the reliance on competitive examinations for appointments to parishes.

[26] Dégert, 1:405-406; Emile Appolis, *Le Jansénisme dans le diocèse de Lodève au XVIIIe siècle* (Albi, 1952); Playoust, 100-109; Claude Langlois, *Le diocèse de Vannes, 1800-1830* (Paris, 1974), 86-88.

[27] Dégert, 2:238-54. See also Augustin Sicard, *L'ancien clergé de France. Tome II. Les évêques avant la Révolution* (Paris, 1899), 413-14; Jean de Viguerie, *Une oeuvre d'éducation sous l'Ancien régime. Les Pères de la Doctrine chrétienne en France et en Italie* (Paris, 1976), 425, 431; Arthur Prévost, *Histoire du diocèse de Troyes pendant la Révolution*, 3 vols. (Troyes, 1908-1909), 1:lvii-lix; Maurice Bordes, "Le Jansénisme dans le diocèse de Lectoure," *ACSS*, 96 (1971), 107-133.

Throughout the entire central portion of France, in dioceses covering perhaps 80 percent of the country, "royal" or "episcopal" Gallicanism had formed an important strand of episcopal and seminary doctrine since at least the seventeenth century. This long-developing tradition had been enunciated most clearly in the "Four Articles," discussed by the General Assembly of the Clergy and formally promulgated by Louis XIV in 1682. Though the Sun King would later draw back from the Four Articles, the doctrine continued to receive the support of most of the French clergy, whether of Jansenist or Molinist persuasion, and it found its way into virtually all of the standard theological manuals. In 1766 a royal declaration would formally require all seminaries to teach the Four Articles.[28] Yet there were a number of regions on the fringes of the French realm in which Gallicanism had never taken strong root or had even been vigorously opposed. This was particularly true of those provinces entering the kingdom after the creation of the General Assembly of the Clergy and which would remain "étrangères" to the Clergy of France to the very end of the Old Regime. In Roussillon, for example, the clergy followed the decisions of the Council of Tarragon in all ecclesiastical matters. The strong influence from Spain was only reinforced by the Jesuit University of Perpignan, which long took an openly ultramontane position and refused to accept the Four Articles.[29] The situation was similar, in many respects, in Flanders, Artois, and Hainaut, where another Jesuit university (Douai) had rejected the Gallican doctrine, and where a Hapsburg brand of ultramontanism had left a deep imprint on the dioceses of Cambrai, Arras, Ypres, Saint-Omer, and Tournai.[30] To the east, Franche-Comté, Lorraine, and Alsace had been linked to the German Concordat rather than to the Concordat of Bologna. Allegiance to the pope was said to have been particularly strong in the diocese of Besançon. In 1791 this allegiance was directly linked by the department directory to the general refusal of the Comtois priests to accept the oath: "the priests of our province have long been nourished on ultramontane principles."[31]

[28] DTC, 4:198-99, 204; also, Dégert, 2:237-43.

[29] Philippe Torreilles, Histoire du clergé dans le département des Pyrénées-Orientales pendant la Révolution française (Perpignan, 1890), p. xix.

[30] Philippe Sagnac and C. Richard, "Le serment à la Constitution civile en 1791 dans la région du Nord," Annales de l'Est et du Nord, 3 (1907), 187; J. Peter and Charles Poulet, Histoire religieuse du département du Nord pendant la Révolution, 2 vols. (Lille, 1930), 1:13-14; Pierre Pierrard, ed., Le diocèse de Cambrai et de Lille (Paris, 1978), 160-61.

[31] Report dated Apr. 27, 1791: A.N., D XXIX bis 22, dos. 239, no. 4. See also Frank Tallett, "Religion and Revolution: the Rural Clergy and Parishioners of the Doubs, 1780-1797," Ph.D.

Somewhat more ambiguous was the case of Brittany. Though this western province was officially joined to the Clergy of France, it maintained special privileges based on its union with France in 1532. Technically, the Concordat of 1516 had never taken force here, and the pope held the collation of at least three-fifths of the cures of the province, cures which were normally granted through special competitive examinations. The peculiarly Breton conjunction of traditions and institutions combined, in the words of one historian, "to make the clergy of the province more Roman than Gallican in character."[32] In 1741, to be sure, the real power of nomination was ceded by the papacy to the Breton bishops. Yet the prelates continued and even expanded the institution of the *concours*, offering rectories only to those who had been most successful in the competition among candidates presenting themselves.[33] In fact, the same or similar institutions existed in virtually all the provinces which had not been incorporated into the original Concordat of Bologna. In Lorraine, all rectories vacated during six months of the year were opened to competition; in Franche-Comté, the same conditions held during eight months of the year.[34] In Flanders, Hainaut, and Artois, the *concours* apparently dated back to the period of Spanish control and had gradually been expanded to include all or nearly all parishes becoming vacant. Individuals were quizzed by an examining committee on theological, historical, and scriptural questions and were also tested on their preaching and singing ability. Though technically the patron of a parish had the right to present any candidate who had passed the exam, in practice the examining committee seems to have designated a specific candidate who was invariably accepted by the patron.[35]

The full influence of these special traditions and institutions in the peripheral provinces is not easy to assess. As we shall discover, there were

Thesis, University of Reading, 1981, 199; and Maurice Rey, ed., *Les diocèses de Besançon et de Saint-Claude* (Paris, 1977), 122-23.

[32] Michel Lagrée, chapter on the Revolution in *Le diocèse de Rennes*, Jean Delumeau, ed. (Paris, 1979), 137. According to Beatrice Hyslop, *French Nationalism in 1789 According to the General Cahiers* (New York, 1934), 278-79, the general cahiers of the clergy in Brittany were the least Gallican of any she examined. See also Robert Gildea and Michel Lagrée, "The Historical Geography of the West of France: the Evidence of Ille-et-Vilaine," *English Historical Review*, 94 (1979), 841.

[33] Berthelot du Chesnay, 82, 329-31; Delumeau, 137; *DDC*, 3:1403-1404.

[34] Eugène Martin, *Histoire des diocèses de Toul, de Nancy et de Saint-Dié*, 3 vols. (Nancy, 1903), 2:323-24; Anne-Marie Kaminski-Parisot de Bernecourt, "Les curés de campagne en Franche-Comté au XVIIIe siècle," Thèse, Ecole des chartes, 1975, 30.

[35] Peter and Poulet, 1:14-15; Pierrard, 161-62; Playoust, 157-58. The *concours* seems also to have existed in Roussillon, Gex, Bugey, and Valromy: Julia, 341.

many other factors which set the frontier areas apart from the core of the realm. Yet it seems likely that the *concours* not only raised the intellectual standards of diocesan clergymen, but gave the bishop much greater potential authority over them, reinforcing a sentiment of deference and hierarchy within the clerical corps as a whole. The sense of hierarchical authority could only have been strengthened by the tradition of strong ties with Rome and the lack of experience with the more independent Gallican stance which characterized these same provinces. It is scarcely surprising that most of the priests of these regions viewed the eminently Gallican legislation of the Civil Constitution through a different optic than many of their colleagues in the core of the kingdom.

The Influence of the Bishops

Aside from seminaries and clerical training, a second element of potential cohesion in the Old-Regime diocese was the bishop himself. Within the context of the Gallican Church, ever jealous of its relative independence of Rome, the bishops stood as the very embodiment of local administrative and theological unity. Yet the relationship between the French prelate and his parish clergy—the social and pastoral distance separating the two—had evolved markedly in the course of the eighteenth century, and by the beginning of the Revolution the bonds within the diocesan hierarchy had often become taut and distended.

In fact, the position of the Old-Regime bishops on the oath, the Civil Constitution, and the Revolution in general is not as easy to characterize as has sometimes been imagined. If the episcopacy ultimately achieved near unanimity in opposition to the oath, it was due in large measure to the long-established *esprit de corps* of that group, born of common family backgrounds, common educational experiences, and the habit of working in concert through the institutions of the "Clergy of France." As individual prelates produced statements on the Revolutionary laws, they were quickly circulated to colleagues along the correspondence network of the former Agents-General. It was no coincidence that Archbishop Boisgelin, one of the principal leaders of the final General Assemblies of the Old Regime, assumed *de facto* leadership of the French episcopacy in 1790, formulating a common statement on the Civil Constitution and ensuring that it was signed and approved by virtually all the bishops.[36]

[36] Michel Peronnet, *Les évêques de l'ancienne France* (Lille, 1977), 1192; A. Sicard, *Le clergé de France pendant la Révolution*, 3 vols. (Paris, 1912-27), 2:83. See also Paul Pisani, *Répertoire biographique de l'épiscopat constitutionnel (1791-1802)* (Paris, 1907), 18-19.

But this ultimate unity, forged by the spring of 1791, concealed a wide divergence of attitudes and tactics on the part of individual bishops. There can be no doubt that, before the passage of the oath decree, a significant number, perhaps the majority of bishops, had demonstrated a certain readiness to cooperate with the Revolutionary authorities. In Besançon, Blois, Chartres, Rodez, Aire, Cahors, and undoubtedly in many other dioceses, the Old-Regime prelates all acquiesced in the reorganization of the parish boundaries in compliance with the guidelines of the Civil Constitution.[37] The bishop of Poitiers seemed prepared to accept new diocesan boundaries, despite the fact that the boundaries in question entailed a significant reduction in the size of his see. Elsewhere, the bishop of Tarbes had begun organizing his new "episcopal council," as prescribed by the revolutionary laws, while his counterpart in Vannes seemed to have resigned himself to the suppression of his cathedral chapter.[38] Indeed, Boisgelin's statement, the *Exposition des principes*, was essentially a moderate, conciliatory document, expressing a willingness to cooperate with the reforms—with the major proviso that the Church be allowed to ratify formally all such changes.[39]

Nevertheless, by the autumn of 1790, if not earlier, a significant minority of the episcopal corps had taken up openly intransigent positions and was doing everything in its power to influence the parish clergy against the Civil Constitution. The bishop of Amiens, who had abandoned his seat in the National Assembly following the October Days, was publicly repudiating both the religious reforms and the Declaration of the Rights of Man and the Citizen.[40] In Strasbourg the crusty old Cardinal de Rohan—former casualty of the Diamond Necklace Affair—insinuated that he might reject the Civil Constitution even if the pope accepted it.[41] And the newly appointed bishop of Vienne, who had seen his see sup-

---

[37] Henri Grégoire, *Mémoires*, 2 vols., H. Carnot, ed. (Paris, 1840), 1:16; Antoine Dégert, *L'ancien diocèse d'Aire* (Auch, 1907), 1:271-73; letter from the bishop of Cahors to the department of Lot, Oct. 21, 1790: A.N., D XXIX bis 20, dos. 212, nos. 11-12.

[38] Marquis Marie de Roux, *La Révolution à Poitiers et dans la Vienne* (Paris, 1911), 367-70; Castex, 109; Augustin Cariou, "La Constitution civile du Clergé dans le département du Morbihan," *Mémoire de la Société d'histoire et d'archéologie de la Bretagne*, 45 (1965), 59-98.

[39] Marcel Reinhard, *Religion, Révolution et Contre-Révolution* (Paris, 1960), 75. See also Philippe Sagnac, "L'Eglise de France et le serment à la Constitution civile du clergé (1790-1791)," *Révolution française*, 53 (1907), 290.

[40] Michel Destombes, *Le clergé du diocèse d'Amiens et le serment à la Constitution civile, 1790-91* (Amiens, 1971), 336-41.

[41] Rodolphe Reuss, *La Constitution civile du clergé et la crise religieuse en Alsace (1790-1795)*, 2 vols. (Strasbourg, 1922), 1:10-13.

pressed in 1790, condemned the religious reforms as "impious, heretical, and blasphemous."[42] A particular cluster of opposition and intransigence was to be found in the province of Brittany. Here, the prelates had experienced an especially bitter defeat in the elections of 1789, a defeat which prevented their being chosen as deputies to Versailles, and which left several of them fuming and raging—but in residence in their dioceses and thus in a position to exercise more immediate pressure on their parish clergies.[43] The extreme case, no doubt, was the bishop of Tréguier, whose vitriolic attacks on the whole Revolution had been pronounced in pastoral letters since the autumn of 1789. But the bishops of Dol, Quimper, and Saint-Pol-de-Léon had also taken strong positions against the Civil Constitution well before the decree on the oath.[44]

Even after the passage of the oath legislation, the bishops continued to respond with a wide array of strategies or non-strategies. Several of the bishops immediately launched vigorous campaigns to influence their curés against the oath. As early as December 12 the bishop of Le Puy sent out hand-signed pastoral letters to all his parish priests, explaining and approving the *Exposition des principes*. He advanced confirmation ceremonies from the spring to the late autumn, specifically for the purpose of condemning the Civil Constitution.[45] La Tour du Pin, archbishop of Auch, was present and active in his diocese, personally appearing before Revolutionary officials to oppose the election of a curé. On the day set for the oath ceremony in Auch, the prelate was the first to arrive, ostentatiously protesting the whole procedure.[46] By Christmas of 1790, Bishop Amelot of Vannes was distributing letters to his clergy, strongly denouncing both the oath and the Civil Constitution, while in Amiens Machault sent all his curés printed copies of the restrictive oath which they were expected to take.[47] Perhaps even more effective were those pleas or condemnations which prelates personally addressed to individual

---

[42] Charles Jolivet, *La Révolution en Ardèche* (Largentière, 1930), 256-57.

[43] Barthélémy Pocquet, *Les origines de la Révolution en Bretagne*, 2 vols. (Paris, 1885), 2:315.

[44] Georges Minois, "Le rôle politique des recteurs de campagne en Basse-Bretagne (1750-1790)," *Annales de Bretagne*, 89 (1982), 161; Barruel, 1:373-92; J. Savina, *Le clergé de Cornouaille à la fin de l'Ancien régime et sa convocation aux Etats-généraux* (Quimper, 1926), 73; letter from bishop of Dol, before May 25, 1790: A.N., C 116, dos. 320; letters from the town of Morlaix, July 5-18, 1790: A.N., D XXIX bis 7, dos. 104.

[45] Ernest Gonnet, *Essai sur l'histoire du diocèse du Puy-en-Velay (1789-1802)* (Paris, 1907), 102-103.

[46] G. Brégail, *Le Gers pendant la Révolution (1789-1804)* (Auch, 1934), 368-69.

[47] Cariou, 63-64; and report by Chasset for the Ecclesiastical Committee, Jan. 25, 1791: *AP*, 22:487-88.

clergymen. In early February, the bishop of Ypres was apparently sending such denunciations directly to the jurors in his diocese, castigating each in the harshest possible terms and forbidding them all sacerdotal functions until they had formally retracted. Likewise, the bishop of Mende was personally rebuking parish priests, calling them "heretics" and "apostates" for having so much as published the Civil Constitution in their parishes.[48] And in Bayeux, the aged and irascible Bishop Cheylus reactivated many of the procedures once used for battling the Jansenists, soliciting signatures from all curés and vicaires, organized for deliberation by deanery on this new kind of *formulaire*. "Let us do battle like the Children of Israel," he wrote, "to save the ark of the Covenant. Let us take courage in the face of the forces of Hell now unleashed against the Faith." To this clarion call, the bishop ultimately obtained over 600 adherences among his diocesan clergy.[49]

Yet such forcible action by bishops present in their dioceses was probably not the norm. There is no reason to believe that episcopal residence was any more conscientious after 1789 than it had been before the Revolution. Archbishop Marbeuf of Lyon was not the only prelate who would leave France as an emigrant without ever having set foot in his diocese. The bishop of Valence appeared at his seat for only thirteen days in January before leaving for good; while the bishop of Die left for Paris, never to return as soon as he received word that his bishopric had been abolished and that he had been granted a pension.[50] Already, by the end of 1789, at least three of the bishops—those of Paris, Apt, and Pamiers—had permanently fled the country. Some seven or eight more would follow in 1790, before the flood tide of emigration began in early 1791 at the time of the oath itself.[51] Another thirty of the bishops, deputies to the Estates-General, would remain in Paris through the end of the Constituent Assembly. Although a few unusually able vicars-general—like Brigeat de Lambert in Avranches or the suffragan Otrope in Metz—might play an important role locally, the continued absence from their

[48] Letters from bishop, Feb. 8 and 11, 1791: A.N., D XXIX bis 21, dos. 224, no. 26 and dos. 226, no. 36; Pierre-Jean-Baptiste Delon, *La Révolution en Lozère* (Mende, 1922), 70-71; and deliberations of the town of Marvejols, Dec. 20, 1790: A.N., D XXIX bis 20, dos. 216, no. 20.

[49] Emile Sévestre, *Les problèmes religieux de la Révolution et de l'Empire en Normandie, 1787-1815*, 2 vols. (Paris, 1924), 210-21.

[50] Maurice Wahl, *Les premières années de la Révolution à Lyon (1788-1792)* (Paris, 1894), 292; Jules Chevalier, *L'Eglise constitutionnelle et la persécution religieuse dans le département de la Drôme pendant la Révolution* (Valence, 1919), 78-94.

[51] Sicard, *Le clergé pendant la Révolution*, 2:110-13; Albert Mathiez, *Rome et le clergé français sous la Constituante. La Constitution civile du clergé. L'affaire d'Avignon* (Paris, 1911), 115.

dioceses of so many prelates at the critical juncture of January-February 1791 could hardly have strengthened episcopal influence.[52] And present or absent, a great many, perhaps the majority, of the diocesan leaders seem to have exercised anything but decisive leadership. The bishops of Normandy were said to be far more active in defending their own benefices and in attacking the elections of their replacements than in instructing and organizing their parish clergies against the oath.[53] And, in many instances, when the bishop had finally taken an unambiguous stand and had explicitly instructed his clergy on the position he expected them to take, the oath ceremonies themselves had already come and gone. It was apparently late January before the prelate had enunciated his position in the diocese of Besançon, February in the diocese of Lyon, March in Lectoure and Coutances, April in Albi, and May in the diocese of Toul.[54] The bishop of Bellay would die in January 1791 without ever having taken a stance; and the archbishop of Bourges, we are told, "neither did nor said nor wrote anything at all" before leaving the country as an emigrant in 1791.[55] In all, perhaps a third of the Old-Regime bishops formally articulated their positions only after the majority of their diocesan clergymen had already been forced to make a decision.[56]

That the massive episcopal rejection of the oath did make a difference

[52] Bindet, 28, 43-44; P. Lesprand, *Le clergé de la Moselle pendant la Révolution. Les débuts de la Révolution et la suppression des ordres religieux*, 4 vols. (Montguy-lès-Metz, 1934-39), 3:32-34. Unfortunately, it has proved impossible to make a systematic survey of the whereabouts of all of the bishops in early 1791.

[53] Emile Sévestre, *L'acceptation de la Constitution civile du clergé en Normandie* (Paris, 1922), 380.

[54] Jean Girardot, *Le département de la Haute-Saône pendant la Révolution*, 3 vols. (Vesoul, 1973), 2:55; Brégail, 368-69; Sévestre, *Problèmes religieux*, 207-208; Louis Pérouas, "Le clergé creusois durant la période révolutionnaire," *Mémoires de la Société des sciences naturelles et archéologiques de la Creuse*, 39 (1976), 561-62; C. Constantin, *L'évêché du département de la Meurthe de 1791 à 1801. Tome 1. La fin de l'Eglise d'Ancien régime et l'établissement de l'Eglise constitutionnelle* (Nancy, 1935), 179n; E. A. Rossignol, *Histoire de l'arrondissement de Gaillac pendant la Révolution* (Albi, 1895), 171-72; Eugène Dubois, *Histoire de la Révolution dans le département de l'Ain*, 6 vols. (Bourg, 1931-35), 2:183-93.

[55] Dubois, 2:16-17; M. Bruneau, *Les débuts de la Révolution dans les départements du Cher et de l'Indre* (Paris, 1902), 351-52.

[56] An attempt has been made to date the earliest pastoral letters or other statements by which bishops instructed their clergies on the stance which they were expected to take. Out of 83 such statements so identified, 29 seem to have been dated after late January, after most oath ceremonies had already transpired. Conclusions based especially on Barruel, vols. 2, 3, 9, 12, and 13; and on A.N., D XXIX bis 20-21, as complemented and completed by a wide variety of local studies. It seems certain, however, that far more than 83 Old-Regime bishops actually sent such pastoral letters.

in the decisions of certain curés can scarcely be doubted. Many clergymen, as we have seen, specifically said as much in their oath explanations.[57] For some patriot administrators, there could be little doubt that the bishops were a major motivating force behind the decisions of the local refractories.[58] Those bishops who were actually present in their dioceses and actively working to win the allegiance of the local curés may have been particularly successful in swaying opinion. Perhaps it was the personal ascendancy of individual bishops which helps to explain those small islands of refractory curés near diocesan capitals in areas that were otherwise massively constitutional—in the dioceses of Langres or Nevers or Poitiers, for example.[59] In fact, the overall oath-taking rate in the episcopal towns was somewhat less than that which might have been predicted on the basis of the towns' population alone.[60]

But, despite the inevitable success of individual bishops in winning over individual clergymen, episcopal leadership, or lack thereof, seems little related to the oath decisions of the great majority of ecclesiastics. There were seemingly as many or even more letters from patriots announcing the failure of episcopal efforts to stimulate curé opposition.[61] In the former diocese of Limoges many of the bishop's personal letters to the curés were publicly denounced by parish clergymen themselves. In the Breton diocese of Saint-Brieuc, by contrast, where the bishop had not resided for years, the curés themselves organized a petition against the oath which was rapidly signed by nearly two hundred colleagues.[62] The priests of the diocese of Albi, whose bishop had been absent for twenty-five years, overwhelmingly refused the oath, while those in Soissons and Amiens seemed largely immune to the vigorous efforts of their

[57] See above, chp. 3.

[58] See, for example, the reports by the department of Ille-et-Vilaine, Jan. 17, 1791: A.N., D XXIX bis 20, dos. 217, no. 15; and by the district of Revel (Haute-Garonne), Feb. 14, 1791: A.N., D XIX 81, dos. 619.

[59] Letter from the Jacobins of Bourbonne, Mar. 12, 1791: A.N., D XXIX bis 21, dos. 331, no. 21; from the departments of Nièvre, Jan. 19, 1791, and Vienne, Jan. 23, 1791: A.N., D XXIX bis 20, dos. 220, nos. 11 and 23.

[60] The sample consists of 74 episcopal towns for which figures are available. The predicted oath rate, based on the population of these towns, is 41 percent. The actual oath rate was 37 percent. See above, chp. 2, for sources.

[61] From the department of Eure, Jan. 19, 1791: A.N., D XXIX bis, dos. 219, nos. 6-7; from Cantal, n.d.: D XIX 22, dos. 364; from Hautes-Pyrénées, May 21, 1791: F19 462; from a tribunal judge in Remiremont (Vosges), Jan. 28, 1791: D XIX 82, dos. 645, no. 11.

[62] Letter by the *procureur-général-syndic* of Haute-Vienne and adjoining documents, Jan. 18, 1791: A.N., D XXIX bis 20, dos. 218, no. 22; and Hervé Pommeret, *L'esprit public dans le département des Côtes-du-Nord pendant la Révolution* (Saint-Brieuc, 1921), 20, 121.

respective prelates. Among those fourteen dioceses whose prelates are described by Sicard or Mathiez as being most intransigent, oath rates ranged from 7 percent in Saint-Pol-de-Léon and 14 percent in Castres to 86 percent in Narbonne and 89 percent in Toulon. The average for the fourteen was 53.5 percent, almost precisely the national mean.[63] On the contrary, in five dioceses where the bishop or the auxiliary took the oath and cooperated with the Civil Constitution, the rates ranged from 38 percent in the French portion of Basel to 87 or 88 percent in Orléans and Sens. While there can be no doubt that the constitutional archbishop Loménie de Brienne strove vigorously to obtain a large oath percentage within his diocese of Sens, it is also evident that the whole section of central France, inside and outside the boundaries of Sens, opted over-whelmingly for the oath.[64] By contrast, in the diocese of Autun, one group of curés openly took Bishop Talleyrand to task for his defense of the oath and countered with their own arguments in opposition. Ultimately, the young bishop-deputy could obtain only a little more than 50 percent adhesions from the clergy of his diocese.[65] And within the department of Ardèche there were far more refractories in the former diocese of Viviers, whose bishops accepted the oath, than in the diocese of Vienne, whose bishop vigorously opposed it.[66]

One arrives at much the same conclusion if one systematically examines the oath-taking rates in the Old-Regime dioceses throughout the king-dom. (See Appendix IV.) To be sure, some of these dioceses do indeed emerge with distinct and coherent oath-taking patterns in striking con-trast to the surrounding regions. Toul in Lorraine, Lodève in Languedoc, Angoulême in the southwest, Tarbes in the Pyrenees; all had average juring rates decidedly higher than the neighboring dioceses; while Saint-Pol-de-Léon in Lower Brittany and Meaux and Senlis in the Parisian Basin stood out with relatively lower rates. Yet cases such as these are exceptions. On the whole, one is even more impressed by the contrasts *within* dioceses and by the gradual changes shading from one region to another, cutting sharply across the former diocesan boundaries. For the larger dioceses, these internal variations were sometimes immense: from

[63] Sicard, *Le clergé pendant la Révolution*, 2:78-80; Mathiez, 114.

[64] Bridoux, 1:37, 44-50.

[65] Louis Bauzon, Paul Muguet and Louis Chaumont, *Recherches historiques sur la persécution religieuse dans le département de Saône-et-Loire pendant la Révolution*, 4 vols. (Chalon-sur-Saône, 1889-1903), 2:84-92. In fact, Talleyrand had just resigned his bishopric when the requirement of the oath was initiated.

[66] Jolivet, 256-59.

14 percent oath-taking in the west of the diocese of Le Mans to 84 percent in the east; from 25 to 83 percent in the diocese of Langres; from 38 to 100 percent in the diocese of Limoges. But a lack of coherence was also visible in medium-sized dioceses. The western portion of the diocese of Auch (the district of Nogaro) was far closer in its oath-taking patterns to the neighboring diocese of Aire. The diocese of Bayeux would be sharply split between a western section closely resembling the diocese of Coutances (higher percentages) and a western section more akin to the diocese of Lisieux (lower percentages)—this, despite the efforts of the bishop of Bayeux to win over all members of his clergy. In Brittany, a strong constitutional area emerged directly astride the frontier between Tréguier and Saint-Brieuc. The adjoining dioceses of Cahors and Rodez were both cut through the middle by a strikingly higher constitutional zone that roughly followed the river Lot. The dioceses of Bordeaux, Châlons-sur-Marne, La Rochelle, Autun, Metz, and Saintes, to name only a few, all revealed internal oath variations of 30 percentage points or more. Indeed, the average range for all dioceses containing three districts or more was precisely 30 points. When oath-taking variations are calculated for the departments, the newly created administrative units whose boundaries corresponded but rarely to those of the dioceses, the average range is found to be almost the same (34 percentage points)—this, despite the fact that the departments were larger, on the average, and contained more districts than the dioceses.[67] Whatever it was that generated the regional patterns of the oath, it seems to have been only marginally related to the policies of the bishops and the existence of the Old-Regime dioceses.

Relations among Peers

For many of the priests of 1791, grappling with the intellectual and emotional complexities of the oath decision, both the seminary and the leaders of the ecclesiastical hierarchy were remote realities to which the ties of influence had been badly frayed or long since shorn away. But there was another potentially more immediate and tangible set of influences arising from within the ecclesiastical milieu: the influence of clerical

[67] Sixty Old-Regime dioceses containing three or more districts have been analyzed. The average range in oath-taking rates between the highest and the lowest districts is 30.0 percentage points. There were an average of 5.9 districts per diocese. Seventy-seven departments for which such data are available have also been analyzed. With an average of 6.7 districts per department, the average range was 34.4 percentage points. In the kingdom of 1791 there were a total of 83 departments and all or part of 139 Old-Regime dioceses.

peers on one another. To be sure, the bonds that linked individuals together at this level are far more difficult to detect in documents generated by official institutions. Yet the memoirs and letters of the period are replete with anecdotes on the informal discussions and consultations between clergymen during the late winter and early spring of 1791. Thus, Descharrières, curé of Saint-Loup in Haute-Saône, told of inviting in priests from as far away as the Vosges to discuss the question that so agonized his conscience. Nicolas Alaidon of Toul described his consultations with numerous friends over the issue—though, in his case, opinion was so divided that he ultimately found little assistance.[68] In all likelihood, influence of this sort operated along lines of association formed long before the Revolution. Under the Old Regime, the common bonds of professional experience and the common need for friendship and social intercourse had established what by many accounts were lively and active local clerical groupings. The correspondence of the period gives us glimpses of the occasional soirées among priests of the same neighborhood for dining or cards or versifying or the sharing of a glass—or a bottle— of wine. Perhaps even more important, given the curés' parish responsibilities and the difficulties of transportation during much of the year, were the contacts maintained in epistolary fashion, in which individuals exchanged books or poems or the latest political news, with a zest and enthusiasm that can only be understood in the context of the crushing monotony of rural village life.[69] When they were faced with the dilemma of the oath, it was far more natural for clergymen to fall back on local networks of this kind than to seek advice from distant prelates.

In this way, because of their better education, their reputation for integrity, or the sheer force of their personalities, individual clergymen like the curés of Ballon in Upper Maine, of Rémeling in German Alsace, of Saint-Loup in Franche-Comté might swing whole small groups of ecclesiastics one way or the other.[70] Etienne Delcher, parish priest in Brioude (Haute-Loire) and doctor of theology, was said to have exerted a powerful influence in favor of the oath throughout his district; while

[68] Girardot, 2:53-54; and H. Thédenat, *Journal d'un prêtre lorrain pendant la Révolution (1791-99)* (Paris, 1912), 2-4.

[69] Lesprand, 3:25; Pierre de Vaissière, *Curés de campagne de l'ancienne France* (Paris, 1932), 234-35. One curé in the diocese of Gap cited the difficulty of obtaining mail in his mountain parish as an important reason why he wished to be transferred: Tackett, 112. See also Mandon, 222-31.

[70] Maurice Giraud, *Essai sur l'histoire religieuse de la Sarthe de 1789 à l'an IV* (Paris, 1920), 249-64; Girardot, 2:53-54; Jean Eich, *Histoire religieuse du département de la Moselle pendant la Révolution* (Metz, 1964), 181-82.

the curé and dean of Bourg d'Iré, in the district of Segré (Maine-et-Loire), seems to have led a whole contingent of his neighbors into the refractory camp.[71] It is perhaps peer pressure and influence of this kind which explains the occasional small clusters of rural clergymen taking positions sharply counter to the overall trends of a particular region.[72]

The existence of pre-Revolutionary networks of association may also help illuminate the terrible confrontations between ecclesiastical factions which emerged in certain localities in 1791—like the one which pitted jurors against non-jurors near the Lower-Norman town of Valogne. In this case, two "clans" of priests, as Emile Sévestre describes them, had already been defined prior to 1789 along lines of ideological orientation and personality disposition—two factions whose rivalries were only intensified by the opposing positions which they took on the ecclesiastical oath.[73] And whenever the bonds of association were reinforced by biology, the interaction might be especially strong. Families of priests—as there were families of lawyers or butchers or bakers—were relatively common under the Old Regime, and the influence of brother upon brother was clearly in evidence in 1791. "My brother and I have taken a conditional oath," wrote Curé Beucher near Le Mans, as though the decision was inherently a joint one.[74] Other brothers are found following identical strategies even to the extent of retracting oaths at almost the same time—and in virtually the same language.[75] Out of 175 priests in four sample provinces who had one or more brothers in the clergy, 83 percent opted in the same fashion as their brother or brothers.[76]

The status of deputy to the National Assembly seemed to give some

[71] Gonnet, 110-16, 123-25; Paul Bardou, "Le clergé angevin et la reconstruction concordataire du diocèse d'Angers," Thèse de 3e cycle, Université de Paris-Sorbonne, 1981, 61.

[72] In Ille-et-Vilaine, for example: Roger Dupuy, *La garde nationale et les débuts de la Révolution en Ille-et-Vilaine (1789-mars 1793)* (Paris, 1972), map, p. 233.

[73] Emile Sévestre, *La vie religieuse dans les principales villes normandes pendant la Révolution (1787-1801). Troisième série. Manche* (Paris, 1943), 42-61.

[74] H. Roquet, *Observation de Me. Beucher, curé de Brûlon* (Le Mans, 1929), 48.

[75] E.g., the brothers Guilhem and the three brothers Jouy in the department of Aude: A. Sabarthès, *Histoire du clergé de l'Aude de 1789 à 1803. Répertoire onomastique* (Carcassonne, 1939), 215, 237-39.

[76] The sample consisted of sets of brothers (pairs or trios) in the departments of Aude (24 sets), Haut-Rhin (26), Moselle (13), and the Old-Regime diocese of Gap (21): for sources, see above, chp. 4, Table 5. Of the 84 sets, 33 (39 percent) unanimously took the oath, 37 (44 percent) unanimously refused, and 14 (17 percent) split. Of the entire sample, 84 of 175 individuals (48 percent) took the oath, compared to 55 percent oath-takers in the four areas generally. This lower oath rate for groups of brothers may reinforce the conclusion later in the chapter about collective reactions to the oath.

clergymen a particular ascendancy over elements of their constituencies. Thus, the deputy Allain, curé of Josselin (Morbihan) and a former Jesuit, was described as "exercising a veritable apostolate" through a constant stream of letters against the oath to the vicars in his home district. So too Collinet, curé in Moselle, returned home without authorization to lobby successfully against a juring position;[77] and the diatribes against the oath by Mathias, deputy and curé of Egliseneuve-d'Entraigues in the district of Besse (Puy-de-Dôme), may well have had an effect on local opinion.[78] Other deputies, like Henri Grégoire, succeeded in influencing clergymen in favor of the constitutional cause.[79] Yet not all deputies were equally successful in advancing their opinions among their colleagues at home. If Mathias found a responsive chord for his opposition to the oath in Puy-de-Dôme, his fellow deputy, Brignon, was totally unsuccessful in promoting the Civil Constitution in another district of the same department. Returning home in September 1791 at the end of his mandate, Brignon would encounter hostility from lay and clergy alike and would find himself, as he sadly commented, "a stranger in the midst of my own flock."[80] On the whole, the positions taken by the clerical deputies seem to have been remarkably little related to the evolving reactions of the constituencies which they represented. Of all the provinces in France, none had a larger number of juring clerical deputies than Brittany—a total of thirteen, representing every diocese in the province—and yet no province would itself be more massively refractory. Similar conflicts between oath-taking delegates and refractory constituencies were to be found in Franche-Comté and in the northern frontier provinces of Flanders, Hainaut, and Artois. By contrast, none of the deputies from the strongly constitutional areas of Berry and Orléanais would accept the oath.[81]

But one can also find instances in which collective action on the part

---

[77] J. Le Falher, *Le royaume de Bignan (1789-1805)* (Hennebont, 1913), 78; letter from the district of Josselin, Jan. 18, 1791: A.N., D XXIX bis 20, dos. 218, no. 23; letter from the national guard of Ville-sur-Yron, Apr. 26, 1791: D XXIX bis 22, dos. 237, no. 10.

[78] Yvon-Georges Paillard, "Fanatiques et patriotes dans le Puy-de-Dôme: histoire religieuse d'un département de 1792 à Thermidor," *AHRF*, 42 (1970), 300.

[79] See the oath speech by Allier, curé of Bouillonville (Moselle), Jan. 30, 1791: A.N., F19 450.

[80] Letter from Brignon, Sept. 26, 1791: A.N., F19 460. See also Maurice Giraud, *Essai sur l'histoire religieuse de la Sarthe de 1789 à l'an IV* (Paris, 1920), 133.

[81] See above, chp. 2. Note that some provincial delegations, notably that of Brittany, contained replacement deputies who had taken their seats between the initial meeting of the Estates General and the period of the oath. But all of these substitutes had been chosen at the same time as the original deputies.

of the clergy was substantially more formalized and widespread, transcending the influence of a few local leaders. Already, at the time of the Dom Gerle affair in April 1790, there were examples of priests in whole deaneries, or even in whole dioceses, coming together to sign joint petitions. In at least three of the Breton dioceses—Rennes, Quimper, and Nantes—and in a certain number of towns (e.g., Autun and Troyes), numerous curés and vicaires would jointly protest the National Assembly's deliberation of April 13 which refused to declare Catholicism the state religion.[82]

With the crisis of the oath some nine months later, the collective organization of groups of parish clergymen would assume even greater proportions. Under the prodding of the bishop at least thirteen of the seventeen deaneries of the Old-Regime diocese of Bayeux formally adhered to Cheylus' statement condemning and rejecting the oath legislation.[83] Similar petitions are known to have been drawn up and signed in the dioceses of Rennes, Nantes, Tréguier, Saint-Malo, Saint-Brieuc, and Quimper (all in Brittany); in the dioceses of Boulogne, Saint-Omer, Tournai, Speyer, and Metz (along the northern frontier); as well as in the diocese of Le Mans and portions of the dioceses of Chartres and Autun.[84] The origins of these various collective actions may never be known precisely. In both the dioceses of Saint-Brieuc and of Tournai—and unlike the diocese of Bayeux—the initiative appears to have come from individual parish clergymen.[85] Yet, whatever the role of the bishops and their vicars-general, the most remarkable fact is that the clerical corps in these areas were so willing to accept episcopal authority and to act together as a group, as an ecclesiastical society.

[82] Barruel, 14:33-34, 53-58, 81-83; Pierre Le Goué, "Aspects sociaux du problème religieux en Ille-et-Vilaine, 1789-1793," D.E.S., Université de Rennes II, 1970, 47. In a few cases small groups of parish clergymen signed petitions in favor of the National Assembly's position: see, for example, E. Brossard, *Histoire du département de la Loire pendant la Révolution*, 2 vols. (Paris, 1904-07), 1:250-52.

[83] Sévestre, *L'acceptation*, 213-15.

[84] Barruel, 14:471-521; Yvonnick Le Cornec, "Les débuts de la Contre-Révolution dans les districts de Saint-Brieuc et de Lamballe, 1789-1793," Mémoire de maîtrise, Université de Rennes II, 1976, 37-38; Pommeret, 120-21; Lesprand, 3:90-91, 4:14; Sévestre, *L'acceptation*, 311-14; A. Lallié, *Le diocèse de Nantes pendant la Révolution*, 2 vols. (Nantes, 1893), 1:51-52; A. Deramecourt, *Le clergé du diocèse d'Arras, Boulogne et Saint-Omer pendant la Révolution (1789-1802)*, 4 vols. (Arras, 1884-86), 2:131-35, 140-42; letter from a curé of the diocese of Tréguier, Dec. 19, 1790: A.N., D XXIX bis 20, dos. 213, nos. 7-8; letter from the department of Ille-et-Vilaine, Feb. 4, 1791: D XIX 80, dos. 612, no. 3; letter from the department of Nièvre, Feb. 6, 1791: D XXIX bis 21, dos. 224, no. 7.

[85] Peter and Poulet, 1:117; Pommeret, 120-21.

But there was a second set of clergymen among whom joint action seems to have been unusually common: the curés and vicaires of the larger towns. Here, it was not just a question of signing petitions, but of meeting repeatedly in face-to-face discussions. In Montpellier the entire urban corps of parish clergymen convened at the home of Abbé Poujols for a lengthy debate, after which all determined on a joint refusal. Much the same verdict was reached in Cambrai after the local clergy passed a night-long vigil near one of the parish alters. In Amiens, curés and vicaires went one step farther: not only refusing the oath *en masse*, but printing the justification of their refusal and distributing it to the rural curés throughout the diocese. In this case, however, the efforts of the urban corps seems to have had no more effect on the rural clergy than the efforts of the bishop of Amiens himself.[86]

To be sure, not all such organizing efforts proved equally successful. Despite a joint statement of opposition by the clergy of the *archiprêtré* of Luzy, in the diocese of Autun, many of the individual members eventually opted for the Constitution.[87] Nor did all those who signed Bishop Cheylus' statement ultimately refuse the oath. Tentative efforts to organize the clergy near Provins seems scarcely to have had any effect. Here, one curé confessed that he had signed a "profession of faith" against the oath "out of respect for the good relations and friendship which [his colleagues] had always shared with him," but that he had no intention of rejecting the Civil Constitution.[88] In this instance, at least, the honor and respect owed to friends was clearly outweighed by other considerations.

Perhaps the most interesting aspect of all such collective actions is that, where they were successful, they seemed invariably to involve positions taken in *opposition* to the Civil Constitution. Resolutions by groups of clergymen in *favor* of adherence to the oath are extremely rare.[89] When-

[86] F. Saurel, *Histoire religieuse du département de l'Hérault pendant la Révolution*, 4 vols. (Paris, 1894-96), 2:19-20; Destombes, 52-53; Peter and Poulet, 1:118; letter from the town of Cambrai, Jan. 29, 1791: A.N., D XXIX bis 21, dos. 221, no. 1. Also, for Bordeaux: Barruel, 14:417-56, 465-71; for Angoulême: J.P.G. Blanchet, *Le clergé charentais pendant la Révolution* (Angoulême, 1898), 58-59; for Angers: Yves-François Besnard, *Souvenirs d'un nonagénaire*, 2 vols. (Paris, 1880), 2:44-45; for Troyes: Prévost, 1:409-410; for Béziers: A.N., D XXIX bis 21, dos. 226, nos. 5-25.

[87] Jules Charrier, *Histoire religieuse du département de la Nièvre pendant la Révolution*, 2 vols. (Paris, 1926), 1:104-107. In fact, the *archiprêtré* would split, eight priests taking the oath and eight refusing.

[88] Statement by Le Rat, curé of Bréau: A.D. Seine-et-Marne, L 282.

[89] I have found only one example, in the context of a single canton in Orne: letter from the curé of Courménil, Jan. 2, 1791: A.N., D XXIX bis 20, dos. 216, no. 22. No such cases have been found for entire dioceses or departments.

ever large numbers of priests seriously joined forces on the issue, they seem consistently to have come down in support of their bishops. In this respect, the patterns of clerical concertation in early 1791 help throw light on oath options of two important segments of the refractory clergy. First, among the rural clergy, one cannot but note the particular concentration of collective action in Brittany, in the north, and in the northeast of the kingdom. In all these areas, areas in which the ultramontane tradition was particularly strong, the success of the petitions would provide additional evidence of a particular sensitivity to hierarchy and authority and an accrued identification with "ecclesiastical society." Second, the analysis can provide some partial clues as to the distinctive character of the oath experience in the towns. If there was a marked tendency for town clergymen to refuse the oath, it was not simply that they were better educated or that they were more likely to be influenced by bishops and seminary professors; urban ecclesiastics would also find it much easier than their rural colleagues to consult and discuss with one another, and to goad each other's consciences. Perhaps the very existence of large numbers of ecclesiastics in the towns, present and in regular contact with one another, reinforced their specific ecclesiastical identity, their sense of ecclesiastical society, setting them more distinctly apart from lay society.

Clerical Interaction in the Rural Parishes

The hypothesis is intriguing: that the sheer size of the clerical contingent residing in a given community may have influenced the members of that contingent in their views on the oath and the Civil Constitution. But if such a theory is valid, similar patterns of reaction should be visible in the rural areas of the realm as well as in the towns. Unfortunately, the enumeration of all ecclesiastics residing in the rural parishes is no simple task. If the canons, monks, and mendicants were largely concentrated in the towns, the village parishes in certain French provinces were inhabited by substantial numbers of non-beneficed or semi-beneficed clergymen without cure of souls—called *habitués, prêtres libres, prêtres consorces, mé-partistes,* or *familiers,* depending on the region.[90] By the nature of their functions, such individuals were seldom required to swear the oath, and they are thus difficult to locate in official enumerations of the clergy. Yet another approach to the problem would seem possible: the analysis of

[90] On this rural, non-parish clergy, see below, chp. 10.

the total number of specifically *parish* clergymen—curés, vicaires, and desservants—living in the various regions of the realm.

In reality, there was a strong tendency for curés and vicaires in the same parish to act together on the issue of the oath. Statistics in this regard have been assembled for over 1,200 rural parishes in eight of the ten sample provinces described in the previous chapter. For reasons of standardization and simplification only those villages with a curé and one vicaire have been taken into account. (See Table 13.) If oath options had been taken entirely independently, one would expect the two clergymen to have divided on the issue in roughly half of the parishes. Yet in none of the provinces considered here did the figure even approach the 50 percent mark, and in two of the regions, Normandy and Dauphiné, the proportion of curé/vicaire disaccord fell to only about 15 percent. The weighted average would suggest that overall only about one-fourth of the parishes witnessed such a split.[91] Among priests such as these, working together on a day-to-day basis and sometimes even sharing the same

TABLE 13

Oath-taking of Curés and Vicaires in the Same Parish

(Rural Parishes with One Curé and One Vicaire or One Curé Only)

Province Sampled	No. of Parishes Considered	Percentage by Category			Percentage Oath-takers	
		Both are Jur.	One Jur. One Rfr.	Both are Rfr.	Where 1 Curé and 1 Vicaire Are Present	Where 1 Priest Is Alone In Parish
Alsace	89	25	35	40	42	38
Berry	58	68	23	9	79	81
Burgundy	89	22	38	40	40	71
Dauphiné	71	85	14	1	92	88
Maine	234	33	35	32	47	75
Normandy (Manche)	401	43	15	42	52	55
Picardy	145	54	22	24	66	58
Poitou	122	15	24	61	26	46
Total	1,209					
Weighted average		43	26	31	56	64

Sources: see above, Chp. 4, Table 5.

[91] A similar tendency is found if one considers those relatively rare parishes with more than one vicaire. Thus, in 73 percent of such parishes in Normandy the clergy acted in unison; in Berry 67 percent acted in unison; in Picardy 53 percent acted in unison.

rectory, there was clearly a tendency for close consultation and a common position in the face of the quandary. More importantly, the average juring rate for priests who lived in society with other clergymen was significantly less than for those solitary curés who manned parishes all by themselves. To be sure, in several of the individual provinces the differences in percentage were relatively small, and, on occasion, they even ran slightly counter to the overall trend. But in Burgundy, Maine, and Lower Poitou the presence of more than one clergyman was associated with an enormously lower juring rate. And, overall, the weighted average was some eight percentage points lower in those parishes with a multiple clerical presence.

To go one step farther, the oath statistics themselves enable us to estimate the regional variation in the number of vicaires per parish at the beginning of the Revolution throughout the entire kingdom. (See Appendix II and Figure D.)[92] Based on these calculations, it seems clear that in some parts of the kingdom vicaires were actually relatively uncommon. In a broad zone from Picardy and Champagne southward into Aquitaine, and in much of central France north of the Massif-Central there was often no more than one vicaire for every three to five parishes— a ratio that would fall even lower if the urban parishes were excluded. But, elsewhere, the numbers of vicaires were substantially larger, sometimes with an average even surpassing one vicaire per parish. Among the areas with the highest such ratios were the western provinces of Brittany, Normandy, Maine, and Anjou; as well as sections of Lorraine, Franche-Comté, the Massif Central, and the Alpine southeast. Indeed, the geography of the "parish clerical density" which emerges is strikingly similar to the now familiar pattern of regional oath-taking. To be sure, the relationship between non-juring rates and vicaires-per-parish ratios was not everywhere equally pronounced. It was most in evidence among the districts of the northwest of the kingdom—in the quadrant including the west, the Parisian Basin, and the middle Loire Valley. It was moderately strong in the southwest, weaker in the northeast, and did not hold at all in the southeast. In the following chapter, we shall examine the particular political trends in Lorraine, Dauphiné, and Provence which may have substantially modified the situation in these sectors of the country. Yet everywhere outside the southeast the correlation was positive and statistically significant: the more auxiliary priests present in the rural

---

[92] Calculations are based on the priests present in the various departments at the time of the oath. In fact, the ratio determined is for vicaires per curé, rather than for vicaires per parish. But parishes with more than one curé were extremely rare.

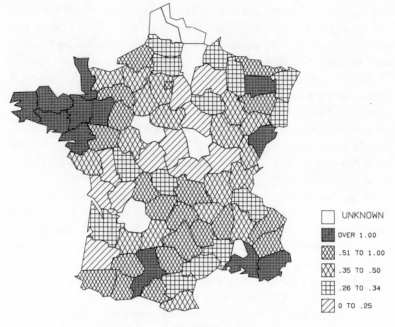

	UNKNOWN
	OVER 1.00
	.51 TO 1.00
	.35 TO .50
	.26 TO .34
	0 TO .25

FIGURE D
Number of Vicaires per Curé by Department at the
Time of the Oath.

villages of a department or district, the more likely it was that the clergy
would reject the oath.[93]

That decisions made in group situations frequently differ in character
and outcome from those made by single individuals is amply confirmed
in the findings of social psychology.[94] In the case of the oath of 1791, we
have already noted that the clergy tended massively to refuse the oath

[93] For France as a whole, the correlation between the rate of oath refusals per department
and the proportion of vicaires per parish is 0.42. If departments for which oath data are uncertain
are excluded, the coefficient is 0.41. When the departments of Dauphiné and Provence are
excluded, the coefficient is 0.57. For the 380 districts for which data are available, the coefficient
is 0.41. Broken down by quadrant: for the northwest (Brittany, Normandy, Maine, Anjou,
Poitou, Parisian Basin, Berry, Bourbonnais) the coefficient is 0.77; for the southwest (Quercy,
Bordelais, Landes, Saintonge, Limousin, southern Languedoc, Roussillon, Gascony, Béarn, Pays-
Basque): 0.39; for the northeast (Alsace, Lorraine, Franche-Comté, Burgundy, Picardy, Champagne, Flanders): 0.29; and for the southeast (northern Languedoc, Rouergue, Auvergne, Lyonnais, Dauphiné, Provence): -0.22.

[94] E.g., Harold Kelly and John Thibaut, "Group Problem Solving," in The Handbook of Social
Psychology, Gardner Lindsey, ed., 5 vols. (Reading, Mass., 1969), 4:1-101.

wherever its members were most organized for joint action on the question. Clearly, a similar effect was at work in many individual parishes: the presence of other clergymen in a parish meant not only that those clergymen would tend to act together on the issue, but that they would tend to act in a specific manner, registering a refusal to accept the simple oath. Indeed, this peculiar pattern of collective reactions may help us understand the strongly refractory stance of two other groups previously identified. If a higher percentage of town clergymen refused the oath, it was partly because the towns held unusually high concentrations of parish clergymen residing in the same community. And if a greater proportion of vicaires refused their adherence, it was not only that the vicaires were less rooted in their careers and in their parishes, but that, in most instances, they lived in the presence of at least one other clergyman.

Yet the precise meaning and explanation of this striking correlation is undoubtedly complex. Our analysis of the clergymen's own explanations of their oaths has already suggested the strong difference in self-image between jurors and refractories. There was a clear tendency for the latter to identify themselves with the ecclesiastical hierarchy and the society of fellow priests, while the jurors linked themselves more commonly to the lay community, envisioning themselves as much the servants of mankind as the servants of God.[95] Perhaps the very existence of mini-hierarchies of clergymen—if only the curé and his subordinate—helped sensitize local clergymen to hierarchical authority in general. Though on occasion the relations between the curé and his assistant were far from cordial, nevertheless the presence of another cleric living in the same village, the possibility of mutual surveillance or emulation may have helped reinforce the sense of clerical identity, strengthening the Tridentine role model of the priest, separate, distinct, and aloof from the laity among whom he lived. In such a context and in the dilemma in which he found himself, it was all the more natural for an individual to refer and defer to the opinions of the ecclesiastical hierarchy and, in consequence, to reject the oath. But the position of the solitary curés of the Parisian Basin, the center, and the southwest of the kingdom was decidedly different. One can speculate that the very nature of the priestly order in these villages made it more difficult to maintain the sense and the reality of clerical separation and clerical hierarchy. Residing for decades, essentially alone in the midst of the peasantry, such clergymen were probably relatively

[95] See above, chp. 3.

less receptive to the lines of clerical authority and relatively more de-pendent and vulnerable in their relations with their flock.

Of course, in all likelihood, the link between parish density and re-actions to the oath was a good deal more complicated than this. In a later chapter it will be necessary to explore the ways in which the nature of the clerical presence may also have affected the lay parishioners and their perceptions of both the clergy and the oath. For the present, we must turn to another important form of collective clerical action, a form which predated the Revolution: the evolution of clerical politics in the course of the eighteenth century.

SIX

Clerical Politics

O NE of the major discoveries of the previous chapter was the importance of collective experience in molding clerical opinion on the Civil Constitution. For this reason, it would seem all the more important that we step back into the Old Regime and explore the tradition of interclerical political organization which had been evolving in the midst of the Gallican Church during the previous two or three generations. It is at least possible that the so-called "revolt of the curés" during the last decades of the eighteenth century was equally or even more important than the seminary experience or the actions of the bishops in the formation of clerical attitudes and perspectives.[1] But how widespread and homogeneous were such movements? To what extent did the near millenarian fervor for unity in 1789 conceal more profound regional divisions in ultimate objectives and assumptions among the curés—as it most certainly did gloss over social and geographic differences within the Third Estate? The purpose of the present chapter is to explore briefly the nature and origins of clerical politicization and its possible relationship to the oath of 1791.

Jansenism and Richerism

At least since the seventeenth century occasional organized manifestations of unrest and dissatisfaction had made their presence felt among the parish clergy. Some of these movements had been almost entirely economic in nature, centering primarily on the problems of the *portion congrue* and the distribution of ecclesiastical wealth: thus the protest activities in the diocese of Grenoble in 1605, in the diocese of Valence in the 1630's, and among the curés of Auvergne in the 1660's.[2] But other incidents were principally related to theological and ecclesiological con-

---

[1] On the curés' "revolt" see Charles-Louis Chassin, *Les cahiers des curés* (Paris, 1882); Maurice G. Hutt, "The Curés and the Third Estate: the Ideas of Reform in the Pamphlets of the French Lower Clergy in the Period, 1787-1789," *Journal of Ecclesiastical History*, 8 (1957), 74-92; Ruth Necheles, "The Curés in the Estates General of 1789," *JMH*, 46 (1974), 425-44.

[2] *Procès-verbal de l'Assemblée générale du Clergé de France ... en l'année 1780* (Paris, 1782), 103-106; *Précis des rapports de l'Agence du Clergé de France par ordre de matières* (Paris, 1786), 147-48.

troversies. The early seventeenth-century doctrine of Richerism, which stipulated the divine origin of the office of curé and elevated the curé's status in the diocese to a position superior to all but that of the bishop, was in this regard particularly influential.[3] Motivated in large measure by Richerism and by animosity toward the Jesuits, the "religious Fronde" of the 1650's saw a full-fledged insubordination against the episcopacy on the part of parish priests in Paris and in several other towns of the realm.[4] The situation appeared serious enough to the ecclesiastical hierarchy and the royal government to justify an ordinance in 1659 forbidding the curés to form independent corporations, elect representatives ("syndics"), or organize meetings not specifically sanctioned by the bishops.[5] Yet, despite this ordinance, the parish clergy in certain regions would continue to hold illegal meetings intermittently throughout the eighteenth century. Moreover, the creation of the rural "ecclesiastical conferences" by the reforming bishops of the late seventeenth century (also called "synods," "deanery assemblies," etc., depending on the region) brought into being a new institutional structure which might easily be politicized and serve much the same function as an illegal assembly. The assemblies of clergymen, legal or illegal, for the voicing of grievances against the bishops or tithe owners would often be greatly facilitated by the royal courts, sympathetic to certain of the curés' complaints, and, at the same time, delighted with the possibility of further encroaching on the jurisdiction of the Church.[6] On several occasions, parish clergymen would attempt to bypass episcopal authority altogether and appeal their cases directly to the parlements.

During the first half of the eighteenth century, one issue in diocesan politics dominated all others: the issue of Jansenism. Though French Jansenism had once boasted a respectable contingent of supporters within the episcopacy, the near totality of Jansenist-sympathizing prelates had disappeared by mid-century and had been systematically replaced by staunch opponents of the movement. Thus, wherever sizable numbers of

[3] Edmond Préclin, *Les Jansénistes du XVIIIe siècle et la Constitution civile du clergé* (Paris, 1929), 1-33.

[4] Richard Golden, "The Mentality of Opposition: the Jansenism of the Parisian Curés during the Religious Fronde," *CHR*, 64 (1978), 565-80; and, by the same, *The Godly Rebellion: Parisian Curés and the Religious Fronde, 1652-1662* (Chapel Hill, 1981).

[5] Golden, *The Godly Rebellion*, 93-95.

[6] Norman Ravitch, "The Taxing of the Clergy in Eighteenth-Century France," *Church History*, 33 (1964), 34-50; B. Robert Kreiser, *Miracles, Convulsions, and Ecclesiastical Politics in Eighteenth-Century Paris* (Princeton, 1978), 30.

parish clergymen had been attracted to Jansenism, a deep-seated core of opposition to the existing power structure was called into being.

While the exact number of Jansenist clergymen will probably never be known, and while the very definition of "Jansenist" is always subject to debate, the research of Edmond Préclin does allow us an approximate image of two of the most important political manifestations of eighteenth-century Jansenism: first, the appeals launched between 1715 and the early 1720's, calling for a council to judge the validity of the anti-Jansenist bull *Unigenitus*; and, second, the expressions of support for the Jansenist bishop of Senez, Soanen, suspended from his see in 1727 by the Council of Embrun.[7] Not all the clergymen so identified were members of the parish corps, though, unfortunately, Préclin does not distinguish between regulars, canons, and other diocesans. Yet the maps—adapted from Préclin for more ready comparison (see Figures E and F)[8]—do provide a good preliminary sketch of the geography of the movement. For the most part, one is impressed by the relatively wide distribution of the first "appelants," a few of whom represented virtually every diocese in northern France from Lorraine to Brittany and from Artois to the Gironde and the upper Loire. There were also minor centers across the lowlands of the Midi from the Atlantic to Provence. Those zones which were apparently untouched by the movement were largely at the peripheries of the kingdom: in Lower Brittany, Flanders-Hainaut, Alsace, Franche-Comté, and portions of the Alps, the Pyrenees, and the Massif-Central. This initial geography presents some interesting comparisons with the map of adhesions to Bishop Soanen some ten years after the first appeals. Overall, the number of Jansenist manifestations had declined substantially. By this time, the royal government, controlled by Cardinal Fleury, was taking a firm position in opposition to the movement, and orthodox bishops in many dioceses had already organized repressive measures. By and large, an open position in favor of Soanen carried much greater danger for the careers of individual clergymen.[9] Yet one can suppose that this second distribution represents precisely those clergymen who were most dedicated and willing to make personal sacrifices in the name of their cause. At any rate, according to this index, Jansenism would now seem largely

[7] Préclin, maps opposite 84 and 124.

[8] Unfortunately, there are some uncertainties about Préclin's maps. Thus, his use of the designation "refractory to Jansenism" curiously excludes a number of dioceses for which there is no indication on the maps of the presence of *appelants*. The author does not explain this. Nor is it altogether clear what is meant by "Jansenist refuges" on the second map.

[9] Préclin, 124-26.

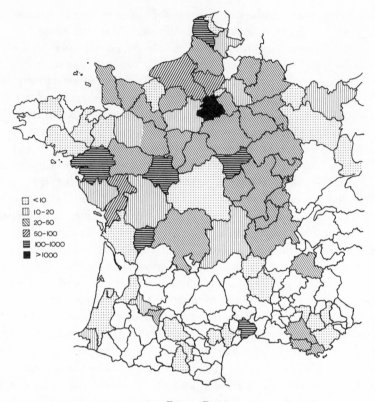

FIGURE E

Jansenism, 1716-25. (Number of *appelants* per diocese
according to Préclin.)

to have faded throughout the southern portion of the kingdom—with
the exceptions of Provence and the diocese of Montpellier. But, in the
north, as well, overt Jansenist sympathies had diminished or disappeared
in most areas. In this context, those few regions where their presence
had actually become more concentrated loom all the more significant:
the diocese of Toul, the Breton dioceses of Vannes and Saint-Malo, and,
above all, the cross of dioceses stamped onto the Parisian Basin from
Paris to Auxerre and from Blois to Troyes. The reasons for this particular
distribution of the Jansenist clergy and its apparent concentration after
1725 are difficult to determine. The specific protection and encouragement
given by Jansenist sympathizing bishops has to rank high among factors.

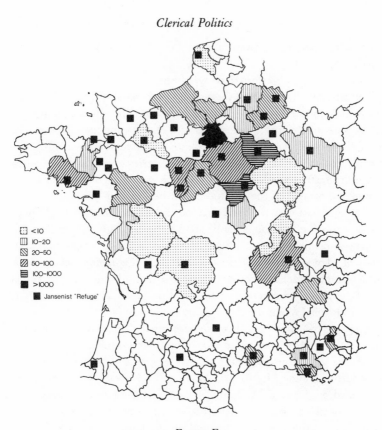

FIGURE F

Jansenism, 1725-50. (Number of adhesions to the bishop of Senez
and location of Jansenist "refuges" according to Préclin.)

At one point, the Parisian Basin, Champagne, and southern Lorraine
became refuges where numerous Jansenists fled to assume benefices in
relatively protected milieus. One would also have to explore the influence
of specific seminaries and sympathetic Parlements—most notably the
Parlement of Paris. Yet it is still significant that the movement never
took hold in most of the south, despite the presence of Jansenist prelates
and seminaries.[10] It should also be noted that in the greater Parisian
Basin, Jansenism would wield considerable influence over both the rural
and the urban clergy. In Brittany, by contrast, it would seem to have

[10] Ibid., 84-88, 208.

been overwhelmingly concentrated in a few towns only and to have been rapidly repressed.[11]

Unfortunately, no efforts have yet been made to plot a geography of Jansenism in the later part of the century. In general, the repressive tactics of the bishops after 1730 seem to have substantially reduced the numbers of the Jansenist clergy in most dioceses of the kingdom. Nevertheless, the followers of Quesnel did survive in a few major town refuges, especially within certain chapters and monasteries over which the bishops had more restricted authority. In addition, they may have become even more concentrated in the rural areas of the Parisian Basin, with its two appendages, eastward toward Lorraine and southward to Lyon. Though a few sympathetic bishops continued to slip through the *feuille des bénéfices*—most notably, Archbishop Montazet in Lyons (1758-1786)[12]—the relatively dense presence of Jansenists in these few regions seems to have become independently rooted in local parish traditions. In this respect, the ecclesiastical conferences of the local deaneries played a particularly important role. When the arch-enemy of the Jansenists, Bishop Languet de Gergy, arrived in Sens in 1730, he estimated that only one-fourth of his clergy could be counted among those "who think correctly." All of his efforts for the next twenty years were opposed measure for measure by a corps of some fifty to sixty curés and other clergymen, frequently organized by deanery. Here, and in others of the Jansenist dioceses, the earlier conciliarism of the *appelants* was increasingly transformed into Richerism, as the curés now focused on the local hierarchy rather than on the church universal, and as they claimed the right to participate with the bishop in all aspects of the government of the diocese. In the diocese of Sens, as later in the diocese of Toul, the prelate eventually attempted to strike at the heart of the local Jansenist tradition by abolishing the ecclesiastical conferences altogether.[13] The irony was evident. Created by the seventeenth-century episcopacy for the reform of the clergy, the conferences were now attempting unilaterally to pursue reforms which the bishops themselves would not tolerate.

The difficulties of defining and identifying late eighteenth-century Jansenists makes the direct comparison between Jansenism and the oath

[11] Alcime Bachelier, *Le Jansénisme à Nantes* (Angers, 1934), 159-77; also Claude Langlois, *Le diocèse de Vannes, 1800-1830* (Paris, 1974), 86-88.

[12] Préclin, 296, 303-304.

[13] Ibid., 143-49; René Taveneaux, *Le Jansénisme en Lorraine* (Paris, 1960), 704; Jean-Marie Gouesse, "Assemblées et associations cléricales, synodes et conférences ecclésiastiques dans le diocèse de Coutances aux XVIIe et XVIIIe siècles," *Annales de Normandie*, 24 (1974), 57.

tenuous and uncertain. Préclin concluded that the leadership of the "party" split sharply over the Civil Constitution.[14] No evident relationship exists between the geography of oath-takers in 1791 and the distribution of the *appelants* against the bull *Unigenitus* seventy years earlier. Yet there is a weak correlation with the distribution of appeals against the treatment of the bishop of Senez.[15] Wherever the movement survived the initial repression of the 1720's and, in particular, wherever it became increasingly concentrated in the first half of the century—in the Parisian Basin, and in parts of Lorraine and Lyonnais—it may well have helped establish traditions of clerical independence and opposition to the ecclesiastical status quo, traditions which could directly color the parish clergy's reception of the Civil Constitution. It is clear that by 1789, even within these regional "refuges," only a tiny minority of curés continued to profess the initial Jansenist tenets of the seventeenth century. Yet even among that majority of clergymen which did not adhere to theological Jansenism, many had been profoundly shocked and critical of the evident tactics of repression used by the episcopacy against their colleagues—tactics which included not only the requirement of adhesion to a pro-*Unigenitus formulaire*, but also the use of *lettres de cachet*, forced detention in seminaries, and the threat of the denial of sacraments. To reprimand a man for doctrinal error—not heresy—was one thing, but to put in danger his eternal soul by withholding the Church's last rites was another matter altogether. Within the former Jansenist strongholds, it was perhaps, in part, a revulsion against this "episcopal despotism" toward errant colleagues which helped transmit a tradition of opposition to the essentially orthodox clergymen of the later eighteenth century.

Clerical Collective Action, 1730-1786

But even though Jansenism declined greatly among the parish clergy in the course of the eighteenth century, other economic, political, and ideological issues continued to stir up diocesan priests and incite them to various forms of group action through the eve of the Revolution. In order to explore the geography and chronology of such activities, an attempt has been made to enumerate the illegal assemblies and other unsanctioned

[14] Préclin, 503.

[15] Excluding those departments in which oath rates are less certain, the correlation coefficient between the percentage of oath-takers and the number of *appelants* as a proportion of the population is −0.023. Compared with the number of protestors against the verdict on Soanan as a proportion of the population, the coefficient is 0.225.

collective efforts by parish clergymen during the sixty years prior to the Civil Constitution.[16] (See Appendix V.) Given the difficulties posed by the sources, any such enumeration is likely to be incomplete. Yet the bureaucracies of both the royal government and the General Assembly of the Clergy made it their business to keep informed of happenings of this kind, and insofar as the records are complete, they undoubtedly make mention of the great majority of curé activities.[17]

Viewed in its kingdom-wide distribution over the entire period, 1730-1786, the map of collective clerical protest does reveal certain regional concentrations. (See Figure G.) Particularly noteworthy are the clusters of dioceses in the Alpine southeast and in the extreme southwest, but also in evidence is a broad band of dioceses across northern France from Lorraine to Brittany. Conspicuously untouched were most of the dioceses in the provinces of Languedoc and Roussillon, and in a central zone from Limousin and Berry to Auvergne, Burgundy, and Franche-Comté. Yet more important than such cartographic impressions are the chronology and specific character of the protest activities in the various regions of the country.

In the northeast of Lorraine and Barrois, the link with the earlier Jansenist experience seems especially clear.[18] Much of the long-lived tenacity of Jansenism in Lorraine can be attributed to the unusual political

---

[16] For this purpose, three principal sources have been searched. Of primary importance is the study of Préclin, cited above. Though it relies almost entirely on printed sources, Préclin's work brings together a massive amount of research and provides short descriptions of a wide variety of collective political actions organized within the clergy throughout the period. But Préclin must be supplemented, first, by the archives of the foreign ministry, whose portfolio dealt with internal problems in a number of provinces; and, second, by the collection of correspondence and reports preserved in the archives of the Clergy of France. For the latter, I have gone systematically through the series A.N., G[8] by means of the alphabetical tables, G[8]* 2467, 2555, 2622-26, 2632 (end), 2832, and 2834. I have also gone through the Clergy's printed collections: *Précis des rapports de l'Agence*, cited above; *Collection des procès-verbaux des Assemblées générales du Clergé de France*, 9 vols. (Paris, 1767-80); and *Procès-verbaux* of the General Assemblies held in 1780, 1782, and 1785 (Paris, 1782-89). Additional information has been culled from a wide variety of local monographs. Details are in Appendix V.

[17] I have eliminated incidents known or believed to have involved less than five clergymen. But indication of the numbers participating is given only rarely and probably ranged from a mere handful to several hundred. Note has been taken, however, of reoccurring incidents in the same diocese, whenever such reoccurrences seem to have been distinct and separated by periods of several years. An effort has also been made to isolate the principal objectives of collective action, but frequently several different problems seem to have been intertwined. Thus, it is often particularly difficult to determine the extent to which Jansenism may still have been a factor in a given incident.

[18] Taveneaux, 56-63, 265.

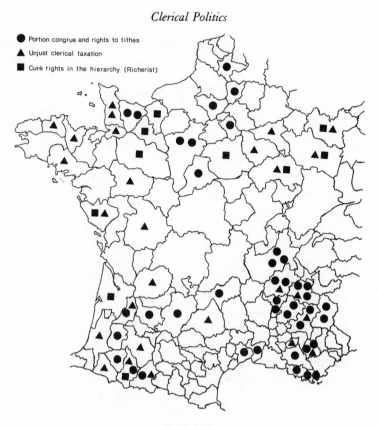

● Portion congrue and rights to tithes
▲ Unjust clerical taxation
■ Curé rights in the hierarchy (Richerist)

FIGURE G
Primary Focus of Collective Political Activities among
Parish Clergy, 1730-86.

and ecclesiastical conditions of the province. A general detachment from
the absolutist trends of the French kingdom prior to 1766 (when Lorraine
was joined to France) and the internal power struggles between the dukes
of Lorraine and the "Three Bishoprics" (Toul, Verdun, and Metz) had
left the local parish clergy exceptionally independent. This was particularly true in the diocese of Toul, where the parish clergy had obtained
the right to hold yearly local "synods" in which virtually any subject
might be discussed.[19] This institutional presbyterianism would be reinforced intellectually after 1768 when the direction of the University of

[19] Louis Jérôme, *Les élections et les cahiers du clergé lorrain aux Etats-généraux de 1789* (Paris,
1899), 164-65.

Pont-à-Mousson passed from the Jesuits to individuals of Richerist and Jansenist persuasion.[20] With their strong local organization, the curés of the diocese of Toul carried on a running battle against the bishop over a whole array of issues: over the *billets de confession* in the 1750's, over the effort to create homes for elderly priests—seen as an insidious means of punishing dissenters—and the attempted reduction and consolidation of feast days in the 1760's. By the later eighteenth century the rural synods were also claiming the right to accept or reject any of the bishops' ordinances—a power similar to that claimed by the Parlements over royal edicts and decrees.[21] In 1773, in near desperation, the bishop attempted to abolish the synods outright, and a veritable insurrection broke out. Organized by the curés of Nancy and backed by local magistrates, a petition was sent throughout the diocese, ultimately signed by all but forty curés, and then carried to Paris by a special delegation. The curés won a temporary victory, but, when Toul was divided into three new dioceses in 1778, the first bishop of Nancy reverted to the earlier suppression, and a new struggle began which would continue into the pre-Revolutionary period.[22] In northern Lorraine, within the diocese of Metz, the curés seem never to have evolved the same degree of independent organization. Yet here too, a series of disputes—notably over feast days and clerical taxation—divided curés and prelates throughout much of the period. Effective leadership of such protests soon fell to François-Martin Thiébaut, professor in the seminary and later curé of Metz. By the 1780's Thiébaut had established a fundamentally egalitarian ecclesiology in which even the distinctions between bishop and curé were said to be based more on a kind of practical division of labor than on divine hierarchical rights.[23]

Nowhere else in northern France does the diocesan clergy appear to have developed such a high level of organization or breadth of involvement. In the Parisian Basin and in the "west"—both taken in their broadest geographic meaning—the collective activities of the curés focused on a wide assortment of objectives. In several zones immediately adjoining the capital, as we have seen, the Jansenist legacy continued to

[20] Taveneaux, 715.

[21] Ibid., 694-705.

[22] Ibid., 704; Eugène Martin, *Histoire des diocèses de Toul, de Nancy, et de Saint-Dié*, 3 vols. (Nancy, 1903), 2:606-611, 3:12-14; *Rapport de l'Agence ... du clergé depuis 1780 jusqu'en 1785* (Paris, 1788), dlix-dlxiii, and 306. In Saint-Dié the synods continued even after the declaration of 1782: *Règlements et ordonnances* (Saint-Dié, 1785), 13, 18-19.

[23] Taveneaux, 694, 710, 713.

inform the local clergy's attitude toward their bishops. But farther to the west, movements more purely Richerist in nature emerged in a number of dioceses where Jansenism had never inspired a wide following or had long since been eliminated.[24] Thus, sixty-nine curés in the Norman diocese of Sées had leagued together in opposition to episcopal innovations in the administration of Penance—innovations which more tightly restricted the curés' confessional authority to the limits of their parishes. In neighboring Lisieux over sixty curés protested their bishop's efforts to impose regular conferences and retreats, viewed as a means of unwarranted discipline. In both Le Mans and Luçon curés would struggle to have all important changes in diocesan affairs approved by synods of parish clergymen.[25]

But there were also certain clusterings of collective manifestations directed toward more purely economic objectives. Throughout the 1760's and 1770's the problem of the *portion congrue* mobilized parish clergymen from Artois to Orléanais and from Bayeux to Meaux. For the most part, there was nothing specifically Richerist or Jansenist in the demands emanating from these groups. They consisted essentially of straightforward requests for higher salaries to ensure a sufficient standard of living and a decent life style.[26] Most probably came from relatively small groups of clergymen, especially from the articulate members of the parish clergy serving in the towns, the one group of curés in northern France among whom the *portion congrue* was relatively common. More important—at least in terms of the number of participants—were those political efforts animated by the issue of clerical taxation. Although there had been a scattering of such complaints earlier in the century,[27] it was the Edict of 1768 which focused widespread attention on the problem. The edict in question not only raised the *portion congrue* but also invited the bishops and their administrations to reassess ecclesiastical tax payments (the *décime*) for all curés who had received increases in their salaries. This measure, coupled with the overall rise in clerical taxes and the successive, halfhearted efforts of the General Assembly to reorganize the taxation

[24] Préclin, 308 ff.

[25] *Précis de l'Agence*, 143-44; Préclin, 310-11, 313-20, 324-30.

[26] See, for example, the demands by the curés of the diocese of Noyon in December 1763 and the letter of the vicar-general of Noyon to the Agents-General, Dec. 14, 1763: A.N., G⁸ 185.

[27] Thus, for example, in the diocese of Avranches during the mid-1750's: Jean Bindet, "Contestataires au diocèse d'Avranches pendant le XVIIe et le XVIIIe siècles," *Revue de l' Avranchin*, 88 (1970), 271-83.

system, helped focus discussion on the management and mismanagement of the diocesan tax assessment boards.[28] A landmark case occurred in the diocese of Troyes in the late 1760's. Led by five curés from the town of Troyes—all of whom, significantly, were "more or less" associated with Jansenism—the local clergy succeeded in obtaining a decision from the king's council, allowing them to choose periodically their own representatives to the tax boards through indirect elections in their deaneries.[29] Thereafter, numerous other clergymen across northern France would organize themselves in an effort to force similar changes. Small movements of this sort were even to be found in dioceses of Brittany, otherwise untouched in the late eighteenth century by movements of curé protest.[30]

In the southern half of the kingdom, there was likewise a considerable diversity of grievances on the part of the curés. Yet, in most dioceses of this zone, where Jansenism had never established strong roots, the real impetus to organization came from the characteristic economic structures of the local church. Thus, in the two Pyrenean dioceses of Comminges and Tarbes, neither with known traditions of Jansenist sympathies, complaints were already being voiced before mid-century over the problems of tax assessments and the *portion congrue*. In Tarbes, parish clergymen met in independent assemblies to elect syndics and to appeal their case *comme d'abus* before the Parlement of Toulouse, expanding their grievances to include a number of other local problems.[31] Elsewhere in the southwest complaints over taxes were registered in the dioceses of Périgueux, Bazas, Dax, Oloron, Auch, and Rodez; while demands for reform of the *portion congrue* came from Saint-Flour, Cahors, Agen, Bazas, Aire, and Lescar.[32]

Yet it is in the southeast of the kingdom, from the Rhône to the Alps, that curé political organization attained its greatest extension. Nowhere did collective action involve a greater proportion of clergymen or reoccur with such frequency—from the early seventeenth century through the eve of the Revolution. Here, with 50 to 90 percent of parish priests receiving only moneyed salaries, it was the issues revolving around the *portion congrue* which dominated all others—a whole nexus of issues,

[28] On the composition of the boards, varying greatly from diocese to diocese, see A.N., G[8] 30.

[29] Préclin, 395; *Collection des procès-verbaux*, vol. 8, pt. 2, 1858.

[30] Charles Berthelot du Chesnay, "Les prêtres séculiers en Haute-Bretagne au XVIIIe siècle," Thèse d'état, Université de Rennes II, 1974, 729-35.

[31] *Précis de l'Agence*, 144; A.A.E., 1488.

[32] See Appendix V.

including not only the priests' standard of living, but also the upkeep of the church, the provision of certain articles necessary for religious service, and the status of the clergymen within both clerical and lay societies. Organized by diocese and deanery, electing independent syndics to make legal appeals, collecting contributions, maintaining ongoing correspondence networks, the curés of Dauphiné and Provence were described by the Agents-General in 1765 as being possessed of a spirit of "impatience and revolt."[33] In this respect, it is curious that the parish clergy in Languedoc, to the west of the Rhône, where the *portion congrue* was also predominant, seem never to have developed a tradition of organized opposition. Perhaps it was the fact that curé salaries in Languedoc were more frequently paid in kind than in money—and thus better protected from inflation. Perhaps—and we shall return to this in a later chapter— it was the presence of greater concentrations of Protestants, a presence engendering a defensive mentality which reinforced the bonds between upper and lower clergy. But we should also not overlook the importance of one individual in unifying the curé movement throughout Dauphiné and Provence: Henri Reymond, curé of Saint-Georges in Vienne.

The career and writings of Reymond have been described elsewhere in some detail.[34] Through highly publicized court suits and an ongoing correspondence with deaneries throughout the province, Reymond helped forge the lower clergy in Dauphiné into the most independent and politically aware corps anywhere in the kingdom. His book *Les droits des curés*, published in 1776 and soon passing through several successive editions, was a popularized compendium of all the grievances which had been exercising the parish clergymen of his own province for the previous quarter century, grievances that were ultimately economic in nature: the problems of clerical salaries, of the inequitable distribution of revenues, of the tax assessment boards, and of the financial responsibilities of tithe owners. As justification, he drew fully on the Richerist doctrine, a doctrine from which he excluded, nevertheless, all Jansenist connotations. But he also developed certain themes taken from Enlightenment writers, picturing the curé as a public servant, tutoring and educating the masses, ensuring the "happiness" of the population and the "progress" of religion. While many of the specific problems and conditions which Reymond described were scarcely typical of any area outside the southeast, the book obviously struck a responsive chord in wide areas of the kingdom. It was

[33] *Collection des procès-verbaux*, vol. 8, pt. 2, 1451.
[34] See the author's *Priest and Parish in Eighteenth-Century France* (Princeton, 1977), 241-48.

enormously influential in strengthening the pride and self-esteem, the sense of idealism and of mission, among certain elements of the lower clergy. In particular, it could be read as a veritable manifesto for the "citizen priest," the new role model for the clergyman and his place in society which was rapidly emerging as a viable alternative to the older Tridentine model.[35]

But what continuity was there between the regional patterns of inter-clerical hostilities under the Old Regime and the distribution of oath-takers in 1791? Superficially, the correspondence would seem to be very loose indeed. Taken together, all the dioceses with known incidents of illegal collective actions on the part of the parish clergy would have aggregate oath-taking rates of 57 percent, only very slightly higher than the average for the entire kingdom.[36] Yet it is clear that there was an enormous range in both the degree of clerical participation and the degree of intensity of the movements in question. In those few regions where large numbers of curés had been exceptionally well organized over con-siderable periods of time—in the southeast, in the central Pyrenees, in the Jansenist dioceses near Paris, and in the diocese of Toul—the pro-portion of clergymen accepting the oath was unusually high. In Dauphiné, at least, the parish clergy would reveal a strong continuity of organization and commitment between the later decades of the Old Regime and the early years of the Revolution.[37]

It is also essential to take note of the principal subjects of grievance in the different areas of the country. In general, the incidence of oath-taking would seem to have been particularly unrelated to the distribution of those movements focusing primarily on the honorific and status rights of the curés or on the problem of clerical taxation. In the dioceses con-cerned the aggregate oath-taking rate of 52 percent was even very slightly below the kingdom-wide average. By contrast, in nearly all the dioceses where the local clergy was primarily protesting the economic problems of salaries or the tithes, support for the oath was notably strong: a full 66 percent oath-taking overall.[38] Among the regions in this category were

[35] See ibid. and the author's article, "The Citizen Priests: Politics and Ideology among the Parish Clergy of Eighteenth-Century Dauphiné," *Studies in Eighteenth-Century Culture*, 7 (1978), 307-28.

[36] For the methodology used in determining diocesan oath rates, see above, chp. 5.

[37] Tackett, *Priest and Parish*, chps. 10-12. First another curé leader of the Old Regime and then Reymond himself would be elected bishops of the department of Isère. For a similar case in Manche, see Jean Bindet, "Le diocèse d'Avranches sous l'épiscopat de Mgr. Godart de Belboeuf, dernier évêque d'Avranches," *Revue de l'Avranchin*, 87 (1969), 34-35.

[38] In ten dioceses known to have protested various problems of general curé rights, the oath

the southeast of Lyonnais, Dauphiné, and Provence, as well as the central Pyrenees and the central provinces of Beauce and Orléanais. But even in the dioceses of Bayeux, Cahors, and Saint-Flour, where overall oath rates were lower, one could find strong nuclei of oath-taking clergy, especially noteworthy by comparison with the surrounding areas. Thus, the evidence would suggest that wherever a longstanding tradition of collective protest had evolved, and wherever that protest focused primarily on the economic injustices of the Church, such traditions may well have colored the optic through which the Civil Constitution was viewed by individual priests.

Electoral Politics, 1787-1789

The numbers of dioceses touched by clerical political activities gradually increased over the last decades of the Old Regime to reach a peak in the years 1779-1780. Finally, in response to a stream of appeals to the king and his ministers from the General Assemblies of the Clergy and their Agents-General, a royal declaration was issued in 1782, renewing the injunction against all curé assemblies convening without the permission of their bishops.[39] Yet the developing "Pre-Revolution" in France after 1786 would stimulate a new flurry of collective action in general disregard of the law. It was during these final years of the Old Regime that organized clerical protest began to emerge in virtually every corner of the kingdom, including numerous areas previously untouched by such movements. The "revolt of the curés," as a national phenomenon, was much more a recent and short-term occurrence than has often been realized.

The government's plan for the organization of provincial assemblies in 1787 officially associated the parish priests with the local political process, making them automatic members of the municipal assemblies, the cellular units of the newly constructed administrative scheme. Though individual priests had never been reticent to exercise indirect influence in village assemblies under the Old Regime, they had been previously forbidden to hold office. The new system, wherever it was actually implemented, helped prepare clergymen for the considerable role which

---

rate was 51 percent oath-taking. In 24 protesting clerical taxation, the rate was 53 percent. In 26 protesting problems of the *portion congrue* and the tithes, it was 66 percent.

[39] *Procès-verbal de 1780*, 107, 197; *Rapport de l'Agence-générale du Clergé depuis 1780 jusqu'en 1785* (Paris, 1788), 304-307.

they were to play in local politics in the early years of the Revolution.[40] In the provincial assemblies themselves, however, and in the provincial estates which took their place in certain regions, the upper clergy seems generally to have succeeded in excluding or severely limiting the participation of the lower clergy. In the politically heated and intense atmosphere of 1787-1789, such blatant maneuvers by the clerical hierarchy frequently incited the hostility of the parish corps and helped project the illusion that interclerical confrontations were closely parallel to those then emerging between the Third Estate and the nobility. Wherever a tradition of curé opposition already existed, such power plays by the upper clergy helped further polarize the situation. Thus, the token representation granted to the parish clergy in the first Provincial Assembly of Lorraine incited the curés of Nancy to organize their colleagues throughout the former diocese of Toul, an operation which drew on the experience of three generations of curé opposition.[41] In similar fashion, the curés of Dauphiné, all but excluded from participation in the Provincial Estates at Romans and, ultimately, from the electoral process of 1789, reactivated their interdiocesan correspondence. Under the leadership of Reymond, they virtually declared their independence from the existing ecclesiastical hierarchy.[42] But, elsewhere, the pre-Revolution seems to have provided the first impetus for such collective efforts. The near exclusion of the curés from the Estates of Franche-Comté in 1788 was apparently crucial in the politicization of the rural conferences of the diocese of Besançon.[43] So too in Brittany, the tumultuous meetings of the Estates in Rennes were a powerful factor in forging curé opposition to local prelates in a province previously marked by docility and discipline on the part of the parish corps.[44]

The convocation of the Estates General, first announced in July 1788,

---

[40] Pierre Renouvin, *Les assemblées provinciales de 1787: origines, développement, résultats* (Paris, 1921), 102, 133; Marquis Marie de Roux, *La Révolution à Poitiers et dans la Vienne* (Paris, 1911), 98-99.

[41] Renouvin, 157; Jérôme, 11-16; C. Constantin, *L'évêché du département de la Meurthe de 1791 à 1801. Tome 1. La fin de l'Eglise d'Ancien régime et l'établissement de l'Eglise constitutionnelle* (Nancy, 1935), 8-9.

[42] Tackett, *Priest and Parish*, chp. 10.

[43] Jean Girardot, *Le département de la Haute-Saône pendant la Révolution*, 3 vols. (Vesoul, 1973), 1:66.

[44] J. Savina, *Le clergé de Cornouaille à la fin de l'Ancien régime et sa convocation aux Etats-généraux* (Quimper, 1926), 76-95. Compare also the situation in Artois where numerous pamphlets appeared on the curés' "humiliation" at being excluded from the Estates of Artois in 1788-89: A. Deramecourt, *Le clergé du diocèse d'Arras, Boulogne et Saint-Omer pendant la Révolution (1789-1802)*, 4 vols. (Arras, 1884-86), 1:358-69.

brought an enormous surge in pamphlet activity from parish clergymen all over France, denouncing the injustice of the provincial assemblies and demanding that the curés be given representation in proportion to their numbers and their importance in the clerical order.[45] The electoral regulations, promulgated by the king in January 1789, proved remarkably responsive to the demands of the lower clergy. Almost everywhere in the kingdom—the principal exceptions being Dauphiné and Béarn— parish clergymen were given one vote per individual with full right of proxy for those who were absent; while the chapters, regulars, and simple benefice holders disposed of only one vote per community or per ten or twenty members.[46]

From January through March 1789 various local, self-appointed leaders of the lower clergy concentrated their efforts on organizing their colleagues to take maximum advantage of the electoral laws. Though a systematic survey would be all but impossible, it seems likely that some measure of advanced preparation was carried out almost everywhere. In Poitou, the curés of Poitiers sent circulars to all their colleagues in the bailliage, requesting blank proxies from those who could not be present. When the meeting convened, virtually every curé actually in attendance would hold three votes—his own and the maximum two proxies allowed to each individual.[47] In Rennes curés were said to be distributing the "minutes" of the meetings before they took place; in Franche-Comté electoral strategies were being busily organized beforehand in the deanery assemblies; and in Lorraine the local associational networks were mobilized once again to control individual electoral assemblies and to coordinate strategy for all the bailliages of the province.[48] Even in dioceses with no previous record of curé politicization—like Tulle, Bourges, and Tours—preliminary committees or commissions were set up to ensure the organization of voting discipline and, in some cases, to determine in advance the deputies to be elected. Once the assemblies were actually under way, the lower clergy frequently held nightly planning sessions to

[45] Hutt, article cited; L. Boivin-Champeaux, *Notices historiques sur la Révolution dans le département de l'Eure*, 2nd ed., 2 vols. (Evreux, 1893-94), 1:28; Eugène Sol, *La Révolution en Quercy*, 4 vols. (Paris, 1932), 1:113.

[46] Armand Brette, ed., *Recueil de documents relatifs à la convocation des Etats-Généraux de 1789*, 4 vols. (Paris, 1894-1915), 1:71-75, and, on Béarn, 4:209-215. On Dauphiné, Jean Egret, *Les derniers Etats de Dauphiné* (Grenoble, 1942), 8-35.

[47] Roux, 157.

[48] Jérôme, 10-15, 20-21, 34-35; Girardot, 1:66; Barthélémy Pocquet, *Les origines de la Révolution en Bretagne*, 2 vols. (Paris, 1885), 2:345.

discuss the next day's tactics.[49] It is a measure of the success of such efforts that close to 90 percent of all parish clergymen were present or represented in the electoral meetings—compared to some 70 percent of the non-parish clergy.[50]

Almost everywhere the assemblies of the clerical order seem to have been more contentious and divisive than those of the other two estates.[51] There were, to be sure, a few bailliages where electoral proceedings were carried out in seeming dispassion: notably in circumscriptions like Abbeville, Montbrison, or Alençon, where no bishops were present and where curé liberals held an overwhelming preponderance.[52] But the great majority of the meetings would seem to have been highly embittered if not tumultuous affairs. A number of the assemblies ran aground in their opening sessions over the question of the presiding officer.[53] In Troyes, the curés were said to have set up a cry at the very mention of the non-parish clergy, even suggesting that canons, regulars, and simple benefice holders were outside the ecclesiastical hierarchy and should not be represented at all.[54] The canons in Draguignon showed themselves equally tactful by arguing that congruist curés—the majority of those present—should be denied voting rights because they paid insufficient taxes.[55] In Le Mans the presiding bishop was openly confronted and addressed by his curés as "Monsieur" rather than by the customary "Monseigneur."[56]

---

[49] Brette, 3:580; 4:363; Deramecourt, 1:378; Jérôme, 45-48; Boivin-Champeaux, 1:28; Arthur Prévost, *Histoire du diocèse de Troyes pendant la Révolution*, 3 vols. (Troyes, 1908-1909), 1:30; F. Saurel, *Histoire religieuse du département de l'Hérault pendant la Révolution*, 4 vols. (Paris, 1894-96), 1:188-94.

[50] In 38 bailliages for which complete data are given in Brette, 5,141 curés were either present or represented out of a total of 5,848 who should have voted (89 percent). Among non-parish clergy for which there are data, 1,520 of 2,122 (72 percent) were present or represented.

[51] Many of the *procès-verbaux* of the meetings are incomplete or have been lost; and even where they do exist, they are often little informative of interclerical relationships. I have relied on Brette, vols. 3 and 4, and on a wide range of secondary studies. The most valuable evidence comes from individual reports and letters of protest sent to the royal government. But a systematic regional typology of the electoral assemblies will probably be impossible.

[52] P. Le Sueur, *Le clergé picard et la Révolution*, 2 vols. (Amiens, 1904-05), 1:214-22; Adhémard Leclère, *La Révolution à Alençon*, 2 vols. (Alençon and Paris, 1912-14), 1:30-37; E. Brossard, *Histoire du département de la Loire pendant la Révolution*, 2 vols. (Paris, 1904-07), 1:112-13.

[53] Thus, for example, in the bailliages of Meaux and Etampes, Brette, 3:336, 380. Normally, the bishop would preside, but if no prelate were present, the question could give rise to endless haggling.

[54] Prévost, 1:33.

[55] François Laugier, *Le schisme constitutionnel et la persécution dans le Var* (Draguignan, 1897), 5 ff.

[56] Paul Piolin, *L'église du Mans durant la Révolution*, 4 vols (Le Mans, 1868-71), 1:12-16.

At least four assemblies witnessed protest boycotts, either by the bishops and their supporters (Périgueux, Béziers, Coutances) or by the curés (Le Puy)—invariably to the advantage of the rump remaining, which went ahead with business as usual.[57]

Generally, the most critical confrontation came over the actual election of deputies to the Estates General. The remarkable success of the lower clergy in these elections, overturning all tradition, has often been noted. In 1614, at the previous Estates General, curés had constituted less than 10 percent of the clerical delegation. But in 1789 some two-thirds of the ecclesiastical deputies leaving for Versailles came from the ranks of the parish clergy.[58] A number of bishops—those of Metz, of Evreux, of Dax, of Aire, of Coutances—were spurned by their own clergies, despite their evident desire to be elected.[59] Several of those bishops who did receive mandates were forced to resort to vigorous electioneering tactics of their own—sometimes of dubious legality—and they were commonly chosen after several ballots in extremely close contests with lower clergymen.[60] In Le Mans the bishop was elected as the last of four clerical deputies only after a previously elected curé representative threatened to resign.[61] In Nîmes, it was apparently the bishop's effective exploitation of Protestant fears—the influential pastor Rabaut-Saint-Etienne had already been chosen by the Third Estate—which ensured his victory.[62] Even the rectors of Brittany were anything but docile and subservient toward their clerical superiors. Special electoral regulations for this province specified that bishops and parish priests would initially meet separately. But when the bishops, allied with the Breton nobility, resolved to boycott the Estates General altogether, the rectors in all but one of the dioceses of the province

---

[57] Saurel, 1:188-94; Lucien Ampoulange, *Le clergé et la convocation aux Etats-généraux de 1789 dans la sénéchaussée de Périgord* (Montpellier, 1912), 135-55; Jean Bindet, *François Bécherel, 1732-1815*, 2nd ed. (Coutances, 1971), 30-31; Ernest Gonnet, *Essai sur l'histoire du diocèse du Puy-en-Velay (1789-1802)* (Paris, 1907), 56-65.

[58] J. Michael Hayden, *France and the Estates General of 1614* (Cambridge, 1974), 93-94.

[59] Bindet, *Bécherel*, 30-31; Boivin-Champeaux, 1:28; Joseph Légé, *Les diocèses d'Aire et de Dax ou le département des Landes sous la Révolution française, 1789-1803*, 2 vols. (Aire, 1875), 1:45; Jean Eich, *Histoire religieuse du département de la Moselle pendant la Révolution* (Metz, 1964), 67; Philippe Torreilles, *Histoire du clergé dans le département des Pyrénées-Orientales pendant la Révolution française* (Perpignan, 1890), 15-16.

[60] Le Sueur, 1:137-67; Saurel, 1:194-95; Brette, 4:170-71; Roux, 162; J.P.G. Blanchet, *Le clergé charentais pendant la Révolution* (Angoulême, 1898), 18-24.

[61] Piolin, 1:12-16.

[62] Albert Durand, *Histoire religieuse du département du Gard pendant la Révolution française, Tome I (1788-92)* (Nîmes, 1918), 34n. The bishop of Bourges used a similar tactic: Brette, 3:482.

resisted pressure from the prelates to adhere to their position.[63] It is only in the light of the recent and very extraordinary political events of 1788-1789 that one can understand the delegation chosen to represent the Breton clergy—a delegation which was soon to prove among the most progressive of any province of France.[64]

The Cahiers of the Clergy of 1789

By 1789 the polarization of opinion within the French clergy, the hostilities between the upper and lower ranks of the ecclesiastical hierarchy, were certainly more accrued and more widespread than ever before. But to what extent had this political movement genuinely transformed the conceptions of common clergymen as to the nature of the Church and the clergy's relationship with society? And to what degree might these political experiences have rendered individual ecclesiastics more sympathetic and receptive to the Civil Constitution of 1790? Certain tentative responses to these questions are suggested by an analysis of the *cahiers de doléances* drawn up by the clergy on the eve of the Revolution.

To be sure, an assessment of the clerical cahiers presents certain problems, some associated with the use of all such documents, others specific to the ecclesiastical grievances alone.[65] While numerous cahiers were undoubtedly written by individual clergymen, there were no specific provisions for these in the official convocation declaration, and the great majority seem to have been subsequently lost.[66] Thus, for the most part, one must rely on the "general" cahiers of the clergy, those collective statements drawn up to be carried by the delegates directly to Versailles. Like the general cahiers, those of the clergy were often influenced by various "model" grievance lists circulated in the kingdom. In their non-religious grievances many were invariably swayed by Jacques Necker's highly publicized statement of December 27, 1788.[67] Perhaps even more influential were the "instructions" systematically circulated to all dioceses by the Agents-General of the Clergy. Though the document itself has

[63] Savina, 76-95.

[64] See also Léon Dubreuil, "Le clergé de Bretagne aux Etats-généraux," *La Révolution française*, 70 (1917), 496; and Donald Sutherland, *The Chouans: the Social Origins of Popular Counterrevolution in Upper Brittany* (Oxford, 1982), 225-26.

[65] See, especially, Beatrice Hyslop, *A Guide to the General Cahiers of 1789* (New York, 1936), 48-106; also, by the same, *French Nationalism in 1789 According to the General Cahiers* (New York, 1934). See also below, chp. 11.

[66] See Charles Porée, *Cahiers des curés et des communautés ecclésiastiques du bailliage d'Auxerre pour les Etats généraux de 1789* (Auxerre, 1927), introduction.

[67] Hyslop, *Guide*, 66-67.

not been located, it probably contained a resumé of positions taken by the General Assembly of the Clergy in its most recent meeting.[68] An additional problem in the interpretation of the clerical cahiers arises out of the very divisions and turmoil within the ecclesiastical assemblies. In at least five instances—of which four, significantly, were in the southeast—it proved impossible for lower and upper clergy to reach a consensus, and two or more separate or successive cahiers had to be drafted.[69] On occasion, the bishop legally or illegally seized control of the cahiers committee and virtually wrote the document himself.[70]

Yet, in most of the electoral regions, the parish clergymen were as well organized for the cahier drafting as they were for the election of deputies. In twenty-six bailliages or sénéchaussées for which the exact composition of the cahier committees has been determined, the curés constituted over two-thirds of all delegates and in only a single case— the bailliage of Amiens—were they less than 50 percent.[71] Many of the committees in question are known to have carefully read the preliminary cahiers of individuals or of groups of ecclesiastics, treating the official document as a compilation of individual grievances.[72] In any case, the finished draft had to be read before the general clerical assembly and was frequently discussed point by point.[73] Though some curés protested the undue influence of upper clergymen on cahier composition, far more common were the letters sent by non-parish clergymen complaining of the dominance of the curés.[74] In sum, it is likely that the general cahiers of the clergy represent, by and large, the collective opinion of precisely

[68] Ibid., 64, 122.

[69] The sénéchaussées of Cahors, Castellane, Digne, Draguignan, and Grasse.

[70] *E.g.*, in Clermont-Ferrand, Amiens, and Langres: Yvon-Georges Paillard, "Fanatiques et patriotes dans le Puy-de-Dôme: histoire religieuse d'un département de 1792 à Thermidor," *AHRF*, 42 (1970), 296; and Brette, 3:72-73, 248.

[71] The following bailliages and sénéchaussées were included: Abbeville, Alençon, Amiens, Angoulême, Arras, Auxerre, Béziers, Castres, Châtellerault, Chaumont, Clermont-en-Beauvaisis, Comminges, Coutances, Dieuze, Etain, Gex, Le Mans, Limoges, Loudun, Montbrison, Paris-hors-les-murs, Toul, Ustaritz, Villefranches-sur-Saône, Villeneuve-de-Berg. In these districts, there were a total of 203 out of 296 (68.5 percent) curé members on the cahier committees. Sources: *AP*, vols. 1-7, *passim*; Charles Jolivet, *La Révolution en Ardèche* (Largentière, 1930), 103-106; Leclère, 1:30-37; Blanchet, 18-24; Saurel, 1:188-94; Deramecourt, 1:387; Le Sueur, 1:137-67, 214-22; Brossard, 1:112-13; Bindet, *Bécherel*, 28-30; Maurice Giraud, *Essai sur l'histoire religieuse de la Sarthe de 1789 à l'an IV* (Paris, 1920), 133-35; A. Lecler, *Martyrs et confesseurs de la foi du diocèse de Limoges pendant la Révolution française*, 4 vols. (Limoges, 1897-1904), 1:134-35.

[72] Thus, in Vannes, in Châtellerault, in Lorraine: J. Le Falher, *Le royaume de Bignan (1789-1805)* (Hennebont, 1913), 25-29; *AP*, 2:686; Jérôme, 48.

[73] Hyslop, *Guide*, 51.

[74] Brette, vols. 3 and 4, *passim*.

that group of clergymen soon to be thrust before the quandary of the oath.[75]

Although the bulk of demands in most of the clerical cahiers was concerned with ecclesiastical questions, only three of the documents did not give some treatment to non-religious questions.[76] At the core of most such demands—occurring in from two-thirds to over three-fourths of all cahiers—was a basic program for constitutional reform which included requests for periodic meetings of the Estates General, for legislative power to approve taxation, and for the suppression of *lettres de cachet* and/or the institution of some form of *habeas corpus*. In return, over 85 percent of the clerical assemblies offered to cede all fiscal privileges and to pay taxes at the same rate as everyone else.[77] On the key issue of the voting system to be followed in the Estates General, only 14 percent of the cahiers called for an imperative vote by head on all issues. Yet close to half of the documents took no position at all on the question. If one considers only those which did take a stance, almost two-thirds seemed willing to accept some form of vote by head, at least on certain questions.[78]

[75] Among previous works dealing with the clerical cahiers, see especially A. Denys-Buirette, *Les questions religieuses dans les cahiers de 1789* (Paris, 1919) and the studies by Hyslop cited above. But a new reading of these documents was found necessary in order to standardize the analysis and to explore the possibilities of regional variation. Of 194 clerical cahiers originally written—not including joint cahiers with other estates—158 had been located as of 1936: Hyslop, *Guide*, 144. Of these, 147 have been analyzed for the present study (essentially, those available in the Library of Congress). See Hyslop, *Guide*, 113-52, for sources. The cahiers used represent virtually all areas of the French kingdom, with the exceptions of the provinces of Dauphiné and Roussillon, and of significant portions of the Pyrenees and Lower Brittany. No attempt has been made to tabulate all the grievances. I have sought rather to take note of grievances related to selected issues defined primarily by the specific problems at hand in the present study. Note, that the Shapiro-Markoff computerized coding of the cahiers does not yet include the clerical cahiers. See below, chp. 11.

[76] Those containing no non-religious grievances: Arles-ville, Digne, and Sisteron. Two others, both very short, mentioned no religious grievances: Pont-à-Mousson and Saint-Jean-d'Angély.

[77] Demands for a permanent or periodic Estates General were found in 76 percent of the clerical cahiers; for the Estates General to approve all taxes: 71 percent; for the abolishing of *lettres de cachet*: 61 percent; for the clergy to pay equal taxes in proportion to their resources: 86 percent. Another 35 percent demanded a written constitution or charter.

[78] Of the 147 cahiers studied, 82 (56 percent) were found to take a position on the issue. Of these, 38 percent demanded a vote by order, 24 percent demanded a vote by head, 29 percent called for a vote by head on specific issues or under certain circumstances; and 9 percent were willing to accept any decision which the Estates General itself should make on the question. The demands for a vote by head were scattered in most parts of the kingdom with the major exception of the southwest. Compare Guy Chaussinand-Nogaret, *La noblesse au XVIIIe siècle* (Paris, 1976), 189-91, 204-216. Most of the grievances in question appeared with only slightly greater frequency in the cahiers of the nobility.

As for religious grievances, the cahiers help reveal the degree to which the protest rhetoric and reform ideas explored earlier in the chapter had penetrated the clergy. One notes, first of all, the near absence of Jansenist demands. Nothing is to be found on the bull *Unigenitus* or the *Formulaire* of Alexander VII. The cahiers would thus seem to confirm the sharp decline in Jansenist influence by the end of the Old Regime.[79] By contrast, there was a scattering of Richerist demands, grievances calling for the reestablishment of curé honorific rights in processions and liturgical ceremonies, for the suppression of the *curés primitifs*, and for modifications of the Edict of 1695 in favor of greater curé independence in the parishes. Yet such demands were generally scarce—found in no more than 10 percent of the documents. The fundamental Richerist contention—that the office of curé was of divine institution—appeared only twice in the 147 cahiers examined.[80]

Relatively more common, however, were the various economic demands of the type inspired by Henri Reymond. Complaints and reform proposals relating to the *portion congrue* were almost universal, not only in the cahiers of the clergy but in those of the other two orders as well. Only slightly less frequent were demands that would reduce or eliminate various "useless benefices"—such as chapels or priories without residence or abbeys *in commendam*—for the benefit of the parish clergy and for various charitable and educational institutions; and those which would ensure the security of parish clergymen in sickness and old age. Fifteen percent of the cahiers even called for the return of all or part of the tithes to the curés.[81] Of the various requests promoting the democratization of the Church, the most frequent demand concerned curé representation on the clerical tax boards.[82] A fourth of the clerical assemblies also asked that the lower clergy be given a greater voice in synods and councils and

[79] Préclin, 443-58.

[80] Fifteen cahiers (10 percent) affirmed the curés' rights of precedence over canons and monks in religious functions; 16 (11 percent) asked that the *curés primitifs* be abolished; 10 (7 percent) asked that the Edicts of 1695 and 1698 be modified; 2 (1 percent) affirmed that the curés were of divine institution; 7 (5 percent) asked in various ways that the role and power of the curés be augmented within the clergy.

[81] I have made no count of the demands to raise the *portion congrue*—which certainly appeared in the overwhelming majority of the cahiers. Other frequencies were as follows: grievances for the reduction or suppression of simple benefices: 52 (35 percent); for the creation of retirement arrangements for curés: 22 (15 percent).

[82] Such demands were found in 59 (40 percent) of the cahiers. But a number of others refrained from similar demands, with the assumption that a unified tax system for all citizens would imply the suppression of the clerical tax boards.

in the General Assemblies of the Clergy, and a few developed detailed plans for the governing of dioceses based on joint councils of bishops and curés, partly anticipating the provisions of the Civil Constitution. An additional 20 percent called for a repeal of the declaration of 1782, urging that parish clergymen have the right to meet in independent assemblies and elect their own legal representatives.[83]

Taking into account all of the grievances calling for an expansion of curé rights in the Church—whether of Richerist or "Reymondist" inspiration—one can transform the "scores" from bailliages to departments and present the results cartographically.[84] (See Figure H.) The geography which emerges is perhaps surprising in some respects. The single highest concentration of such demands was in the northwest and west center of Normandy, Maine, and Touraine. South of the Loire, clusters of grievances for curé power were to be found between the Massif-Central and the Pyrenees and in the extreme southeast. The latter region would undoubtedly stand out far more emphatically if the clergy of Dauphiné had produced their own cahiers. In fact, the unofficial cahiers of the curés of Dauphiné, organized by Reymond and signed by parish clergymen throughout the province, reveal this corps to have been the most radical in France in 1789.[85] Yet one must also take into account the significant differences in the principal thrust of cahier demands between the north and the south. There was a clear tendency for more grievances concerning honorific rights to appear in the north: grievances involving the *curés primitifs*, for example, or the rights of curés in processions. In

---

[83] Frequency of demands for greater curé power in the General Assemblies: 37 (25 percent); for greater power in synods and/or councils: 32 (22 percent); for the right of curés to meet independently: 29 (20 percent). Among those clerical assemblies demanding full cooperation of the curés and bishops in the government of the dioceses were Digne, Etampes, and Villeneuve-de-Berg.

[84] The following grievances were considered in the aggregate count of "curé rights": increase curé power in *chambres ecclésiastiques*; increase power in General Assemblies of the Clergy; increase power in synods and/or councils; declare curés descendants of the 72 disciples; expand curés' rights of precedence; abolish or limit *curés primitifs*; modify Edict of 1695 in curés' favor; allow independent curé assemblies and elections of *syndics* to represent them; return all or part of the tithes to the curés; generally augment the power and/or role of the curés in the Church. For each such grievance appearing in a cahier, one point was assigned to the cahier's score. The scores tallied for each of the electoral districts (bailliages or sénéchaussées) were then transformed into scores for departments through a weighting procedure based on proportionate overlapping territorial areas. See John Markoff and Gilbert Shapiro, "The Linkage of Data Describing Overlapping Geographical Units," *Historical Methods Newsletter*, 7 (1973), 34-46.

[85] Tackett, *Priest and Parish*, 258-68. The only official "cahier" drawn up in Dauphiné was the brief statement produced jointly by the three orders in the Estates of Dauphiné meeting in Romans.

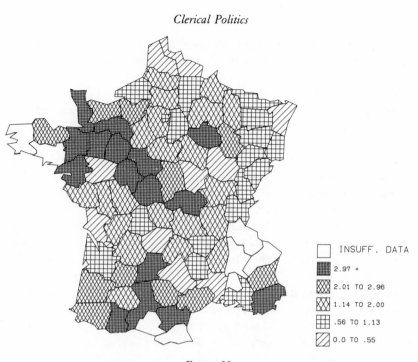

FIGURE H
Grievances for Curé Rights in Clerical Cahiers of 1789.

the south, and especially the southeast, there were far more requests for
an expansion of curé political rights, and notably for the right to hold
independent curé assemblies.[86] But equally significant was the general
paucity of all such demands among the clergy of the northern and northeastern border provinces of Flanders, Artois, Lorraine, Alsace, and
Franche-Comté. Despite the long history of curé opposition movements
in Lorraine, despite the energetic organization of elements of the parish
clergy to assure the election of curés to the Estates General, the cahiers
produced by this province proved surprisingly conservative. The entire
region of the northeastern frontier, outside the Gallican organization of
the Clergy of France, and with a generally strong ultramontane tradition,
was substantially less sensitive to the problems of the honorific, economic,

---

[86] Of demands for the suppression of the *curés primitifs*, 12 of 16 came from clergymen north
of this line; also 10 of 15 demanding greater curé rights in processions, *etc.*, came from the
north. But of those asking that curés be allowed to meet in independent assemblies, 18 of 29
came from the south.

and political rights of the parish clergy. It is of interest that most of these clergymen would later opt in massive proportions to follow their bishops into opposition against the Civil Constitution.

But one can also directly confront the anticipation of the Civil Constitution by comparing the demands in the clerical cahiers with fifteen of the most important religious reforms incorporated into the Revolutionary legislation.[87] Several of these "anticipation" grievances have already been discussed: the participation of the parish clergy in the diocesan administration, the creation of pensions for sick and aged priests, the suppression of all or part of the simple benefices. All were registered with considerable frequency in the general cahiers. A full 40 percent were also prepared to abolish the *casuel*, the requisite pastoral fees long decried by the curés for the animosities which they engendered among the laity. A fourth of the grievance lists demanded that all benefice holders, or at least all bishops, be held to maintain residence. And four out of ten cahiers asked for opening of clerical careers to talent, regardless of birth or "favor"—often by requiring all bishops or canons to have previously served several years in the parish clergy. Limiting bishoprics to members of the nobility was, as one cahier put it, "contrary to the spirit of religion itself."[88] Yet grievances anticipating the most radical measures of the Civil Constitution were scarcely to be found anywhere. Though most clergymen were prepared to give up their tax privilege, no cahier made mention of the suppression of all clerical privileges. Nor was there any consideration of the sale of even a portion of Church property—and indeed 15 percent specifically demanded that Church lands be preserved. Two cahiers, both in Provence, suggested the abolition of the tithes in kind, but there was no suggestion anywhere that all clergymen might be placed on salaries. Nowhere did the cahiers consider the lay election of bishops and curés—though one document demanded

[87] The following are the grievances counted as anticipating the Civil Constitution with their frequencies of appearance in the clerical cahiers: abolish all or some clerical privilege: 126 (86 percent); abolish all or part of regular clergy: 8 (5 percent); sell all or some of Church property: 0; change boundaries of parishes or dioceses: 17 (12 percent); elect priests to clerical posts: 2 (1 percent); make all clerical posts open to talent: 58 (39 percent); abolish all or some chapters: 10 (7 percent); abolish all or some simple benefices: 52 (35 percent); abolish all or some of the tithes: 3 (2 percent); abolish the *casuel*: 59 (40 percent); abrogate the Concordat of Boulogna or reinstate the Pragmatic Sanction: 9 (6 percent); require residence of all benefice holders: 36 (24 percent); reduce the wealth of the bishops: 1 (1 percent); provide pensions for old and sick priests: 100 (68 percent); give diocesan clergy a greater voice in diocesan affairs: 65 (44 percent). In scoring, one point was assigned to a cahier for each grievance which appeared. In those where all or part (some) of an institution was at stake, a score of one was given when a partial suppression was requested; a score of two, if the request was for a total suppression.

[88] Cahier of the sénéchaussée of Digne: *AP*, 3:337.

that bishops be elected by the parish clergy. And if a handful considered the suppression of certain regular houses and collegiate chapters whose revenues or membership were insufficient, none would envision the complete disappearance of such institutions. In fact, over half of the cahiers called for the *preservation* of the regulars threatened—in the eyes of many—by the reforms of Loménie de Brienne's Commission twenty years earlier.[89]

In general, the geography of this "degree of anticipation" appears substantially less coherent than the geography of the demands for curé rights. (See Figure I.) One finds a number of isolated, especially progressive departments—Aveyron, Seine-et-Oise, and Basses-Alpes ranked the highest—peppered over a grey landscape of moderate electoral districts.[90] If the southwest from Bordelais to Poitou seems somewhat more moderate, and the Parisian Basin somewhat more progressive, the Massif-

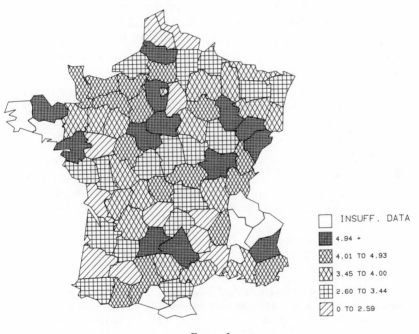

INSUFF. DATA

4.94 +

4.01 TO 4.93

3.45 TO 4.00

2.60 TO 3.44

0 TO 2.59

FIGURE I

Anticipation of the Civil Constitution in Clerical Cahiers of 1789.

[89] The request appeared in 79 (54 percent) of the clerical cahiers.

[90] The bailliages of Rodez, Digne, and Etampes had scores of 11, 13, and 11, respectively—much higher than any other cahiers or than the mean score of 3.8.

Central and the northeastern border provinces do not appear with the same cohesiveness as on the previous map. There is no statistical correlation whatsoever between this degree of anticipation of the Civil Constitution and the percentage of oath-takers per department.[91]

Moreover, to judge the clerical cahiers solely on the degree to which they match preconceived patterns—of the anticipation of the Civil Constitution, of the voicing of grievances on curé rights—is to miss an important conservative element found in even the most "progressive" cahiers. In numerous cases, the opening statement is a stern and elaborate demand for the implementation of all religious strictures on lay society: the mandatory honoring of Sundays and feast days, the enforcement of Lenten alimentary codes, the diligent policing of all those social misdeeds which were daily affronts to the authority of the Church: drinking and gambling, blasphemy and sacrilege, prostitution, dueling, and general "libertine" behavior.[92] In an overwhelming proportion, the clergy opposed any form of freedom of the press, demanding rather a renewed and aggressive censorship policy. And if a few cahiers were willing to concede the very rudimentary "Edict of Toleration" for the Protestants passed in 1787, none even considered the possibility that Catholicism might not remain the sole state religion.[93]

And there was another critical issue on which most of the clerical cahiers were patently vague and inarticulate: the issue of how, under whose aegis and authority, the needed changes were to be effected. A few of the documents suggested that the approval of the French bishops would be necessary; others affirmed that a national council or a series of diocesan synods would be required to ratify decisions of the Estates General; and still others appeared to be granting the ultimate authority to the Estates themselves.[94] But the great majority of the cahiers remained

[91] The correlation coefficient is 0.02. The correlation coefficient between the oath and the number of demands for curé rights was an even lower −0.009.

[92] A careful count was not kept, but appeals to end the "profanations" of Sundays and feast days appeared in close to half of the cahiers.

[93] Only 11 (7 percent) of the cahiers asked specifically for freedom of the press in anything resembling the modern sense. Many others would allow such "freedom" as long as nothing was written against religion or the monarchy. Some 76 (52 percent) specifically demanded that censorship be enforced or strengthened.

[94] Those emphasizing the authority of the bishops: Auch, Bigorre, Boulogne-sur-Mer. Those calling for councils or synods for ratification: Digne and Chaumont. Vitry called for reforms by means of a national council, but if the council failed, the Estates General itself was urged to take charge. Besançon suggested that several specific major reforms (the surveillance of the regulars, the suppression of simple benefices, *etc.*) be carried out by the Estates.

inexplicit as to the manner of accomplishing the reforms, couching their grievances in an impersonal or passive voice. Nowhere, moreover, do they reflect on the power which the papacy might wield in the reforming process. To be sure, there were numerous pronouncements of allegiance to the "Catholic, Apostolic, and Roman Church," and four of the cahiers made specific references to their affection and commitment to the pope.[95] But, for the most part, the cahiers divulge very little about clerical attitudes toward the role of Rome in the future transformations. On the question of the legitimization of ecclesiastical change, as on the question of the nature of the reforms to be consummated, the general cahiers of the clergy of 1789 suggest a clerical corps of which the majority was largely unprepared to confront either the Civil Constitution of the Clergy or the ecclesiastical oath of 1791.

Conclusion

Nowhere had the collective opinion of the clergy closely anticipated the Revolutionary transformations of the Church. Yet it does seem clear that past political activities in certain regions may have helped prepare some clerical corps better than others to accept the new laws once they had been promulgated. For, as we have seen, the protest efforts of the eighteenth-century curés against bishops and the upper clergy in general varied conspicuously in objectives and intensity from province to province. Two long-developing strands of curé opposition, in particular, had served to undercut respect for episcopal authority and to inspire a broad reevaluation of traditional ecclesiology. First were those movements born of Jansenist affiliations or sympathies. Second was the deep disaffection engendered by the peculiar economic structures of the Church in certain regions, structures which left large numbers of curés disinherited from ecclesiastical wealth and property and reduced to a fixed moneyed salary. In Dauphiné and Provence, in the Parisian Basin and Central Lorraine, clerical opposition impelled by Jansenism or the *portion congrue* had become virtually institutionalized within the rural synods or the ecclesiastical conferences. In each of these areas the majority of curés and

[95] The stock phrase was found in 50 of the 147 cahiers, distributed in virtually all regions of the country. The specific references to the pope were in the cahiers of Gien, Longwy, Loudun, and Etampes. A few also complained against papal privileges. The *prévention* was condemned in 28 cahiers, the *résignation* in 7. Eight others complained against the papal right of the *annates*. "Gallican liberties" were specifically affirmed in Poitou, Soissons, and Saint-Quentin, among others.

vicaires would accept the Civil Constitution with relatively little hesitation. Many, like Henri Reymond himself, were astounded by the sweep of the reforms. Yet they had effectively declared their independence from the ecclesiastical hierarchy even before 1791, and the oath would rarely pose any serious crisis of conscience.[96]

But the curés of these provinces were clearly atypical of the French clergy generally. For most of the kingdom the "revolt" of the parish clergy, so often alluded to in the historical literature, was but a short-term epiphenomenon. Whatever the anger of the curés of Franche-Comté in 1788 over their near exclusion from the provincial assembly, whatever the relative progressivism of the cahiers of the Rouergue clergy, the parish priests of both provinces had long histories of docility and deference to ecclesiastical hierarchy.[97] Political opposition to the aristocratic bishops in 1789 would have little bearing on religious allegiance to these same prelates when the stakes had been raised in the winter of 1791.

[96] For Dauphiné, see the author's *Priest and Parish*, 269-86; and "Citizen Priests," 321-22.

[97] Nicole Lemaître, "Pour l'indépendance des curés au XVIIIe siècle: le curé de la cathédrale contre son évêque," *Actes du colloque du VIIe centenaire de la cathédrale de Rodez. Rodez, 20 mai 1977* (Rodez, 1979); Edmond Préclin, "La situation ecclésiastique et religieuse de la Franche-Comté à la veille de la Révolution," *Bulletin de la Fédération des sociétés savantes de Franche-Comté*, no. 2 (1955), 12, 26-27.

PART THREE

FRENCHMEN CONFRONT THE OATH

SEVEN

Clerical Leadership and the Voice from Below

THROUGHOUT the first part of this study, we have focused primarily on the clergymen themselves as they confronted the oath of 1791: on individual careers and ecclesiastical experiences as well as on the broader clerical society to which those individuals belonged. Yet, in a number of instances, our inquiry has suggested the potential interaction between the priest and his lay parishioners. Despite the efforts of bishops and seminary directors to set the clergy aloof and apart from "the world," no clergyman could ever immure himself altogether from the opinions and sentiments of his flock. In certain regions, in the eyes of contemporaries, the ecclesiastical crisis of 1791 was associated with a major shift in popular attitudes with regard to the Revolution itself. It was thus a critical crossroads for French rural history as well as for French ecclesiastical history.[1] But what was the nature of this interaction between clergyman and laity? And who ultimately was the leader, and who was the led?

Clerical Leadership and the Battle of the Sacraments

For the Revolutionaries, there could be little doubt of the essential independence of the clergy's actions on the question of the oath. Under the Old Regime, Frenchmen had grown accustomed to considering the parish clergy as the leaders and tutors of the local community and as pivotal figures in the maintenance of social cohesion and stability. As overt popular opposition to the Revolution's religious policies began to grow after 1789, it was initially assumed to be the work of a bitter and jealous upper clergy. But when agitation arose in some parishes over the oath itself, the conclusion seemed inescapable that it was the handiwork of the non-juring parish clergymen. How else could one explain the perversion of popular opinion against a regime that saw itself as the embodiment of popular sovereignty? The refractories soon took their place beside the "aristocrats" in the rogues' gallery of enemies of the Revolution, prime instigators of counterrevolution. And by and large,

[1] See above, chp. 1.

most historians—whether republican or clerical—have tended to agree: insofar as the population held any views on the oath at all, they had been received from the clergy.

Indeed, the letters streaming into the National Assembly and the Ministry of the Interior seemed to give ample evidence that some refractory clergymen were stirring up trouble.[2] In Rouergue, the non-juring clergy was said to be actively riling up the people against the Constitution, treating their juring colleagues with "une répugnance qui semble tenir au délire." Everywhere in Ille-et-Vilaine, according to the departmental directory, curés were spreading trouble and discord, taking advantage of the people's ignorance and credulity to sow fears that religion itself was under attack. In Calvados, the curé of Le Buisson was preaching revolt and "semant la zizanie dans les coeurs." In the overwhelmingly constitutional department of Creuse, it was only in the rare parishes with refractory curés that people were said to be upset by the ecclesiastical changes. This had transpired, we are told, because priests were widely announcing the National Assembly's intention of "changing the religion" of France.[3]

Certain refractories were said to be making full use of their control over the parish's ritual life to frighten the population against the Civil Constitution. Above all, there was the unsettling pronouncement that sacraments performed by the constitutional clergy would be inefficacious or, worse yet, the works of the devil. In point of fact, most theologians were careful to make the distinction between oath-taking curés originally consecrated by an Old-Regime bishop and the genuine "intrus" elected by the districts after 1790. In the judgment of the orthodox canonists, it

[2] The single most important source for the development that follows consists of the papers of the Committee for Research of the National Assembly. A large number of letters, reports, petitions, etc.—well over a thousand pieces—concerning the implementation of the oath seem to have been centralized in the four large cartons: A.N., D XXIX bis 20-23. I have also examined a series of correspondence received by the Ecclesiastical Committee: especially A.N., D XIX 80-88, using D XIX 102 as an index. But most correspondence relating to difficulties with the oath seems to have been passed on to the Committee for Research. In addition, I have looked through portions of the papers received by the Ministry of the Interior concerning religious questions: A.N., F^{19} 398-481; and by the Committee for Reports: A.N., D XXIX. The latter, however, are filed by place rather than by subject and are thus extremely awkward to use.

[3] Letters from the district of Sévérac, Nov. 20, 1791: A.D. Aveyron, L 1937; from the department of Ille-et-Vilaine, Feb. 23, 1791: A.N., D XIX 80, dos. 613, no. 19; and from the department of Creuse: A.N., D XXIX bis 22, dos. 237, no. 2. Also, Emile Sévestre, *Liste critique des ecclésiastiques fonctionnaires publics insermentés et assermentés en Normandie* (Paris, 1922), 345-46.

was only the latter whose commission would be ineffective. Yet many refractories issued blanket condemnations of the sacraments of all jurors without exception.[4] A marriage performed by a Constitutional priest— no different than one presided over by a Protestant pastor—would be null and void, and the children issuing from such a union would be bastards in the eyes of God.[5] When the wafer of the Eucharist had been consecrated by a juror—according to some refractories in Alsace—it was not the body of Christ but of the devil that would be elevated before them.[6] In Auvergne non-conformist clergymen were openly preaching that all constitutionals had already been damned, that the people would be damned as well if they received absolution from them, and that it was "better to confess to a tree than to a constitutional curé."[7] The Revolutionaries were particularly uneasy about the use which non-jurors were presumed to be making of the sacrament of Penance. The "secrets of the confessional" elicited many of the same fears and suspicions among the patriots as the "Masonic secrets" had formerly caused among the Old-Regime clergy—particularly since many of the patriot leaders themselves may have had little recent experience in the confessional.[8]

To believe the reports of the Revolutionary administrators, the non-jurors took advantage of every possible occasion to preach against the constitution. The vicaire of Plounérin in Côtes-du-Nord was accused of reading such a protest in the middle of a marriage ceremony. The bishop of Le Puy had advanced his scheduled pastoral visits in order to intone against the new legislation during confirmation rites. In Franche-Comté and in Normandy priests were attacked for pressuring children in their first communion classes, requiring them all to swear an oath never to attend mass or confession with a constitutional priest. Haas, curé of Bitche in German Lorraine, attracted large numbers of people through the ploy

[4] See the letter from the Abbé Guillon in Paris to two refractories in Lorient, spring 1791: A.N., D XXIX bis 22, dos. 233, no. 9; and the letter from the municipality of Yvetot, Apr. 20, 1791: A.N., D XXIX bis 22, dos. 235, no. 16. See also the article by C. Constantin on "Constitution civile du clergé" in the *DTC*, vol. 3, pt. 2, cols. 1537-1604.

[5] Letter from Lefebvre, bourgeois of Gisors, Mar. 13, 1791: A.N., D XXIX bis 21, dos. 229, no. 19.

[6] Letter from ten curés in the district of Belfort, July 18, 1791: A.N., D XXIX 85.

[7] Letter from an unnamed constitutional priest in the district of Brioude, April 1, 1791: A.N., D XXIX bis 22, dos. 237, no. 1. For a similar case, see the letter from Fayl-Billot, near Langres, Mar. 22, 1791: A.N., D XXIX bis 21, dos. 232, no. 4.

[8] For example, in the district of Ustaritz (Basses-Pyrénées): Abbé Haristoy, *Les paroisses du pays basque pendant la période révolutionnaire*, 2 vols. (Pau, 1895-99), 1:123.

of offering a special exposition of the Blessed Sacrament. He then used the occasion to read the papal bull condemning the Constitution and the Revolution.[9]

In truth, however, refractory clergymen had little need to search for special opportunities to exert their influence on the population. From the point of view of the opponents of the Civil Constitution the oath crisis could not have occurred at a more opportune moment in the liturgical cycle. Easter would fall that year on April 24, later than in any year of the entire Revolutionary decade. During those critical weeks of Lent, to within a few weeks or days of the district elections for the replacement of curés, virtually every member of the parish would come in for his requisite confession as part of his "Easter Duties." From every corner of France came expressions of fear over the use and abuse which refractories were thought to be making of the annual "tribunal of the conscience." Many refractories in Normandy were said to be profiting from this last intimate contact with their congregations "to indict in advance those who would come to replace them" and to indoctrinate the people with the idea that it was an open sacrilege to attend mass or confession with an "intrus." The departmental directors of Haute-Garonne decried the "unhappy coincidence" that elections of new curés were being organized in a period of maximum church attendance when refractories had their best occasion of the year to "scrutinize consciences" and to "direct impressions in the manner they saw fit." A patriot priest in Issoudun was particularly appalled at a letter received from his twelve-year-old niece who, under the influence of a non-juring curé, was trying to influence her uncle against the Civil Constitution.[10] In Yvetot, near Rouen, both curé and vicaire were refusing Easter absolution to anyone who did not first acknowledge the Old-Regime bishop as their sole legitimate prelate. According to one witness, as soon as he stepped into the booth, the priest accosted him with the single question: "What side are you on?" If the answer was wrong, the subject was simply sent away.[11] Similar treatment of penitents by parish clergymen, threatening to refuse absolution to

[9] Interrogation of the vicaire of Plounérin, Nov. 11, 1790: A.N., F[19] 418; Ernest Gonnet, *Essai sur l'histoire du diocèse du Puy-en-Velay (1789-1802)* (Paris, 1907), 102-103; letter from department of Doubs, Apr. 27, 1791: A.N., D XXIX bis 22, dos. 239, nos. 4-5; P. Lesprand, *Le clergé de la Moselle pendant la Révolution*, 4 vols. (Montguy-lès-Metz, 1934-39), 3:48.

[10] Emile Sévestre, *Les problèmes religieux de la Révolution et de l'Empire en Normandie*, 2 vols. (Paris, 1924), 1:545-47; letter from department of Haute-Garonne, Mar. 8, 1791: A.N., D XXIX bis 21, dos. 229, no. 15; letter from Jacobins of Issoudun, *ca.* early 1791: A.N., D XIX 45.

[11] Minutes of the meeting of the Yvetot municipal council, Apr. 20, 1791: A.N., D XXIX bis 22, dos. 235, no. 16.

supporters of the Civil Constitution, was also reported in Anjou, where the action aroused considerable anxiety among administrators.[12] More than a few clergymen were apparently falling back on the same refusal of sacrament tactics which the oldest among them had first seen practiced against the Jansenists during the decade of the 1750's.

In certain instances, ecclesiastics seem to have organized a veritable sacramental blackmail to coerce their parishioners. Rectors in the district of Clisson near Nantes declared that as soon as the delay for taking the oath had expired, they would immediately cease all clerical functions. The directors of this Breton district found themselves in the ironic position of ordering the refractories to continue in their pastoral duties until they were replaced—this under the threat of being prosecuted as "perturbateurs du repos public."[13] A number of curés in the Landes region of the southwest were more bluntly materialistic in their approach: they would terminate all curial duties unless the population both repudiated the new laws and continued paying them as under the Old Regime.[14] In Côtes-du-Nord there was a refusal by the refractory vicar-general to issue marriage dispensations; in Anjou and Lorraine there were reports of refractory curés abruptly ceasing to contribute to poor relief, thus causing widespread alarm and discontent among the population. Colt, curé of Forbach, sarcastically recommended that the poor henceforth address themselves directly to the Constituent Assembly for charity. If the national body had enough money to erect an epitaph to Jean-Jacques Rousseau, it could certainly spare something for the poor.[15]

It would not be difficult to mobilize many other anecdotal examples of refractory parish clergymen vigorously working to raise the hostilities of the population against the Civil Constitution and the oath. But how typical were they of the clergy as a whole, and how successful were they in winning the sympathy of their parishioners? There is at least some

[12] Paul Bardon, "Le clergé angevin et la reconstruction concordataire du diocèse d'Angers" Thèse de 3e cycle, Univ. Paris-Sorbonne, 1981, 62. On the difficult position of the administrators over the question see Emile Sévestre, *L'acceptation de la Constitution civile du clergé en Normandie* (Paris, 1922), 518-20.

[13] Letter, Jan. 18, 1791: A.N., D XXIX bis 20, dos. 220, no. 2.

[14] Jean Lacouture, "La Constitution civile du clergé dans les Landes," *Bulletin de la Société de Borda*, 52 (1928), 90; and letter from the municipality of Urgons, *ca.* Feb. 1, 1791: A.N., D XXIX bis 21, dos. 230, no. 20.

[15] Letter from the department of Côtes-du-Nord, Feb. 4, 1791: A.N., D XIX 80, dos. 612, no. 13; Maurice Giraud, *Essai sur l'histoire religieuse de la Sarthe de 1789 à l'an VI* (Paris, 1920), 387-88; letter from the district of Sarreguemines, mid-Feb. 1791: A.N., D XXIX bis 21, dos. 225, no. 11.

indication that the aggressive rabble-rousers among the non-jurors were considerably less common than the nervous and suspicious administrators suspected. By law any non-juror promoting disobedience to the decrees—either to the Civil Constitution or to the oath—was to be denounced and prosecuted in the criminal courts. Everywhere the Jacobin clubs and other groups of patriots rapidly and self-consciously established themselves as watchdogs over any such "anti-constitutional" activities by clergymen.[16] Yet, despite these efforts and despite the notoriety given to the clergymen indicted for counterrevolutionary activities in almost every department, the number of priests actually prosecuted for such misdeeds probably represented only a small minority of the local parish corps.[17] In point of fact, the pastoral letters circulated by the Old-Regime bishops usually emphasized that the clergy should in no way use or encourage force in the matter, that their only weapons should be the passive "signs and sobs" of sadness, the traditional mode of the martyrs.[18]

Indeed, as we have already seen, numerous of the clergymen who swore restrictive oaths—perhaps the majority of all refractories—took great pains to insist on their desire to remain good citizens despite their forced retirement. In this, they were but affirming a tradition of the Old Regime, reinforced by their seminary training, to maintain their support for civil obedience to the government in power. Though such cases were far less dramatic, and thus seldom noted by contemporaries, there were undoubtedly instances of refractory curés offering their passive or even active cooperation to their elected successors.[19]

For, whatever a curé's personal convictions on the issue, how far would he be willing to pursue his case if he sensed a widespread opposition to

[16] See articles 6-8 of the decree of Nov. 27, 1791: *AP*, 21:80-81. On the activities of the Jacobins, see Michael L. Kennedy, *The Jacobin Club in the French Revolution. The First Years* (Princeton, 1982), 152-77.

[17] Following the general amnesty decree of Sept. 14, 1791, the *commissaires du roi* in each district were asked to report on the individuals touched by the law. In 54 districts for which the information in the National Archives would seem to be complete, 182 priests had been indicted prior to that date for various forms of "counterrevolutionary" action. This represents only 5.7 percent of the refractories and less than 3 percent of all the parish clergymen in these districts: A.N., BB³.

[18] See the descriptions, for example, of the pastoral letters of the bishops of Trève and Verdun: A.N., D XXIX bis 20, dos. 215, no. 25; and of the bishop of Boulogne: A. Deramecourt, *Le clergé du diocèse d'Arras, Boulogne, et Saint-Omer pendant la Révolution*, 4 vols. (Arras, 1884-86), 2:131-37.

[19] Thus, in Valogne: Emile Sévestre, *La vie religieuse dans les principales villes normandes pendant la Révolution (1787-1801). Troisième série. Manche* (Paris, 1943), 65-66; in the Pays de Caux: A.N., D XIX 22, dos. 364.

that position on the part of his parishioners? And herein lay the error of both the revolutionaries and of most historians: in wide areas of France the lay populations were anything but malleable clay in the hands of the clergy, ready to be formed in their own image. It is rare indeed that we are permitted to attend the Sunday sermon or penetrate the confessional and actually observe the interaction between priest and parishioners over the question of the Civil Constitution. But in Yvetot (Seine-Inférieure) the municipal administrators actually launched an inquest into the confessional practices of the local clergy during the oath crisis.[20] One of the witnesses called in for testimony, Félicité Aillard, recounted her experience. As soon as she appeared before the vicaire for her Easter duties, he asked her opinion of the "affaires du temps." When she responded that she had come to confess and not to talk about all that, he immediately criticized her for displaying too much pride and for "reasoning like a woman." It was essential that she tell him if she would recognize the elected replacements for her bishop and curé and would abandon her "legitimate pastors." She would not, she answered, abandon them: it was they who were abandoning her. She would always be the sheep of the pastor who came to care for her. And, in any case, how was she to know which priest to believe when those of the two sides were constantly contradicting each other? The vicaire exhorted her to follow "the greatest number and the most enlightened" and to remember that hardly any of the bishops had taken the oath. She answered that she would be mad to listen to the bishops, who, as everyone knew, were only interested in holding onto their immense wealth. And with this the vicaire dismissed her, refusing to hear her Easter confession.

As wife of a lawyer and municipal administrator, Félicité Aillard was hardly a typical citizen of Yvetot. But three other witnesses came forward to testify in a similar vein, two from merchant families and one humble woman unable to sign her name. The testimony is revealing of the potential complexities in the relationship between clergy and laity and the potential independence of the latter. It would be an error to underestimate the possible influence of this voice from below.

The Parish Community Confronts the Oath

In the long historiography of the oath, surprisingly little attention has been given to the other side of the parish equation: the masses of the lay

[20] Municipal minutes, Apr. 20, 1791: A.N., D XXIX bis 22, dos. 235, no. 16.

population. In an oft-cited passage of his thesis on the peasants of Nord during the French Revolution, Georges Lefebvre argued that the rural inhabitants had little understanding or interest in either the Civil Constitution or the oath, and that it was only when their curé had refused the oath and was scheduled to be replaced that the cultural inertia of the village was upset and the population became enraged. The great majority of historians, whether clerical, anticlerical, or something in between, have tended to concur with the Lefebvre position.[21] Though the countrypeople are usually deemed fully capable of independent political judgment and action where their economic interests are at stake, they have been curiously transformed into non-entities or automatons in the religious crisis of 1791, reacting reflexively to the pressure of events and the decisions of their clergy. To be sure, the vast majority of the laity could never have understood the fine theological subtleties debated by ecclesiastics in the battle of the oath.[22] But the people had their own logic in such matters, their own theology of sorts.

Under the Old Regime a dialectical relationship between priest and parishioner had been clearly in evidence over a wide range of issues, secular and religious. The villagers had a sharply defined image of what the priest should be in his conduct and outward appearance, and they were often disposed to various forms of passive or violent coercion in attempts to impose their views. This had been true not only for the clergyman's secular activities but for his role as religious leader as well. Every priest was conscious of the critical need to maintain the confidence of his "flock," without which his very leadership would be impotent. In the crisis of the oath, no less than under the Old Regime, the opinions of the flock were a force to be reckoned with.[23]

The enormous popular outrage in some areas over official efforts to implement the oath is often in evidence in the records. The mere publication or attempted publication of the November 26 decree ignited riots

---

[21] Georges Lefebvre, *Les paysans du Nord pendant la Révolution française* (Paris, 1924), 780. Perhaps the major exception among recent historians has been Paul Bois, *Paysans de l'Ouest*, abridged ed. (Paris, 1971), 292.

[22] See, for example, Augustin Sicard, *Le clergé de France pendant la Révolution*, 3 vols. (Paris, 1912-27), 2:149; Sévestre, *L'acceptation*, 326-27. Note the case of the municipality of Dugny near Paris, whose members were unable to understand the pastoral letter of the archbishop of Paris when it was read to them by the curé: minutes, Jan. 23, 1791: A.N., D XXIX bis 20, dos. 220, no. 22.

[23] See the author's *Priest and Parish in Eighteenth-Century France* (Princeton, 1977), 194-221; also Marie-Hélène Froeschlé-Chopard, *La religion populaire en Provence orientale au XVIIIe siècle* (Paris, 1980), 259-349; and Gérard Bouchard, *Le village immobile* (Paris, 1972), 285-343.

in Frévent (Pas-de-Calais) and Le Vigan (Gard) and a general uprising in several villages of the future *Vendée militaire*.[24] But the enforcement of the oath itself brought even greater turmoil. Throughout the Massif-Central, Alsace, and much of the west large crowds formed on numerous occasions to prevent officials from administering the civic ceremony. In the region around Le Puy, mayors and municipal officers despaired for their lives and were largely ignored by the national guard when they pleaded for help and protection. In Morbihan several thousand peasants marched on Vannes on the eve of the scheduled oath, as district officials predicted their own impending massacre.[25] Though most historians have seen in these and in many similar incidents the pernicious (or salutary) machinations of the parish clergy, the explanation is far from simple. In the first place, the popular fury in such regions might be directed not only against the administration and the elected replacement curés—the "intrus"—but against Old-Regime parish clergymen of longstanding who had dared to take the oath. The rector of La Chapelle-Janson would bitterly complain of being jeered by his parish and pelted with stones as he attempted to perform his civic oath: they "treated me like an *intrus*," "I who have been in the rectory for forty years." In the Alsatian parish of Thannenkirch the Abbé Bernauer lamented that since he had sworn the oath he had lost the respect of his parishioners. He was hooted as "impious, sacrilegious, and heretical," and the children had ceased attending his catechism classes. Those curés in Lozère who dared to become jurors might be chased from their parishes or threatened with death by knife-wielding women. And in Vendée one constitutional vicaire was ambushed and shot as he left the rectory.[26] To the independent few willing to confront similar manifestations of popular rage in regions such as these, how many others chose the better part of valor, yielding in advance to the popular will which long years of service had taught them to detect if not to sympathize with?

Moreover, it was not uncommon for clergymen to make specific ref-

[24] Report from Frévent, Mar. 6, 1791: A.N., D XXIX bis 21, dos. 229, no. 5; municipal minutes of Le Vigan, Feb. 20, 1791: D XXIX bis, dos. 228, no. 14; letter from the directory of Maine-et-Loire, Feb. 13, 1791: D XXIX bis 21, dos. 225, no. 20.

[25] Gonnet, 119, 138-44; Augustin Cariou, "La Constitution civile du clergé dans le département du Morbihan," *Mémoire de la Société d'histoire et d'archéologie de la Bretagne*, 45 (1965), 67-70.

[26] Donald Sutherland, *The Chouans: The Social Origins of Popular Counterrevolution in Upper Brittany* (Oxford, 1982), 239; letter from the curé of Thannenkirche, June 5, 1791: A.N., D XIX 86, dos. 677, no. 7; Pierre Pourcher, *L'épiscopat français et constitutionnel et le clergé de la Lozère durant la Révolution*, 3 vols. (Saint-Martin-de-Bourbaux, 1896-1900), 1:542-44; 2:163; Report from the district of Challans, Apr. 11, 1791: A.N., D XXIX bis 22, dos. 235, no. 3.

erences to parish sentiments in their speeches or letters explaining their oaths. The curé of Sainte-Honorine in Calvados declared that if he accepted the Civil Constitution, he would not only act against his conscience but would be regarded with scorn by local society. Two nearby parish priests in Verson described the vocal sentiment registered in the church against their taking anything but a restrictive oath and concluded that "they would prefer exposing themselves to all the rigors of the law rather than to lose the esteem of their parishioners." And one of the curés of Bayeux, greeted with a similar expression of opposition within his own church, was convinced to cede to the "will of his parishioners."[27]

Other priests, who had convinced themselves that the will of the majority was not necessarily the General Will, tried to maintain a double standard before parishioners and administrators. The curé and vicaire of Belfort, like the curé of Reviers in Calvados, vigorously maintained in letters to the district their intention of accepting the Civil Constitution. In the presence of their parishioners, however, they could take restrictive oaths only, "pour tranquilliser les esprits."[28] So, too, the curé of Heuilley near Dijon justified his restrictions with the need to assuage the population, widely convinced that the oath was part of a plot to "force them to change their religion."[29] But the reconciliation of divided loyalties, difficult enough in any age, is all but impossible in a time of revolution. And the curés' day-to-day existence was not in the patriot centers of the district or departmental capitals, but in the midst of their parishioners.

In a bitter, almost mocking, letter sent directly to Voidel—the deputy who had introduced the oath legislation in the National Assembly—one parish clergyman of the district of Brioude described the plight of the juring priests in a region where the population utterly rejected the Civil Constitution. Though he and many of his colleagues had initially backed the new law, its implementation had proved an unmitigated disaster in the department of Haute-Loire. Everywhere the population was treating the refractories as "saints and heroes," while the jurors were viewed as so many "animals, Judases, traitors, and tyrants." He and his fellow constitutionals no longer held the confidence of their flocks, and if something was not done soon, they would have no other choice but to retract: not because of the decision of the pope—which the clergyman never

---

[27] Sévestre, *Liste*, 340-43; and *L'acceptation*, 331.

[28] Letter from the *procureur* of the district of Belfort, Feb. 14, 1791: A.N., D XIX 86, dos. 677, no. 2; and Sévestre, *Liste*, 327.

[29] Entry for Jean-Baptiste Jobard, curé of Heuilley, in the manuscript catalog of the clergy of Côte-d'Or during the Revolution: B.M. Dijon, Ms. Reinert.

mentioned in his letter—but because of the verdict of the people.[30] "Vox populi, vox dei": perhaps under the circumstances, the old adage was not inappropriate.

Yet by no means was the people's verdict always opposed to the oath and the Civil Constitution. There were also numerous and widespread examples of popular pressures exerted on clergymen to accept the religious legislation. Already in April 1790, in the reverberations produced by the Dom Gerle affair, there had been evidence of the potential for lay scrutiny over the local clergy's politico-theological positions.[31] A number of priests and groups of priests, in their letters of adhesion to the National Assembly's deliberation of April 13, described their fears of losing the confidence of the people. The minority protest against that deliberation, signed by numerous clerical deputies, had generated a first rustling of anticlericalism among the laity and a distinct nervousness among the parish clergy of certain areas. Thus, a group of clergymen from the district of Lodève (Hérault) complained that they were, as a group, losing the people's confidence; that they were openly called "aristocrats," despite their loyalty to the Revolution. In order to clear the air of unfounded popular suspicions, they begged the National Assembly to publish the names of all curés known to have opposed the April 13 decision. In both Melle (Deux-Sèvres) and in Limoges ecclesiastics protested the unjust aspersions cast against their patriotism. The municipality of Saint-Denis-de-Pile (Gironde), whose curé had in fact signed the minority protest against the National Assembly, demanded the removal of their pastor for the crime of "lèse-nation" and his immediate replacement by a true patriot.[32]

There were several areas of France in which large segments of the population joined with the Jacobins and the Revolutionary administrators in their energetic support and encouragement of the oath. An earlier chapter bore witness to the enthusiasm and celebration accompanying the successful accomplishment of the curé's "civic duty" in numerous parishes. Frequently, a clergyman's failure to swear the oath incited widespread discontent and even violence. Perhaps nowhere was the pressure on potential non-jurors more intense than in the capital itself. A

[30] A.N., D XXIX bis 22, dos. 234, no. 18.

[31] See above, chp. 1, and below, chp. 9.

[32] Letter from 5 curés near Sallèles, July 2, 1790: A.N., C 119, dos. 353; letter from 13 curés and several nobles near Melle, May 18, 1790: C 115, dos. 314; letter from the municipality of Limoges: C 116, dos. 323; letter from the municipality of Saint-Denis: A.N., D XXIX bis 20, dos. 213, no. 25. Note also the similar case of 20 curés in Beaujolais, deliberating on Apr. 19: C 118, dos. 338.

veritable sea of people overwhelmed the great parish church of Saint-Sulpice on the Sunday designated for the oath ceremony, with some individuals even clambering up the pillars and clinging to the cornices. When Curé Mayneaud de Pancement refused the oath after a lengthy oration, there was a "frightful uproar" and a stampede toward the altar, with the curé making his escape only with the help of church officials and the national guard. Numerous cries of "the oath or the lamp post" seemed to prefigure the logic that would reign in the same neighborhood at the time of the September Massacres.[33] Curé Bossu, in the parish of Saint-Paul across the river, chose a much more prudent course: after unobtrusively leaving a note that he could not accept the oath, he packed up his belongings, paid off his bills, and left town in the middle of the night.[34] Paris was one of the few places in the kingdom where regulars and non-parish clergymen were also coerced into making an oath decision, even though the decree of November 27 in no way held them to such an act.[35]

But Paris was by no means an anomaly as far as popular threats and pressure on the parish clergy were concerned. In the district of Thionville (Moselle) portions of the laity considered an oath refusal to be a "shameful act," and one rural non-juror protested bitterly at being hooted and mocked by the local children because of his refractory stance. In a parish near Saint-Quentin (Aisne) the local national guard assembled with "pikes, antique muskets, and agricultural instruments" and formally excommunicated their non-juring curé for his act of "heresy." In the countryside of Ile-de-France curés who attempted to read the pastoral letters from the Old-Regime bishops might be shouted down by the population and forced to confine themselves to saying mass. Those who ventured explanations of their oaths which seemed in the least restrictive or conditional might be met with angry shouts and with threats of losing their salaries or of being driven out of town.[36] Indeed, the popular violence

[33] Paul Pisani, *L'Eglise de Paris et la Révolution*, 4 vols. (Paris, 1910-11), 1:197-98.

[34] Letter by the curé and comments by the local section, Jan. 4, 1791: A.N., D XXIX bis 20, dos. 216, no. 18.

[35] Bernard Plongeron, *Les réguliers de Paris devant le serment constitutionnel* (Paris, 1964), 76-82.

[36] Lesprand, 3:271; Louis-Victor Pécheur, *Annales du diocèse de Soissons. Volume 8. La Révolution* (Soissons, 1891), 440; minutes of the municipality of Villepreux (Seine-et-Oise), Feb. 21, 1791: A.N., D XXIX bis 21, dos. 227, no. 13; letter from the curé of Attilly (Seine-et-Marne), Jan. 24, 1791: A.D. Seine-et-Marne, L 283. A similar uproar broke out in Montebourg near Coutances when the curé tried to read the bishop's pastoral letter: Sévestre, *L'acceptation*, 327-28.

committed or insinuated against potential non-jurors could be equally as intimidating as that directed toward the constitutionals elsewhere in the kingdom. Guyon, curé of Beuveille near Longwy (Moselle), had prepared an "interpretive speech" describing the meaning—and the limits—of his oath, but as soon as he began he was prevented by the violence of the congregation from actually reading it. He would find courage to retract only a year and a half later. Three non-jurors near Laon were seized by a crowd of two to three hundred men and women who tried to force them to take the oath. They were bombarded with mud and rocks, dragged into a courtyard and beaten, and one was even shot in the arm. In Sarthe there was a series of attacks by crowds on churches, initially directed at ripping up and destroying pews belonging to local noblemen, but which seem also to have been related to popular pressure exerted on potential non-jurors. Such, at least, was the testimony of one clergyman who in 1795 would lament having been terrorized into taking the oath out of fear of the "blinded and misled" population.[37]

In a certain number of communities it was the parishioners themselves who took the initiative in demanding the replacement of their non-juring priests, even forcibly expelling them from the parish. This was all the more striking in that the National Assembly had formally decreed that all non-jurors should be kept at their posts until their replacements could be secured. Thus, after a district assembly in Marne failed to find a successor to the refractory curé of Somme-Vesle-et-Poix, the parishioners barred the door of the church and refused their curé entrance. The unfortunate clergyman found himself slapped in public by women, burned in effigy, and threatened with being thrown into a quarry. Here, in sharp contrast to the situation in the west, it was the refractories, not the jurors, who had to be protected by the national guard.[38] So, too, certain attempts at sacramental blackmail, which proved only too successful in some parts of the kingdom, would seem to have backfired elsewhere. If a curé in Ile-de-France refused to administer the Easter confession and penance to those who accepted the constitutional bishop, his parishioners might simply abandon him and demand a replacement.[39] One historian of the department of Doubs has, in fact, detected an interesting regional concentration of parishes in which citizens took the

[37] Lesprand, 3:240; Pécheur, 413; Giraud, 383-86.

[38] A. D. Millard, *Le clergé du diocèse de Châlons-sur-Marne. Première partie. Le serment* (Châlons-sur-Marne, 1903), 362.

[39] Fernand Bridoux, *Histoire religieuse du département de Seine-et-Marne pendant la Révolution*, 2 vols. (Melun, 1953), 1:89-90.

initiative of requesting such replacements.[40] Similar statistics for other departments, if they are attempted in the future, might be particularly revealing of zones of popular impatience and anger with non-jurors. But it is already clear that lay climates of opinion varied enormously from region to region.

Women and the Oath

In the various lay demonstrations for or against the Civil Constitution or the oath, certain segments of the population invariably stood out. On the constitutional side, the diverse embodiments of the patriotic clubs inevitably lent their presence and support, frequently seconded by municipal officers and the elites of the national guard. There is also a scattering of evidence of the energetic stance sometimes taken by students in the secondary schools of the kingdom. In the royal collège for noblemen's sons located in Pont-à-Mousson (Meurthe), where thirteen of nineteen teachers were said to have accepted the oath, the schoolboys were entirely won over by the refractories and openly insulted the juring clergymen until all class discipline became impossible. There was a similar split and a similar reaction in Amiens, where boys in the upper grades terrorized their constitutional professors with cries of "apostate" and "to the lamp post." By contrast, in Normandy the adolescents both in the schools and outside seem generally to have given their backing to the Civil Constitution. There were class riots against non-jurors in Avranches and Evreux, while in Coutances the schoolboys marched with a small band to meet their constitutional professor, presented him with a tricolored "national waistband," and led him in procession to his desk. In Cherbourg the "youth club" vowed never to participate in a refractory mass.[41] It is unfortunate that so little evidence has been preserved on the activities in 1791 of similar youth groups which undoubtedly persisted elsewhere in the kingdom.[42]

But there was another group whose vociferous presence in public demonstrations during the oath crisis frequently dominated above all

[40] Frank Tallett, "Religion and Revolution: the Rural Clergy and Parishioners of the Doubs, 1780-1797," Ph.D. Thesis, University of Reading, 1981, 219.

[41] Letter from the municipality of Pont-à-Mousson, Feb. 21, 1791: A.N., D XXIX bis 21, dos. 226, no. 45; Michel Destombes, *Le clergé du diocèse d'Amiens et le serment à la Constitution civile* (Amiens, 1971), 48-49; Sévestre, *L'acceptation*, 328-29.

[42] On youth clubs in Provence, see Maurice Agulhon, *Pénitents et Francs-Maçons de l'ancienne Provence* (Paris, 1968), 43-64.

others: the women. On occasion, this support was decidedly in favor of the juring position. The rough treatment offered by women to the non-juring curé of Somme-Vesle-et-Poix has already been mentioned. In a strongly constitutional area like Dauphiné, the ladies of Saint-Marcellin (Isère) could proudly attend Pentecostal services with their daughters, adorned in white dresses and tricolored ribbons, and then proceed to the town hall, where all would swear the same civic oath taken by the clergy.[43] The women's club of the Friends of Truth in Dijon, consisting primarily of the wives of Revolutionary officials, ostentatiously upheld the oath and made a point of supporting the constitutional priests in their religious services.[44]

Yet if one is to judge by the evidence preserved, the positions taken by the ladies of Dijon and of Saint-Marcellin were relatively atypical of women's reactions throughout most of the country. Particularly in those cases where threats or actual violence were involved, a distinct majority of Frenchwomen would seem to have rejected the oath and supported the refractories. According to Abbé Sévestre, "the voices of women dominated" in Normandy wherever riots against the oath erupted; and in many cases it was they alone who protested, sometimes supporting priests who had already opted against the Civil Constitution, sometimes pressuring those who were undecided or leaning toward a juring status. In Les Moûtiers parish women threatened to hang the municipal officials if they attempted to administer the oath; in Saint-Pierre-sur-Dives they ripped down notices of the oath decree, cheered the refractories, and made "scornful faces" at the official administering the legislation. In Balleroy they shouted and screamed in the church for half an hour when the curé's restrictive oath was rejected. In Vendes, as the curé and vicaire stood before the crucifix with hands raised, nearly all the women of the parish rose and swarmed into the choir, bringing a halt to the ceremony and escorting the clergymen out of the church.[45] In a number of towns of Rouergue and Languedoc, women were said to have adamantly opposed the publication of the oath decree and to have badly handled the town criers in charge of proclaiming it. Women and girls in Craponne (Haute-Loire) would refuse to permit the vicaire and four other priests to fulfill the National Assembly's requirements (the harried clergymen were obliged to wait until everyone had left before reading the oath texts

[43] A.N., C 116, dos. 318.
[44] Olwen Hufton, "Women in Revolution, 1789-96," *Past and Present*, no. 53 (1971), 99.
[45] Sévestre, *L'acceptation*, 328, 333; Sévestre, *Liste*, 339-40.

to a few "true [male] citizens"). When the curé of Sainte-Madeleine in Troyes held a special meeting to explain his opposition to the Civil Constitution, it was the women who formed the majority and who forcibly ejected a district director who made the mistake of defending the law in their presence.[46]

In these and in many other examples which might be given, the maneuvers of women seem particularly oriented toward violence. Yet other more pacific support was also offered to the refractories, particularly among women of the non-laboring classes. Individual women seem frequently to have played central roles in the distribution networks for circulating illicit refractory literature among rural priests and laity. Typical, perhaps, was Mademoiselle Faïdide of Ambert (Puy-de-Dôme), who was serving as the prime contact for one of the canons in Riom in his efforts to proselytize the refractory cause in March 1791. An unmarried woman caring for her ailing father, she revealed herself well educated and extremely pious and eager to serve the "Roman" church. Indeed, she soon proved even more *dévote* than the canon himself, who felt obliged to caution her in a letter to "moderate your zeal which is too external." (In the end, it was her very overzealousness which tipped her off to the authorities and led them both afoul of the law.)[47] In Strasbourg a peaceful procession of 250 women presented a petition to the departmental directory announcing their fears for the Catholic religion if the oath were enforced. Rebuffed by the administrators, they courageously took their case to the soldiers garrisoned in the local barracks. But the infantrymen, already won over to the patriot side, met them with derision and spent much of the following night serenading them beneath their windows with patriotic songs.[48] The case of Strasbourg was particularly revealing in that the petitioners seem to have represented a wide range of social backgrounds, from women of the aristocracy and the wife of the president of the department directory to relatively humble members of the common people. Along with women such as these, one should also take into account

---

[46] Bernard Combes de Patris, *Procès-verbaux des séances de la Société populaire de Rodez* (Rodez, 1912), 646; letter from the priests of Craponne, Mar. 10, 1791: A.N., D XXIX bis 21, dos. 230, no. 1; Arthur Prévost, *Histoire du diocèse de Troyes pendant la Révolution*, 3 vols. (Troyes, 1908-1909), 1:426-27.

[47] Correspondence of *ca.* Mar. 1791 confiscated by departmental authorities: A.N., D XXIX bis 22, dos. 233, nos. 2-3. Note also that anti-oath literature was said to be circulating in Ille-et Vilaine through the help of "femmes dévotes": letter from departmental directory, Feb. 4, 1791: A.N., D XIX 80, dos. 612, no. 3.

[48] Rodolph Reuss, *La Constitution civile du clergé et la crise religieuse en Alsace*, 2 vols. (Strasbourg, 1922), 1:37-38.

the contingents of nuns throughout the kingdom who generally proved far more determined to maintain their vows than their masculine counterparts, and whose convents frequently served as local rallying points for the refractory church through 1791 and 1792.[49]

To believe certain contemporaries, the battle of the oath among the laity often lined up as a veritable battle of the sexes, cutting across all social lines. There were numerous examples of local forces of womenfolk, sometimes with their children in tow, facing such male bastions of revolutionary leadership as the municipal councils or the Jacobin clubs. The Jacobins and other patriots, furious at the support given to the non-jurors by these "fanaticized" women, might taunt and insult them as they entered refractory masses.[50] Some patriots were convinced of the existence of a kind of conspiracy between the priests and their own wives which threatened not only the Revolution but their very authority as family patriarchs as well. The women of Ardèche were said to be "tormenting their husbands, children, and servants like so many devils." In the district of Brioude *dévote* wives, supposedly won over by the clergy in the confessional, were acting like "Trojan horses" to corrupt whole households. In Chartres and in Loir-et-Cher there were bitter complaints of the oath crisis' destroying domestic tranquillity and bringing several women to abandon their husbands altogether.[51] Occasionally, one senses a revival of the old fears on the part of the husbands, sometimes expressed under the Old Regime, of the sexual power and attraction of the clergy over their women.[52]

It is difficult to disentangle reality from suspicion and conjecture in many of these accounts, reported with few exceptions by the dominant male segment of the society. The descriptions abound with stereotyped commentaries on female nature, on the inherent "attachment plus vif et plus tendre à la religion," of the weaker sex; or depicting all such women

[49] See, for example, the decision of the department of Charente-Inférieure, June 18, 1791: A.N., F¹⁹ 413.

[50] See, for example, the problems described in Somme by the departmental directory, May 13, 1791: A.N., F¹⁹ 476; also as described by the municipality of Sainte-Foy, Feb. 13, 1791: A.N., D XXIX bis 21, dos. 224, no. 22.

[51] Charles Jolivet, *La Révolution en Ardèche* (Largentière, 1930), 261n; letter from a group of clergymen in the district of Brioude, Apr. 14, 1791: A.N., D XXIX bis 22, dos. 234, no. 18; letter from the mayor of Chartres, Apr. 26, 1791: A.N., F¹⁹ 424; letter from the department of Loir-et-Cher, Apr. 7, 1791: A.N., D XXIX bis 21, dos. 234, no. 2. See also the accusations against the vicaire of Worhmoudt (Nord): A.N., D XXIX bis 21, dos. 230, no. 29.

[52] Note, for example, the deliberations of the department of Loir-et-Cher, Feb. 12, 1791: A.N., D XXIX bis 21, dos. 224, no. 28. See also the author's *Priest and Parish*, 192.

as "béguines" or dévotes"—words which had taken on clear derogatory connotations.[53] Occasionally there were even biblical references: the priests were working "diabolically through women as the Serpent through Eve."[54] It was clearly convenient for the revolutionary leaders—and consistent with their paranoid view of events in general—to denigrate the opposition to their religious policies by reducing it to the overheated effusions of hysterical women manipulated by fanatical priests.[55]

But in point of fact, priests or no priests, women had for centuries played a central role in a whole range of riot activities under the Old Regime, from bread riots to tax uprisings. Given the common assumption of their inferior nature and irresponsible character, they had long been granted a kind of license in activities of this kind which translated as a *de facto* exemption from prosecution. In a certain sense, acts of collective violence pursued by women may have assumed a kind of moral authority, as the embodiment of the collective conscience of the community. Both men and women were well aware of this fact, and there is a scattering of evidence under the Old Regime that men sometimes instigated, even directed, the riots by women; and that on occasion they dressed themselves in feminine garb to join in the fray—whether through a sense for the rites of violence or as a simple disguise for protection from the law.[56] Significantly, in at least one of the larger revolts against the oath, in the town of Millau in Rouergue, there were accusations that the crowds included both women and a number of men dressed up like women.[57]

Thus, one should not overlook the possibility that a great many women viewed the Civil Constitution and the oath through a distinctly different optic than a great many men. For, as we have seen, when women took to the streets in the early weeks of 1791, it was not in support of any village consensus on the oath, but—in the great majority of cases, insofar as the evidence allows one to generalize—it was in support of a specific position *opposing* the oath. Much has been written of the women of Paris during the French Revolution, of the radical violence and terror of the

[53] Combes de Patris, 646; letter from the Jacobins of Craponne, Apr. 3, 1791: A.N., D XXIX bis 22, dos. 234, no. 6.

[54] Letter from an unknown clergyman in the district of Brioude, Apr. 1, 1791: A.N., D XXIX bis 22, dos. 237, no. 1.

[55] See Natalie Z. Davis, "Women on Top," in *Society and Culture in Sixteenth-Century France* (Stanford, 1975), 124-25.

[56] Ibid., 146-49; E.P. Thompson, "The Moral Economy of the English Crowd," *Past and Present*, 50 (1971), 115-17; also the author's *Priest and Parish*, 213.

[57] Combes de Patris, 641-42; and minutes of the municipal council of Millau, Jan. 26, 1791: A.N., D XXIX bis 21, dos. 226, no. 37.

sans-jupons and the *tricoteuses*.[58] But, in the end, it was perhaps the humble women of provincial and rural France, protesting with their whole beings this "change in religion" thrust upon them by the men in Paris, who delivered the single most influential political statement by any women of the revolutionary decade.

The Oath and Village Politics

Although the political life of the Old-Regime village is still poorly known, it seems clear that rivalries involving religion and the clergy were recurrent themes in the power alignments and confrontations of many rural communities. Throughout Provence, according to Maurice Agulhon, the political factions so characteristic of village life in the Midi were above all "religious or parareligious" in nature: "it was the Catholic religion, with its 'parties,' its orders, and its congregations, which traditionally allowed the Provençal communities to manifest a remarkable aptitude for internal divisions and municipal factions." The leadership of confraternities and processions, the control of education and of charitable services, the split between Jesuits and Jansenists: such were but a few of the issues which might polarize a village or reinforce pre-existent political groupings.[59] In such a state of affairs it was usually difficult if not impossible for the local parish clergyman to remain aloof, to avoid taking sides.

During the early months of the Revolution, many villages may have experienced mini-municipal revolutions not unlike those better-documented movements sweeping through most of the larger towns—power struggles based in part on ideological conviction but also on the reactivation of traditional factional rivalries.[60] And, inevitably, many of these power plays entailed attacks on the position of the local clergymen. A significant number of complaints would soon be voiced by curés and vicaires, protesting the new or renewed affronts by local officials against the clergy. Commonly, the ostensible justification was the secularization or partial secularization of institutions controlled in theory by the

[58] Hufton, 106-107; also Mary Jay Durham, "The Sans-Jupons' Crusade for Liberation during the French Revolution," Ph.D. dissertation, Washington University, 1972, 458-61.

[59] *La vie sociale en Provence au lendemain de la Révolution* (Paris, 1970), 229-33.

[60] On village politics see Peter M. Jones, "*La république au village* in the Southern Massif-Central," *The Historical Journal*, 23 (1980), 793-812. Many of the village "revolutions" may not have occurred through a forcible seizure of power, as in the towns, but through the more orderly shifts in the power balance permitted by the first municipal elections in early 1790.

Church—but which had already been the subject of untold disputes between priests and lay elites under the Old Regime. Thus, the curé of Terny in Aisne had a terrible run-in with his new municipal leaders over the right to appoint a schoolmaster, storming out of church in the middle of the mass rather than countenancing the participation of a teacher named by his opponents. Another pair of parish priests from Nord complained to the National Assembly of the growing pretensions of village officials not only to manipulate the choice of all schoolmasters but to dominate utterly the parish treasury. For the curé of Selles near Romorantin (Loir-et-Cher) the Revolution had expelled the "despotism of the aristocracy" only to see a new despotism arise in the form of the village churchwardens who were now lording it over the curés and making life miserable for them to an extent far greater than under the Old Regime. In Riverie, on the other hand, it was the municipal officers who attacked the "despotism" of their curé, "a man who could not get it through his head that the days of his dominance in the village were gone forever."[61]

In the Norman village of Bléville (Calvados) a storm arose over the efforts of the newly elected village officials—"ces espèces de curés manqués," as the clergyman scornfully called them—to install pews for themselves immediately in front of the altar. Ironically, it was the same desire for this symbol of parish status that had formerly caused so many suits between curés and local noblemen. In Saint-Mars-d'Outillé (Sarthe), Joubert, the new mayor, would even order the national guard into the church to prevent the Old-Regime mayor and his officials from occupying the front-row seats and to ensure his own place in this symbolic position of power. When the curé of Saint-Mars tried to order out the guard before beginning his mass, a lengthy "brouhaha" resulted as Joubert charged to the altar and tugged on the curé's cassock and as both sides and their supporters began shouting insults. After the mass, the mayor, like so many noblemen of days gone by, would bitterly complain that he had not properly been bestowed incense by the priest.[62]

Though it is often difficult to demonstrate, one suspects that many of

[61] Minutes of the municipality of Terny, Apr. 20, 1791: A.N., D XXIX bis 22, dos. 235, no. 14; letter from two curés near Tournay, 1791: A.N., D XIX 22, dos. 264; letter from the curé of Selles, Feb. 8, 1791: A.N., D XIX 83, dos. 660, no. 2; letters from the municipality of Riverie, Feb. 14 and Mar. 2, 1791: A.N., D XXIX bis 21, dos. 229, nos. 6-8.

[62] Sévestre, L'acceptation, 361; Sévestre, Problèmes religieux, 361-62; Giraud, 383-85. Note also the anger of the curé of Clamecy (Nièvre) over the national guard's appearance in the church during the oath ceremony: "indécent pour une cérémonie sainte et religieuse": A.D. Nièvre, series L "Cultes," district Clamecy (non-inventoried).

these clashes were essentially sequels to Old-Regime sagas of inter-elite rivalries, now simply adapted to the new system of Revolutionary symbols and rhetoric. In this sense, the oath ceremony, with all its inherent dramatic qualities, would provide an ideal stage on which to prolong the drama. This was especially true since the National Assembly had specifically assigned to the municipal governments the prime responsibility for observing and enforcing the oath.[63] On occasion, the officials might present a list of a curé's wrongdoings under the Old Regime in the same paragraph with vituperations against his lack of patriotism or his refusal of the oath. The standard litany of sins from the previous regime, which villagers had traditionally mobilized when attacking undesirable clergymen, was now joined ingenuously with accusations against the new sins of a new regime.[64] In the parish Louâtre (Aisne), for example, the municipality drew up a list of seventeen grievances against their curé. Beginning with attacks on his refusal to read the oath decree of February 1790, his scandalous remarks against the nation, and his snide comments on the incompetence of the new municipal government, the village leaders then turned to his supposed moral failings: he neglected to give the last rites to a dying woman, he carried on a suspect relationship with his housekeeper, he had launched a civil suit against some of his parishioners, and he took revenge on his enemies by requiring inordinate penitential tasks for absolution and by failing their children in the catechism class.[65] In the district of Melun near Paris another curé claimed that he was being harassed by the village council over the minor observations with which he had framed his oath and which, in his view, did not vitiate his acceptance of the Civil Constitution. According to the curé, the oath was merely being used as a pretext to revive the village's longstanding complaints over his fashion of conducting divine service: his abbreviation of parts of the mass, his refusal to sing vespers and to lead the liturgy of the local confraternity. Though the curé denied all fault, he also admitted that he would almost prefer being replaced, if only to be rid of his ungrateful parishioners.[66] Another lengthy enumeration of grievances was leveled by the inhabitants of Saint-Jean-d'Aubrigoux (Haute-Loire) against their parish priest. He was a tyrant oppressing the parish, frequenting the cabarets, beating his servants, vilifying his parishioners with

[63] *AP*, 21:80-81.

[64] See the author's *Priest and Parish*, 189-93.

[65] Deliberations of the departmental directory of Aisne, Oct. 19, 1790: A.N., D XXIX bis 21, dos. 228, nos. 15-16. Unfortunately, the curé's ultimate decision on the oath has not been determined.

[66] Letters by the curé and the municipal officers, Jan.-Feb. 1791: A.D. Seine-et-Marne, L 283.

indecent language, and overcharging everyone with the tithes. But, in a different twist, perhaps not untypical for the strongly refractory Massif-Central, the curé's greatest crime—in the eyes of the villagers—was not that he had refused but that he had *taken* the oath.[67]

In fact, there are numerous examples of village leaders blatantly using the oath as a lever for gaining the upper hand over a rival or undesirable curé: exploiting the oath legislation for a kind of blackmail of their own. The municipality of Villemer (Seine-et-Marne), for example, refused to accept their curé's perfectly valid oath unless he first got rid of his servant woman. (The department soon overturned the decision, reminding the villagers that a curé "is not an angel, but a man, and you must patiently put up with his weaknesses as our religion requires us to do.")[68] In Mondeville (in Seine-et-Oise), the parish attempted to refuse even to allow the curé to take his oath, hoping thus to rid themselves of "un mauvais caractère de curé." In Juliénas (Rhône-et-Loire), the mayor doctored the records, attempting to insert a restriction on a perfectly valid oath in order to have the parish priest dispossessed; in Itteville (Seine-et-Oise), the mayor refused to allow his curé to remove a restriction, hoping thus to be rid of his longstanding enemy.[69] One suspects similar motives on the part of the municipal officers of Champdeuil (Seine-et-Marne) who interrupted the Sunday service to accuse the curé of only pretending to take a valid oath, while subtly hiding his true sentiments. The priest, furious at this commentary in the middle of his liturgy, completed the mass and then turned and ostentatiously enunciated a simple oath directly in the face of the officers: on the stage of the altar, before the eyes of the assembled village.[70] How many clergymen took— or refused—their oaths out of sheer spite, more concerned with scoring points against their rivals than with any of the loftier problems of theology and national politics?

Symbiosis

The range of examples in the present chapter succeeds in further underlining the considerable complexity of the oath of 1791 as a community

[67] Gonnet, 137-38.
[68] Letter from the district of Nemours to the municipality of Villemer, Feb. 14, 1791: A.D. Seine-et-Marne, L 286.
[69] Minutes of the municipality of Mondeville, Feb. 6, 1791: A.N., D XIX 82, dos. 646, no. 12; letter from the curé of Juliénas, n.d.: *ibid.*, dos. 649, no. 10; letter from the curé of Itteville, n.d.: D XIX 81, dos. 628, no. 13.
[70] Minutes of the municipality of Champdeuil, Jan. 23, 1791: A.D. Seine-et-Marne, L 282.

experience. By their training, by their socioeconomic background, by the very ideology of their age, parish clergymen had been prepared for an elite position of local leadership, aloof and independent from the laity. Yet, immersed as they were in secular society, few could escape being influenced in various degrees by the very flock which they sought to lead; few could escape—in the words of one twentieth-century clerical scholar—"that sociological law which models the curé after the image of his parishioners."[71] The modeling in question might well occur through the direct effects of coercion and intimidation. But it could also be effected through more subtle processes, through the shared experiences and perceptions of people inhabiting the same ecological niche in the kingdom— patterns of experiences which remain to be explored in the following chapters. The symbiotic interaction between clergy and laity during the crisis of the oath was vaguely sensed by some of the departmental administrators. Those of Hérault, for example, describing the broad unrest engendered by the crisis, blamed it in part on the clergy, who "fanaticized" the inhabitants and threatened to cease all sacerdotal services if the oath were enforced. But, in the same report, they also blamed the country-people themselves, who were forcing their priests to refuse the oath. Clergymen became non-jurors "either to avoid hopelessly losing the confidence of their parishioners, or in response to the horrible threats which are directed against them if they should obey [the decree of the National Assembly]."[72]

As with any symbiotic relationship of this kind, the precise weight to be given to the two interacting elements in the parish equation—the parish clergy and the laity—would be difficult, if not impossible, to extract. It seems clear that one or the other of the two forces could have been more or less operative in different parishes and in different regions. A model of interaction would undoubtedly have to leave room for a variety of contingencies: that the village priest might strongly affirm or strongly reject the oath, or that he might be deeply torn and undecided; that the parishioners themselves might be violently for, violently against, or totally indifferent to, the Civil Constitution; or, indeed, that they might be deeply divided by sex or economic class or status group. One may also suspect that the nature of the relationship would depend on the relative prestige or lack thereof of individual clergymen and, perhaps, of clergymen in general. While almost any permutation or combination of these

---

[71] Anonymous, "Le serment de 1791 dans l'Ardèche," *Semaine religieuse du diocèse de Viviers*, 83 (1964), 590.

[72] Report by the departmental directors of Hérault, Jan. 28, 1791: A.N., D XIX 81, dos. 627.

factors might appear in specific villages, a particular goal of the following chapters will be to identify regional configurations that might enable us better to understand the kingdom-wide patterns of oath-taking. In fact, a few initial clues can perhaps be culled from the examples presented above, illustrating popular pressures on priests to accept or reject the oath. While it is not strictly correct to speak of a "sample" of such cases, most are derived from a systematic reading of a large series of letters and reports received by the National Assembly from throughout the kingdom in the winter and spring of 1791.[73] With few exceptions, those parishes whose inhabitants pushed their priests to reject the oath were in districts whose clergy would be overwhelmingly refractory; those where coercion was used in favor of the oath were in districts which were soon to emerge as strongly constitutional.[74] One might thus suggest the tentative hypothesis that areas in which ecclesiastics opted massively in one way or the other were usually associated with vigorous popular positions. It is also noteworthy that most of the examples found of lay elites attacking the power and position of the parish clergy in the early Revolution occurred in zones of strong oath-taking.[75] On the contrary, the instances of women playing an energetic role in opposing the oath seemed to occur almost everywhere, in juring and refractory regions alike.

In the following chapters it will be necessary to change the focus of inquiry from clerical reactions to lay reactions. To do so, inevitably, will be to render the whole problem of causation vastly more complicated and problematic. If it has been possible to circumscribe the French clergy and to sort through the question of motivation in a relatively satisfactory fashion, the motives of the French population as a whole present us with a series of all but insurmountable difficulties. Not only was the lay society immensely larger than the ecclesiastical society, not only was it vastly more complex and heterogeneous, but the documents for assessing that society in a systematic manner are far more sparse and less reliable. And yet neither can the issue be brushed aside.

[73] See above, note 2.

[74] I have included here all those case examples presented in the second section of the present chapter. They have been taken from a wide range of sources, most of which have been examined in the series of the A.N., as described in note 2. Among districts with evidence of popular pressure against the oath, 13 of 16 would have oath rates under 40 percent; the mean for these districts was 29 percent and the median was 23.5 percent oath-takers. Among districts with evidence of pressure for the oath, 8 of 11 would have oath rates over 60 percent; the mean was 63 percent and the median 65 percent oath-takers.

[75] Ten of 13 were in areas of strong oath-taking.

EIGHT

The Oath as a Referendum

The Secular Context of the Oath

B ETWEEN the Great Fear of 1789 and the news of the fall of the
monarchy in August 1792, the ceremony of the ecclesiastical oath
was often the single most dramatic event in the life of a French
community. Yet one must take care not to lose sight of the broader
political climate and social context in which the oath crisis presented
itself to the average Frenchman. The second winter of the Revolution
brought with it a train of new institutions and procedures, thrusting
themselves into the lives of citizens everywhere with a dogged efficiency
rarely seen under the Old Regime. At the head of the list, no doubt,
were the various laws associated with the Church reorganization itself.
Signed into law many months earlier, these measures, with their potentially unsettling effects, were only just being implemented in late 1790
and early 1791. Thus, peasants and townsmen would find themselves
grappling with the dilemma of the oath just as their local chapters and
religious houses were being boarded up or sold. And in most departments
the calendar for the auctioning of Church property closely coincided with
the oath-taking crisis: beginning in early to mid-January and reaching a
peak of sales in March or April 1791.[1] Even more traumatic was the
threat of an impending suppression and consolidation of rural parishes,
a measure blocked up until then by the Old-Regime bishops, but already
widely discussed by the patriot administrators.[2]

Yet January 1791 also ushered in a number of major non-ecclesiastical
laws passed during the previous months but scheduled to take effect only
at the beginning of the new year. The most important of these concerned

[1] See, for example, Joseph Lacouture, *La politique religieuse de la Révolution* (Paris, 1940), 36-
37; Pierre de la Gorce, *L'histoire religieuse de la Révolution française*, 5 vols. (Paris, 1909-23),
1:185; Philippe Sagnac, *La législation civile de la Révolution* (Paris, 1898), 182; Maurice Giraud,
Essai sur l'histoire religieuse de la Sarthe de 1789 à l'an IV (Paris, 1920), 189; Emile Sévestre, *Les
problèmes religieux de la Révolution et de l'Empire en Normandie, 1787-1815*, 2 vols. (Paris, 1924),
1:125-26; Charles Aimond, *Histoire religieuse de la Révolution dans le département de la Meuse et
le diocèse de Verdun (1789-1802)* (Paris, 1949), 84-85. On the dates of Church land auctions, see,
for example, Paul Moulin, *Département des Bouches-du-Rhône. Documents relatifs à la vente des
biens nationaux dans le district de Sens*, 2 vols. (Auxerre, 1912-13), 2:lxxi-lxxxiii.

[2] See above, chp. 1.

the reformulation of the tax laws which the National Assembly had decided to institute. As we shall soon discover, certain elements of society stood to be deeply affected by the new fiscal machinery being set in motion at the very moment when priest and parish were confronting the oath. More intangible, but perceptible nevertheless, was the subtle change of mood touching increasing segments of the French population in the last weeks of 1790. The initial events of the Revolution—from the electoral assemblies and the composition of the cahiers through the night of August 4—had stimulated an extraordinary enthusiasm, a near millenarian optimism at all levels of society. But nearly a year and a half had transpired since those heady days of the summer of 1789. The period of passage, betwixt and between the old and the new, where each man might hope for his private utopia—such days were rapidly coming to a close.[3] The outlines of the "new" regime created by the patriots in Paris were now well delineated for everyone to see. And, inevitably, for a great many citizens that regime fell far short of expectations. Even before the oath crisis broke, the honeymoon mood had largely waned.

Indeed, for one noted historian, Paul Bois, clerical responses to the oath are impossible to understand outside the immediate secular context in which they were manifested. In his classic study of the *Paysans de l'Ouest*, Bois presents an argument similar in certain respects to that developed in the previous chapter. Apart from a few particularly strong personalities among the parish clergy who reached their decisions in a genuinely independent fashion—and who may have constituted, according to Bois, some 20 percent of all clergymen—ecclesiastical reactions essentially mirrored the local attitudes and mind-set of the population toward the Revolution in general as it was perceived in early 1791. But what is more—and this was actually a second proposition—the "prise de conscience" of the rural masses registered by the oath was only indirectly related to the specific problems of the clergy and religion. Religious opinion, as described by Bois, was a kind of superstructure, a convenient ideology which buttressed choices initially made for social, economic, or political reasons. The oath, then, could be construed as a plebiscite, a popular referendum on the non-religious innovations of the Revolution as a whole.[4]

Bois's suggestions are intriguing, and obviously they must be placed

---

[3] Victor Turner's analysis of the psychology of rites of transition seems to apply particularly well to the early French Revolution: see, especially, *The Ritual Process: Structure and Anti-Structure* (Chicago, 1969).

[4] Paul Bois, *Paysans de l'Ouest*, abr. ed. (Paris, 1971), esp. 292-94.

at the head of our agenda for the investigation of popular responses to the oath. But, unfortunately, the difficulties of exploring and testing such propositions are considerable. The twelve months prior to the oath saw neither the composition of *cahiers de doléances* nor the holding of general elections, events which might have been used for the probing of popular opinion. One would need to know a great deal more about the regional history of the Revolution in the year or so prior to the oath. Yet by comparison with works on the origins of the Revolution or the period of the Convention, studies devoted to the so-called "quiet year" of 1790 are relatively meager, especially in regard to provincial history.

The approach of the present chapter must necessarily be somewhat indirect and tentative. First, we will attempt to examine one aspect of regional attitudes toward the Revolution through an overview of the patterns of collective violence during the twelve months prior to January 1791. For it is clear that throughout 1790 many Frenchmen were actively voting with their feet, that the period was anything but the "année heureuse" frequently portrayed in the historical literature.[5] Second, we will explore several recent hypotheses related to the socioeconomic and political analysis of the Old Regime, hypotheses which aim primarily at explaining popular counterrevolutionary movements but which must be considered here in our assessment of the oath as a referendum. If we can never enter into the inner sentiments of townsmen and countrypeople as they witnessed and participated in the oath proceedings, we can at least hope to isolate the regions where popular unrest was particularly prominent and assess the extent to which such a geography does or does not correspond to the regional patterns of oath-taking.

Popular Violence in 1790

If the year and a half after October 1789 marked a relative hiatus in the popular violence of the French capital, many of the provinces were experiencing repeated outbreaks of rioting, approaching the intensity of the Great Fear. The origins of these uprisings are not simple to isolate. Like the great waves of peasant protest in the seventeenth century, those of 1790 were commonly complex and multi-sided. But, based on a systematic reading of the printed documents in the *Archives parlementaires* and on a variety of national and local studies, certain preliminary conclusions

[5] On the reinterpretation of the year 1790, see Michel Vovelle, *La chute de la monarchie, 1787-1792* (Paris, 1972), 138-39; and Samuel Scott, "The Problem of Law and Order during 1790, the 'Peaceful' Year of the French Revolution," *AHR*, 80 (1975), 859-88.

would seem possible.[6] An obvious underlying cause of the violence was the very breakdown in authority engendered by the collapse of the Old-Regime administrative structures and the consequent interregnum, lasting a period of several months, before the institutions of the new regime could be put into operation.[7] Yet, beyond this temporary power vacuum, there were apparently three fundamental sources of popular violence: the problem of grain provisioning, the transformation of the seigneurial system, and the reforms of the tax structures. Of the grain riots there is relatively little to be said here. In the first place, uprisings of this kind, compelled by the primary logic of finding enough to eat for oneself and one's family, would appear to have occurred in virtually every corner of the kingdom. There seems little hope of identifying regional concentrations of such activities that might subsequently be compared with the geography of the oath. In the second place, such riots represented a generalization of a type of protest, the "subsistence" riot, already widely experienced under the Old Regime. In any case, anxieties caused by the threat of famine were probably subsiding—at least in the rural areas—after the summer of 1790 and the relatively ample harvest which that year provided.[8] But the other two focuses of protest—the seigneurial system and the tax structures—will require a more careful scrutiny.

For a great many peasants, the National Assembly's policies toward the seigneurial system were probably the source of an immense disappointment and disenchantment. The flood of rural violence in the spring and summer of 1789 had been largely directed against the nobles, the noble estates, and their agents.[9] This rural crisis had been partly responsible for the night of August 4 and the National Assembly's decrees

[6] Two principal general sources have been used: *AP*, vols. 11-21, in which I have systematically taken note of all entries indexed under the key word "troubles"; and A. V. Ado, *Krest'yanskoe dvizheniye vo Frantsii vo vremia velikoi burzhuaznoi revolyutsii kontsa XVIII veka* (The Peasant Movement in France during the Great Bourgeois Revolution at the End of the Eighteenth Century) (Moscow, 1971), table printed on pp. 415-35. Other relevant studies and manuscript sources used will be mentioned below in the notes.

[7] Henri Sée, "Les troubles agraires en Haute-Bretagne (1790 et 1791)," *Bulletin d'histoire économique de la Révolution* (1920-1921), 254-56; and Jean Boutier, "Jacqueries en pays croquant. Les révoltes paysannes en Aquitaine (décembre 1789-mars 1790)," *Annales E.S.C.*, 34 (1979), 766-68.

[8] George Rudé, *The Crowd in the French Revolution* (Oxford, 1959), 80-81; M. Bruneau, *Les débuts de la Révolution dans les départements du Cher et de l'Indre* (Paris, 1902), 132-33; Pierre-Jean-Baptiste Delon, *La Révolution en Lozère* (Mende, 1922), 50. More generally, on the Old Regime, see Steven L. Kaplan, *The Famine Plot Persuasion in Eighteenth-Century France* (Philadelphia, 1982).

[9] Georges Lefebvre, *La Grande Peur de 1789* (Paris, 1932). Also Vovelle, 122-31.

ostensibly abolishing "the feudal system." Yet, as the details of these grand pronouncements were worked out during the following weeks, it became clear that many of the seigneurial dues were to be treated as forms of property which could be collected indefinitely until they were redeemed in cash by the peasantry: a capital outlay which would be all but prohibitive for the majority of the population. Even many of the hated "personal" and honorific rights would have to be "purchased" if the lord could prove that they had been collected during the previous forty years. To make matters worse, no procedure was created to force a lord to sell his "property" if he did not so desire. For the present, the seigneurs could continue collecting most of their dues as under the Old Regime.[10] By the end of the year, a number of antiseigneurial riots and uprisings had broken out and would continue sporadically through 1790, recurring repeatedly until the summer of 1792.

If Bois were correct, one might expect these antiseigneurial sentiments to have been powerful ingredients in raising hostilities against the National Assembly and influencing, in consequence, the rejection of the "plebiscite" of the oath. The problem is to compare the actual geography of the antiseigneurial riots of 1790 with the regional patterns of oath-taking. Though it was once thought that attacks of this kind broke out "everywhere" in the year before the oath,[11] the research of the Soviet historian A. V. Ado reveals that their incidence was relatively restricted.[12] (See Figure J.) If one focuses only on those instances touching more than a single community, one finds some 38 districts in 17 departments—out of a total of well over 500 districts—known to have been touched by acts of collective violence which were predominantly antiseigneurial in nature.[13] To be sure, the centers of the two largest and most violent sectors of such protest, Brittany and Aquitaine, were located in regions where

[10] Jacques Godechot, *Les institutions de la France sous la Révolution et l'Empire*, 2nd ed. (Paris, 1968), 192-95.

[11] Sagnac, 126.

[12] Cited above.

[13] The districts concerned were as follows: Vervins (Aisne); Mirepoix (Ariège); Rodez, Sauveterre (Aveyron); Murat (Cantal); Saint-Jean-d'Angély, Saintes (Charente-Inférieure); Brive, Tulle, Uzerche (Corrèze); Belvès, Bergerac, Montignac, Périgueux, Sarlat (Dordogne); Bain, Redon, Montfort (Ille-et-Vilaine); Châteaubriant, Nantes (Loire-Inférieure); Montargis (Loiret); Cahors, Figeac, Gourdon, Lauzerte, Saint-Céré (Lot); Agen, Lauzun, Monflanquin, Valence, Villeneuve-d'Agen (Lot-et-Garonne); Ploërmel, Rochefort (Morbihan); Charolles (Saône-et-Loire); Nemours (Seine-et-Marne); Albi (Tarn); Joigny, Sens (Yonne). The list is based on the *AP*, Ado, and various other monographs. Inevitably, the list must remain provisional and may well be incomplete.

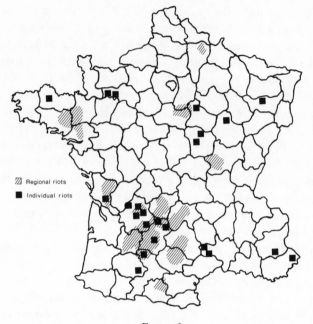

FIGURE J
Incidence of Antiseigneurial Riots, 1790.

the populations would soon strongly support the refractory clergy. Yet the correspondence is far from perfect. Though they were centered in the future refractory zones of Quercy and Rouergue, the insurrections of the southwest overlapped amply into the strongly constitutional territories of Agenais and Périgord. Rioting in the Gâtinais region south of Paris and in the department of Charente occurred in zones which would support the Civil Constitution as strongly as any groups in the kingdom. Of the 38 districts in which widespread violence of this kind is known to have taken place, the proportion of oath-taking varied between 0 (Redon) and 98 percent (Nemours and Montargis). Overall, 51 percent of the clergy in these districts accepted the oath—only 3 or 4 percentage points below the national average.[14] In sum, if the oath was a plebiscite

[14] The average was 51.3 percent oath-takers in the 38 districts, compared to about 55 percent in the kingdom generally. Unfortunately, the printed sources usually do not permit parish-by-parish statistics. In the department of Lot, a total of 62 parishes are specifically named by Eugène Sol as being the sites of violent uprisings in 1790. In the 51 of these parishes for which oath data are available, 18 (35 percent) of the curés would be ranked as jurors in 1791. This is

on the Revolution, it seems to have been little related before 1791 to the population's outwardly manifested sentiments toward the National Assembly's policies on the seigneurial system. Even in those zones where antiseigneurial riots did coincide with massive refusals of the oath, it is difficult to find any direct evidence that the two were linked in the minds of the countrypeople. The uprisings seem to have taken place, first, in regions not previously inoculated by the trauma of violence during 1789; and, second—and above all—in areas where the seigneurial dues were the most onerous and where they were paid in kind rather than in moneyed rents.[15] Significantly, it was only *after* the crisis of the oath had begun, during the first six months of 1791, that a certain correspondence could be detected between opposition to the Civil Constitution and antiseigneurial violence. The oath-taking rate in the twenty-two districts experiencing riots during this period was only 40 percent.[16]

But the movements against Revolutionary tax policies present a somewhat different picture. In Lower Brittany, at least, there seems to be evidence of a direct fusion between opposition to the oath and opposition to taxes. From the moment the decree of November 27 arrived in the department of Morbihan in early 1791, the countryside reverberated with open manifestations of popular outrage. Several municipalities refused even to consider the law, returning it indignantly to the district authorities; others sent petitions or even marched on the department capital of Vannes to deliver their demands. On February 9 rumors arose of an attempt on the life of the Old-Regime bishop, and thousands of peasants from throughout the region descended on Vannes, there to clash violently with national guardsmen.[17] Yet it is also clear that the anger of the rural Vannetais must be placed in the context of the long months of opposition aroused by various non-ecclesiastical issues, of which the foremost was probably the tax question. From the beginning of January, a series of local meetings had been held, drawing up petitions concerning the taxes

---

slightly less than the 40 percent of curé oath-takers in the department as a whole, but the difference is probably too small to be significant: Sol, *La Révolution en Quercy*, 4 vols. (Paris, 1932), 1:232-50, for peasant uprisings; and *Le clergé du Lot et le serment exigé des fonctionnaires publics ecclésiastiques* (Paris, 1927), 153-234, for the oath.

[15] Boutier, 766; Albert Soboul, "A propos d'une thèse récente sur le mouvement paysan dans la Révolution française," *AHRF*, 45 (1973), 90-91.

[16] Thus, if there was a causal relation in 1791, perhaps it worked in the opposite direction.

[17] Joseph-Marie Le Mené, *Histoire du diocèse de Vannes*, 2 vols. (Vannes, 1888-89), 2:260-62; J. Le Falher, *Le royaume de Bignan (1789-1805)* (Hennebont, 1913), 72-73; T.J.A. Le Goff, *Vannes and Its Region* (Oxford, 1981), 348; Yves Moizo, "La Contre-Révolution dans le district de La Roche-Bernard (1789-1793)," *thèse de maîtrise*, Université de Rennes II, 1978, 74-76.

which were found to have risen substantially under the new regime, as well as the new stamp duty and the problems of poor relief. For the mayor of Saint-Jean-Brévelay, writing in late 1790, it was the tax increase which had already "pushed local discontent to its limits." In the eyes of the department directors, the root of all the unrest was to be found in a combination of "religion and taxes."[18]

Yet it is by no means certain that the scenario of Lower Brittany was commonly replayed elsewhere in the kingdom. Though movements of tax protest were probably widespread in 1790, no one has yet attempted to determine their geography, as Ado has done for movements opposed to seigneurial rights. Clearly, much of the Revolution's tax problem arose from the National Assembly's awkward attempts to provide for an orderly transition, from its insistence on maintaining the Old-Regime tax and tithing systems throughout 1790, until new local administrations could be organized and new fiscal arrangements implemented. To be sure, the former privileged classes were soon incorporated into the tax base through a new set of tax rolls requiring them to assume a respectable share of the fiscal burden. And, nevertheless, such generally cautious and conservative policies seemed little suited to the highly charged political atmosphere and the revolutionary psychology of a peasantry impatient for immediate changes.

In examining the widespread reactions to the deputies' policies, we need to distinguish the different categories of taxes and their differential effects on various social groups. Under the Old Regime, few institutions had been more generally decried than the *gabelle*, the *aides*, and the other indirect taxes. Thus, the National Assembly's decision to maintain these taxes until January 1791 ignited a veritable fury of complaints. To rely on a survey by Marcel Marion, protests ranging from passive resistance to armed revolts broke out in numerous areas of the kingdom: from Picardy, Artois, and Normandy in the north and west, through the Paris Basin, the Loire Valley, the lower Rhône Valley and Roussillon in the extreme south. Thus, insofar as can presently be determined, there was no correlation between anger over the *gabelle* and anger over the Civil Constitution. Indeed, the most vigorous tax reactions apparently transpired in Picardy and the Parisian Basin, both of which tended massively to approve the oath of 1791. In any case, much of the animosity seems to have dissipated by the end of the year, once it became evident that

[18] Le Goff, 350; Le Falher, 116; department of Morbihan to the Ecclesiastical Committee, Jan. 29, 1791: A.N., D XIX 80, dos. 612, no. 9.

the deputies in Paris genuinely intended to suppress the indirect taxes—and once it became evident, even earlier, that a generalized refusal was in progress against which the government could do little or nothing.[19]

Ultimately, much the same might be said of both the tithes and the royal direct taxes. Though the night of August 4 had initially abolished the ecclesiastical taxes, the declaration of August 11, 1789 temporarily reinstated them until later unspecified arrangements could be made. It was only on April 20, 1790, that a definitive procedure was set up for liquidating the tithes, one which required their continued payment through the end of 1790. As in the case of the ex-*gabelle*, the deputies in Paris were bombarded with complaints concerning peasants who refused the tithes outright or who tried to reduce their payments or convert them to fixed sums of money—complaints which continued even after the Constituent threatened tough legal action against the recalcitrant. Most of the antiseigneurial protests—in Brittany and Aquitaine, as in Gâtinais and Aunis-Saintonge—were apparently associated with attacks of varying magnitude on the tithes. But incidents seem to have arisen in virtually every province—in Flanders, Picardy, Champagne, Lorraine, the Paris Basin, Nivernais, Gascony, and Languedoc, for example.[20]

As for the royal taxes—the *taille, capitation*, and *vingtième*—the widespread rumor that the Revolution had abolished all such payments rendered their collection virtually impossible in many provinces. Collection was hindered even further by the Constituent's decision that assessments be made in the village where property was located rather than in the village where the property's owner resided. Widespread chaos arose as the newly elected municipalities struggled to understand and execute the decrees, and as they soon found themselves the targets of harassment by a disappointed population.[21]

But if the changeover on January 1, 1791, resolved most of the conflicts over the indirect taxes, the unhappiness of certain taxpayers over the *taille* and the tithes would long persist. Perhaps the most serious and potentially dangerous problem was the outright perpetuation of these two taxes for one important segment of the French peasantry: the tenant

[19] R. B. Rose, "Tax Revolt and Popular Organization in Picardy, 1789-1791," *Past and Present*, 43 (1969), 92-93, 99-100; Marcel Marion, "Le recouvrement des impôts en 1790," *RH*, 121 (1916), 33-34, 39; R. Schnerb, *Les contributions directes à l'époque de la Révolution dans le Puy-de-Dôme* (Paris, 1933), 92-94.

[20] Henri Marion, *La dîme ecclésiastique en France au XVIIIe siècle et sa suppression* (Bordeaux, 1912), 275-86.

[21] M. Marion, 4, 6-8, 13-15; Schnerb, 78-83.

farmers. The core of the difficulty was the National Assembly's law of December 1-10, 1790, which permitted landlords to augment their tenants' rents in an amount equal to the abolished *taille* and tithes. Lease values, it was argued, had originally been determined with the assumption that both taxes would be paid by the leaseholder. Now that the owner was to be given the direct responsibility of discharging the *impôts fonciers*, it was only just that he pass along the former charge to his tenants. Yet, to many tenants, it appeared for all the world that the landlords had simply seized control of the Old Regime taxes, creating a "dîme bourgeoise" and a "taille bourgeoise," as they would still be called in the nineteenth century. A similar procedure would also be followed in the summer of 1792, when the seigneurial dues were largely abolished. Once again, the leaseholders found their rents hiked up in proportion to the suppressed dues. Thus, wherever tenant farmers formed a large segment of the rural population, local opinion might shift sharply against the Revolution and all its policies.[22]

Such observations are important because most of the new tax laws, including those concerned with tenant farmers, were being implemented at precisely the moment when priest and parish were confronting the oath. Thus, in the region of Vannes, numerous peasants worked the land under the system of *domaine congéable*, a form of precarious tenure similar in many respects to that of the long-term leaseholder. In point of fact, it was the dissatisfaction of these Breton farmers over this aspect of the new tax system—as well as the National Assembly's failure to abolish the *domaine congéable* altogether—which particularly envenomed the political atmosphere in early 1791, and helped incite the unusually violent reaction in much of Lower Brittany to the Civil Constitution.[23]

Unfortunately, the lengthy research necessary for the analysis of landholding patterns and their effects on mentality have never been attempted in most other regions of France. The situation in southern Anjou would seem similar in many respects to that in Brittany. Here a population dominated by small leaseholders would react with determined opposition to the new tax system during a period when their hostility toward the

[22] Here, I follow the arguments of Donald Sutherland and T.J.A. Le Goff: Sutherland, *The Chouans* (Oxford, 1982), 142-43; Le Goff and Sutherland, "The Social Origins of Counter-Revolution in Western France," *Past and Present*, no. 99 (May 1983), 75. See also H. Marion, 273-74; Albert Soboul, "Survivances 'féodales' dans la société rurale française au XIXe siècle," *Annales E.S.C.*, 23 (1968), 965-86; Claude Petitfrère, "Paysannerie et militantisme politique en Anjou au début de la Révolution," *Annales de Bretagne*, 89 (1982), 181-82.

[23] Sutherland, esp. 138-43, 308-310; Le Goff and Sutherland, 65-87.

Civil Constitution was growing ever more embittered.[24] A similar correspondence between tax opposition and religious protest in a tenant-farming region may well have been operative in Gascony and the Landes of southwestern France—though, here, the precise articulation of popular opinion remains to be worked out. In the southeastern sector of France, Michel Vovelle would stipulate a rough correlation between peasant ownership and "revolutionary conformity" in Upper Provence—a region where the oath would also be generally accepted by the clergy and the lay population. In Lower Provence, by contrast, the predominance of elite landlords in rural areas was associated with widespread confrontations between revolutionaries and counterrevolutionaries and with relatively greater opposition to the Civil Constitution.[25]

Nevertheless, a correspondence of this kind was not consistently present in all parts of the kingdom. In Aunis-Saintonge, the important tenant-farming class seems massively to have supported the Civil Constitution, while the peasants of Quercy, owning 50 percent of all the land, appear generally to have opposed it. And, even within the west, there were zones of greater peasant proprietorship, like the eastern Côtes-du-Nord, which refused the oath and embraced the counterrevolution; and others, like the eastern Sarthe, where tenant-farming peasants never openly rejected the Revolution and apparently backed the oath.[26] Thus, while the animosities engendered by taxes may sometimes have reinforced popular religious discontent, the relationship does not seem to have operated everywhere in the same manner.

Town and Country Interaction

The apparent link between the presence of tenant farmers and options on the oath is interesting and suggestive. If the oath were indeed a referendum, the popular discontent revealed by a refractory stance might be examined as a function not only of particular Revolutionary policies, but also of the regional socioeconomic conditions within which those policies were implemented. For Paul Bois in his study of Sarthe, the key

[24] Petitfrère, 180-82; Charles Tilly, *The Vendée* (Cambridge, Mass., 1964), 119-32.

[25] Antoine Richard, "Les troubles agraires des Landes en 1791 et 1792," *AHRF*, 4 (1927), 564-77; Michel Vovelle, "Formes de politisation de la société rurale en Provence sous la Révolution française: entre jacobinisme et contre-révolution au village," *Annales de Bretagne*, 89 (1982), 187.

[26] Georges Frêche, *Toulouse et la région Midi-Pyrénées au siècle des Lumières* (Toulouse, 1974), 188-89; Léon Dubreuil, *La vente des biens nationaux dans le département des Côtes-du-Nord* (Paris, 1912), 7-27; Bois, 148-49. Sutherland and Le Goff have themselves noted that not all of the west fits the same landholding pattern: article cited, p. 66.

to the regional patterns of both the refractory clergy and the later Chouannerie was to be found, above all, in the nature of the interaction between
the major towns and the surrounding rural society. Though his full
explanation is carefully nuanced, it could ultimately be reduced to the
analysis of the extent to which the countryside was integrated into the
urban economic system. Those rural areas least closely tied to the towns
economically were the most likely to show recalcitrance to the political
positions of the urban patriots; those best integrated into the urban world
tended to accept, or were at least indifferent to the gamut of Revolutionary
changes. Similar, in many respects, is the study by Charles Tilly of
counterrevolution in the northern portion of the future "Vendée." To be
sure, Tilly's explanation is perhaps even more complex; and, unlike the
Bois thesis, it treats religious attitudes as an essentially independent variable. Nevertheless, Tilly too places particular stress on the ongoing *process*
of what he calls "urbanization." The non-juring and counterrevolutionary
sectors of the region he studied were characterized by the recent but
rapidly expanding influence of town-based merchants and royal officials,
a transformation which threatened the rural elites and the traditional
social structures and thus helped to energize opposition to the Revolutionary policies emanating from the towns.[27]

Unfortunately, careful local studies of this kind are still relatively rare,
and it would be difficult to devise any general measures of town and
country interaction or of the rate of "urbanization" for the whole of
France on the eve of the Revolution. Yet a scrutiny of certain preliminary
indices suggests that the process of "urbanization" or "modernization"
may not help us very much in explaining kingdom-wide patterns of oath-
taking—whatever their value for interpreting counterrevolution in the
microcosms observed by Bois and Tilly. It seems clear that the actual
physical isolation of the rural areas was largely unrelated to the distribution of oath-taking. If the single most isolated sector of the kingdom—
the mountains of the Massif-Central—was generally refractory, other
provinces with relatively inaccessible hinterlands, like Limousin, Upper
Dauphiné, and Upper Provence, seemed generally receptive to the Civil
Constitution and the oath. Indeed, one should not underestimate the
continued isolation of portions of the flat country of central France—
Sologne or Nivernais or Berry, for example—where early nineteenth-
century travelers to rural villages were still confined to simple footpaths,
but where the oath of 1791 was massively accepted. In point of fact, the
eighteenth-century postal road system—the major commercial link be-

[27] Bois and Tilly, cited above.

tween inland towns and villages—was more densely implanted in refractory Brittany and Artois than in the constitutional zones of Berry,
Sologne, and the Alps of the southeast.[28]

At the same time, there is no evident connection between the size of
the "urban" population within each department and regional reactions
to the oath. One notes, for example, the provinces along the entire northern frontier from Flanders and Hainaut to Lorraine and Alsace. These
regions were among the most highly "urbanized" in eighteenth-century
France—and were also covered by one of the densest road networks in
the country—yet all tended to reject overwhelmingly the religious policies
of the Constituent. Overall, there was no statistical relationship between
either the density of the postal roads or the proportion of the urban
population, on the one hand, and the regional reaction to the oath, on
the other.[29]

As for the elements of society which might have affected relations
between town and country, the conclusions of Bois and Tilly would seem,
in at least one respect, to be at odds with one another. For the former,
the presence of domestic industry in the countryside was a key ingredient
in successfully linking the rural hinterlands to the urban Revolution; but,
for the latter, rural artisans, under the control of town merchants, posed
a prime threat to rural elites and the more traditional agricultural complex, thus helping to stimulate suspicion and hostility toward the towns.[30]
Unfortunately, no figures on the regional strength of domestic industry
are presently available for France as a whole. Empirically, however, other
case studies would seem to confirm the inconsistent relationship between
the presence of a town-dominated putting-out system and local options
on the oath.[31] For the most part, the patterns of economic development
in Old-Regime France, as they are presently known, would seem relatively

[28] See Emmanuel Le Roy Ladurie, "Introduction" to Adolphe d'Angeville, *Essai sur la statistique de la population française*, new ed. (Paris, 1969), xxii. Also, Georges Duby and Robert
Mandrou, *Histoire de la civilisation française*, 2 vols. (Paris, 1958), 2:91.

[29] The proportion of the urban population in each department has been estimated from René
Le Mée, "Population agglomérée, population éparse au début du XIXe siècle," *Annales de
démographie historique, 1971* (Paris, 1972), 467-93. The correlation coefficient between the oath-
taking rate per department and the length of postal roads per square kilometer is 0.08 (with
data for 78 departments). With the density of the urban population (in relation to the total
population), the correlation is −0.05.

[30] Bois, esp. 270-71; Tilly, esp. 35-37, 157-58.

[31] Thus, in strongly refractory and counterrevolutionary Ille-et-Vilaine, to the west of Sarthe,
rural industry played only a very minor part in the local economy and "did not decisively affect
political attitudes": Sutherland, 17-23. In Dauphiné, widespread rural industry was associated
with massive acceptance of the oath: Pierre Léon, *La naissance de la grande industrie en Dauphiné*,
2 vols. (Paris, 1953), 1:55-57, 303-304.

little helpful for our understanding of the regional reception of the Civil Constitution.

Of course, it is possible that the critical factor in the relationship of town and country depended less on the physical and economic links between the two than on settlement patterns in the rural communities. The predominance in western France and the Massif-Central of small hamlets and isolated farms has frequently been cited as a fundamental structural feature, reinforcing the isolation of the population which resided there. Outside ideas, in general, and the political ideology of the Revolutionaries, in particular, are said to have had greater difficulty in penetrating the diffused and dispersed society of the *bocage*—especially by comparison with the more typical clustered villages of the north, east, and southeast.[32] The problem arises when one attempts to define more carefully the extent of dispersed communities in Old-Regime France. To rely on the descriptions of eighteenth-century travelers, they were apparently far more widespread than is sometimes realized and were generally typical not only of the west but of much of France south of a line from Rouen to Geneva—an impression that would seem to be confirmed by the results of nineteenth-century censuses. The correlation coefficient between the oath of 1791 and the dispersal of the population in the nineteenth century is essentially insignificant.[33]

Reactions to Centralization

Closely, perhaps inseparably, related to the problem of urban-rural interaction was the issue of the general increase in state activity in local affairs. Indeed, for Charles Tilly the very concept of "urbanization" includes not only the growing importance of urban elites and market forces, but also the general process of centralization.[34] Clearly, this was a process which had long been evolving in France. At the end of the Old Regime, as Alexis de Tocqueville first argued, the modern centralized French state had already taken form. Nevertheless, during the first two

[32] Tilly, 86. On dispersed settlements in the Massif-Central, see Peter Jones, "Parish, Seigneurie, and the Community of Inhabitants in Southern Central France during the Eighteenth and Nineteenth Centuries," *Past and Present*, 91 (1981), 74-108.

[33] *Statistique de la France. 1876* (Paris, 1878), 76-79. For all of France, the correlation coefficient between the proportion of oath-takers and the dispersion of the population is −0.233. But when the five Breton departments are excluded, the coefficient drops to −0.100. For a map of the distribution of dispersed populations, see Emmanuel Le Roy Ladurie and André Zysberg, "Géographie des hagiotoponymes en France," *Annales. E.S.C.*, 38 (1983), 1321.

[34] Tilly, 16-17, 26-37.

years of the Revolution, state encroachment into the individual's daily life accelerated dramatically, attaining a level substantially greater than anything previously experienced. The oath itself, with all that it entailed, must have appeared particularly symbolic of those accumulated intrusions.[35]

In fact, the threat of such intrusions might generate irritation and hostility in both urban and rural areas. For the town dwellers, the full impact of the Revolutionary changes became particularly manifest as the Paris deputies began modifying and rearranging the various bureaucracies, establishing new systems of courts, tax collectors, and general administrators—in addition to the extensively transformed and simplified clerical hierarchy. The overall result was to create a greater concentration of bureaucratic machinery in a more limited number of towns. Inevitably, a number of municipalities would deeply resent the decisions of "popular sovereignty" in Paris which so utterly ignored local interests and which prevented their towns from sharing in the full benefits of the organization of power—the "fruits of the constitution," as they were sometimes called. As many towns rightly perceived, the failure to be designated as the seat of a new department or diocese might have major detrimental effects on the local economy. The proud old town of Montauban would encounter a particularly cruel fate at the hands of the Revolutionaries. Formerly the site of an intendancy, a *cours des aides*, and a bishopric, as well as of several lesser courts and a number of chapters and monasteries, Montauban lost virtually everything and found itself abruptly reduced to the status of a district *chef-lieu*. Many among the Catholic majority of the town were convinced that the influential pastor, Rabaut-Saint-Etienne, had engineered their city's defeat in revenge for the town's earlier treatment of the Calvinists. In late 1790, the Catholic townsmen would be easily convinced that the Civil Constitution was itself a Protestant document intended to force them to abandon their faith.[36] A similar lot fell to the town of Le Buis in Dauphiné, which lost a number of ecclesiastical and judicial institutions and found itself only the insignificant seat of a canton. One historian has concluded that the town's disappointment over its treatment by the National Assembly was a key element in the local

---

[35] For a more detailed analysis, see especially T.J.A. Le Goff and D.M.G. Sutherland, "The Revolution and the Rural Community in Eighteenth-Century Brittany," *Past and Present,* no. 62 (Feb. 1974), 96, 108-119. Also, Alexis de Tocqueville, *L'Ancien régime et la Révolution française*, J. P. Mayer, ed. (Paris, 1952), esp. 107-122.

[36] Léon Lévy-Schneider, *Le conventionnel Jeanbon Saint-André*, 2 vols. (Paris, 1901), 1:47-50, 61. See also the following chapter.

population's rejection of the Civil Constitution and the oath.[37] Contemporaries themselves made similar arguments to explain local opposition to the new ecclesiastical laws in Aire (Pas-de-Calais) and Saint-Pol-de Léon (Finistère).[38]

One might also anticipate a less than favorable reception for the new legislation from those towns—like Saint-Pol and Montauban—which found their bishoprics abruptly suppressed by the National Assembly. Communities as diverse as Alet, Dax, Saint-Bertrand-de-Comminges, Lisieux, and Noyon all complained bitterly of the Revolution's injustice in depriving them of their dioceses—and of the economic benefits which a bishop's presence generated.[39] Complaints of this sort were especially common in the Midi, where the elimination of the plethora of minuscule Old-Regime dioceses aroused resentment in numerous small and medium-sized towns. One scholar has even cited this concentration of aggrieved towns in the south as a relevant factor in the strength of counterrevolutionary activities throughout the region.[40] Yet if the suppression of bishoprics and of other key Old-Regime institutions was undoubtedly important in a number of specific cases, it would seem of only limited value for explaining refractory opinion in urban France as a whole. Statistically, the proportion of oath-takers in towns which lost their bishops was virtually the same as that in towns which conserved their sees— 37 percent in the first case, 36 percent in the second.[41] To judge by the hundreds of appeals flooding into the secretariat of the National Assembly, virtually every town in France was presenting itself as seriously aggrieved in one manner or another.[42] Yet long experience in pleading

[37] F. Baboin, "L'application de la Constitution civile du clergé dans la Drôme," *Révolution française*, 37 (1899), 245-48.

[38] Jacobin club of Saint-Omer to Committee for Research, Mar. 9, 1791: A.N., D XXIX bis 21, dos. 230, no. 7; and municipality of Saint-Pol-de-Léon to same, Dec. 10, 1790: A.N., D XXIX bis 20, dos. 212, no. 1.

[39] *Adresse de la ville d'Alet à l'Assemblée nationale* (Carcassonne, 1790): A.N., C 115, dos. 308; municipality of Saint-Bertrand-de-Comminges to the minister of the interior, Apr. 11, 1790: A.N., F[19] 462; municipality of Lisieux to the Committee for Research, Dec. 18, 1790: A.N., D XXIX bis 20, dos. 213, nos. 11-13; and deliberations of the municipality of Noyon, May 9, 1790: A.N., F[19] 457.

[40] Colin Lucas, "The Problem of the Midi in the French Revolution," *Transactions of the Royal Historical Society*, 28 (1978), 13.

[41] In the 47 episcopal towns which maintained their bishoprics for which data are available, 308 of 867 clergymen (36 percent) took the oath. Among 27 towns which found their bishoprics suppressed, 74 of 200 clergymen (37 percent) were jurors.

[42] Ted W. Margadant, "Urban Crisis, Bourgeois Ambition, and Revolutionary Ideology in the 1790s," paper given at the meeting of the Society for French Historical Studies, New York, April 1982.

their case before the royal tax collectors had given the town fathers ample experience in the art of exaggerating economic disaster. Injustice as flagrant as that dealt out to Montauban and Le Buis was probably relatively rare. (Indeed, the case of Montauban was so unusual that Bonaparte would later promote it to the rank of *chef-lieu* over a new department created specifically for this purpose.) All things considered, one is compelled to maintain a measure of skepticism toward the mass of pleas received in Paris against the bureaucratic reorganization.

For the rural areas, the problem of state intrusion and dominance presented itself in rather different terms. Though there were proposals for the suppression and reduction of parishes, such plans seldom materialized outside the larger towns. In many sectors of the countryside, the principal problem would seem to have been a more general and pervasive reaction to a wide range of state activities touching the peasant community. In the context of rural Brittany, for example, Le Goff and Sutherland have argued that a veritable "administrative revolution" occurred between 1790 and 1791.[43] For the first time, a nationwide, standardized bureaucratic system was put in place which facilitated both the gathering of local information and the implementation of the dozens of new decrees emanating monthly from Paris. Within the space of a year, the municipalities would be asked to draw up new tax rolls, survey landholdings, establish a census, survey the grain trade, certify lists of local poor, and oversee the Church reorganization. Though some of these operations had already been attempted in a sporadic manner by the intendants, the Revolutionary directories would now supervise and goad the municipalities with far greater vigor and efficiency than ever before. And whenever the municipalities failed to comply or encountered local opposition, the district and department patriots felt no qualms about sending in commissioners or even detachments of the urban national guard to compel compliance. As we shall see in a later chapter, not all departmental authorities were as domineering and insensitive to local practices as those in Brittany. But, in the context of rural traditions, such insistent prodding and prying could easily be viewed as arbitrary and authoritarian, as an attack on the community's own time-tested manner of handling its problems. A village notable who chose to cooperate with such tactics might be rapidly grouped with the town patriots as an "intrus." In this sense, the Civil Constitution and the oath could be viewed as a particularly "shocking intrusion into the solidarity of the rural com-

[43] Le Goff and Sutherland, "The Revolution and the Rural Community," 100-116. See also above, chp. 11.

munity," threatening the "destruction of the . . . community as a cohesive, morally defined unit."[44]

Yet why was it that some areas of the country were apparently so much more sensitive than others to the threats of such outside encroachment? Contemporaries themselves were puzzled by the fact that most of the refractory departments were situated at the periphery of the country. For the minister of the interior, Cahier de Gerville, it was "as if the light of reason which shines steadily at the center of the Empire had not yet succeeded in penetrating the circumference."[45] But, obviously, the problem entailed much more than the mere physical distance from Paris and Versailles. Many of the provinces in question had long traditions of opposition to royal authority under the Old Regime. The generally refractory western and southern provinces of Normandy, Brittany, Poitou, Saintonge, Quercy, and Languedoc all had experienced successive waves of armed peasant uprisings in the sixteenth and seventeenth centuries, revolts directed in large measure against the royal government.[46] Several of the peripheral provinces in question—Brittany, Roussillon, Franche-Comté, Artois, Lorraine, Alsace—had entered into the French realm relatively recently. In these and in a number of other provinces, the historical tradition of independence was reinforced institutionally through the perpetuation of regional estates and/or Parlements. As we have seen, many of these same provinces had also preserved their independence from the bureaucracy of the Gallican Church and were considered, to the end of the Old Regime, as "provinces étrangères," linked as strongly with neighboring German or Spanish or Austrian Churches as with the French Church itself. The lively tradition of royal opposition, maintained to the very end of the Old Regime in provinces like Brittany and Franche-Comté, helped to neutralize the royal intendancies and to preserve a sense of local autonomy not only at the provincial level but at the village level as well.[47] In fact, the departments located within the former *pays d'état*

---

[44] Sutherland, 223, 242.

[45] Speech by Cahier de Gerville, Feb. 18, 1792: *AP*, 38:623.

[46] For a preliminary chronology and geography of sixteenth and seventeenth-century peasant uprisings, see Jean Jacquart, "Immobilisme et catastrophes (1560-1690)" in *Histoire de la France rurale. Tome 2. L'Age classique des paysans*, Emmanuel Le Roy Ladurie, ed. (Paris, 1975), 339-53. Most of the principal regions of peasant revolts would emerge as refractory in 1791. There were some exceptions, however: Upper Poitou, Angoumois, and Agenais, which were largely constitutional.

[47] Le Goff and Sutherland stress the meagerness of the royal bureaucracy in its real effects within the Breton village: article cited. See also Henri de Fréville, *L'intendance de Bretagne (1689-1790)*, 3 vols. (Rennes, 1953), esp. vol. 3. On the ecclesiastical "provinces étrangères" see

were notably more refractory than those within the *pays d'élection*—
particularly if one excepts Provence, where the estates system and Parlement had long been virtually coopted by the royal government.[48] Oath-
taking rates within the departments outside the domain of the "Clergé
de France" were also decidedly lower than the national mean.[49]

But there was another reason why the "light" of Parisian logic had
difficulty in attaining the circumference. For many, though not all, of
the refractory regions at the edges of the kingdom spoke languages other
than French. The suspicions of the Revolutionary leadership toward *patois*
and other "foreign" languages within the nation has often been pointed
out. Many patriots were convinced of a strong link between the failure
to understand French and the failure to comprehend and accept the
national Revolutionary objectives.[50] Though eighteenth-century linguistic
geography is still not perfectly known, it is evident that the majority of
the population in Lower Brittany, Flanders, eastern Lorraine, most of
Alsace, Roussillon, and the Pays-Basque had great difficulty in penetrating
the documents and the rhetoric emanating from Paris. In Lorraine, Alsace, and Roussillon even large numbers of the elite, including many
curés, were scarcely conversant in the French language. Thus, in the
diocesan seminary of Metz, astride the linguistic frontier between French
and German Lorraine, notes were carefully made as to which students
spoke German—perhaps 45 percent of the total—and which spoke
French or were bilingual. In Roussillon, Curé Molas of Palada complained
of his difficulty in communicating in French: "28 years of service in a
region where the national language is unknown have made French almost
foreign to me." Many of Molas' clerical colleagues would consistently use
Catalan in all their correspondence with the departmental authorities.[51]

---

above, chp. 5. On Franche-Comté, see Maurice Gresset, "Les Franc-Comtois entre la France
et l'Empire," in *Régions et régionalisme en France du XVIIIe siècle à nos jours* (Paris, 1977), 103-
116.

[48] In the departments within the former *pays d'état*, the oath-taking rate was 44.4 percent; if
Provence is excluded, the rate was 40.5 percent.

[49] In the departments within the former *diocèses réputés étrangers*, the oath-taking rate was
36.5 percent.

[50] See Michel de Certeau, Dominique Julia, and Jacques Revel, *La politique de la langue: La
Révolution française et les patois: L'enquête de Grégoire* (Paris, 1975). Note also the speech of
Barère in 1794, cited in Albert Soboul, "De l'Ancien régime à la Révolution: problème régional
et réalités sociales," in *Régions et régionalisme*, 41; and the speech by Grégoire, Feb. 9, 1790: *AP*,
11:419.

[51] A.D. Moselle, papers of the Old-Regime bishopric of Metz, provisional carton 21⁴; Pierre
Vidal, *Histoire de la Révolution française dans le département des Pyrénées-Orientales*, 3 vols. (Per-
pignan, 1885-89), 1:168, 193. See also Emmanuel Todd and Hervé Le Bras, *L'invention de la
France* (Paris, 1981), 277-79.

In zones such as these, both clergymen and parishioners might feel particularly unhappy with the efforts of the "French nation" to impose its values and centralizing systems. Where even the elites had held little contact with the intellectual and political trends originating in the capital over the previous decades, the efforts of the National Assembly toward standardization and "national regeneration" might seem altogether alien. In 1791 a geographic correspondence would be strikingly in evidence between the inability to speak French, on the one hand, and a refractory status on the part of the clergy, on the other. In southwestern France, as one observer put it, "Without instruction in the Basque language, true patriotism will have great difficulty in spreading." And since, for the most part, only the clergy was capable of interpreting the new reforms to the masses, the urban patriot minority was extremely pessimistic about the possibilities of success.[52] In Brittany, the Breton language was frequently cited as the prime obstacle to patriotism, especially since in this province, as in the Basque country, the local rectors played a dominant role as cultural intermediaries. On the eastern frontier administrators in the bilingual district of Belfort contrasted the refractory "German" curés and countrypeople with the "French" who generally accepted the oath.[53] Test studies within both the district of Belfort and the department of Moselle reveal an impressive correspondence between zones speaking German and zones refusing the oath.[54] Among all those regions, without exception, where a non-French language was not only spoken but written—provinces like Alsace, Lorraine, Flanders, and Roussillon—the oath would be massively rejected.

Counterrevolution and the Oath

That there was some kind of relationship between the various manifestations of counterrevolution and the geographic incidence of the oath

[52] Abbé Haristoy, *Les paroisses du pays basque pendant la période révolutionnaire*, 2 vols. (Pau, 1895-99), 1:116-17; and F. Brunot, *Histoire de la langue française*, 12 vols. (Paris, 1977), 9:176.

[53] See the letter of the *procureur syndic* of the district of Lannion (Côtes-du-Nord) to the Minister of the Interior, Nov. 16, 1790: A.N., F19 418; and the letter of the *procureur syndic* of the district of Belfort to the Ecclesiastical Committee, Feb. 14, 1791: D XIX 86, dos. 677, no. 2.

[54] In the district of Belfort, the oath-taking rate was 69 percent in the French-speaking parishes and 31 percent in the German-speaking areas: based on notes by Jules Joachim, B.M. Colmar, ms. 972. In the department of Moselle, 46 percent of the clergy in the French-speaking sectors and 19 percent of the clergy in the German-speaking sectors took the oath: based on Jean Eich, *Les prêtres mosellans pendant la Révolution. Répertoire biographique*, 2 vols. (Metz, 1959).

seems scarcely to be denied. Those zones in which major movements of violent opposition to the governments in power would make themselves felt after 1791 would mark off virtually all the areas where a majority of clergymen were refractory to the Civil Constitution. The parallels are even more striking if we concentrate on the regions of popular counter-revolution and exclude those departments—like Gironde or Rhône-et-Loire or Var—where opposition consisted primarily of the urban-based and elitist-led "Federalist" uprisings of 1793.[55]

Yet the ultimate causal link between the two phenomena is by no means obvious. The proposition of Paul Bois—that oath options were primarily the effect, the mirror of broader secular grievances toward the Revolution as a whole—has proved less successful than we might orig-inally have expected. To be sure, there does seem to have been something of a correlation between refractory regions and societies dominated by tenant farmers—a group which, as we have seen, stood to be particularly dissatisfied and disadvantaged by the Revolutionary reforms. Yet the tenant-farmer syndrome does not seem to have operated everywhere in the same manner and can in no way serve as a general explanation of refractory France. A second promising mode of socioeconomic analysis, involving the interaction of towns and rural areas, proved generally inconclusive and disappointing for the comprehension of the broader national patterns of reactions. Likewise, our efforts to discover a con-nection between popular riots in 1790 and oath responses yielded rather meager results. In general, those questions raised by the Revolution which most exercised the French population in the months prior to the eccle-siastical oath—the perpetuation of the seigneurial system, the reorgani-zation of taxes, the breakdown of adequate grain distribution—seem little related to the patterns of clerical options at the beginning of 1791. Indeed, it was only *after* the oath had been required, in the period during the first six months of 1791, that one begins to detect a link between antiseigneurial riots and the oath—suggesting the possibility that the religious issues raised by the Civil Constitution may themselves have been a powerful force galvanizing public opinion.

[55] Compare the oath map with the incidence of counterrevolution as identified by Donald Greer, *The Incidence of the Terror during the French Revolution* (Cambridge, Mass., 1935), unpaginated map at the beginning of the book. The correlation coefficient by department between oath-taking and Greer's map is −0.526. The correlation would be higher if the de-partments registering only Federalist activities were excluded. See also the map of peasant movements during the French Revolution by T.J.A. Le Goff and D.M.G. Sutherland, "Religion and Rural Revolt in the French Revolution: An Overview," in *Religion and Rural Revolt*, Janos M. Bak and Gerhard Benecke, eds. (Manchester, 1984), 127.

A more fruitful approach has been to explore the question of general reactions to state centralization. All evidence points to the existence of a patriotic core of the kingdom which contrasted sharply with various peripheral regions in which the population appeared far more reticent toward Revolutionary developments. But the existence of such a general dichotomy seems to have depended less on the patterns of communication or economic "modernization" than on deeply rooted political, cultural, and linguistic traditions. Though there were notable exceptions, most of the towns of the realm came rapidly under the control of the patriots, who dutifully followed and enforced the decrees radiating from Paris. Yet in many regions at the circumference, such patriots would soon find themselves in danger of being overwhelmed by the suspicion and incomprehension of the surrounding countryside. For the present, the linguistic factor would appear to have been particularly significant. In areas where even many members of the rural elite scarcely understood the language of Rousseau and Voltaire, of Sieyès and Mirabeau, a stubborn resistance was soon to be manifested against the Revolution in general, and the religious legislation in particular.

But here, too, a number of regions would not seem to fit the pattern. One is hard pressed to adapt such a scheme to provinces like Anjou, Maine, and Poitou: provinces where the clergy was strongly refractory, but where the French language was understood by almost everyone, where the political systems had been integrated into the central monarchy for centuries, and where the ecological and economic characteristics differed little from the constitutional regions immediately to the east. And, by most accounts, Breton-speaking Lower Brittany, was less recalcitrant to Revolutionary policies than was Upper Brittany where a French dialect predominated.[56]

In the following chapters it will be necessary to take a rather different tack. Without rejecting or disregarding the "secular" aspects of popular discontent in the period of the oath, we will argue that disappointment or satisfaction with the Revolution cannot be separated from the specific disappointment or satisfaction with the Civil Constitution itself; and that there was a largely independent, religious dimension to regional reactions on the part of the populace.

[56] Hervé Pommeret, *L'esprit public dans le département des Côtes-du-Nord pendant la Révolution* (Saint-Brieuc, 1921), 112-17.

NINE

The Protestant Menace

HE men who made the Revolution of 1789 were particularly sensitive to the problems of the French Protestants. Few could have been unaware that tolerance toward non-Catholics had been a major theme among Enlightenment writers since the middle of the century, that the Revocation of the Edict of Nantes was commonly portrayed as the prime example of the pernicious powers wielded by the Church, that Voltaire himself had long waged a personal battle in behalf of religious toleration. Indeed, in the months following the fall of the Bastille, revolutionary discourse was commonly laced with references to the sixteenth-century Wars of Religion and the Saint Bartholomew's Day Massacre, epitome of the horrors wrought by religious prejudice and intolerance. And, nevertheless, one must be wary of generalizations based solely on the pronouncements of a certain literate elite. In order to explore the possible connections between Protestantism and reactions to the oath, it will first be necessary to examine briefly the situation of the non-Catholics on the eve of the Revolution and then turn to the evolution of Catholic-Protestant relations through the winter and spring of 1791.

Eighteenth-Century Background

As near as can be estimated, the Protestant portion of the French population at the end of Old Regime amounted to something approaching 700,000 individuals—perhaps 2 to 3 percent of all French men and women.[1] Of these, approximately one-third were Lutherans, most of whom lived in Alsace and in small portions of Lorraine and Franche-Comté (near Montbéliard). The remaining two-thirds, the true "Huguenots," belonged to the Calvinist confession and were concentrated primarily in a crescent of provinces extending from northern Languedoc and Dauphiné south and west along the southern fringes of the Massif-

[1] I have used Samuel Mours, *Les églises réformées en France: tableaux et cartes* (Paris, 1958), 188-89, for the Calvinist population; and Marcel Scheidhauer, *Les églises luthériennes en France, 1800-1815* (Strasbourg, 1975), 1-33, for the Lutheran population in Alsace and the region near Montbéliard. Mours' estimates are actually for 1815, but the relative proportion of Protestants had probably not changed very much since 1790.

Central and then northward through Guyenne, Saintonge, and Poitou. There were also a few isolated groups clinging to existence in northern and central France. Constituting 30 to 40 percent of the population of Lower Alsace and Lower Languedoc, the Protestants also represented substantial minorities of 5 percent or better in Vivarais, southwestern Dauphiné, the Cévennes, Albigeois, and Poitou.[2] Though they had once been strongly centered in the towns of the kingdom, by the late eighteenth century some 80 percent of the Huguenots lived in rural areas—virtually the same proportion as among the Catholics. The "typical" Calvinist, as the typical Frenchman, was a peasant or rural artisan.[3]

More difficult to gauge, however, is the degree of cohesion and vitality of the Protestant populations, factors which varied regionally not only as a function of their numbers but as a function of their specific historical experiences. Thus, the Lutherans of Alsace and Montbéliard, essentially untouched by the Revocation of 1685, had maintained a strong legal and institutional identity since the sixteenth century, making them a powerful, self-conscious force to be reckoned with in all Alsatian affairs.[4] Many Calvinists, on the contrary, had been badly isolated and disorganized by the royal repression and the large-scale emigration, both of which continued after the Revocation well into the eighteenth century. Thus, for a variety of reasons, their forces had greatly diminished and had lost much of their vigor in Aunis, Saintonge, and Poitou, the provinces adjoining the former Huguenot stronghold of La Rochelle.[5] The vital center of the sect in the eighteenth century had shifted to Languedoc, within the confines of the future departments of Gard, Ardèche, and Lozère. It was here that the popular rebellion of the "Camisards" had raged for

[2] In addition to the pages cited above, see the maps in Mours, 143, and in Scheidhauer, 21. The percentage of the Protestant population for each department has been calculated based on the overall population in 1806 as published in René Le Mée, "Population agglomérée, population éparse au début du XIXe siècle," *Annales de démographie historique, 1971* (Paris, 1972), 455-510. Note, that there was also a small Calvinist population in Alsace.

[3] Daniel Ligou and Philippe Joutard, "Les déserts (1685-1800)," in Robert Mandrou, ed., *Histoire des Protestants en France* (Toulouse, 1977), 245. I have not located any such estimates for the Alsatian Protestants.

[4] Henri Strohl, *Le protestantisme en Alsace* (Strasbourg, 1950), 2e partie; Rodolphe Reuss, *L'église Luthérienne de Strasbourg au XVIIIe siècle* (Paris, 1892), and, by the same, *Les églises Protestantes en Alsace pendant la Révolution (1789-1802)* (Paris, 1906), 1-13. Also Bernard Vogler, "En Alsace: orthodoxie et territorialisme," in *Histoire des Protestants*, 151-88. On Montbéliard, see Jean-Marc Debard, "Piété populaire et Réforme dans la principauté de Montbéliard du XVIe au XVIIIe siècle," *ACSS*, 99 (1974), 1:7-34.

[5] Louis Pérouas, *Le diocèse de La Rochelle de 1648 à 1724* (Paris, 1964), 418-21. Also Marquis Marie de Roux, *La Révolution à Poitiers et dans la Vienne* (Paris, 1911), 47.

almost a decade at the beginning of the century: the quasi-millenarian revolt that marked the Huguenots' sole large-scale uprising against Louis XIV's repressive edicts. But, despite the repression and despite a significant movement of emigration, certain elements of the Protestant or crypto-Protestant population maintained a prominent position in the local economic elite. Throughout the century, the principal Calvinist leaders, from Antoine Court to Paul Rabaut and Rabaut-Saint-Etienne, originated in this province. As early as 1715, even before the death of Louis XIV, the Calvinists of Lower Languedoc and the Cévennes had succeeded in secretly reorganizing themselves into "synods." Within a few years similar synods would be constituted in Vivarais and Dauphiné. But it would be almost mid-century before such institutionalized "churches of the desert" were created in Guyenne, Poitou, and Saintonge, and only in the later eighteenth century in Normandy and northern France.[6]

A great deal has been written about the general Protestant revival and the growth of official toleration in the course of the eighteenth century. There was a clear trend after 1750 toward the *de facto* acceptance of non-Catholics by the royal administration and judiciary: a period often referred to in Protestant histories as the "second desert." Gradually, the prisons incarcerating recalcitrant Huguenot women were opened and the ships of the Mediterranean were emptied of their "heretic" galley slaves. By the 1770's Protestant leaders were openly negotiating with the government and Turgot would employ the pastors of the Midi—as he used curés elsewhere—to help disseminate governmental directives to the population. Ultimately, elite attitudes toward the Protestants were also transformed by the efforts of the *philosophes*, of which the various *causes célèbres* stirred up by Voltaire were only the best known. While Enlightened philosophers and Protestant divines initially made unlikely bedfellows, a decline in the intensity of doctrinal controversy and a growing rationalism among many Calvinist theologians greatly diminished the incongruity.[7]

Unfortunately, much less is presently known of Protestant-Catholic relations in the rural communities during the eighteenth century. But if a "toleration of indifference" had apparently prevailed within most governmental and elite circles, the old hatreds and antagonisms seem scarcely

[6] Ligou and Joutard, 193, 214, 220, 221.

[7] Burdette Poland, *French Protestantism and the French Revolution* (Princeton, 1957), 27-82; David Bien, *The Calas Affair: Persecution, Toleration and Heresy in Eighteenth-Century Toulouse* (Princeton, 1960), 25-76; Alice Wemyss, *Les Protestants du Mas-d'Azil, histoire d'une résistance, 1680-1830* (Toulouse, 1961), 189-201; Ligou and Joutard, 220-23.

to have abated among the lower classes and in the rural milieus where most of the Protestants actually lived. Particularly in Languedoc, the memories of the Camisards episode, with its brutal savagery on both sides, remained vivid and vibrant among both Protestants and Catholics.[8] The sporadic reassertion of repression through 1760 ignited a number of incidents of counterviolence on the part of the Huguenots—despite the teachings of the Calvinist leadership in favor of patience and passivity.[9] In 1752 one curé was killed and another was wounded in the Cévennes, exciting wide anticipation of the renewal of civil war. A rural panic broke out near Montauban in 1761, sparked by the fear of Protestant "brigands" supposedly seeking revenge for the arrest of one of their pastors. And there was a near riot in Nîmes in 1771 over an imagined insult to a Catholic procession.[10] In his examination of the town and region of Nîmes, James Hood was particularly impressed by the continuing cycles of real or threatened violence still in evidence throughout the second half of the eighteenth century. He discovered an intensely "nervous behavior," a collective tension among both populations, based on the assumption of a general conspiracy on the part of the opposing religious community.[11] David Bien found that similar conspiracy theories were widely held by the Catholic populace of Toulouse in the 1760's.[12]

By most accounts, the Edict of November 1787, the so-called "Edict of Toleration" which regularized the civil status of the Calvinists, served inadvertently to reheat simmering religious hostilities in many of those regions where Protestants were present. Both the General Assembly of the Clergy and the provincial Parlements were quick to point out the "dangers" of such an edict—though they accepted the general principle of a Protestant *état civil*.[13] But many Protestants themselves were rapidly disillusioned with the law, especially after they discovered the meagerness

[8] See Philippe Joutard, *La légende des Camisards* (Paris, 1977); and Robert Sauzet, "La religion populaire en Bas-Languedoc au XVIIe siècle," in *La religion populaire. Paris, 17-19 octobre 1977*. (Colloques internationaux du Centre national de la recherche scientifique, no. 576) (Paris, 1979), 107-108.

[9] Ligou and Joutard, 214-15, 219.

[10] Bien, 77-82 Ligou and Joutard, 214-15; James N. Hood, "The Riots in Nîmes in 1790," Ph.D. dissertation, Princeton University, 1968; and Daniel Ligou, *Documents sur le Protestantisme montalbanais au XVIIIe siècle* (Toulouse, 1955), lxv, lxxi.

[11] James N. Hood, "Protestant-Catholic Relations and the Roots of the First Popular Counterrevolutionary Movement in France," *JMH*, 43 (1971), 252-53, 260, 268, 270.

[12] Bien, 118-20, 124, 146.

[13] Poland, 86-87; Jean Egret, "La dernière assemblée du Clergé de France," *RH*, 219 (1958), 10-12.

of the gains actually achieved, the inconsistencies and uncertainties of the edict's wording—easily used by begrudging Catholics to block even limited change—and the considerable cost and inconvenience incurred when individuals tried to take advantage of its provisions. If anything the edict only succeeded in wetting the Protestants' appetite for greater freedom and in intensifying Catholic fears of a Calvinist threat. Everywhere there were reports—accompanied by bitter recriminations from the Catholics—of Protestants using the edict as a pretext to celebrate their religion more openly than ever before, to insult and antagonize the Catholics, or to cease paying their tithes to the Catholic clergy.[14] Close to three-fifths of the clerical cahiers of 1789 would specifically request that the Edict of 1787 be revoked or, at least, that Catholicism be the sole religion practiced in public.[15]

Perhaps future research will ultimately reveal a genuine growth of social tolerance between rival religious confessions in other rural regions of the country. It is significant that virtually all the *causes célèbres* of the *philosophes* and all the best-known incidents of violence and panic involving the Protestants can be situated in the general sector between Nîmes and Montauban, previously identified as the major focal point of Calvinist identity. It was here that the collective memory of past atrocities, the peasant suspicions of the non-conformists and "outsiders," and the fundamental fears for the danger to one's soul remained particularly pronounced. The philosophers might seek to banish prejudice and to invoke the reign of universal brotherhood under one Supreme Being. But the Devil—Huguenot or Papist, depending on one's faith—remained alive and afoot in the hill country and plateaus of the Midi. In many of these same regions, the transformations wrought by the Revolution would soon intensify interconfessional animosities more than at any time since the beginning of the eighteenth century.

[14] Louis Mazoyer, "L'application de l'Edit de 1787 dans le Midi de la France," *Bulletin de la Société de l'histoire du Protestantisme français*, 74 (1925), 149-76; Hood, "Protestant-Catholic Relations," 259, 267; Léon Lévy-Schneider, *Le conventionnel Jeanbon Saint-André*, 2 vols. (Paris, 1901), 1:52-53.

[15] Attitudes toward the Protestants have also been studied through the "general cahiers" of the Third Estate, documents which were, however, little indicative of rural and peasant opinion. Of 164 Third-Estate cahiers, Louis Mazoyer found only 35 which even mentioned the Protestant question. Here, the attitude was generally neither hostile nor sympathetic, but basically in favor of a "parsimonious and limited tolerance": Louis Mazoyer, "La question protestante dans les cahiers des Etats-généraux," *Bulletin de la Société de l'histoire du Protestantisme français*, 80 (1931), 65.

Protestantism and the Revolution: The Dom Gerle Affair

The year 1789 would see the rapid achievement by French Protestants of a whole array of new civil and political rights, scarcely conceivable just a few months earlier. The provisions for elections to the Estates General permitted a broad Protestant participation in electoral meetings and resulted in the choice of some fifteen Protestants to serve as representatives in Versailles.[16] Later that summer the Declaration of the Rights of Man and the Citizen would affirm that no one could "be disturbed because of his opinions, even religious." Even more important was the decree introduced on December 21 and passed on Christmas Eve 1789 which assured full political rights to Protestants on an equal footing with Catholics, rights which included the possibility of holding all positions of public office and of practicing all professions.[17] A year later, those whose forefathers had emigrated after the Revocation and whose lands had thus been confiscated were invited to return and reclaim their property wherever it was still held in public trust.[18]

Surprisingly, perhaps, the decree of December 24, reinserting non-Catholics into the political nation, aroused relatively little opposition from the clerical members of the National Assembly—who revealed themselves far more intent on keeping out actors and Jews. The major debate arose, not over the question of Protestant political and economic rights, but over whether Catholicism should be declared the state religion with sole rights to public religious celebration. A motion in favor of such a declaration had first been introduced by the Alsatian Abbé Eymar on August 28, 1789, but was set aside as inappropriate to the discussion at hand.[19] Far more serious had been the motion of February 13, 1790, urged by Bishop La Fare of Nancy. In the midst of a bitter discussion over the fate of clerical property and the religious orders, La Fare and several of his colleagues had become increasingly convinced that elements of the Left in the National Assembly harbored underlying antireligious intentions. A speech by the deputy Garat, seen as blasphemous by the clergy, triggered the demand that the Assembly immediately take a position in favor of the Catholic religion. After a brief and heated exchange, the motion was again tabled as being out of order.[20] But the April 12 motion

[16] Poland, 291.
[17] *AP*, 10:693-95.
[18] *AP*, 27:35, and 21:358.
[19] *AP*, 8:505.
[20] *AP*, 11:589-90.

by Dom Gerle—himself a Jacobin sympathizer—could not be so easily suppressed and would stimulate a bitter, tumultuous, and impassioned two-day debate.[21] It would also send reverberations throughout the kingdom. Numerous copies of the minority declaration of April 19, affirming the original Dom Gerle motion, were soon printed and circulated extensively.[22] A particularly early and vigorous reaction in favor of the same propositions was taken on April 20 by the Catholics of the town of Nîmes. Led by the future royalist counterrevolutionary, François Froment, the town's deliberations were published and would serve as an additional relay in the dissemination of the protest.[23] An examination of reactions to the Dom Gerle affair allows us to probe the opinions of provincial Frenchmen on the National Assembly's position toward Protestants— and toward religious reform in general—just eight months before the same population would confront the question of the ecclesiastical oath.

If one were to judge solely from the letters received in Paris, the predominant reaction to the declaration of April 19 and to the deliberations of Nîmes would seem to have been one of shock and outrage.[24] Within a few weeks, close to ninety collective statements had been received in Paris, either adhering to the April 13 deliberations or condemning the actions of the minority of deputies or of the town of Nîmes.[25] The messages arrived from almost every corner of the kingdom—a fur-

[21] See above, chp. 1.

[22] For the minority opinion, see *Déclaration d'une partie de l'Assemblée nationale sur le décret rendu le 13 avril 1790 concernant la religion* (Paris, April 19, 1790). I have used the copy in A.N., C 116, dos. 316. The letters received by the National Assembly occasionally gave indication of how the declaration of April 19 was being circulated: *e.g.,* by the vicar-general of Angoulême or by the deputy, Abbé Royer, in Jura: see the letter from the municipality of Montbron (Charente): A.N., D XXIX bis 6, dos. 84; and the letter from the electoral assembly of Jura: A.N., C 115, dos. 311'. Copies of the *Déclaration* seem commonly to have been sent not only to the municipalities, but also to numerous religious corporations and individual curés.

[23] It is not clear if Nîmes had already received word of the Dom Gerle motion at this time, though the participants were well aware of the events immediately preceding it and would certainly have received news by April 29, when the published version first began to be distributed. See Gwynne Lewis, *The Second Vendée* (Oxford, 1978), 20-21. The original deliberation is in Barruel, 14:154-64. A copy of the cover letter which accompanied it, dated April 29, is in A.N., C 115, dos. 309.

[24] I have examined A.N., C 113-118 and D XXIX bis 5-7, the two principal series in which such letters were apparently deposited. Without a doubt, the list compiled here is incomplete. I have counted only those statements which specifically mentioned the deliberations of April 13 and 19 or those issued in Nîmes. Many others seem to allude to these deliberations without explicitly mentioning them.

[25] Fifty-seven adhered to the April 13 deliberation or condemned the April 19 declaration. Thirty-eight condemned the deliberations of Nîmes. Seven mentioned both.

ther indication of the extent to which the protest had been circulated—though there was a slightly greater number from the southern half of the country.[26] Most came from individual municipalities, from town councils or general assemblies, but a few emanated from cantonal assemblies or units of the national guard.[27] Many of the adherences conveyed a sense of urgency, even panic. The moment the town of Ussel received a copy of the April 19 declaration, an extraordinary assembly of all active citizens was convened. In Saint-Martin-en-Ré there was even a public burning of the minority publication.[28] Almost everywhere the Jacobin clubs were galvanized into action to defend vigorously the majority of the National Assembly.[29] Part of the uproar was clearly related to political and constitutional issues. In the first place, there was the disturbing assertion that the National Assembly was no longer free in its deliberations. Equally critical, the minority declaration served to put into question the status of the Assembly as the undivided embodiment of popular sovereignty. If the deputies ceased following a majority rule, was there not the danger of a complete collapse into anarchy—"the dissolution of the National Assembly," as the citizens of Saint-Brieuc put it?[30] In their near obsession with the necessity of unity, many of the groups sending in adhesions ended their statements with collective oaths of unambiguous allegiance to all the decrees which the National Assembly had already passed or would pass in the future.

But few of the statements of adherence overlooked the central religious question. Several included veritable professions of faith, accepting the Left's contention that one cannot legislate religious belief, but also taking the occasion to affirm their fundamental devotion to Catholicism and their satisfaction with the whole gamut of religious reforms already passed or pending: "We are told that religion is lost! Ah, let us say that it has been saved!"[31] Others, however, revealed sentiments of undisguised anticlericalism, accusing the clergy of causing such a fuss merely because

[26] Fifty-two of the 88 separate demands came from south of the line from La Rochelle to Geneva.

[27] I have excluded those coming from Jacobin clubs or departmental directors.

[28] Letter from Ussel, May 9, 1790: A.N., C 115, dos. 308; letter from Saint-Martin-en-Ré, May 14, 1790: ibid., dos. 311¹.

[29] The Dom Gerle affair has been described as "pivotal" in the history of the Jacobin clubs: Michael L. Kennedy, *The Jacobin Club in the French Revolution. The First Years* (Princeton, 1982), 153.

[30] Letter of May 10, 1790: A.N., C 115, dos. 309.

[31] The quote is from Rodez: letter of May 16: A.N., C 115, dos. 312. For a profession of faith: letter of May 11 from Morlaix: ibid., dos. 310.

they feared losing their excessive wealth. Religion had been invoked, it was argued, as a mere pretext, as a means of defending all the abuses of the Old Regime.[32] Yet there was also evidence of an underlying fear on the part of the local patriots that the widely distributed minority declaration was beginning to influence the popular classes. In Poligny in the province of Franche-Comté it was said to have caused much "fermentation" within the town; in Châteauneuf-sur-Charente it had aroused "defiance" among many citizens; and throughout the countryside near Rodez the rumor that "religion was in danger" was spreading far and wide. As one curé in Poitou put it, the Dom Gerle Affair had "broken the unity of the patriotic faith."[33]

In all, only a handful of citizens' groups or municipalities sent in statements to the National Assembly adhering to the April 19 minority declaration. Yet this is hardly an adequate indication of the full spectrum of opinion. Many undoubtedly preferred to direct their adherences to the individual leaders of the minority rather than to the National Assembly per se. Through a broad assortment of sources—accusations sent in by patriots, local monographs, and a collection of such protests assembled later by Abbé Barruel—it has been possible to identify thirty-two communities in which there were meetings protesting the April 13 or accepting the April 19 deliberations, or expressing sentiments directly parallel to the minority views.[34] Though the list is certainly incomplete, it can nevertheless provide us with an initial impression of the range and distribution of the protest.

[32] Thus, the canton of Mercoeur, May 24: ibid., dos. 319; the towns of Sévérac-le-Château, May 30: A.N., C 116, dos. 324; and of Gien, June 2: C 117, dos. 327.

[33] Poligny, May 30: A.N., C 315, dos. 324; Rodez, May 16: ibid., dos. 312; Châteauneuf-sur-Charente, May 20: D XXIX bis 6; Roux, 278.

[34] Nîmes, April 20, 1790; Montauban, April; Uzès (Gard), Feb. 16 and May 3; Alès (Gard), Mar. 25; Toulouse, Apr. 18-20; Lautrec (Tarn), ? ; Albi (Tarn), Apr. 30; Saint-Pons (Hérault), May 2; Villefranche-de-Lauragais (Haute-Garonne), May 6; Nogaro (Gers), before May 28; Pampelonne (Tarn), before May 18; Saint-Martin-des-Noyers (Vendée), ? ; Tarbes (Hautes-Pyrénées), before May 14; Murasson (Aveyron), May 24; Saint-Juéry (Aveyron), May 24; Rebourguil (Aveyron), May 30; La Rochepot (Côte-d'Or), May 30; Belmont (Aveyron), May 24; Castres (Tarn), Apr. 18; Moissac (Lot), ? ; Cahors (Lot), ? ; Perpignan (Pyrénées-Orientales), before May 3; Châteauneuf-sur-Charente (Charente), before May 20; Rouans (Loire-Atlantique), before May 30; Loriol (Drôme), ? ; Livron, (Drôme), ? ; Bagnols (Lozère), ? ; Saint-Paul-les-Trois-Châteaux (Drôme), ? ; Pézenas (Hérault), ? ; Montélimar (Drôme), ? ; Voiron (Isère), ? ; Vinézac (Ardèche), ? . Sources: Barruel, 14:84-113; Lévy-Schneider, 1:66; Albert Durand, *Histoire religieuse du département du Gard pendant la Révolution française, Tome I (1788-92)* (Nîmes, 1918), 65-69; Jean-Claude Meyer, *La vie religieuse en Haute-Garonne sous la Révolution (1789-1801)* (Toulouse, 1982), 51; Charles Jolivet, *La Révolution en Ardèche* (Largentière, 1930), 210; A.N., C 115-16; D XXIX bis 5-11; F19 408.

Of the thirty-two sites, half were "towns" by the Napoleonic definition of the word, and three—Nîmes, Toulouse, and Montauban—were major regional capitals. Eleven were the seats of bishoprics and thus, perhaps, more directly in touch with the upper clergy in the Assembly; but only four were bishoprics scheduled for suppression under the reorganization of the Church.[35] The majority, however, were small to medium-sized communities of a few hundred or a few thousand inhabitants, most of which had not yet seen the formation of Jacobin clubs.[36] Of particular interest is the small scattering of genuine agricultural villages, all situated, significantly, within the southern Massif-Central or the future *Vendée militaire*. Unfortunately, the numbers and classes of the population participating in such protests are seldom known: several thousand in Nîmes, over a thousand in Castres, only a few hundred in Toulouse and Tarbes, but virtually the entire community of the Vendéean village of Saint-Martin-des-Noyers.[37] Though members of the clergy were almost always present, so too were substantial contingents from the elite of the middle class and the nobility, and it was often the latter two groups which provided the leadership.[38]

Clear and unambiguous, however, was the geographic distribution of the protest. (See Figure K.) It presents, over all, a close replication of the crescent of the Calvinist population from the Rhône around the southern Massif-Central and north to Poitou. Twenty-six of the thirty-two sites were within or immediately adjoining Protestant settlements. To be sure, a few of the Protestant-populated sectors were apparently untouched. It is at least tempting to speculate that the apparent absence of protest in Béarn, Périgord, Agenais, and most of Dauphiné (with the major exception of the Rhône and the Isère valleys) may indicate local Catholic populations which felt generally less threatened by their Protestant neigh-

[35] The "towns," as defined by Le Mée, were Nîmes, Montauban, Uzès, Alès, Toulouse, Albi, Saint-Pons, Villefranche, Tarbes, Castres, Moissac, Cahors, Perpignan, Pézenas, Montélimar, and Voiron. The seats of bishoprics were Nîmes, Uzès, Alès, Toulouse, Albi, Saint-Pons, Tarbes, Castres, Cahors, Perpignan, and Saint-Paul-les-Trois-Châteaux.

[36] See the list of clubs and their foundations in Kennedy, 345-61.

[37] Barruel, 14:105-111, 154-64; A.N., D XXIX bis 6; *Inventaire sommaire des Archives communales de Castres* (Castres, 1881), GG 5.

[38] In Nîmes all the members of the commission established to write up their grievances for the king were apparently elite commoners: Lewis, 21. In Castres, the leader seems to have been the Baron de Sénégas. In Tarbes, there was no indication of participation by the clergy, and the curé seems to have avoided taking sides: A.N., D XXIX bis 6, dos. 81. In Uzès the committee to petition the king was made up of a *chevalier*, an *avocat au Parlement*, and a notary; while the Baron de Fontarèches was presiding officer.

FIGURE K
Lay Appeals that Catholicism be Declared the State Religion.
(Each dot indicates one appeal.)

bors.[39] Clearly, the greatest concentration of protest was in the province of Languedoc, in precisely that Nîmes-Montauban axis previously identified as a center of Protestant-Catholic hostilities under the Old Regime.

The specific rationales for protesting the April 13 deliberation were often quite complex.[40] A number of communities criticized the whole range of impending ecclesiastical changes because of their potential effects on the local economies. Both Nîmes and Uzès also linked their religious grievances to the political situation. For the Catholic leaders of these two towns, the fact that such a resolution could be passed at all proved that the National Assembly was being coerced and was no longer free to express the will of the people. It was suggested that the king himself was

[39] While no specific protests have been located in Alsace, it is known, nevertheless, that a German translation of the Nîmes deliberation, circulated in and near Strasbourg, caused "unrest" among the inhabitants: Lewis, 21n.

[40] Unfortunately, detailed rationales have been found for only 18 of the 32 protests.

under duress in Paris and that he should immediately transfer his residence elsewhere in the country.[41] Given the prominence of the nobility in several of the protest meetings, it was only too tempting for the patriots to see the whole affair as an aristocratic plot. Such suspicions seemed amply justified, moreover, after the openly counterrevolutionary Camp de Jalès had been organized as a direct outgrowth of the anti-Protestant hostility in Languedoc.[42]

Yet the dominant theme of protest almost everywhere was the need to protect the Catholic Church in all its integrity from the Protestant menace. Catholics had watched with growing alarm the successive gains of the Protestants in the Revolution and the actions of such powerful Calvinist deputies as Barnave and Rabaut-Saint-Etienne. They were convinced that men such as these were laying siege to Catholicism, that they were putting its very survival in danger.[43] To allow the open practice of two religions in the same country, it was argued, was a sure formula for a return to the civil war of the sixteenth century.[44] If the Church were forced to sell its lands, it was the Huguenots and the Jews who would buy up everything, leaving no resources to the Catholic poor and no Catholic education for the children.[45] There must be no reduction in the number of clergymen, all of whom were necessary for the spiritual needs of the people and for the pomp and circumstance requisite if young Catholics were not to be attracted to the more "facile religion" of Calvin.[46] In this sense, the Catholics of the Midi seemed openly to defend the "baroque" form of religious practice, a baroque which seemed under direct attack from Paris. Was not the National Assembly continually calling for a return to a simplified and purified pristine Christianity and the elimination of all "superfluous" non-parish clergymen? In fact, an ample clergy was essential for religion itself. As the Catholics of Nîmes put it, "the people see in the clergy the firmest support of religion."[47]

Particularly in the smaller rural communities the grievances tended to be almost exclusively religious in their formulation. For La Rochepot in the province of Burgundy—where a small Calvinist contingent survived

[41] For Nîmes and Uzès see Barruel, 14:85, 96-97. For comments on the economic effects, see the statements from Toulouse: A.N., D XXIX bis 6, dos. 86.

[42] Jolivet, 210-11.

[43] Statement from Alès: Barruel, 14:100.

[44] Statement from Toulouse: Barruel, 14:105-111.

[45] Statement from Tarbes: A.N., D XXIX bis 6, dos. 81.

[46] Statements from Uzès: Barruel, 14:167; and from Alès: ibid., 99-103.

[47] Statement from Nîmes: ibid., 84-87.

in nearby Charollais—it was clear that the National Assembly was seeking to destroy the Catholic religion and make Protestantism dominant. For the Rouergat village of Belmont, it was essential that Catholicism alone be the state religion and that it be passed on to the next generation of children without any change whatsoever. For those in the neighboring village of Saint-Juéry, the National Assembly had given the Protestants free rein to insult the Catholics at will and to attempt to dominate them. Was it any wonder that the people were now beginning to lose confidence in all the Revolution's decrees?[48]

This pronouncement by the citizens of Saint-Juéry was revealing and symptomatic. The longstanding tradition of interconfessional hostility, fear, and vendetta through many sectors of Languedoc and Rouergue invariably affected the way in which the local populations viewed not only the religious transformations but the whole Revolutionary constitution. It was scarcely surprising that the Protestants, almost to a man, should enthusiastically throw in their lot with a new regime which had liberated them politically and economically, which had allowed them and their families to come out of the desert.[49] But neither could it be surprising, as James Hood has argued, that the Catholics of the Midi were quickly deterred from viewing the Revolution sympathetically by the very presence in the Revolutionary ranks of the "ideas and men they had learned to hate."[50] The friends of your enemies were your enemies. An oversimplification perhaps: but in the atmosphere of suspicion and assumed conspiracy that pervaded these regions of the south, the old adage may provide more than a small measure of explanation for the political options of both the rural and urban inhabitants.

In the spring of 1790, with word coming in regularly of the imminent sale of Church property, of the imposed retirement of a major segment of the Catholic clergy, of the election of Rabaut-Saint-Etienne as president of the National Assembly, the Dom Gerle affair would serve as a catalyst, binding together with a sense of unity and urgency substantial elements of the Catholic population of Alsace and the Midi. "The Alliance is

[48] Statements from La Rochepot: A.N., D XXIX bis 6, dos. 94; from Saint-Juéry: ibid., dos. 91; from Belmont: F[19] 408.

[49] In Alsace, the Protestants had initially been wary that a transformation engineered by Catholics might integrate their province more fully into post-Revocation France and leave them worse off than before. But with the Declaration of the Rights of Man they enthusiastically embraced the Revolution: Roland Marx, *Recherches sur la vie politique de l'Alsace pré-révolutionnaire et révolutionnaire* (Strasbourg, 1966), 129.

[50] Hood, "Protestant-Catholic Relations," 273-75.

formed," wrote a pamphleteer in Alsace. "The Rabauts and the Barnaves have triumphed in the Assembly. In the provinces of the south Calvinism has taken charge of the committees, it is drawing up speeches, it is seizing control of the forces of the national guard, and it is furiously propagating ... the sentiments of hate, intolerance, and vengeance which animated Calvin, its founder."[51] Talk of an impending "war of religion" was already widespread in the Midi when two major incidents occurred which could only confirm the population in their fears. On May 10 a riot broke out in Montauban which led to the death of five national guardsmen and to a massive temporary exodus of the Protestants from the town.[52] A month later a veritable civil war between Catholics and Protestants exploded in Nîmes, leaving some three hundred dead—most of them Catholic—after three days of combat.[53] There can be no doubt that in both instances religious hatreds reinforced and were reinforced by class conflicts between a Protestant power elite of merchants and manufacturers and an essentially Catholic working force. Yet both incidents would also serve to polarize an already tense religious confrontation in numerous towns and villages where economic conflict played only a minor role.[54] Though open violence tended to subside in the Midi during the following months, the Dom Gerle affair, in many regions of the country, would serve as a veritable dress rehearsal for the oath crisis of 1791.

The Protestant Presence and the Application of the Oath

To anyone, clergyman or layman, already obsessed by the Protestant "menace," the Civil Constitution of the Clergy might well be perceived as a Protestant document. The seizure of Church property by the state, the suppression of religious vows, the elimination of all chapters: measures such as these were immediately compared to the actions of Henry VIII at the beginning of the English Reformation.[55] The selection of parish

[51] Rodolphe Reuss, *La Constitution civile du clergé et la crise religieuse en Alsace (1790-1795)*, 2 vols. (Strasbourg, 1922), 1:18-19.

[52] Poland, 112-18; Lévy-Schneider, 1:65-67; Daniel Ligou, *Montauban à la fin de l'Ancien régime et au début de la Révolution* (Paris, 1958), 231-40.

[53] Durand, 1:123-26; Lewis, 1-40.

[54] Hood argues that no "separate noble interest group opposed to the Revolution emerged in Languedoc" due to "the absence of significant personal privileges for nobles" in the province. The local oligarchs tended to see the Revolution as "primarily ... a threat to the legal and economic position of the Catholic Church": "Protestant-Catholic Relations," 274.

[55] See, for example, Louis Trénard, "Eglise et état: le clergé face à la Révolution dans les diocèses du Nord de la France, 1788-1792," in *Christianisme et pouvoirs politiques* (Lille, 1973), 76.

clergymen by the laity seemed dangerously close to the Calvinist practice. And the weakening of bonds with the Papacy could be viewed only with apprehension. The patriots, including a substantial proportion of the French clergy, might insist that such actions marked a renewal of religion, a return to the primitive simplicity of the religion of Jesus and the early church fathers. But the argument itself was suspiciously evocative of sixteenth-century statements by Luther and Calvin. Indeed, the very idea of a simplified and purified religion, of the religious austerity apparently embraced by the Revolutionary leadership, might smack of Calvinism and clash with the aesthetic sensitivities of people who still identified themselves with the "baroque" expressions of the Counter-Reformation.

With the advent of the oath of 1791, the actions of certain Protestants could only further confirm such fears. Though prudence might have dictated a neutral position on an issue which did not directly concern them, many Protestants eagerly affirmed their patriotic devotion to the new laws and openly savored the decline in power and wealth suffered by the Catholic clergy, their former persecutors. Pastor Lacombe in the region of Foix published a tract defending the Civil Constitution, much to the irritation of the local Catholics.[56] A number of Alsatian pastors would voluntarily swear the same oath required of the priests—as a prelude, some suggested, to demanding full status as state-paid *fonctionnaires publics*.[57] In Millau, the Calvinists were described as doing everything they could to "torment" the Catholics, even to the point of ostentatiously attending the religious services given by the constitutional curé, services which were shunned by the Catholic laity.[58] In Strasbourg the Protestant leadership felt obliged to take its congregation to task for "irritating our Catholic brothers," in the midst of their predicament before the oath. "We are convinced that your ridicule will never increase the numbers of the true friends of truth and liberty. We strongly disapprove of the sarcasm and insulting words which certain thoughtless members of our confession have allowed themselves to utter against the partisans of a different faith."[59]

Throughout Alsace and the southeast—and in certain other areas as well—numerous priests pictured the oath as a Protestant plot from the very beginning. Curés near Foix announced that the National Assembly

---

[56] Wemyss, 54.

[57] Letter from a municipal officer in Strasbourg, May 1, 1791: A.N., D IV 56, no. 1651.

[58] Report by the Ministry of the Interior on the troubles in Millau in 1791: A.N., F¹⁹ 408.

[59] Statement of Jan. 16, 1791: Rodolphe Reuss, *L'Alsace pendant la Révolution française*, 2 vols. (Paris, 1881-84), 2:117-18.

which had imposed the oath was "made up of Protestants," and that anyone who accepted the oath could only be a Calvinist or a Lutheran at heart. A similar statement emerged from the curé of Le Fenouiller in Vendée, who protested that the Civil Constitution had "trampled Catholicism underfoot." In Haute-Saône, not far from the Protestant stronghold of Montbéliard, the curé of Dambenoît advised those recognizing the constitutional bishop to begin attending services with the Huguenots.[60] And a number of priests in Lozère proclaimed that it was the Protestants who were forcing the refractory parish priests to abandon their flocks. According to the curé of Banassac, the National Assembly was striving to abolish five of the seven sacraments, just as the Calvinists had done.[61]

Yet, as always, the opinions and pressures of the people themselves were equally important in influencing the positions of the clergy. A number of parish clergymen in Vivarais justified their refusals of the oath by invoking the popular belief that the Revolutionary government wished to force them to embrace Protestantism. "Any priest taking the oath in this area," wrote the curé of Saint-Etienne-de-Lugdarès, "would run the risk of being thrown out of his parish and perhaps assassinated."[62] Farther south in the department of Tarn, twenty-two mayors and municipal officers representing nine communities signed a statement formally refusing their cooperation with the oath legislation, which, it was said, would annihilate the Catholic religion and favor the Protestants.[63] As usual, women often formed the vanguard, the agents of "popular opinion" brought to bear on the priests. Thus, in a Tarn village near Castres, it was a "mob" of women who rioted and forbade their priests to swear the oath: any clergyman harboring such a thought "might as well leave his head at home, for he would surely lose it if he came there." And some two-hundred women in Vabre, a neighboring community in southern Languedoc, physically seized the oath decree of November 27 and tore it to shreds, threatening any priest with a stoning if he should even consider

---

[60] Wemyss, 219; G. Arnaud, *Histoire de la Révolution dans le département de l'Ariège* (Toulouse, 1904), 228; A.N., D XXIX bis 21, dos. 227, no. 19; Jean Girardot, "Clergé réfractaire et clergé constitutionnel en Haute-Saône pendant la Révolution," *Mémoires de la Société pour l'histoire du droit et des institutions des anciens pays bourguignons, comtois et romands*, 24 (1963), 128-29.

[61] See the deliberations of the directory of the department of Lozère, Aug. 4, 1791: A.N., D XIX 22, dos. 365; and Ferdinand André, ed., *Délibérations de l'administration départementale de la Lozère et de son directoire de 1790 à 1800*, 4 vols. (Mende, 1882-84), 1:438.

[62] "Le serment de 1791 dans l'Ardèche," *Semaine religieuse du diocèse de Viviers*, 83-84 (1964-65), 476-77; and Jolivet, 262.

[63] A.N., D XXIX bis 21, dos. 224, no. 23.

taking the oath.[64] In fact, if we believe one of the rare patriot priests of Vabre, the entire local society, nobles and commoners, the masses and the elites—including the entire municipal administration—were ignoring the new legislation on religion and the oath and were openly talking of an impending "civil war."[65]

The potential for violence over the question of the oath increased considerably in those towns of the Midi in which individual Protestants had succeeded in entering or even gaining control of the local power structure—either through the municipal council or the national guard. In 1790 the political struggles between Catholics and Protestants had already played an important role in both the Montauban riots and the "bagarre" in Nîmes. The Aveyron town of Millau saw a similar, if less bloody, uprising shortly after the implementation of the oath laws was announced.[66] In this case, since a portion of the Millau town council was Calvinist, it was literally the Protestants who were imposing the oath on the Catholic clergy. On January 25, 1791, some two hundred active citizens met in the chapel of the Penitents to petition the city government not to enforce the oath "against the constitution of the Roman Church." Shortly thereafter some four to five hundred women and, it was said, "men dressed as women," besieged the city hall, and finally succeeded in dragging the mayor and one Calvinist councilman into the public square and forcing both of them to resign their posts. The Jacobins of Rodez, in reporting the incident, were especially appalled that neither the national guard nor the district directory of Millau lifted a finger to help the mayor. In its response the district simply appealed to the principle of popular sovereignty, arguing that their first duty was to their constituents and that the overwhelming majority of the local population was determined that no oath should be imposed.

Though most of the conflicts described thus far occurred in Languedoc or Rouergue, similar incidents linking opposition to Protestantism with opposition to the oath would transpire in Alsace. At the beginning of January 1791 departmental officials in Bas-Rhin predicted that lower-class hostility between Catholics and Protestants might explode at any moment.[67] And, in fact, a riot broke out in Strasbourg on January 3 over

[64] Ibid., dos. 231, nos. 2 and 4.

[65] Ibid., no. 2.

[66] Ibid., dos. 226, no. 37; A.D. Aveyron, 6 L 273; B. Combes de Patris, *Procès-verbaux des séances de la société populaire de Rodez* (Carrère, 1912), 641-42, 646-47. I have also profited from a conversation with Peter Jones.

[67] Reuss, *La Constitution civile*, 1:28-29.

the government's attempts to close the collegiate church of Saint-Pierre-le-Vieux and to confiscate its archives and sacred ornaments. Rumors had spread widely that it was all part of a plot by the Protestants to seize control of the town's Catholic churches—including the cathedral itself—for their own use. When a group of women found that the workers present to collect the church possessions and board up the building were themselves Protestants, they began throwing rocks and threatening the accompanying national guard.[68] Two weeks later a large meeting was held in the seminary opposing the transference of any Catholic churches to the Protestants and announcing that the Catholic citizens of the city "would never permit their priests to take the oath."[69] The Alsatians were particularly exasperated by the laws on the election of curés, since there were districts in Bas-Rhin where Lutherans and Calvinists were in the majority and where, consequently, the Protestants could not only take charge in enforcing the oath but might easily dictate the appointment of clergymen to Catholic parishes. The fears of Lutherans' meddling in Catholic affairs seemed amply confirmed by the presence of over a hundred Protestants in the electoral assembly which selected a constitutional bishop for the Bas-Rhin.[70]

In the coming months, as repressive measures against the refractory clergy tightened, the outcome of events seemed only too bitterly ironic to many Catholics. The very Revolution which brought the Protestants out of the desert had now created a new desert to which the refractory Catholic clergy was henceforth to be exiled. Was it not all a mockery of the religious freedom guaranteed by the Declaration of the Rights of Man?[71] In a long petition to the king, the Catholic citizens of Lunel in Hérault would describe their bitterness and humiliation at being treated unequally to "Moslems and Calvinists."[72] In a similar petition from Lédenon in Gard, Catholics lamented the loss of their curé, taken away from them by "outsiders (étrangers) who profess a religion different than ours."[73] In Upper Vivarais, to believe the curé of Joannas, "the population sincerely believes that the government wants them to embrace the Protestant religion." In Alsace a great many Catholics referred to the con-

[68] Ibid., 19-25.

[69] Reuss, L'Alsace pendant la Révolution, 2:121.

[70] Reuss, La Constitution civile, 1:5-9, 146-52.

[71] The directory of the department of Bas-Rhin had already mused on this paradox in November of 1790: ibid., 7-9.

[72] Letter dated Oct. 31, 1791: A.N., F¹⁹ 430.

[73] Letter dated Nov. 1, 1791: A.N., F¹⁹ 426.

stitutional clergy as the "Lutheran Church."[74] For the peoples of the southeast and of Alsace, all the apprehensions of a Protestant conspiracy to take over seemed only too close to reality. In circumstances such as these one could scarcely expect a willing acceptance of either the Civil Constitution or of the Revolution that had spawned it.

Conclusion: Religious Frontiers?

That a connection frequently existed between a Protestant presence and an antipathy toward the Civil Constitution on the part of the Catholic population can scarcely be put into question. Yet it is also evident that the relationship was far from simple, that the mere existence of Calvinists or Lutherans did not everywhere have the same effect. Nearly all the examples presented here originated in Languedoc and Alsace. One is hard put to find similar confirmation in such traditional Protestant strongholds as Dauphiné, Saintonge, or Guyenne. In point of fact, the correlation coefficient for all departments in France between the percentage of oath-takers and the size of the Protestant population—whether in absolute numbers or as a proportion of the total population—is statistically insignificant.[75] Even if one focuses only on those departments with greater numbers of Protestants—over 1 percent or over 5 percent of the total population—the correlation is probably not significant. The twenty-five departments with 1 percent Protestant populations had aggregate oath rates of just over 50 percent, only a very little less than the kingdom-wide average. For the nine departments with 5 percent Protestant contingents, the oath-taking proportion dropped to 38 percent, but included departments ranging from 16 percent (Lozère) to 84 percent (Drôme).[76]

The picture becomes even more complex if one examines in greater detail the sub-regions within the individual departments. Often the sectors with the greatest Protestant densities are found to have somewhat higher oath rates than other nearby areas: thus, Lower Vivarais in Ardèche, the

[74] Letter to the district of Tanargue, Feb. 1, 1791: Jolivet, 262; Marx, 123.

[75] On the Protestant population in 1815, see above, note 1. For 82 departments, excluding Corsica, the correlation between the oath percentage and the proportion of Protestants is -0.262. But when the two "outliers" of Gard and Bas-Rhin are excluded—both with much higher Protestant populations than in any other department—the coefficient drops to -0.097. With the absolute numbers of Protestants, the coefficients are -0.258 and -0.058, respectively.

[76] In the 25 departments with Protestant populations less than or equal to 1 percent of the total, the coefficient is -0.460, but -0.081 when Gard and Bas-Rhin are excluded. In the 9 departments with Protestant populations less than or equal to 5 percent, the coefficients are -0.361 and 0.198, respectively.

highlands of Gard, the cantons near Montbéliard in Doubs, southern Vendée and Deux-Sèvres near Fontenay, the mountainous portions of Drôme, and the central Agenais. If one attempts an approximate characterization, it would seem that the lowest oath rates in the "Protestant" departments were often within relatively isolated and strongly agrarian sectors just outside and immediately confronting the major Calvinist or Lutheran concentrations: in Upper Vivariais, Velay, Gévaudan, Rouergue, Albigeois, the Basque area, the Jura plateau (confronting the Swiss cantons as well as Montbéliard), and northwestern Poitou (within the future "Vendée militaire"). Such a confrontational effect would seem distinctly less operative, however, in many of those adjoining areas like the Rhône Valley, the Mediterranean coast, and the middle and lower Garonne Valley which were more "urbanized" in character: regions with a greater presence of clustered towns exhibiting more differentiated social structures and tighter links to communication networks.[77] Obviously and perhaps inevitably, there are a certain number of cases which do not seem to fit this summary generalization: Lower Alsace, for example—where the largest Protestant populations were directly associated with the lowest oath-taking rates—or the "urbanized" but refractory sectors of Nîmes and the central Rhône delta. But, as we have also seen, it is essential to take note of the quality as well as the quantity of the Protestant presence. In both Alsace and in the Nîmes-Montauban axis, the Protestants were economically powerful and had been particularly active, well-organized, and aggressive throughout the eighteenth century. In the case of Languedoc there was also a deep collective memory of Protestant violence, a collective memory which undoubtedly conditioned the Catholic reaction to the Dom Gerle affair in the spring of 1790. This partial pattern would at least seem to justify a reexamination of a thesis suggested by Pierre Chaunu, stipulating the existence of a series of internal "frontiers of Catholicism" in seventeenth- and eighteenth-century France.[78] In those regions where Catholic populations confronted substantial contingents of Protestants, the contact and friction might engender a peculiar mental outlook on the part of the Catholics, an outlook that was at once aggressive

[77] On "urbanization" see the previous chapter and Charles Tilly, *The Vendée: A Sociological Analysis of the Counterrevolution of 1793* (Cambridge, Mass., 1964), 16-37.

[78] See especially Pierre Chaunu, "Une histoire religieuse sérielle. A propos du diocèse de La Rochelle (1648-1724) et sur quelques exemples normands," *RHMC*, 12 (1965), 24-32; and "Jansénisme et frontière de catholicité," *RH*, 127 (1962), 115-38; also, Jean Orcibal, *Etat présent des recherches sur la répartition géographique des 'Nouveaux catholiques' à la fin du XVIIe siècle* (Paris, 1948).

for the propagation of the true faith and defensive of the Catholic values and traditions threatened by the adjacent "foreigners." In the light of the present analysis, one might add some additional refinements to the thesis. In the first place, it would be necessary to take into account the strength of the local Calvinist or Lutheran identity and cohesion, factors partly— but only partly—related to the sheer numbers of Protestants. And, secondly, one would need to give some consideration to the effects of local social structures on Protestant-Catholic relations. All else being equal, it seems probable that the Protestant "threat" appeared most menacing and frightening in rural, dispersed, and essentially closed societies in which there was a greater premium on conservative and conformative values and behavior, but in which there was also a greater physical separation from social intercourse with neighboring Protestants.[79] If such distinctions are valid, they may also help explain the differential "thickness" of the frontier effect, the distance to which a Protestant presence was still conceived as a threat: the fact that whole provinces, like the overwhelmingly agrarian Rouergue and Gévaudan, might be sensitive to a "Protestant menace" on their southeastern frontiers.

It seems likely that in large segments of northern and central France, the Civil Constitution of the Clergy was perceived by the mass of the population as a straightforward piece of legislation, badly needed to reform abuses in the Church and the clergy. Yet, through substantial sectors of the Midi and Alsace, the existence of Lutherans and Calvinists had helped to make traditional Catholicism integral and central to the basic self-image of the inhabitants. For people such as these, the Civil Constitution and the oath imposed on their priests might well be perceived as a frontal attack on a fundamental element of their very identity.

[79] Worth citing in this regard is the evidence of David Bien taken from witnesses testifying in the Calas affair. Those with no personal contact with Calas were the most convinced of a vast Protestant plot. Those who had known Calas personally were much more sympathetic to his plight and less inclined toward the conspiracy theory: Bien, 145-47.

TEN

Clericalism and the Oath[1]

THE preceding exploration of the Protestant "menace" has demonstrated the importance of more purely religious issues in the
popular reception of the Civil Constitution and the oath. Yet this
anti-Protestant syndrome seems to have been largely confined to several
specific regions of France. Beyond the confessional battle lines in Alsace-
Lorraine and the Languedoc-Rouergue sector of the Midi, accusations of
a Huguenot influence on Revolutionary policies might be found scattered
in a number of provinces—even in western and northern France. Several
priests in Brittany were said to be linking the juring clergy to the Protestants, comparing the reforms of 1790 with those of Henry VIII, or
announcing the formation of a Calvinist plot to create a "Huguenot
republic" and take revenge for the Revocation of 1685.[2] But nowhere
outside the Midi and the northeast does the issue appear to have aroused
such intense popular emotions, such an obsessional preoccupation among
the laity. The single largest cluster of refractory provinces—the "West"
of Normandy, Brittany, Maine, Anjou, and Lower Poitou—contained
only a few tiny Calvinist congregations clinging to existence, virtually
unseen and unnoticed by the overwhelmingly dominant Catholic population. Indeed, the position on the oath of this great western sector of
the kingdom remains something of a mystery.

And, nevertheless, our examination of the Protestant provinces may
provide us with an additional clue for understanding reactions to the
Revolution elsewhere in the kingdom. We have noted the laity's frequent
emphasis on the clergy as a central element in the Catholic cult, as "the

[1] Portions of this chapter originally appeared in the author's articles, "The 'West' in France
in 1789: the Religious Factor in the Origins of the Counterrevolution," *JMH*, 54 (1982), 715-
45; and "French Clericalism under the Old Regime and the Ecclesiastical Oath of 1791" in
Proceedings of the Eleventh Annual Meeting of the Western Society for French History, John F.
Sweet, ed. (Lawrence, Kansas, 1984), 156-65. They are reproduced in part here with the permission of the editors of the respective publications. See also the author's "Ecclesiastical Structures
and Clerical Geography on the eve of the French Revolution," *FHS*, 11 (1980), 352-70 (published
with Claude Langlois).

[2] Donald Sutherland, *The Chouans: the Social Origins of the Popular Counter-Revolution in
Upper Brittany, 1770-1796* (Oxford, 1982), 248; J. Le Falher, *Le royaume de Bignan (1789-1905)*
(Hennebont, 1913), 103; René Kerviler, *Recherches et notices sur les députés de la Bretagne aux
Etats-Généraux*, 2 vols. (Rennes, 1889), 1:143.

firmest support of religion." In precisely this respect, the complex of ecclesiastical changes embodied in the new laws had the potential for producing a powerful effect on popular perceptions of the Revolution. For, whatever else it did, the Civil Constitution clearly effected a sweeping transformation in the social, cultural, and economic status of the priest. To be sure, the Revolutionaries of 1790 never publicly questioned the basic sacerdotal powers of clergymen in the religious mysteries of the Catholic faith—even though a few, like Mirabeau and Robespierre, had little personal understanding of such mysteries and tended to view the priest as an "ecclesiastical functionary" charged with responsibilities over "public happiness."[3] Yet these same Revolutionaries did, without a doubt, substantially chip away at the clergy's secular powers and sources of prestige: powers which, in the mind of the rural population, were perhaps never altogether disassociated from the priests' supernatural capacities. Thus, the destruction of the local clergy's economic independence through the suppression of the tithes and the nationalization of Church lands was a distinct blow to the curé's "notability" in the rural society. The appointment of all parish priests through elections in the district assembly, rather than through the nomination of an ecclesiastical superior, served to underscore the clergyman's new position as a kind of government bureaucrat increasingly under the control of the civil authorities. This impression could only have been reinforced by the Constituent's requirement of a civil oath on the part of all "ecclesiastical public functionaries," as they were now officially designated.

But equally important was the extraordinary "rationalization" or "functionalization" of the clergy: the Revolution's wholesale elimination of all clerical positions not involved in "useful" functions within the Church, where utility was defined exclusively as the cure of souls and the dispensing of sacraments. As the new laws were implemented in late 1790 and early 1791, a hundred thousand ecclesiastics and religious, close to three-fifths of the men and women of the Old-Regime clergy, would find themselves abruptly forced into varying degrees of early retirement—unless, of course, they opted to join the parish clergy and "make something useful of themselves."[4] The enforced retirement of all regulars, canons, and lesser chapter clergymen would perhaps have had relatively little importance in the countryside, where most of the population resided. But the new laws would also affect a host of minor clergymen—chaplains,

[3] See, for example, the speech by Robespierre on May 31, 1790: *AP*, 16:3.
[4] Tackett and Langlois, 357. See also the development in chp. 1 above.

227

habitués, and members of rural "societies of priests"—who played an integral part in the parish service and ritual life in certain regions of the country. Numerous complaints would soon be voiced against this standardization of clerical posts and its effects on local religious practice. As early as January 8, 1791, one deputy in the National Assembly relayed the anxieties of his constituency that the retirement of all chaplains and *habitués* would seriously disrupt feast-day celebrations, thus "inciting the discontent of weaker souls." A few months later, a village in Lower Brittany would protest that the five to seven priests formerly serving the parish in pastoral functions had now been reduced to a single curé—an extreme case, perhaps, but indicative of the apprehension engendered in a number of regions over the massive reductions in clerical service.[5] Equally serious, the wholesale elimination of all non-parish clergymen entailed the effective closing of numerous rural chapels and pilgrimage sites manned by such ecclesiastics and the profound disruption of the rites and processions associated with the chapels. Closings of this kind were pushed even more vigorously in the spring and summer of 1791, after many such chapels came to be viewed as the haunts of refractory priests pursuing "anti-constitutional" activities. In the summer of 1791, a number of departments would push for the immediate closing of every church or chapel not used by a parish or by a specific social institution such as a prison or a hospital.[6] But frequently the suppression of the non-parish chapels was launched even earlier. In February 1791 two commissioners of Bas-Rhin were already attempting to close down the important Alsatian pilgrimage sites at Marienthal and Sainte-Odile. On their arrival, the commissioners were met by several thousand people demanding that the laws not be enforced.[7]

In fact, from a certain point of view, the Civil Constitution of the Clergy and the associated religious legislation might easily be construed as "anticlerical" documents. For anyone who took seriously the official doctrine establishing the clergy as a necessary element in religious practice, the Revolutionary laws might even appear as an attack on religion itself. But how seriously was this doctrine taken? And to what extent might opinions have differed in the various regions of Old-Regime France? In order to explore these issues more fully, it is first necessary to examine

[5] Speech by an unnamed deputy, Jan. 8, 1791: *AP,* 22:81; and letter from the community of Taulé, autumn 1791: A.N., F¹⁹ 425 (Finistère).

[6] See, for example, the arrêt in Haute-Marne of July 1791: A.N., F¹⁹ 448.

[7] A.N., D XIX 82, dos. 641, no. 3.

the long-term development of clericalism in the kingdom and its relation to popular religion.

The Clericalization of Popular Religion

In the context of Old-Regime France, the term "clericalism" may be thought to signify, first, the integration of the clergy and of clerical powers into the general belief system, to the extent that the priest would be viewed as necessary for the pursuance of religious practice and the attaining of supernatural objectives; and, second, the readiness on the part of the population to accept and, in some cases, to *require* the leadership of the priest over the parish. There was, in fact, a curious paradox inherent in this position, a paradox which must be carefully noted from the outset. For clericalism, as such, did not imply blind obedience by the population toward all ecclesiastics. First, it primarily concerned those clergymen encountered within the community on a day-to-day basis, and it might altogether exclude monks, canons, and even bishops, perceived as outsiders and perhaps exploiters of the community. But, second, clericalism also entailed a complex of lay expectations concerning the proper role and behavior of the priest. It was in this sense that local ecclesiastics might literally be compelled by the laity to provide them with leadership, a leadership informed, in large measure, by the norms and conventions of the community.[8] Clearly, clericalism must be construed as having both a sociopolitical and a religious-theological dimension.

It is a curious fact that while a great deal has been written on the origins and nature of French anticlericalism, the history of clericalism itself has been only peripherally explored. Yet recent research into the implementation of the Catholic Reformation in France and the attitudes of the reformers toward the pre-existent "popular religion" of the masses may help illuminate certain aspects of the question. It seems clear that one of the central concerns of the clerical hierarchy in the seventeenth and eighteenth centuries had been to organize a veritable purge and acculturation of the local religious practices of large segments of the rural population.[9] Under attack was a complex profusion of popular beliefs

---

[8] Compares the analysis of the peasants' attitude toward the "leadership" of the nobility in Sutherland, 167-94. Note also the cases of curés enlisted or forced to lead the insurrectionary movements of their parishioners in the seventeenth century: Madeleine Foisil, *La révolte des nu-pieds et les révoltes normandes de 1639* (Paris, 1970), 203-206; and Yves-Marie Bercé, *Histoire des Croquants* (Paris, 1974), 665-66.

[9] Among the extensive recent literature touching on "popular religion" and the effects of the Tridentine reforms, see Jean Delumeau, *Le catholicisme entre Luther et Voltaire* (Paris, 1971)

with substantial variations from region to region. Included were numerous embellishments of Catholic rites and liturgical cycles, often entailing virtual parallel cults accompanying the celebration of the sacraments or the Easter and Christmas rituals. Many such practices were distinctly magical in character, with specific functions for curing ailments, bringing rain, or ensuring the fertility of crops, animals, and human kind. Also to be associated with "popular religion" were cults devoted to certain saints or relics, cults which developed with particular vigor in the late Middle Ages and which frequently took on a polytheistic character.[10] Finally, there was the specifically festive character which "popular religion" lent to Catholic rites, with sacred feast days called upon as the occasions for widespread revelry and merrymaking. A great many of these practices were followed independently or semi-independently from the supervision of the Catholic clergy. As people in the region of Nice put it, "the priest sings the mass, but the saint leads the festival."[11]

Though the official hierarchy had long disapproved of certain of these practices, the challenge of the Protestant Reformation had pushed the Church into a new and far more aggressive stance. First, in response to the attacks on Catholic "superstition" and the "profanation" of religious rites, the Church undertook vigorous efforts to "purify" religion, to operate wherever possible a radical growth in the distance between the sacred and the profane.[12] Second, in order to effect this purification and, at the same time, to counter the Protestant call for a universal priesthood, the Catholic leadership placed a far stronger emphasis than ever before on the distinct and essential role of sacerdotal powers and the hierarchical society of the clergy in the pursuance of religious objectives.[13] Even though

and *La mort des pays de Cocagne* (Paris, 1976); Yves-Marie Bercé, *Fête et révolte. Des mentalités populaires du XVIe au XVIIIe siècle* (Paris, 1976); Robert Muchembled, *Culture populaire et culture des élites dans la France moderne* (Paris, 1978); Bernard Plongeron and Robert Panet, *Le christianisme populaire* (Paris, 1976); *La religion populaire. Paris, 17-19 octobre 1977.* (Colloques internationaux du Centre national de la recherche scientifique, no. 576) (Paris, 1979); Marie-Hélène Froeschlé-Chopard, *La religion populaire en Provence orientale au XVIIIe siècle* (Paris, 1980); François Lebrun, ed., *L'histoire des catholiques en France* (Toulouse, 1980); Marc Venard, *L'Eglise d'Avignon au XVIe siècle*, 5 vols. (Lille, 1980); Philip T. Hoffman, *Church and Community in the Diocese of Lyon, 1500-1789* (New Haven, 1984).

[10] Bernard Plongeron, "Le procès de la fête de l'Ancien régime," *Le christianisme populaire*, 175.

[11] Ibid.

[12] Dominique Julia, "Discipline ecclésiastique et culture paysanne aux XVIIe et XVIIIe siècles," in *La religion populaire*, 199-201.

[13] Robert Sauzet, "Présence rénovée du catholicisme, 1520-1670," in *Histoire des catholiques*, 85-86.

the acts of the Council of Trent were never officially promulgated in France, the French episcopacy gradually adopted the spirit of Trent in their own reforming efforts, efforts coordinated, in large measure, through the General Assemblies of the Clergy. Throughout the seventeenth century one of the bishops' principal tasks was to recapture clerical control over the proliferation of popular religious activities: first, by the direct repression of the most blatantly offensive practices; second, by the indoctrination of the population through the systematic use of the catechisms and missionary preaching; and, third, by the redirection of popular religious energies into forms of devotion more easily dominated and supervised by the clergy.

Indeed, some recent writers have described what they see as a confrontation in the seventeenth and eighteenth centuries between two distinct cultures, two different religions, with an initially urban-based clergy, soon supported by members of the urban lay elite, seeking to instigate a true "cultural revolution" among a country populace which they openly described as "pagan" or "savage."[14] In this sense, the "Christianization" of the French countryside described by the Catholic historian Jean Delumeau and others as reaching its pinnacle in the eighteenth century might more aptly be described as an attempted "clericalization" of popular religion.[15]

The goals of the clergy and the nature of the confrontation can be illustrated through the examination of two particularly important focuses of reform: the attack on popular feast-day celebrations and the efforts to control and redirect the religious confraternities. In the first instance, the aim was never to eliminate feast-day observances altogether but to reduce their numbers substantially and to regulate their celebration more closely. Thus, the bishops commonly sought, first, to have all parish patron-saint feast days celebrated on the same date throughout the diocese—to prevent the populations of adjoining villages from attending one another's festivals—and, second, to reduce to a minimum, under careful clerical control, the secular hilarity and festivity traditionally associated with such celebrations. A first peak of repression was reached in the later seventeenth century when the efforts of the General Assembly of the Clergy to root out "scandal and superstition" were encouraged by Colbert—who was probably more interested in increasing the number of working days

[14] Froeschlé-Chopard, esp. 139-40. Also Sauzet, 129-30; and Plongeron, 172.

[15] Delumeau, *Le catholicisme*, 256-92. *Cf.* also Delumeau's later interpretation in "Déchristianisation ou nouveau modèle de christianisme?" *Archives de sciences sociales des religions*, 40 (1975), 3-20. Dominique Julia suggests this interpretation in the article cited, 208-209.

in the kingdom.[16] But there was a second wave of attacks in the later half of the eighteenth century, prompted by the logic of the Catholic Enlightenment as much as by the more traditional arguments. The *fêtes* were now castigated as affronts not only to religion and morality, but to reason as well. Many such celebrations were, after all, centered on saints proved apocryphal by historical criticism. And the secular festivities accompanying them were seen as frightful wastes of time, money, and food and as frequently leading to overindulgence in strong drink. There were numerous diocesan rulings after 1760 severely limiting the number of feast days to be celebrated.[17]

But as they struggled to reduce and control the popular festivals, the reforming clergy also sought to emphasize selected older forms of religious expression and to encourage new ones which the Church might more easily direct and monitor. Certain confraternities, popular since the Middle Ages, had often given rise to uncontrolled parallel devotions in competition with the official parish cult. Such was the case, for example, with many of the confraternities of Penitents, particularly popular in the southern provinces of the realm, and forever the subject of discord between the curés and their male parishioners. But, from the sixteenth century on, some of the relatively newer devotional confraternities found particular favor with the reforming clergy, in part because of the theological orientation of these confraternities and in part because of their greater malleability before clerical authority. Such, in particular, were the confraternities of the Rosary and of the Blessed Sacrament, with their emphasis on highly orthodox devotion within the confines of the parish church.[18] Such too was the devotion to the Sacred Heart, originally dating

[16] Plongeron, 172-73; Maarten Ultée, "The Suppression of *Fêtes* in France, 1666," *CHR*, 62 (1976), esp. 182-84.

[17] Plongeron, "Le procès de la fête," 173-74, 180-83; and "Le fait religieux dans l'histoire de la Révolution française," *AHRF*, 47 (1975), 105-106; Ultée, 182; Michel Peronnet, *Les évêques de l'ancienne France* (Lille, 1977), 917-18. The new offensive against feast-day celebrations was perhaps also inspired, in part, by the Jansenists: see Anne-Marie Poynet, "Jansénisme et *Aufklärung* catholique devant la fête chrétienne à la fin de l'Ancien régime," in *Les fêtes de la Révolution. Colloque de Clermont-Ferrand (juin 1974)*, Jean Ehrard and Paul Viallaneix, eds. (Paris, 1977), 99-113.

[18] Gabriel Le Bras, "Les confréries chrétiennes, problèmes et propositions," *Revue historique de droit français et étranger*, 4e série, vols. 19-20 (1940-41), 310-63; Maurice Agulhon, *Pénitents et Francs-Maçons de l'ancienne Provence* (Paris, 1968); the author's *Priest and Parish in Eighteenth-Century France* (Princeton, 1977), 194-202; Froeschlé-Chopard, 143-255; Louis Pérouas, "La diffusion de la confrérie du Rosaire au XVIIe siècle dans les pays creusois," *Mémoires de la Société des sciences naturelles et archéologiques de la Creuse*, 38 (1975), 431-48; Jean Quéniart, *Les hommes, l'église et Dieu dans la France du XVIIIe siècle* (Paris, 1978), 215; Hoffman, 105-114.

to the thirteenth century, but revived and increasingly supported by bishops and curés in the late seventeenth and eighteenth centuries. Confraternities of both the Sacred Heart and the Rosary were frequently created in the wake of missionary campaigns—such as those of Jean Eudes and his followers in western France. Certain of the missionaries even publicized the cults through the distribution of cheap paperback books in the manner of the *bibliothèque bleue*. By the later eighteenth century a number of bishops were also encouraging the creation of Sacred Heart confraternities.[19]

But if most historians now recognize the hierarchy's attempts to establish a more clerically controlled religion, the real success of these efforts remains somewhat uncertain. To what extent had the rural masses of the population genuinely internalized the changes inculcated from above? And why might some areas of the country have been more affected than others?

Ecclesiastical Strategies and the Limits of Clericalization

From one perspective, at least, it would seem that the French clergy had been remarkably successful in the campaign to reassert its influence. By the eighteenth century the overwhelming majority of the rural population was apparently fulfilling the basic requirements of religious practice: the yearly confession before their priest and communion at Eastertime in their parish church.[20] Yet the full significance of this practice appears far from clear, particularly since the "Easter duties" had become an obligation not only by the laws of the Church but by royal decree as well.[21] In fact, there is reason to believe that in many regions of the kingdom, and perhaps in almost all rural areas, a substantial body of popular religious beliefs continued to prosper or was, at best, only partially concealed by clerically approved practices. Regardless of episcopal interdictions, many countrypeople continued to observe and celebrate their preferred feast days, only slightly annoyed when clergymen refused to participate. In-

[19] Plongeron, "Le procès de la fête," 186-88. For an interesting example of a priest's struggle and eventual success in arousing his parishioners' interest in the creation of a Sacred Heart confraternity, see the letters of the curé of La Chapelle-en-Valgaudemar to the bishop of Gap, Dec. 1787-Aug. 1789: A.D. Hautes-Alpes, G 986. Ultimately, it was only after an epidemic had struck the parish that the people came to accept the proposal with enthusiasm.

[20] Gabriel Le Bras, *Etudes de sociologie religieuse*, 2 vols. (Paris, 1955-56), 1:275-77. There are, to be sure, signs of far less assiduous practice in many of the towns of the realm, though these are still rather poorly known: see ibid., 277-79; and the following chapter.

[21] Delumeau, "Déchristianisation," 8.

deed, the bishops' efforts to reduce or displace feast days might even incite forms of popular rebellion. Thus, when the bishop of Toul attempted such a procedure in 1767, his actions ignited "violent remonstrances" throughout the diocese from people protesting the suppression of these "eminently popular institutions." Far more dramatic was the reaction to the bishop of Cahors, who not only transferred all *fêtes* to the same day everywhere in his diocese, but also forbade the ringing of church bells during thunderstorms to drive away evil spirits threatening the crops. In the midst of the Great Fear of 1789, there was a riot against the bishop and an attack on his episcopal palace that was directly linked to his earlier tampering with popular beliefs.[22]

On the front lines, so to speak, charged with the direct application of episcopal policies, the curés were often particularly harried and disconcerted by the "superstitions" of the troops in their care. Some expressed their irritation at having to witness such dubious activities as processions to isolated holy fountains or special rites for crop fertility or excommunications of grasshoppers and caterpillars. And a certain number, determined to assert their authority, steadfastly refused to countenance or cooperate with practices of this kind. Thus, Henri Reymond, curé of La Bâtie-Neuve in Dauphiné, was prepared to confront a virtual revolt of his parish rather than participate in a "high-mountain" procession which he considered indecent for the clergy and the mysteries of the Church.[23]

Yet many other curés were sensitive to the need for devising some form of compromise with rural beliefs. After all, if they were too strict or intolerant, they risked losing the confidence of the parish, falling behind perhaps in the competition with local witches and magicians.[24] Such would seem to have been the approach ultimately taken by Curé Christophle Sauvageon in the late seventeenth century during his long encounter with the "superstition" of the peasants in the depths of Sologne. To follow the eighteenth-century writings of Jean-Baptiste Michon, parish priest in Limousin, there was always a necessary gap between the directives of the bishops on feast days or saints' cults and their actual enforcement in his parish. By the end of the Old Regime in the dioceses of Toul and of Gap, the parish clergy was sometimes coming to the support of

[22] Eugène Martin, *Histoire des diocèses de Toul, de Nancy et de Saint-Dié*, 3 vols. (Paris, 1903), 2:421, 603-605; Eugène Sol, *L'église de Cahors au XVIIIe siècle* (Aurillac, 1948), 80, 85-86; and A.D. Lot, G 16. See also Bercé, 156-62; Julia, 207; Tackett, *Priest and Parish*, 208.

[23] Tackett, *Priest and Parish*, 208-209. The curé in question is not to be confused with the political leader of the province.

[24] Julia, 205-206.

the population and was strongly opposing their bishop over the issue of reorganizing the feast days. Perhaps the curé of Rilly-sur-Aisne near Reims expressed the ambiguous feelings of many curés: a curious oscillation between exasperation and resignation. He was convinced that it could even be dangerous for a curé to raise his hand "against the crude country religion"; "... the peasant who willingly accepts criticisms on questions of morality will never forgive a priest for ridiculing his Gothic observances; for he believes these observances are directly tied to religious doctrine."[25]

These remarks by the curé of Rilly are perceptive and suggestive of an interesting new dimension to the problem. Perhaps, in practical terms, the ultimate measure of success of the great push toward clericalization under the Old Regime was not the extent to which the clergy was able to crush popular religion—which was all but impossible in the short term—but rather the extent to which the clergy was able to impose its influence while still maintaining a viable and flexible *modus vivendi* with the popular expressions of religious sentiment.

In fact, there is some evidence of certain regional clusterings of clerical attitudes, more or less hostile, more or less accommodating to the aberrations of the countryfolk from the reigning orthodoxy. Thus, those diocesan clergies which had been influenced by Jansenism may well have manifested particular impatience and intransigence. Where religious practice is concerned, flexibility and accommodation were hardly virtues in the Augustinian ethos. It has been argued that the austere and confrontational Jansenist position taken by large segments of the curés and vicaires of certain regions—notably in the Auxerrois and the Parisian Basin—may have contributed to alienating permanently much of the laity and may have helped generate widespread rural anticlericalism. Philip Hoffman has suggested a possible link between Jansenism in the diocese of Lyon and a growing atmosphere of conflict between priests and parishioners as measured by the numbers of court suits initiated between these two groups.[26] Thus, the same Jansenist tradition which stimulated the

[25] Gérard Bouchard, *Le village immobile* (Paris, 1972), 288-323; Louis Pérouas, "Entre le XVIe et le XIXe siècles. Des regards différents sur le culte des saints en Limousin," in *La religion populaire*, 92; Martin, 2:603-605; Tackett, *Priest and Parish*, 208; Nicole Perin, "La religion populaire: mythe et réalité. L'exemple du diocèse de Reims sous l'Ancien régime," in *La religion populaire*, 222.

[26] Alfred Lajusan, "La carte des opinions françaises," *Annales. E.S.C.*, 4 (1949), 406-14; Pierre Chaunu, "Jansénisme et frontière de catholicité," *RH*, 127 (1962), 121-22; Hoffman, 160-61. For Hoffman, Jansenism is only one of several possible explanations for the rise in priest-parishioner conflict.

disaffection of parish clergymen from their bishops may also have been a factor in alienating the people from their curés.[27]

But other strands of thought among the post-Tridentine clergy were relatively more tolerant, or at least more pragmatically flexible toward popular belief systems and sensitive to the problems faced by the curés. Alain Lottin has attributed a large measure of the Catholic Reformation's success in Flanders and Hainaut to the Church's skill in adapting itself to local religion. Of particular importance was the role of the Jesuits, especially strong and influential in northern France, and known for their attempts to conciliate indigenous traditions and popular religious aspirations. When a Jansenist-sympathizing bishop later initiated a policy of rigorism and repression in the diocese of Tournai, a widespread and successful movement of protest quickly arose, with the Jesuits and Franciscans, as well as the parish clergy, staunchly defending popular demands against the bishop.[28] A similar approach toward the religion of the people may help explain the considerable success of the rural missions in western France led by Grignion de Montfort, Jean Eudes, and their followers.[29] The secret of Grignion de Montfort, and to a lesser extent of Jean Eudes, seems to have been a particular talent for talking to the common people, adopting their language, and sympathizing with their religious perspectives. According to Louis Pérouas, Grignion "fought against the pro-Jansenist, Augustinian current [of spirituality], above all ... in order to defend popular religion." His approach to preaching had many parallels to the popular literature of the *Bibliothèque bleue*, adapting to the people's taste for the miraculous, the exotic, and the secretive, and developing particularly simple, straightforward, and practical steps for becoming good Christians. He also put great stress on processions and festivals, orchestrated in a fully baroque manner, though always carefully supervised by an ample clergy.[30]

[27] See above, chp. 6.

[28] Alain Lottin, "Contre-réforme et religion populaire: un mariage difficile mais réussi aux XVIe et XVIIe siècles en Flandre et en Hainaut," in *La religion populaire*, 53-63.

[29] See the issue of *XVIIe siècle*, no. 41 (1958) devoted to seventeenth-century internal missionaries, notably articles by Louis Pérouas, "Saint Louis Grignion de Montfort," 375-95; and Charles Berthelot du Chesnay, "Les missions de Saint Jean Eudes," 328-48. Also the issue of *Annales de Bretagne*, 81, no. 3 (1974) on preaching and popular theology in the age of Grignion de Montfort.

[30] Louis Pérouas, *Grignion de Montfort* (Paris, 1966), 78-79, 122-24; *Ce que croyait Grignion de Montfort* (Paris, 1973), 189-93; and "La piété populaire au travail sur la mémoire d'un saint, Grignion de Montfort," *ACSS*, 99 (1974), 1:269-70. In the opinion of Alain Croix, a dense presence of clergymen in a given area made a substantial contribution to the success of a mission: *La Bretagne aux 16e et 17e siècles. La vie, la mort, la foi*, 2 vols. (Paris, 1981), 2:1240-41. Missions

And, nevertheless, the success of such an achievement in certain regions of France cannot be attributed solely to the finesse and accommodation of clerical leaders and religious orders. The fact remains that some populations were distinctly more *receptive* to such efforts than others. The triumphs of Grignion de Montfort in western France were impressive indeed by all accounts. But once he ventured beyond certain geographic limits, once he had left the *bocage* country of Brittany and Lower Poitou and had ventured southward into Aunis and Saintonge, the missionary magic seemed to fail him.[31] Later generations of "Montfortains" would have much the same experience.[32] And there were other areas where the energetic efforts of the reforming bishops could apparently achieve only temporary gains which never took root. The research of Louis Pérouas in Lower Marche would suggest that between 1680 and 1720 the bishops of Limoges may have succeeded in substantially reducing the number of popular feast days celebrated locally, as well as in implanting large numbers of the preferred Rosary and Blessed Sacrament confraternities. But, after 1720, the popular feast days seemed to revive more strongly than ever, and the new confraternities themselves were soon subordinated and incorporated into the celebrations.[33]

It is the hypothesis of the present chapter that, while vigorous measures were prosecuted almost everywhere in the seventeenth and eighteenth centuries to clericalize Catholicism, and while the ecclesiastical leadership achieved a certain real success in virtually every diocese, there was considerable variation in the reception and permanent rooting of this clericalization within differing regions. More importantly, the regional and social variation in receptivity had potentially significant effects on popular perceptions of the Civil Constitution of the Clergy in many areas of the country. But if such a hypothesis is plausible, it is by no means simple to prove conclusively. For the present, the case to be made must be

---

may have been less successful in the Parisian Basin precisely because of the sparsity of clergymen in the rural areas: Jeanne Ferté, *La vie religieuse dans les campagnes parisiennes* (Paris, 1962), 231-41.

[31] Pérouas, "La piété populaire," 259-60; and *Grignion de Montfort*, 49 (map).

[32] Louis Pérouas, *Pierre-François Hacquet. Mémoires des missions des Montfortains dans l'ouest (1740-1779). Contribution à la sociologie religieuse historique* (Fontenay-le-Comte, 1964), 149-61. The seventeenth century was the heyday of mission activity almost everywhere in the country, though such efforts fell on far more fertile ground in some areas than in others. On the Parisian Basin, for example, see Robert Sauzet, "Prédication et missions dans le diocèse de Chartres au début du XVIIe siècle," *Annales de Bretagne*, 81 (1974), 491-500.

[33] Pérouas, "Entre le XVIe et le XIXe siècle," 85, 93; "La confrérie du Rosaire," 434, 443-46.

somewhat indirect and circumstantial. The problem is to sort through the scattering of isolated evidence, indicative, one might hope, of a regional propensity toward clericalism at the end of the eighteenth century, and determine to what extent it does or does not relate to the geography of oath-taking in 1791.

The Geography of Eighteenth-Century Clericalism

Contemporaries of the Revolution were themselves convinced that certain regions of the country—and notably the refractory regions—were markedly more receptive to the influence of the clergy than were others. Writing in March of 1791, department directors in Toulouse took special note of the "dominance which the clergy has taken over this region." In Brittany, officials described the parish clergymen as, "so to speak, the souls of the municipalities." In Alsace they were "accustomed to using a host of stratagems in order to dominate" the countryside; while Rouergue was said to be, "for the most part, turned over to sacerdotal authority."[34] Yet assessments such as these, written by patriots in the heat of revolution, are hardly the best sources for an evaluation of the regional receptivity of clericalization.

One more objective indication of popular attitudes on the eve of the Revolution can be gathered from the patterns of clerical recruitment during the last decades of the Old Regime. To be sure, motives for entering the clergy in the eighteenth century were invariably complex and were linked not only to the accomplishment of a religious vocation, but also to the need to establish oneself in a remunerative profession. In the majority of cases, it was probably a young man's family who determined his decision to enter the priesthood. Nevertheless, the existence of sharp social and regional differences in recruitment rates—the number of young men ordained to the clergy in relation to the local population— may still tell us something about the relative interest and willingness of families in particular regions or particular milieus to direct a portion of their progeny into the service of the Church, as opposed to other possible careers.[35] In sum, recruitment patterns may provide us with some initial

[34] Letter from the directory of Haute-Garonne, Mar. 8, 1791: A.N., D XXIX bis 21, dos. 229, no. 15; from the municipality of Bourgneuf-en-Retz (Loire-Inférieure), May 30, 1790: C 116, dos. 324; from Jacobins of Strasbourg, before July 7, 1791: D XIX 86, dos. 678, no. 5; and report of prefect of Aveyron, 14 Thermidor IX: F19 865.

[35] On motives for entering the clergy, see Louis Pérouas, "Le nombre des vocations sacerdotales, est-il un critère valable en sociologie religieuse historique aux XVIIe et XVIIIe siècles," ACSS, 89 (1962), 35-40; also, Tackett, Priest and Parish, 41-47.

suggestions about the potential receptivity to clericalization of different populations of the kingdom.

In fact, for France as a whole at the end of the eighteenth century, there does not seem to have been a significant correlation between the recruitment rates by department and the local proportion of oath-takers.[36] But as was also the case with the distribution of the Protestant population, it is important to look beyond the rough national statistics. A more careful analysis can divulge certain clues about a number of specific regions. In the first place, one must take note of the regional extremes in clerical recruitment. Among the strongest recruitment centers for the secular clergy were portions of Lower Normandy, the Jura, the Massif-Central, and the Alps. Each of these areas produced clergymen not only for their own dense networks of local posts, but also for export to surrounding provinces. The weakest recruitment rates—often only one-fourth to one-fifth as great—were the Parisian Basin, the central, and the southwest of Upper Poitou and Aquitaine, zones in which there was always an insufficiency of clergymen to fill the necessary posts. It is significant that, with the obvious exception of the Alps, all the prime breeding grounds of priests would be refractory in 1791, all of those zones most impoverished in "vocations" would be strongly constitutional.

In addition, one must take note of the important disparities in the character of clerical recruitment from region to region. Though some three-fifths of clergymen in France as a whole came from rural parishes, there was a thick horseshoe of provinces from Bordeaux, northward through Upper Poitou, the middle Loire valley, and Ile-de-France, and then southward through Burgundy, in which rural vocations were rare, often extremely rare, and in which most of the limited local recruitment was a product of the towns.[37] In truth, virtually all the rural areas in question, so generally poor in local vocations, would massively accept the Civil Constitution. The corresponding relationship between a greater rural recruitment and a refractory stance is much less clear. But here it is important to make certain distinctions as to the family backgrounds of those entering the priesthood. Through much of the kingdom, the clergy was essentially middle class in character, originating in families of

---

[36] For this and the following paragraph, see the author's, "L'histoire sociale du clergé diocésain dans la France du XVIIIe siècle," *RHMC*, 26 (1979), 221, 228; also Tackett and Langlois, "Clerical Geography," 360-61. The correlation coefficient between the proportion of oath-takers and the departments of origin of the clergy of 1790 still alive in 1817 was −0.05. Some caution must be taken with this figure, however, because of differential regional mortality rates: see the above article for details.

[37] "L'histoire sociale," 223, 229; "Clerical Geography," 367.

officeholders, members of the liberal professions, merchants, and artisans (though the precise proportions of these individual groups varied somewhat from region to region). In most cases only a tiny proportion, usually under 10 percent, came from agricultural milieus—the wealthier peasantry, wine-growers, and agricultural merchants, for the most part. Yet there were also a few striking exceptions in which the agricultural segment of the clergy rose to 40 or 50 percent, or even higher: notably in the Massif-Central, the Basque country of the extreme southwest, and in an Atlantic coastal zone running apparently from Boulonnais through Normandy and Brittany.[38] (See Figure L.) It seems evident that in all of those areas, without exception, where the clerical corps came out of the local peasant population itself, laity and clergy would generally reject the ecclesiastical reforms of the Revolution.

Many of these contrasts in clerical origins were paralleled, moreover, by markedly different patterns of clerical density. Everywhere in the kingdom, there were always important concentrations of clergymen in the towns: clergymen manning the cathedrals and chapters, the monasteries and convents, the hospitals and secondary schools—institutions which had best survived and had even prospered in the urban environment. The critical factor for the present inquiry is the rural "parish density," the numbers of priests sustained in the countryside where the bulk of the population actually lived. We have already noted the significant variations from province to province in the numbers of resident vicaires, and the strong regional correlation in evidence between the ratio of vicaires per parish and the local proportion of oath-takers.[39] Many of these same provinces with greater concentrations of assistant parish priests also had substantial contingents of seculars other than curés or vicaires active in parish service. First, there were the various kinds of priests holding simple benefices (without residence requirements) or with no benefices at all, living off the revenues of incidental masses or small endowed chapels: the *habitués, prêtres libres, consorces, obitiers,* chaplains,

---

[38] "L'histoire sociale," 209-16, 227, 231-34; supplemented by the following: for Lyon: Hoffman, 359; for Tréguier: Georges Minois, "Les vocations sacerdotales dans le diocèse de Tréguier au XVIIIe siècle," *Annales de Bretagne*, 86 (1979), 53; for Paris: Jacques Staes, "La vie religieuse dans l'archidiaconé de Josas à la fin de l'Ancien régime," Thèse, Ecole des chartes, 1969, p. 288; for Saumurois: Louis Gallard, "Le clergé saumurois de 1789 à 1795," D.E.S., Université de Poitiers, 1960, pp. 13-19; for Creuse: Pérouas, "Le clergé creusois," 556-57; for Lons-le-Saunier: Vernus, 69; for Mende: Frédéric Izard, "Le clergé paroissial gévaudanais à la fin du XVIIIe siècle," Mémoire de maîtrise, Université de Montpellier III, 1978, p. 24; for Périgueux: Mandon, 26 and tables.

[39] See above, chp. 5

FIGURE L
Clerical Recruitment from Agricultural Milieus at the End of the
Old Regime. (Data exclude rural "merchants" and are for
Old-Regime dioceses unless otherwise indicated.)

etc. Second, there were the members of various kinds of "societies of
priests," called *mépartistes, familiers, fraternisants,* or *sociétaires,* depending
on the region: those belonging to institutions resembling miniature rural
chapters whose constitutions often required them to be native sons of the
parish where the "society" was located.[40]

[40] Le Goff, *Vannes,* 245; Antoine Dupuy, *Etudes sur l'administration municipale en Bretagne au
XVIIIe siècle* (Paris, 1891), 116-17, 121-22; Emile Sévestre, *L'organisation du clergé paroissial à la
veille de la Révolution* (Paris, 1911), 28-29; Jean Bindet, "Le diocèse d'Avranches sous l'épiscopat
de Mgr. Godart de Belboeuf, dernier évêque d'Avranches," *Revue de l'Avranchin et du pays de
Granville,* 46 (1969), 55; Yves Chaille, "Livre d'or du clergé vendéen," *Archives du diocèse de
Luçon,* nouv. sér., 32 (1960), 18-23; Maurice Giraud, *Essai sur l'histoire religieuse de la Sarthe de
1789 à l'an VI* (Paris, 1920), 86-87; G. de Léotoing-d'Anjony, "Les communautés des prêtres
filleuls de l'église N.D. d'Aurillac," *Revue de la Haute-Auvergne,* 33 (1952-53), 372-77; Louise
Welter, "Les communautés de prêtres dans le diocèse de Clermont du XIIe au XVIIIe siècle,"
RHEF, 35 (1949), 9-10; A.D. Cantal, Fonds Delmas, ms. 224; Michel Vernus, "Le clergé du
doyenné de Lons-le-Saunier, diocèse de Besançon (1662-1790)," thèse de 3e cycle, Université de

Such relative concentrations of rural priests were partly dependent on local benefice structures perpetuated from the distant past. Yet they were also indicative of a certain willingness on the part of the local population of these regions to tolerate and even to support a more numerous clergy. Though many of the clergymen in question held beneficed lands and portions of the tithes, others were partly or totally dependent on the payment of an ample "casuel" and on continued contributions from the heirs of long-deceased founders of perpetual masses. Certain of the parishes also contributed directly to the upkeep of their vicaires. There was undoubtedly a tight relationship between the "supply" of higher recruitment rates in most of these provinces and the "demand" for more priests to fill such local posts. The fact is clear that many provinces—Lower Marche or Burgundy, for example—had once possessed similar plethoras of priests but had seen their numbers decline sharply by the eighteenth century.[41] Yet in Lower Normandy, Brittany, Maine, and Anjou, and in much of the Massif-Central, Lorraine, and Franche-Comté—all provinces soon to opt against the Civil Constitution—the rural *habitués*, the *sociétaires*, and the multitude of vicaires would remain alive and well to the very end of the Old Regime.

Indeed, the analysis of clerical recruitment and density can also suggest ways in which the clericalism of certain regions may have been self-reinforcing. In the first place, the greater "parish density" of certain regions, the presence of several clergymen in the same community, was undoubtedly important not only for the priests' view of themselves—as already examined in an earlier chapter—but also for lay perceptions of the priest.[42] In those areas where the clergy was represented not by a solitary individual but by a miniature society of ecclesiastics, it may have

---

Nancy, 1975, pp. 25-26; Martin, 2:326-27; Charles Guyot, "La communauté des enfants-prêtres de la paroisse de Mirecourt," *Mémoires de la Société d'archéologie lorraine*, 42 (1892), 154-87.

[41] Dominique Julia, "La réforme posttridentine en France d'après les procès-verbaux de visites pastorales: ordre et résistances," in *Società religiosa nell'età moderna* (Naples, 1973), 342-43; Paul-Exupère Ousset, "Etat des paroisses du diocèse de Toulouse en 1763-1764," A.D. Haute-Garonne, W ms. 91, pp. 13 and 18; Thérèse-Jeanne Schmitt, *L'organisation ecclésiastique et la pratique religieuse dans l'archidiaconé d'Autun de 1650 à 1750* (Autun, 1957), 25; Nicole Lemaître, "La communauté des prêtres-filleuls d'Ussel à la fin de l'Ancien régime," *ACSS*, 102 (1977), 1:295-309; Louis Pérouas, "Le clergé creusois durant la période révolutionnaire," *Mémoires de la Société des sciences naturelles et archéologiques de la Creuse*, 39 (1976), 553; Hoffman, 354-55; Philippe Torreilles, *Histoire du clergé dans le département des Pyrénées-Orientales pendant la Révolution française* (Perpignan, 1890), xii-xiii. Also, the ordinance of the archbishop of Lyon, July 1, 1749: A.D. Rhône, 1 G 12.

[42] See above, chp. 5.

greatly accentuated the separation of clergy and laity, and enhanced the impression of clerical distinctiveness, setting the priest apart and aloof in the minds of both the laity and the clergy. In the second place, the patterns of recruitment prevalent in certain provinces may have affected regional perceptions of the clergy. It seems clear that throughout much of the west, the Massif-Central, the Basque country, and perhaps the Jura, the curés and vicaires were primarily local men and that a large number were from the same rural and/or peasant backgrounds as their parishioners. Many, in fact, originated in those wealthier elite families who stood to dominate the local social and political life. The local roots and family influence of such clergymen may well have enhanced their status and position in the parish community. Their firsthand experience with the popular religious culture may have increased their sympathy and understanding for such beliefs and have facilitated the creation of a *modus vivendi*. In 1791 the departmental administrators of Ille-et-Vilaine would take note of—and lament—the particularly strong influence wielded by all those clergymen who were native to their parishes.[43]

In certain other regions, by contrast—in the Parisian Basin, the central, and the west-central provinces from Upper Poitou to Bordelais—a much greater proportion of parish clergymen, sometimes the majority, were outsiders to their parishioners. Imported from elsewhere to compensate for the insufficiency of priests in the rural areas, they were outsiders who came from the towns rather than the countryside, and often from other dioceses and provinces altogether. From unknown families, little familiar or even unfamiliar with local customs, popular religious practices, and the language or dialect, many must have encountered much greater difficulty integrating themselves into their parishes. One should not overlook the frequent complaints of bishops in these regions that the migrant priests arriving to fill local posts tended to be precisely those men who had been unable to succeed in their home dioceses—through either lack of ability or rejection for faulty morals—and that such an influx of outsiders was diminishing the populations' respect for their clergy.[44] With only a few exceptions, those regions where a large proportion—over one-third—of parish clergymen were imported from other dioceses would

[43] Departmental deliberations, Dec. 14, 1791: A.N., F[19] 431. Note also the assessment of a citizen in the neighboring Loire-Inférieure that the local people were particularly unhappy with the replacements of the refractories because so many were "des étrangers et peu connus" among the parishioners: letter from Devineau in Nantes, Dec. 14, 1791: A.N., F[19] 440.

[44] See, for example, Staes, 276; and Mandon, 48-49.

opt strongly in favor of the Civil Constitution and the revised conception of the clergyman embodied in that legislation.[45]

Beyond the suggestions of ecclesiastical recruitment and clerical density, other systematic, homogeneous indices of the regional sensitivity to clericalization are more difficult to find. Yet four additional sets of evidence deserve to be mentioned briefly, particularly insofar as they corroborate and reinforce certain of the regional clusters previously identified. First, it would seem logical that the presence and density of pious confraternities—and notably of those approved by the Catholic Reformation—might be indicative of populations amenable to clerical control. A pioneering study by Louis Pérouas identified a remarkable dichotomy in the distribution of Rosary confraternities within the seventeenth-century diocese of La Rochelle. Their concentration in the north, in the bocage area of the future *Vendée militaire*, and their relative paucity in the southern lowlands surrounding La Rochelle nicely describe the predominantly refractory and predominantly constitutional zones of 1791.[46] Similar approximate regional correspondences can be found between the oath and the seventeenth-century Rosary confraternities in the diocese of Nîmes—where the confraternities also marked the greatest concentrations of the Catholic population—or the eighteenth-century Rosary confraternities in the diocese of Rodez or the confraternities of *la charité* in the diocese of Rouen.[47] But, clearly, the correspondence between oath and confraternities was not always so clearcut. In much of the southeast, the association was weak or non-existent; and the strongly constitutional Creuse would seem to have contained as dense a concentration of Rosary confraternities as the future Vendée.[48] Unfortunately, a kingdom-wide inventory of these pious organizations remains to be made.[49] Yet, even

---

[45] Among the 22 departments in which more than one-third of the clergymen are thought to have originated in other departments, the oath-taking rate was 64 percent. See Tackett and Langlois, "Clerical Geography," 361.

[46] Louis Pérouas, *Le diocèse de La Rochelle de 1648 à 1724* (Paris, 1964), 501; and "Le nombre des vocations," 39.

[47] Robert Sauzet, *Contre-Réforme et Réforme catholique en Bas-Languedoc. Le diocèse de Nîmes au XVIIe siècle* (Louvain, 1979), 460-63, and for Protestant population, 53; André Dubuc, "Les charités du diocèse de Rouen au XVIIIe siècle," *ACSS*, 99 (1976), 1:228; Pierre Lançon, "Les confréries du Rosaire en Rouergue aux XVIe et XVIIe siècles," *Annales du Midi*, 96 (1984), 124-25. Compare also the diocese of Reims, where there were few pious confraternities in the eighteenth century, and where most priests would take the oath in 1791: Perin, 222.

[48] Pérouas, "La confrérie du Rosaire," 437. On confraternities in the diocese of Gap, see Tackett, *Priest and Parish*, 194-202.

[49] See Michel Vovelle, "Géographie des confréries à l'époque moderne," *RHEF*, 69 (1983), 259-68.

when more complete information becomes available, it will also be necessary to take into account the date of foundation and the evolving character of the institutions, the fact that certain took root and prospered while others simply vegetated or disappeared altogether.[50] A map of the eighteenth-century network of Rosary sodalities represents a palimpsest of successive waves of pious foundations, some of which—as we have seen in the case of Lower Marche—may have been largely transformed from their original purpose.

A second approach is to examine the numbers of religious books published in the provinces in the years just prior to the Revolution.[51] The bulk of the great quantity of such books, produced by the regional presses, consisted either of sacred texts and liturgical writings or of reprints of works written by clergymen which generally supported and extolled the orthodox, Tridentine conception of a hierarchical Church in which the clergy occupied a dominant position. Typical, no doubt, was the pious *Ange conducteur dans la dévotion chrétienne*, one of the great best sellers of the age (with fifty-one editions in the last decade of the Old Regime) and described as a "livre dévot par excellence."[52] The publication of this kind of literature might thus provide a kind of rough indication of the regional receptivity, the "market" for clericalization. In fact, the map of the number of religious books published on regional presses presents some remarkable similarities with the geography of the oath—particularly when the results are expressed as a proportion of the local literate population. It was precisely the future refractory zones of the west, the northern frontier, Lorraine, and Languedoc which revealed the highest ratios of religious publications; while the predominantly juring Parisian Basin, the center, and the region of Aquitaine were all particularly impoverished in publications of this kind.[53]

A third tentative measure of regional responsiveness to clericalization is suggested by the historical demographer: the extent to which various populations honored the clergy's longstanding interdiction against marriage during the religious cycles of Lent and Advent. Obedience or recalcitrance in this regard, it might be argued, are revealing of the clergy's influence over even so intimate and personal a decision as the beginning

---

[50] Ibid., 435.

[51] Julien Brancolini and Marie-Thérèse Bouyssy, "La vie provinciale du livre à la fin de l'Ancien régime," in François Furet, ed., *Livre et société dans la France du XVIIIe siècle* (Paris, 1965-70), esp. 11-15, 24-31.

[52] Ibid., 14, 26.

[53] Ibid., 29.

of one's conjugal life. Unfortunately, the statistics presently available are still rather approximate—based as they are on a relatively small sample of parish registers throughout the country—and the results published by Jacques Houdailles are by clusters of provinces which do not always match the groupings found most useful for the analysis of the oath.[54] Nevertheless, one cannot but be impressed by the dichotomy within the northwestern quadrant of France. It is not insignificant that the western provinces of Brittany, Anjou, and Normandy revealed the lowest recalcitrance rates of the entire nation—nearly three times lower than the adjacent Parisian Basin. In the course of the Revolution, the massively non-juring provinces of Brittany and Anjou maintained their standing, while the Paris region soared to the highest recalcitrance rate in France.

A final piece of evidence can perhaps be culled from a sample of the local electoral lists of 1790. In an earlier chapter we examined the parish priests elected as village mayors or *procureurs* and discovered a certain tendency among such individuals to adapt the model of the "citizen curé" and embrace the constitutional position. But the selection of a clergyman to sit in the secondary assembly of the department was indicative of a rather different reality. Unlike the longer-term, day-to-day commitment of the post of mayor, the position of elector required the priest's active service for only a few days each year. The candidate was chosen, not from a single village—where local personality clashes and power struggles might have played an important role—but as the temporary representative of an entire canton for the choice of departmental officials. In brief, the presence of priests on the first electoral lists of the Revolution might be considered an additional indication of the honor and confidence shown toward the local clergy within a whole small region. And, indeed, there does seem to be a certain association between areas with greater numbers of priest-electors and areas soon to emerge as predominantly refractory. Once again, the juxtaposition of the west and the Parisian Basin is particularly noteworthy. In seven of the western departments for which information has been found, priests represented an average of 7 percent of the electoral corps, rising as high as 11 percent in Morbihan and 14 percent in the neighboring Breton department of Côtes-du-Nord. But among three departments of the Parisian Basin, the proportion was only slightly over 1 percent.[55]

[54] Jacques Houdailles, "La célébration saisonnière des mariages avant, pendant et après la Révolution française," *Population*, 33 (1978), esp. 373-75. Grouped together, for example, are such diverse regions as Nord and Picardy, or Languedoc and Provence.

[55] To date, I have found lists of the electors in 27 departments, though many more could undoubtedly be located in the departmental archives. In 1790 most lists continue to give

Clericalization and "Religious Vitality"

In the end, the approach taken here has been somewhat different from that traditionally followed by historians of "religious sociology" in the line of Gabriel Le Bras. The "piety" or "religiosity" or "religious vitality" which this school has attempted to assess would seem to be both overly vague and not altogether useful for the purposes of the present analysis. Indeed, one might argue that virtually all countrypeople of the Old Regime—beset by the same overpowering threats to their crops, to their families, to their physical and mental well-being—felt the need for and actively sought solace from the supernatural. In this sense, all were indeed "religious." If one wishes to analyze "religious vitality," one must also specify *which* religion—or, at least, which tendency within the Catholic religion. For our comprehension of oath patterns in 1791, a more viable approach has been to examine possible variations not in religiosity per se, but in the clerical dominance of religion.

Everywhere in France, from the sixteenth and especially the seventeenth century on, the Church had promoted the clericalization of Catholicism. Yet it is evident that attempts were far more successful in some areas and milieus than in others. The reasons for this success were undoubtedly complex and were linked to the specific symbiotic relationships which existed between clergy and laity, to the delicate balance between the clergy's push of the laity and the laity's pull on their priests. It is possible that in certain regions, pre-Christian or sub-Christian belief systems present in the sixteenth century were in themselves more amenable to the acceptance and integration of the new strand of post-Reformation Catholicism. One must take care not to represent "popular religion" as a monolith throughout France. In his massive study of Brittany in the sixteenth and seventeenth centuries, Alain Croix has argued that it was the existence of certain longstanding beliefs and practices among the Breton rural classes which predisposed them to a rapid as-

---

the "qualités" of the electors. But even where they do not specify the occupations of all of the laymen, they usually take note of the "abbés." Among the 27, the correlation coefficient of the oath-taking percentage vs. the proportion of priest-electors is -0.34. The departments and the percentage of priest electors are as follows: Hautes-Alpes (6.9 percent); Aveyron (4.4); Bouches-du-Rhône (4.7); Côte-d'Or (1.5); Côtes-du-Nord (14.4); Doubs (2.4); Drôme (3.6); Finistère (2.1); Gard (3.6); Haute-Garonne (4.3); Ille-et-Vilaine (7.4); Indre-et-Loire (4.7); Maine-et-Loire (4.2); Manche (3.6); Marne (1.3); Mayenne (2.1); Meurthe (6.3); Morbihan (10.7); Bas-Rhin (9.5); Sarthe (3.4); Haute-Saône (0); Seine-et-Marne (1.3); Seine-et-Oise (1.8); Vendée (6.1); Vienne (7.6); Haute-Vienne (6.1); Vosges (3.2). A wide variety of sources have been used, primarily local departmental studies and diverse series in the A.N.

similation of Tridentine Catholicism during the seventeenth century.[56] But, unfortunately, the mapping and comparative assessment of regional variations in popular culture for the late medieval period is altogether unfeasible in the present state of historical research.

There is also some reason to believe that the Catholic Reformation model was substantially more attractive to women than to men. The sexual dichotomy in religious practice, the "feminization" of religion so well documented for the nineteenth and twentieth centuries, was already crystallizing at the end of the Old Regime. Membership in the various devotional confraternities, for example—especially those like the Rosary, the Scapulaire, the Sacred Heart, particularly favored by the eighteenth-century clergy—was increasingly dominated by women even before the Revolution.[57] Though the statistical evidence would be difficult to muster, it seems plausible that the responsiveness of women to the clericalization of religion helps explain the vigorous opposition which they offered almost everywhere to the Civil Constitution and to the assault on the Tridentine priesthood which that legislation entailed.[58]

In any case, it appears likely that the regional success of clericalization was greatly enhanced by such cultural and structural features as the rural density of the clergy, the patterns of clerical recruitment, and perhaps even the relative wealth of the parish corps.[59] Success also entailed a certain degree of tolerance and accommodation on the part of the ecclesiastical corps: attitudes which themselves might be affected by regional theological positions on the part of the clergy (e.g., Jansenist intransigence or Jesuit flexibility) and perhaps, in certain areas, by ecological features (like the degree of isolation or of settlement dispersion). Clericalism, it

---

[56] Croix, 2:1241-42.

[57] Pérouas, "La confrérie du Rosaire," 442-43; Michel Vovelle, *Piété baroque et déchristianisation en Provence au XVIIIe siècle* (Paris, 1973), 353, 356-57; Tackett, *Priest and Parish*, 196; Jean-Luc Le Gac, "Les confréries de dévotion dans le diocèse de Vannes aux XVIIe et XVIIIe siècles," Mémoire de maîtrise, Université de Rennes II, 1980, p. 52; Jacques Raulet, "Les confréries de dévotion dans l'ancien diocèse de Saint-Brieuc, du concile de Trente à la Révolution," Mémoire de maîtrise, Université de Rennes II, 1981, annexe VIII, p. 24. The clauses in eighteenth-century wills also suggest that women remained more faithful to those "baroque" forms of religious expression strongly identified with the Catholic Reformation of the seventeenth century: Vovelle, 133-40, 298; Pierre Chaunu, *La mort à Paris* (Paris, 1978), 434; unpublished research of Kenneth Fenster for a Ph.D. at Marquette University, kindly shared with me by Mr. Fenster; also, Kathryn Norberg, "Rich and Poor in Old-Regime Grenoble, 1600-1804," Ph.D. dissertation, Yale University, 1978, pp. 297, 331.

[58] See above, chp. 7.

[59] See the author's more general speculations on the origins of clericalization in "French Clericalism under the Old Regime," cited above.

has been argued, involved a relatively greater internalization of sacerdotal functions in one's view of the nature and workings of religion. At the beginning of the Revolution some French men and women had long come to consider a rigidly hierarchical clergy as essential to their world view and to their relations with the supernatural. In the end, a form of clericalism had been incorporated into the popular culture itself. Yet other French inhabitants, it might be suggested, had never entirely integrated clerical functions into their religious culture.

There is substantial evidence, moreover, of the existence of certain regional typologies, of certain clusterings of variables which converged to help foster particularly strong clerical or anticlerical orientations on the part of specific populations. One such clustering is clearly in evidence in the "west" of Brittany, Normandy, Maine, Anjou, and Lower Poitou. Here the unusually dense presence and the overwhelmingly rural recruitment of the parish clergy, coupled perhaps with an unusual clerical wealth and a particular mode of settlement, and a missionary tradition sympathetic to certain aspects of popular religion, all helped to promote a large measure of respect for the rural clergy and a greater degree of acceptance and cooperation with the Church's objective of clericalization.[60] Throughout most of these provinces, the Civil Constitution, a veritable frontal attack on the tradition of post-Tridentine clericalization, would be viewed with suspicion and hostility by both the lay population and the clergy alike.

The sharpest contrast was presented by the Parisian Basin, and by portions of Picardy, Champagne, Orléanais, and the center. Here the clergy was far more sparsely implanted and modestly endowed; its members were primarily of middle-class extraction and consisted in large measure of outsiders to the rural communities: characteristics which did little to facilitate the attempts by the clerical leadership to impose the new model of reformed Catholicism. The task was perhaps further hindered by the rigid and intransigent Jansenist orientation, stronger among the clergy here than anywhere else, and by the spread of the longstanding anticlerical tradition of Paris, more easily disseminated because of the well-developed communications network and the clustered settlement patterns typical of this part of France.

Other areas of France would seem to present configurations similar to these two ideal types. The Massif-Central, the Jura, and the Basque

---

[60] On clerical wealth in the west see above, chp. 4. On the dispersed settlements in the west—and the problems of such an analysis—see chp. 8.

country appear parallel to the west in numerous respects; while Upper Poitou, Saintonge, and Bordelais reveal many cultural and structural similarities with the Parisian Basin. But nowhere were the alignments of conditions and forces exactly the same. And in several other provinces, as we have already seen, the key to understanding the oath reactions of 1791 would seem to be more closely related to the presence and relative dynamism of Protestantism than to the existence of clericalism as such. Yet an additional element must be taken into account before we can attempt any broader conclusions: the influence of the nearby towns and of the urban elites. It is to this question that we must turn in the following chapter.

ELEVEN

The Urban Elites and the Oath

To assay the total cultural and religious chemistry of a region, it is not enough to analyze the masses of the country population, however large the proportion of that population among the total inhabitants of France. One must also examine the islands of urban culture emerging from the sea of rural France, and particularly those commoner urban elites who dominated that culture.[1] The world of the town-dwelling notables was by no means hermetically sealed from the countryside.[2] Yet a more intense contact with literacy and secondary education, a far greater access to communications networks, and tighter links with national politics and intellectual life lent a distinctive character to the middle- and upper-class townsmen, and instilled in them a sense of self-confidence and superiority not to be found among other commoners. Empirically, the group of town "notables"—officeholders, professional men, merchants, and individuals living off land revenues and investments—has often proved a useful and cohesive unit for social analysis.[3] More to the point, it was precisely this group which dominated the local administrative bodies in 1790 and 1791 and which thus took charge of the implementation of the Civil Constitution.

Elite Anticlericalism under the Old Regime

In the seventeenth century this same urban elite had served as one of the principal buttresses of the Catholic Reformation. The Church had turned to the townsmen for support in its efforts to reform and clericalize religion among the less readily attainable countrypeople, and on occasion the lay notables had even taken the initiative in pressing the clergy for

---

[1] The "urban elite" described here will be defined as the town-dwelling office holders, members of the liberal professions, merchants and entrepreneurs, and individuals living off their investments (often calling themselves simply "bourgeois"). For present purposes, we will exclude members of the nobility, whose political role was generally minimal after 1789.

[2] See Pierre Goubert, *L'Ancien régime. Tome I: La société* (Paris, 1969), 197.

[3] Note Michel Vovelle's critique of the use of the category of "elite": "L'élite ou le mensonge des mots," *Annales. E.S.C.*, 29 (1974), 49-72; however, Vovelle is primarily concerned with the distinction between nobles and commoners within the "elite," while we are here distinguishing the commoner elites from the non-urban countrypeople.

more rapid reforms. The families of town notables would provide prime recruiting prospects for both the regular and secular clergy of the Counter-Reformation. Indeed, the Gallican clergy had perhaps never been more elitist in its social origins than in the late seventeenth and early eighteenth centuries.[4] Yet even during this earlier period, sincere religious fervor might easily coexist with strands of anticlericalism. The clergy's immense landholdings, its privileges and material resources, had long been the source of a residual jealousy and resentment among certain elements of the laity, resentment that was sometimes encouraged and inflamed by the actions of the royal government.[5] By the end of the Old Regime, the potential for such conflict had greatly increased as town fathers became interested in urban beautification and the rejuvenation of commerce and industry, but found themselves thwarted by the large blocks of urban property in the hands of the Church. In Vannes, in Angers, in Lyon, and no doubt in many other towns as well, this "institutional anticlericalism" often led to bitter friction between the clergy and municipal leaders.[6]

But quite apart from these "structural" tensions, certain segments of the urban middle class of the later eighteenth century were experiencing striking changes in attitude toward both the clergy and religion. A great deal has been written about the impact of the Enlightenment on the religious outlook of the French population. To believe the testimonies of the clergy itself, a spirit of irreligion was sweeping over the kingdom after 1760 in a veritable flood. Beginning at mid-century and at every meeting thereafter up to the eve of the Revolution, the General Assembly of the Clergy would broadcast its complaints against "this swarm of evil books," "this crowd of impious writers who become more audacious with every passing day."[7] In 1766 the curé of Vézelay described his parishioners as "devouring" impious works, especially those of Rousseau; while Curé Réguis, from his parish near Auxerre, fulminated against the "torrent of

---

[4] Marie-Hélène Froeschlé-Chopard, *La religion populaire en Provence orientale au XVIIIe siècle* (Paris, 1980); and the author's, "L'histoire sociale du clergé diocésain dans la France du XVIIIe siècle," *RHMC*, 26 (1979), 213.

[5] Alec Mellor, *Histoire de l'anticléricalisme français* (Paris, 1978), 45-46.

[6] John McManners, *French Ecclesiastical Society under the Ancien Régime. A Study of Angers in the Eighteenth Century* (Manchester, 1960), 117-28; T.J.A. Le Goff, *Vannes and Its Region* (Oxford, 1981), 123-24; Philip T. Hoffman, *Church and Community in the Diocese of Lyon, 1500-1789* (New Haven, 1984), 18.

[7] *Collection des procès-verbaux des assemblées générales du clergé de France depuis l'année 1560* (Paris, 1767-80), 8:372; also Michel Peronnet, *Les évêques de l'ancienne France* (Lille, 1977), 770, 779-80.

evil and corruption which, after having flooded the capital and rushed over all the dikes, has now swept into the provinces." "Today," wrote Abbé Beucher of Brûlon in his parish register, "all the people *en place* have absolutely no religion. It is only among the humble in the countryside that religious belief remains intact."[8] Yet one must be wary of taking the clergy's testimony altogether at face value—colored, as it almost certainly was, by rhetorical exaggeration and a touch of paranoia. In fact, recent efforts to measure the extent of cultural change in the eighteenth century would suggest a much more complex picture.

Thus, when one examines the consumption of books sold in Parisian bookshops, as indicated by the official censor's lists, one discovers that the total number of religious titles actually increased during the first half of the eighteenth century, reflecting perhaps a substantial interest in the great religious and theological controversies of mid-century. It was only the far greater rise in the number of secular books which brought a percentage decline in the corpus of religious publications. But the forty years after mid-century witnessed a precipitous drop in both the percentage and the number of religious titles. By the end of the Old Regime, the religious sections of the Paris bookstores contained only a few works of antiphilosophical apologetics and specialized theology.[9] One study of the personal libraries of several hundred urban middle-class households in ten western towns reveals trends roughly similar to those found in the book trade of the capital. The number of religious works on the shelves of urban "notables" increased through the 1750's as the members of this milieu followed the religious controversies of the times and continued to fit devotional literature into their overall cultural consumption. But thereafter, and through the decade of the Revolution, there was a dramatic change. With very few exceptions—primarily widows and unmarried women—the number of works on religion declined drastically or disappeared altogether.[10]

And nevertheless, conclusions based on the circulation and possession

[8] Dale Van Kley, "Church, State, and the Ideological Origins of the French Revolution," *JMH*, 51 (1979), 629; Guy Besse, "La représentation du peuple chez un prédicateur: François-Léon Réguis, 1725-1789," in *Images du peuple au XVIIIe siècle* (Paris, 1973), 163; H. Roquet, *Observation de Me. Beucher, curé de Brûlon* (Le Mans, 1929), 36.

[9] François Furet, "La 'librairie' du royaume de France au 18e siècle," in *Livre et société*, 2 vols. (Paris, 1965-70), 1:3-32. In his graphs Furet gives only the percentage of titles published in the different categories, without noting the absolute numbers in each category.

[10] Jean Quéniart, *Culture et société dans la France de l'ouest au XVIIIe siècle* (Paris, 1978), 225-86. Note that Quéniart defines "elites" somewhat differently, as consisting, for the most part, of nobles and prominent office holders.

of books, suggestive though they may be, still leave us one step removed from the culture of the French elite. Aside from the problem of determining the books which were actually read—as opposed to those sitting quietly on a shelf, symbols of conspicuous consumption—there is the fundamental question of reception. To read a book is not necessarily to believe it, or even to understand it. How can one assess the ultimate impact of *La Nouvelle Héloïse* as opposed to a pious and orthodox best seller like the *Ange Conducteur?*[11] Moreover, to judge by the lists of governmental permissions, if books sold in the capital were substantially laicized, they were by no means de-Christianized. The eighteenth century marked an explosion of curiosity and creativity in nearly all aspects of inquiry—in history, geography, science, politics, philosophy, and the arts—all of which combined to replace religion as the central preoccupations in reading matter. And, while Parisian editions may well have dominated the libraries of most lay elites, one should not overlook the more specialized local presses, whose publication lists, as we have seen, contained numerous religious works to the very end of the century.[12]

The contradictions and ambiguities of the Enlightenment as it was experienced in the provinces are further illustrated by studies of three of the more important institutional forms of cultural exchange. Following the research of Daniel Roche it now seems evident that the provincial academies of eighteenth-century France were never openly antireligious. Most of the academicians prided themselves on their stance toward a certain kind of Enlightenment and laced their discourses with the word "lumières." They consciously shunned religious quarrels and avoided undue contact with the regular clergy, excluded from full membership in many academies. Yet, in their public sessions through the end of the Old Regime, they continued to celebrate solemn *Te Deums* and to frame their proceedings with prayers and religious services. Through the century, secular clergymen constituted some 20 percent of the nationwide membership.[13] A second, and even more popular, form of Enlightened association, the Freemasons, included a substantially smaller contingent of clergymen: by best estimates, no more than 4 percent of the 20,000 or 30,000 members of the later eighteenth century. Yet this limited clerical membership can probably be explained by the formal condemnation of the Masons by the pope and the Sorbonne. The theory of an insidious

[11] Julien Brancolini and Marie-Thérèse Bouyssy, "La vie provinciale du livre à la fin de l'Ancien régime," in *Livre et société*, 2:14.

[12] Ibid., 27; see also above, chp. 10.

[13] Daniel Roche, *Le siècle des Lumières en province*, 2 vols. (Paris, 1978), 1:131, 140, 198, 205.

Masonic plot against Church and royalty can no longer be sustained. In fact, it was not uncommon for the lodges to have their own chaplains and to fund special masses. In the Masonic lodges, as in the academies, there was "no fundamental questioning, no blatant manifestations of a crisis of the sacred; but on the contrary, everywhere one finds an attachment to the gestures of religious practice and denunciations of atheism and freethinking."[14] Compared to the lodges and the academies, the local literary societies or *chambres de lectures* are less well known. It is usually impossible to say what went on in private reading organizations of this kind or how they might have affected religious attitudes. Yet, far less rigidly institutionalized, and thus relatively independent and spontaneous—and potentially more radical—such associations may have played an even more important role in the propagation of Enlightenment ideology and in the politicization of the urban elites during the period of the "pre-Revolution."[15] In this respect, it is noteworthy that the *chambres de lectures* were more concentrated in some regions than in others and that there was apparently a particularly dense network among the towns of western France—a point to which we must return below.[16]

More direct evidence of a change in the degree of religious commitment among urban notables is not easy to muster. In certain towns by the end of the eighteenth century churchgoing would seem to have declined substantially below the elevated levels of the countryside—where well over 90 percent continued to perform their "Easter duties." Clergymen could complain of the "small minority" fulfilling these basic requirements in the Parisian parish of Saint-Sulpice; of less than half in Bordeaux; of only two-thirds in the small southern town of Lunel.[17] But, beyond a few isolated reports of this kind, the extent of such urban recalcitrance is still somewhat obscure. More massive evidence has been mobilized in recent years through the analysis of the clauses in wills. Michel Vovelle and others have noted the sharp decline in religious references and overt

[14] Ibid., 2:262-77; Daniel Mornet, *Les origines intellectuelles de la Révolution française, 1715-1787* (Paris, 1933), 358-87; Michel Vovelle, "Essai de cartographie des limites de la sociabilité méridionale à la fin du XVIIIe siècle," *ACSS*, 96 (1971), 169-71.

[15] Roche, 1:61-64 and esp. the maps on 2:477. See also Augustin Cochin, *Les sociétés de pensées et la Révolution en Bretagne* (Paris, 1925), 19-21; François Furet, *Penser la Révolution* (Paris, 1978), 58-59.

[16] Roche, 1:63.

[17] Gabriel Le Bras, *Introduction à l'histoire de la pratique religieuse*, 2 vols. (Paris, 1942-45), 1:97; and "Notes de statistiques et d'histoire religieuse," *RHEF*, 19 (1933), 512-13; Gérard Cholvy, *Religion et société au XIXe siècle. Le diocèse de Montpellier*, 2 vols. (Lille, 1973), 1:22.

adherence to Catholic values in the wills of the upper and middle classes of Marseille, Paris, Bordeaux, and other small towns of the Midi.[18]

Yet, if the evidence from wills per se remains both limited geographically and ambiguous as to ultimate significance,[19] the patterns of clerical recruitment at the end of the Old Regime can provide us with some particularly useful indications on the kingdom-wide transformations in the attitudes of French notables. To be sure, the precise chronology of recruitment trends was not everywhere the same. But in most towns there was a tendency during the eighteenth century for fewer and fewer elite families to send their sons into the secular clergy. In certain dioceses such as Aix-en-Provence or Orléans or Autun, the decline in entries from this group was altogether dramatic—sometimes involving a drop of 50 percent or more within a few decades.[20] Over all, the proportion of new clergymen born in the towns declined from about 45 percent of all recruitment in 1760 to about 27 percent on the eve of the Revolution.[21] Given the complexity of motivation for entries into the priesthood, it would be hazardous to link such trends directly to a rise in anticlericalism. But, at the very least, they suggest a growing distance, a decline in immediate family links, between the lay urban elites and the clergy.

Moreover, the evolution of recruitment rates reveals significant regional differences. The three zones registering the sharpest overall urban decline were Paris itself (down 50 percent between the two periods 1757-1771 and 1776-1791), Provence (down 46 percent), and the central area south of Paris and including Berry, Bourbonnais, and Nivernais (down 43 percent). Other regions with unusually sharp decreases were Languedoc, Aquitaine, Burgundy, and Lyonnais (with declines of from 31 to 40 percent). In truth, this was a period of a general decrease in clerical entries touching most sectors of France, although urban recruitment was declining substantially more rapidly than rural recruitment. It should be noted, however, that sectors of western France significantly diverged from

[18] Michel Vovelle, *Piété baroque et déchristianisation* (Paris, 1973); Pierre Chaunu, *La mort à Paris du XVIe au XVIIIe siècle* (Paris, 1978); and, on Bordeaux, information kindly shared with me by Kenneth Fenster.

[19] See, notably, the comments of John McManners, *Death and the Enlightenment* (Oxford, 1981), 240-42. Because of differences in legal codes, wills cannot be used everywhere for testing religious attitudes: Philippe Goujard, "Echec d'une sensibilité baroque: Les testaments rouennais au XVIIIe siècle," *Annales. E.S.C.*, 36 (1981), 26-43.

[20] See the author's "L'histoire sociale du clergé diocésain dans la France du XVIIIe siècle," *RHMC*, 26 (1979), 212-13.

[21] See the author's article written with Claude Langlois, "Ecclesiastical Structures and Clerical Geography on the Eve of the French Revolution," *FHS*, 11 (1980), 366-67.

the national trend. In the rural areas of Maine, Anjou, and Lower Poitou (the future Vendée), in particular, the numbers of new clergymen actually increased by some 48 percent between the two periods, while those from urban parishes fell by 26 percent. It is a fact worth stressing that nowhere in France was the divergence in recruitment between town and country so great as in this sector of the west.[22]

Figures such as these strongly suggest that among the urban notables, no less than among the countrypeople of France, there were important regional variations in attitudes toward religion and the clergy. Without a doubt, the strongest center of anticlericalism was the capital itself. Nowhere outside Paris were the forces of clerical opposition—whether inspired by the parlements or the Jansenists or the *philosophes*—more powerful, persistent, and articulate. Here a whole series of *affaires* and *causes célèbres*, from the repression of the convulsionnaries in the 1730's through the *billets de confessions* in the 1750's and the expulsion of the Jesuits in the 1760's, had contributed in broadly publicizing and intensifying suspicions and grievances toward the clergy.[23] But how did the provincial urban elites compare to their Parisian counterparts in their perceptions of religion and of the clergy on the eve of the Civil Constitution? And what differences existed among the various towns of the realm? Fortunately, one approach for such a comparison does exist: an examination of the *cahiers de doléances* of the Third Estate.

Elite Opinion before the Revolution: The Third-Estate Cahiers[24]

A whole historiography has grown up over the question of the cahiers of 1789: the various influences exercised in their composition, their value as objective portrayals of economic and social realities, the precise social groups active and involved in their composition. But, in fact, much of the debate concerns the various "preliminary" cahiers—those written by parishes, guilds, towns, or smaller geographic units.[25] The "general" ca-

[22] Figures derived from the analysis in ibid. Between the two periods total rural recruitment would seem to have declined by about 12 percent, total urban recruitment by about 25 percent.

[23] See especially Dale Van Kley, *The Jansenists and the Expulsion of the Jesuits, 1757-1765* (New Haven, 1975); and *The Damiens Affair and the Unraveling of the Ancien Regime, 1750-1770* (Princeton, 1984).

[24] Portions of the following section originally appeared in the author's article "The West in France in 1789: The Religious Factor in the Origins of the Counterrevolution," *JMH*, 54 (1982), 715-45. They are reproduced here with the permission of the editors.

[25] See, for example, Alexandre Onou, "Les élections de 1789 et les cahiers du Tiers-Etat," *Révolution française*, 26 (1909): 525; Henri Sée, "La rédaction et la valeur historique des cahiers

hiers of the Third Estate—the statements of grievances drawn up in the final stage of the electoral process to be presented directly to the king at Versailles—pose far fewer problems. There are ample indications of the progressive elimination of the more humble elements of the population through the successive steps of the elections. The assemblies signing the general cahiers were almost always dominated by petty officials, lawyers, and members of the upper "bourgeoisie."[26] Those committees actually drawing up the cahiers for approval by the general electoral assemblies were probably even more elitist and heavily weighted in favor of the deputies of the largest towns. Though many committees made an effort to examine the preliminary cahiers written by local assemblies, they inevitably gave greatest attention to those grievances which they themselves knew best and with which they could most closely identify. Thus, at least five of the nine members of the cahiers committee for the *sénéchaussée* of Anjou were residents of the town of Angers, and many items in the final document—especially those concerning the Church—were copied almost *verbatim* from the town cahiers. In the *sénéchaussée* of Vannes a small group of politically experienced notables from the town dominated both the election of deputies and the cahier preparation. So too in Brest, Dinan, Lesneven, and probably Rennes, the town cahiers and the town notables seem to have been particularly influential.[27] Indeed, a strong case can be made that the general cahiers of the Third Estate represented primarily that group of non-peasant notables, and especially those from the towns, whose views on religion and the clergy we wish to examine.

Though a number of studies have touched on the "religious question" in 1789 as represented in the cahiers, most have focused on a general "national opinion" for which cahiers from all levels of the electoral process have been lumped together.[28] In order to explore the crucial issue of

---

de paroisses pour les Etats-Généraux de 1789," *RH*, 103 (1918): 292-306; Charles Tilly, *The Vendée* (Cambridge, Mass., 1964), 165-67. Many parish cahiers were in fact written by outsiders to the peasant milieu.

[26] See especially Beatrice Hyslop, *A Guide to the General Cahiers of 1789* (New York, 1936), 82.

[27] Arthur Le Moy, *Cahiers de doléances des corporations de la ville d'Angers et des paroisses de la sénéchaussée particulière d'Angers pour les Etats-Généraux*, 2 vols. (Angers, 1915-16), 1:cii-ciii, cxlvii-cxlviii, and ccxxxii-ccxxxv; Le Goff, 143-44; *AP*, 2:475; Hervé Pommeret, *L'esprit public dans le département des Côtes-du-Nord pendant la Révolution* (Saint-Brieuc, 1921), 38; Henri Sée and André Lessort, *Cahiers de doléances de la sénéchaussée de Rennes*, 4 vols. (Rennes, 1909-12), 1:ciii-cvi; François Roudaut, "Les cahiers de doléances de la sénéchaussée de Lesneven (1789)," *Annales de Bretagne*, 87 (1980), 527.

regional opinion, an entirely new analysis of the general cahiers of the Third Estate has been attempted. Obviously, such documents cannot be equated to a modern public opinion poll. Nothing approaching a national agenda for discussion—not to mention a standardized questionnaire— was ever prepared by the government. While "model cahiers" and other tracts with recommended grievances were undoubtedly in circulation, outside documents such as these seem to have been used discriminately by local cahier committees.[28]

For present purposes, in order to study the urban elites' stated grievances on religion and the clergy, two separately conceived content analyses of the Third-Estate cahiers have been used.[30] Examining the documents in this way, one is immediately impressed by the paucity of demands concerning religion per se, as opposed to those touching the clergy or ecclesiastical institutions.[31] Other than a few rare allusions to Jansenism, there are almost no references to problems of theology or religious prac-

---

[28] See, for example, A. Denys-Buirette, *Les questions religieuses dans les cahiers de 1789* (Paris, 1919), and Edme Champion, *La France d'après les cahiers de 1789* (Paris, 1904). George V. Taylor takes a similar perspective, although he distinguishes between different categories of cahiers, separating Paris, larger towns, and rural parishes: "Revolutionary and Non-Revolutionary Content in the *Cahiers* of 1789," *FHS*, 7 (1972), 479-502.

[29] Hyslop, 63-77.

[30] Both are available in computerized data banks at the University of Pittsburgh. The first is a thematic coding of selected grievances originally prepared by Beatrice Hyslop for her study of nationalism and later adapted by Sasha Weitman. See Sasha Weitman, "Bureaucracy, Democracy, and the French Revolution," Ph.D. dissertation, Washington University, 1968, and Hyslop's *French Nationalism in 1789 According to the General Cahiers* (New York, 1934), appendices, 250-87. The second analysis of the cahiers, undertaken by Gilbert Shapiro and John Markoff, includes all grievances. In many cases, however, I have regrouped the grievances which they coded into clusters relevant to my own specific interests. See their articles, written with Weitman, "Quantitative Studies of the French Revolution," *History and Theory*, 12 (1973), 163-91; and "Toward the Integration of Content Analysis and General Methodology," in *Sociological Methodology*, ed. David R. Heise (San Francisco, 1974), 1-57; also, by Markoff, "Who Wants Bureaucracy? French Public Opinion in 1789," Ph.D. dissertation, Johns Hopkins University, 1972. For the Hyslop-Weitman file, the data base consists of 207 coded cahiers out of a probable original of 236—including several written jointly by the Third Estate and one or both of the other two orders. The Shapiro-Markoff data are based on the analysis of 198 of the 236. I have excluded the province of Dauphiné for which there is only a single, very cursory joint cahier. May I reiterate here my appreciation to Markoff and Shapiro for allowing me to use their data at the University of Pittsburg, and to Robert McIntyre for assisting me with the analysis of the data and the construction of the maps.

[31] An initial attempt was made to score the cahiers in terms of their tone and rhetoric—*e.g.*, the degree of anticlericalism or of clerical deference—but this proved unsatisfactory, requiring an excessively subjective appraisal. Note Beatrice Hyslop's attempt to gauge the "anticlericalism" of the general cahiers, a categorization which seemed too vague and imprecise to be of use here: Hyslop, *French Nationalism*, 107 and 263-64.

tice. One interesting exception, however, involves the demands of some twenty-five commoner cahiers—and of another thirteen noble cahiers—that religious feast days be suppressed, reduced in number, or held only on Sundays.[32] We have already seen that similar demands were relatively common among the clerical leadership in the seventeenth and eighteenth centuries and that they were closely related to the movement of clericalization.[33] But, in the late eighteenth century, the traditional rationales for tampering with the feast days, related to their perceived "scandalous and superstitious" nature, came to be joined with justifications based on economic arguments: the *fêtes* should be modified and reformed in order to increase the number of work days and thus promote productivity. The interest here is that for the Third-Estate notables writing the cahiers it was almost always the economic rationale that was used. Thus, for the notables of Bordeaux, the feast days should be reduced in order "to increase agricultural labor and augment the amount of food available." Those in Châlons-sur-Marne judged them "harmful for the most indigent group of the population," while others thought less of the interests of the poor than of the possibility that a reduction in the *fêtes* would "lower the price of labor and give new activity to commerce and agriculture" (e.g., Saint-Pierre-le-Moûtier).[34] In this sense, such grievances might well indicate a tendency toward a more rationalistic approach to religion, a readiness to subordinate religious practice to a more secular, utilitarian logic: attitudes, in short, not unrelated to certain forms of the Enlightenment. When grievances such as these are represented cartographically, one is particularly impressed by their geographic concentration. (See Figure M.) In addition to smaller clusters near Bordeaux and along the Mediterranean coast, the demands were centered above all in a broad strip of territory from Picardy, Champagne, and the Parisian Basin southeast into Burgundy. During the last decades of the Old Regime most of these regions had in fact experienced precipitous declines in urban vo-

---

[32] The following general cahiers of the Third Estate included such demands: Aix, Arles (town), Autun, Beauvais, Bordeaux, Bourg-en-Bresse, Carcassonne, Châlons-sur-Marne, Charolles, Château-Thierry, Châtillon-sur-Seine, Moulins, La Rochelle, Libourne, Montargis, Montpellier, Nîmes, Nevers, Paris-*intra-muros*, Paris-*hors-murs*, Reims, Saint-Pierre-le-Moûtier, Saint-Quentin, Troyes, Vitry-le-François. The thirteen noble cahiers with such demands were almost without exception from the same regions. There were also six such demands in the cahiers of the clergy in 1789.

[33] See above, chp. 10.

[34] *AP*, 2:397-405, 594; 5:640. Of the 11 Third-Estate cahiers giving justifications for their grievances against *fêtes*, 10 specifically mention or imply economic rationales.

FIGURE M
Demands for Reduction or Concentration of Feast Days among
Third-Estate Cahiers.

cations to the clergy. At the time of the Revolution the clergy in most of the departments in question would be predominantly juring.

Yet we must also be wary of extrapolating too far on the basis of a single, relatively infrequent, demand. As a second approach, we can focus on the total number of grievances in each cahier which mentioned ecclesiastical matters of any kind. Only three Third-Estate assemblies have been found in which nothing whatsoever was written on this score.[35] Yet clearly the Church and the clergy received much fuller treatment in some regions than in others (see Figure N), and the geography which emerges is decidedly different from that which appeared in the previous map.[36]

---

[35] Peronnet, 1128. There were another 21 cahiers of the nobility which did not mention such questions.

[36] Analyzed, in practice, are all grievances coded by Shapiro and Markoff under the general rubric "R" (Religion). Note, that in considering the total number of religious grievances rather than a ratio, I am following the precedent defended by Gilbert Shapiro and Philip Dawson in "Social Mobility and Political Radicalism: The Case of the French Revolution of 1789," in *The*

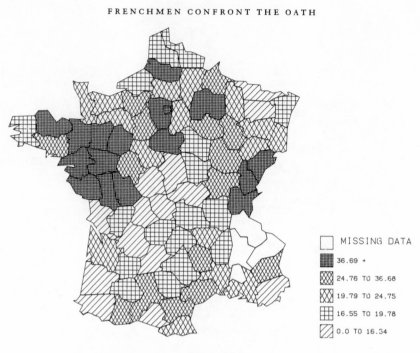

FIGURE N
Total Number of Religious Grievances in Third-Estate Cahiers.

Though Paris and the two adjoining departments stand out once again, a far more prominent and cohesive cluster of departments appears in the "west," a west which would seem to exclude Normandy, however, and to be linked almost in continuity with the Parisian Basin. Evidently, the same western notables who avoided all mention of feast days had a great deal to say about Church personnel and organization. Other areas of greater prominence appear in portions of the Midi and in the eastern provinces of Champagne, Burgundy, and Franche-Comté. By contrast, it was the center, the Massif-Central, the southwest, and Alsace-Lorraine which seemed the least preoccupied with Church questions. A cursory

---

Dimensions of Quantitative Research in History (Princeton, 1972), 178. In order to facilitate the mapping and the comparison with other data, here and in what follows scores tallied for the Old-Regime electoral districts have been transformed into scores for the French departments of 1790 through a weighting procedure based on estimated proportionate populations. See the article by Markoff and Shapiro, "The Linkage of Data Describing Overlapping Geographical Units," *Historical Methods Newsletter*, 7 (1973), 34-46.

reading of the grievances themselves confirms the findings of such simple frequency counts. The differences in tone were striking between the cahiers of such western electoral districts as Nantes, Le Mans, Rennes, or Anjou—with their lengthy and detailed programs for ecclesiastical change—and those of bailliages in the center or northeast—like Saumur, Loudun, Sens, Semur-en-Auxois, or Longuyon—which generally included only five or six dispersed comments on the subject.[37]

Yet if some provincial notables were far more loquacious on matters of the Church, what precisely did they say on the subject? In order to test the relative "progressivism" of the cahiers, scores have been assigned to each document, indicating the number of grievances registering hostility toward specific aspects of the Church and its policies. Counted here is an aggregate of six sets of grievances commonly expressed in reforming literature on the eve of the Revolution: those demanding an end to various forms of clerical privilege, full or partial secularization of key social institutions, full or partial state control of Church property, an end to the legal and fiscal prerogatives of the papacy within the French Church, the institution of greater religious toleration, and a democratization of the Church through the expansion of the power and status of the curés.[38] From this perspective, the geography of the cahiers presents a somewhat different and generally less coherent picture. (See Figure O.) Portions of the Massif-Central and of Aquitaine emerge as more progressive, even though the number of their religious grievances was relatively small; while Franche-Comté, Burgundy, and Upper Languedoc have now faded somewhat. Yet the overall contours of the two maps have many similarities. One notes, above all, the particular progressivism of the west of France. Indeed, the nine departments of this sector had not only the highest total ranking of any comparable cluster of departments in the country, but also ranked highest on all but one of the six subsets of ecclesiastical grievances—the Parisian region itself ranking but a close second.[39]

[37] *AP*, 1:7-10, 38-45, 131-33; 3:596-98, 644-45; 4:94-101; 5:538-50, 723-26, 757-61; Hyslop, *Guide*, 318-26.

[38] The Hyslop-Weitman data were used for this analysis. A score of 1 was attributed to a bailliage cahier each time a designated grievance occurred. The bailliage scores were then transformed to department scores through the procedure of proportionate populations described above. An aggregate of the scores was justified since most of the six sets correlate significantly with one another.

[39] The nine departments considered here as the "West" are Côtes-du-Nord, Morbihan, Ille-et-Vilaine, Manche, Mayenne, Sarthe, Loire-Atlantique, Maine-et-Loire, and Vendée. Considered as the "Paris region" are Oise, Seine-et-Oise, Seine-et-Marne, Seine, and Eure-et-Loir.

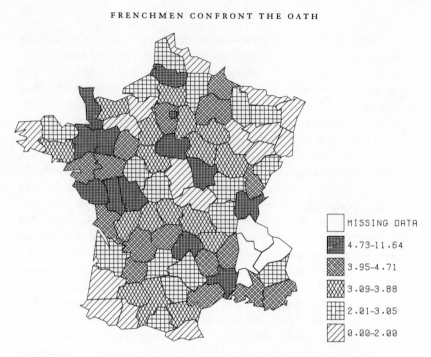

	MISSING DATA
	4.73-11.64
	3.95-4.71
	3.09-3.88
	2.01-3.05
	0.00-2.00

FIGURE O
Scores for Religious "Progressivism" in Third-Estate Cahiers.

The least progressive cluster of departments by this tally would seem to be the northeast of Alsace, Lorraine, and Franche-Comté, along with the extreme southwest and the northernmost provinces of Flanders, Artois, and Hainaut. Obviously, a failure to formulate progressive demands does not necessarily imply conservative attitudes on the part of these notables. But an additional aggregate score of "conservatism" toward the Church has also been generated for each cahier. The resultant map (see Figure P)[40] suggests the presence of a number of bailliages which ranked

---

The west attained an average departmental aggregate score of 5.3. The Paris region had 4.8. The lowest score was in Alsace-Lorraine: 1.7. The west also ranked first in each of the individual sets of grievances, except the demands for tolerance.

[40] The score for "conservatism" toward religion and the clergy consisted of four sets of grievances: those demanding a preservation of the status-quo in Church-state relations and Church privileges and prerogatives; those demanding a preservation and/or increase in censorship; those demanding the preservation of Church property in its various forms; those opposing toleration for non-Catholics. Unlike the progressivism grievances, these sets of grievances did not correlate well between themselves.

high both in "progressivism" and "conservatism."[41] Nevertheless, for many parts of France, the two maps are negative-positive images of one another. One is struck by the general weakness of "conservatism" in most of the western departments, but also by its relative strength in the eastern and northernmost frontier regions—Alsace, Lorraine, Franche-Comté, Artois, and Hainaut. As noted earlier, this group of provinces entered relatively late into the French realm and was generally more ultramontane in orientation.[42] Apparently, on questions of the clergy, the lay notables of the east and the extreme north were particularly cautious.

Whatever the range of opinion on a progressive-conservative scale, none of the cahiers of 1789 came close to prefiguring all of the measures

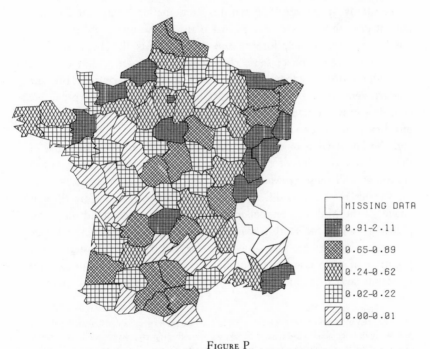

□	MISSING DATA
▨	0.91-2.11
▨	0.65-0.89
▨	0.24-0.62
▨	0.02-0.22
▨	0.00-0.01

FIGURE P
Scores for Religious "Conservatism" in Third-Estate Cahiers.

[41] Such bailliages had perhaps been unable to achieve a consensus and had thus produced documents that were actually pastiches of two or more sets of opinion. Among the areas with particularly strong scores in both progressivism and conservatism were the departments of Ain and Loiret and the city and suburbs of Paris.
[42] See above, chps. 5 and 8.

of the Revolutionary reorganization of the Church. As we have seen, the Constituent Assembly soon moved far beyond the articulated positions of the French notables at the end of the Old Regime.[43] Yet, an analysis of the degree to which the cahiers anticipated or partially anticipated the Civil Constitution is even more revealing of the regional distribution of elite opinion. The content of each cahier has been compared with a list of fifteen of the most important clerical reforms.[44] In the geographic representation (Figure Q) there emerges a scattering of "darker" departments, caused in most cases by solitary, unusually radical, cahiers. But the strongest and most coherent cluster of scores is found once again in the northwestern quadrant of the kingdom, this time in an arc extending from Picardy south through Ile-de-France and then westward into Brittany. If one breaks down this "anticipation" score into its component grievances, one discovers that many of the more moderate proposals—demanding help for sick and elderly priests, the abolition of the *casuel*, the suppression of some clerical privileges—are widely diffused throughout the kingdom, with no easily identifiable centers. But the western zone, from Paris to Nantes, stands out even more sharply if one considers only the five most radical religious measures: the suppression of tithes, of monastic vows, and of chapters; the sale of Church property; and the lay election of curés and bishops. (See Figure R.) The first of the five—the question of the tithes—is particularly illuminating. When one isolates all those grievances which simply *mention* the tithes, calling for various reforms, modifications, or clarifications (see Figure S), it is above all the Midi of Languedoc and Aquitaine which stand out. This preoccupation of the south is scarcely surprising, given the fact that tithe rates were higher here than anywhere else and that there existed a long tradition of tithe opposition among the Parlements of Toulouse and Bordeaux and of recalcitrance to tithe payments by the local popula-

[43] See above, chp. 1, Table 1.

[44] The grievances scored were as follows: abolish clerical privileges (fiscal, seigneurial, political, judicial, honorific); abolish the regular clergy; sell Church property; change the boundaries of dioceses or parishes; choose curés and bishops by election; open all posts to talent, regardless of class or status; abolish simple benefices; abolish the tithes; abolish the *casuel*; abrogate the existing Concordat with Rome; require residence of all clergy with cure of souls; reduce the wealth and income of the bishops; provide pensions for sick and elderly priests; give parish clergy greater voice in diocesan affairs; abolish chapters. The count was made by hand, using the Shapiro-Markoff data as a guide to all Church-related grievances. Each appearance of any of the designated grievances was scored 2. A partial rendering of any of the demands e.g., abolish some regular orders, sell a portion of Church lands for state purposes) was given a score of 1.

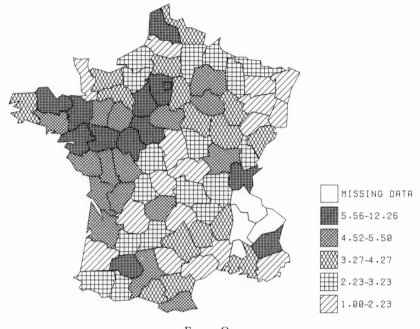

MISSING DATA

5.56-12.26

4.52-5.50

3.27-4.27

2.23-3.23

1.00-2.23

FIGURE Q

Anticipation of the Civil Constitution in Third-Estate Cahiers.

tions.[45] But when one focuses on grievances demanding the total or partial *suppression* of the institution itself, the Midi largely fades from the picture, and it is the northern half of the kingdom, and particularly the west, which appears most radical on the issue. (See Figure T.)

Despite its inevitable limitations, our consideration of the *cahiers de doléances* does permit some interesting observations. In the first place, one might seriously put into question the efforts of certain historians to discover a unified "French opinion" in the cahiers on the eve of the Revolution. At least in the realm of religious opinions, one is more impressed by regional diversity than by national homogeneity. This is not to say that clear and cohesive positions appear in every sector of

[45] Counted here are all grievances in Shapiro and Markoff's category "RDI" (Religion-Dîme). On tithe protests in the south see Pierre Gagnol, *La dîme ecclésiastique en France au XVIIIe siècle* (Paris, 1910), 151; Henri Marion, *La dîme ecclésiastique en France au XVIIIe siècle et sa suppression* (Bordeaux, 1912), 187; and Georges Frêche, *Toulouse et la région Midi-Pyrénées au siècle des Lumières* (Toulouse, 1974), 536-43.

267

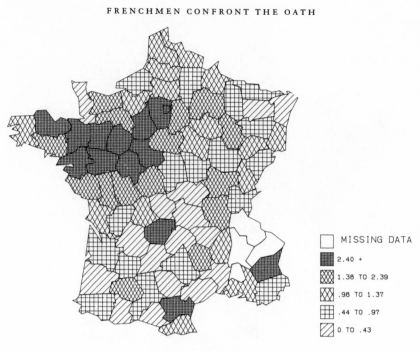

FIGURE R
"Radical" Anticipations of the Civil Constitution in
Third-Estate Cahiers.

France. For some provinces or groups of provinces—much of the Midi, for example—the various strategies employed here have failed to discern a consistent picture. Yet a number of key regions have emerged in which the elite notables seemed to reveal relatively characteristic attitudes. Those living in the eastern frontier provinces and in the extreme north of the kingdom, for example, generally appear moderate, even "conservative," on ecclesiastical concerns, little inclined, for the most part, toward innovation or radical change. By contrast, the most advanced and progressive notables were apparently those in the Paris Basin and the west.

No attempt has been made to analyze systematically the language used in these cahiers. But an impressionistic reading reveals the strong anticlerical tone of several of the cahiers from both the west and the Parisian Basin: the indictment of the notables of Rennes against the "corruption, intrigue, and despotism" involved in the filling of clerical posts; the appeal of the Brestois for a radical disengagement of the clergy from all temporal

268

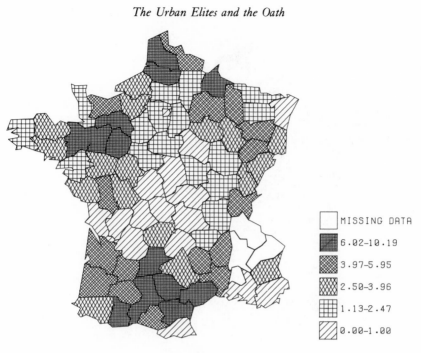

MISSING DATA

6.02-10.19

3.97-5.95

2.50-3.96

1.13-2.47

0.00-1.00

FIGURE S
Grievances Concerning the Reform of the Tithes in
Third-Estate Cahiers.

affairs; the forceful attacks on the regular clergy by the Parisian delegates.[46] To judge by the grievance lists, nowhere were the elite commoners
more adamant to bring under attack the clericalized, "Tridentine" brand
of Catholicism; nowhere were they more prepared to advance ideas that
would anticipate the Civil Constitution and, in particular, the most radical
measures of that Constitution. That such positions should appear among
the urban notables of the Parisian Basin is hardly unexpected, given all
that we know of the religious character of the capital and the towns and
villages nearby. Far more remarkable, however, is the apparent continuity
of elite opinion from the plains of the Seine into the towns of the bocage
of Brittany, Anjou, and Maine—in the very heart of the future Vendée
and Chouans regions. Perhaps it was the intensity of the surrounding
rural clericalism in the west which gave a particular meaning and rel-

[46] *AP*, 1:468-69; 5:286-88; 542.

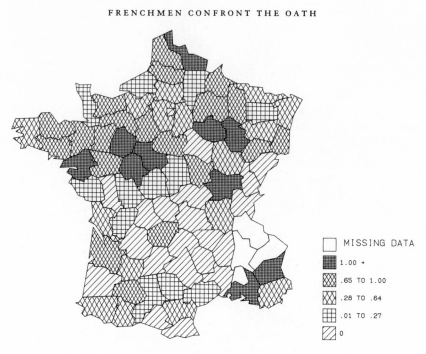

MISSING DATA

1.00 +

.65 TO 1.00

.28 TO .64

.01 TO .27

0

FIGURE T
Grievances Asking the Suppression of All or Part of the Tithes
in Third-Estate Cahiers.

evance to the anticlericalism of the Enlightenment, stimulating and intensifying the feelings of notables toward priests and ecclesiastical
institutions.

It is not surprising, then, that cahier opinion correlates poorly with
the positions soon to be taken by the clergy on the oath. There is, in fact,
no significant association between the oath and cahier progressivism,
cahier conservatism, the anticipation of the Civil Constitution, or the total
number of religious grievances.[47] Nevertheless, a weak *negative* correlation
does appear between the oath and the number of "radical" religious
grievances. Such a finding would suggest the possibility that the clergy,
generally so susceptible to the influence of the local masses of the pop-

[47] The correlation coefficients per department between cahier scores and the proportion of
oath-takers were as follows: with progressivism: −0.049; with conservatism: 0.072; with total
religious grievances: −0.164; with anticipation of the Civil Constitution: −0.089.

270

ulation, may sometimes have reacted *against* the opinion of the neighboring elites.[48] This is a point to which we must return below.

The Urban Elite and the Regional Implementation
of the Religious Legislation

Within a little more than a year many of the same members of the Third Estate who had drawn up the cahiers of their bailliages and sénéchaussées would be called upon to begin organizing the newly created departmental and district administrations. The electoral process of 1789 often served as the first lesson in the education of the nascent political nation, with the most active and successful individuals soon making the transition into the local power elites of the new regime.[49] It was commonly the same individuals who took charge of the regional implementation of the Civil Constitution and the oath legislation in the early months of 1791. In the two previous chapters we have explored the extent to which these laws may have shocked and upset the local religious sensibilities of certain regions. Yet it is also evident that the manner in which the local political elites implemented the laws varied considerably from one department to another. Eventually, the departmental leaders would everywhere be led and goaded into a relatively standardized policy on the ecclesiastical reforms.[50] Yet their initial reactions could play out numerous variations on a theme, and the tone or "style" with which they executed the laws might continue to differ markedly.

From the first, a number of administrations revealed themselves as distinctly moderate and flexible in their implementation of the Civil Constitution. On occasion, the district authorities—though never the departmental authorities, as far as we can tell—were openly recalcitrant in imposing unpopular aspects of the law. The district of Morlaix (Finistère), for example, refused to cooperate in executing the suppression of the bishopric and the cathedral chapter of Saint-Pol-de-Léon. Eventually, the department was forced to commission the leaders of the neighboring district of Brest to perform the delicate and highly unpopular task. There were unverifiable accusations by patriots of Thouars (Deux-

[48] The correlation coefficient between the oath and the number of "radical" religious grievances is −0.350; between the oath and the number of grievances concerning the tithes it is −0.391.

[49] See Le Goff, 108-48; also Lynn Avery Hunt, *Revolution and Urban Politics in Provincial France* (Stanford, 1978).

[50] See above, chp. 1.

Sèvres) that local district leaders were protecting priests and monks and refusing to do anything to replace refractory clergymen. At least two of the districts in German Lorraine—Bitche and Boulay—seem to have refused to cooperate in suppressing monasteries and to have left the overwhelmingly refractory clergy virtually unmolested through September of 1792.[51] More common, perhaps, were those administrations which simply acted in a cautious and circumspect manner when dealing with the problems of the clergy, doing whatever they could to avoid jostling the sensibilities of their constituencies, attempting in this way to ease their departments gently into the oath legislation. They sought to circumvent confrontations, buying time and hoping the storm would soon blow over; aware, moreover, of the potential threats to their physical well-being if they should break too far from popular consensus.[52]

Such would certainly seem to be the approach taken by the notables in power in Lozère. To follow the official departmental deliberations, the problem of the enforcement of the oath legislation was never even raised before late June 1791, despite the fact that the region was one of the most refractory in all of France. Only after a delegation of patriots appeared in person before the officials, complaining that a refractory in their canton was regularly preaching against the constitution—in both its civil and ecclesiastical provisions—was the department directory moved to take action. Only then, concluded the *procureur-général-syndic*, had infractions against the law "become so serious that they could no longer be dismissed."[53] In equally refractory Bas-Rhin, the administration was forced to consider the issue much earlier. But, in this case as well, the directors desperately attempted to avoid a confrontation, writing a lengthy and impassioned plea to the National Assembly that they might avoid the replacement of refractories.[54] Just to the south, in Haute-Saône and Jura, within the former province of Franche-Comté, the efforts toward appeasement and reconciliation may have been even more vigorous. Faced with a large number of restrictive oaths, the departmental directors in Vesoul devised a subtle distinction between restrictions which

[51] For the problems in Saint-Pol-de-Léon, A.N., D XXIX bis 20, dos. 212, no. 1 and dos. 215, no. 36; on Thouars, D XXIX bis 21, dos. 232, no. 22; on German Lorraine, P. Lesprand, *Le Clergé de la Moselle pendant la Révolution. Les débuts de la Révolution et la suppression des ordres religieux*, 4 vols. (Montguy-lès-Metz, 1934-39), 4:2-3, 350.

[52] See above, chp. 7.

[53] Ferdinand André, ed., *Délibérations de l'administration départementale de la Lozère et de son directoire de 1790 à 1800*, 4 vols. (Mende, 1882-84), 1:437-38.

[54] Rodolphe Reuss, *La Constitution civile du clergé et la crise religieuse en Alsace (1790-1795)*, 2 vols. (Strasbourg, 1922), 1:28-29.

totally vitiated the oath and those which did nothing to harm the "spirit of the oath." It was only in the early summer of 1791, when clergymen had been required to acknowledge the constitutional bishop, that administrators were forced to conclude that only one-third, not two-thirds, of the parish corps could be counted as constitutional.[55] Policies were so similar in nearby Doubs that one suspects some degree of consultation between the two departments. Here too, until the directors were compelled to require recognition of the new bishop, curés with a wide variety of restrictive oaths were maintained in their posts. Vicaires and even "vicaires en chef"—who in Franche-Comté had virtually the same responsibilities as curés—were at first not even constrained to an oath, following the argument that it was impossible to determine which vicaires would still be needed after the parishes of the department had been reorganized. By the late spring and summer, several of the district directors began to complain of the "principles of indulgence" adopted by the men in Besançon which encouraged refractories to think they could break the law with impunity. But at least through the middle of summer the department insisted on a policy of tolerance: "in a free country one cannot be punished for a few spoken words"—only for "faits graves" or a "coalition criminelle." The refractories were only "citizens gone astray" who would hopefully come back in time to the correct way of thinking.[56]

Such patience and indulgence on the part of the administrators formed a sharp contrast with the attitudes of men in a number of other departments, men who commonly revealed themselves as intolerant and unsympathetic, not only toward the refractory clergymen but toward the religious sentiments of their lay constituencies as well. The Breton department of Ille-et-Vilaine, which probably had no greater problems with recalcitrant non-jurors in 1791 than the department of Doubs, took a distinctly more hostile and aggressive posture toward the local clergy. Already in April of the previous year several priests who had voted during a seminary retreat to demand that Catholicism be declared the state religion were arrested and accused of treason—a reaction unprec-

[55] Jean Girardot, *Le département de la Haute-Saône pendant la Révolution*, 3 vols. (Vesoul, 1973), 2:65-66; Jean Girardot, "Clergé réfractaire et clergé constitutionnel en Haute-Saône pendant la Révolution," *Mémoires de la Société pour l'histoire du droit et des institutions des anciens pays bourguignons, comtois et romands*, 24 (1963), 126-27.

[56] Department directory of Doubs to the municipality of Blamont, Mar. 25, 1791; and to the district of Ornans, June 20, 1791: A.D. Doubs, L 742; also, the district of Baume-les-Dames to the department, May 31 and July 7, 1791: A.D. Doubs, L 741. See, in addition, the dissertation by Frank Tallett, "Religion and Revolution: the Rural Clergy and Parishioners of the Doubs, 1780-1797," Ph.D. thesis, University of Reading, 1981, esp. 182-83.

edented in its rigor for a departmental administration.[57] With the episode of the oath Ille-et-Vilaine adopted, in the words of Donald Sutherland, "an outlook which is generally associated with the Terror," suspending constitutional guarantees of freedom of speech and association in the name of a greater good. As early as January 1791, they tried to intimidate clergymen by threatening to refuse pensions to non-jurors—an action totally illegal and soon criticized as such by the royal government. Thereafter, they continued to show a "predilection for repressive and coercive measures" against all refractories, eventually even anticipating the Legislative Assembly by requiring a second oath and voting a general deportation to Louisiana for all refractories.[58]

The situation was similar in many respects just to the south in Nantes and the department of Loire-Inférieure. Here, too, priests who refused to read the new laws at the pulpit were summarily denied their salaries and their status as "active" citizens. The same punishment was meted out to all those who signed a statement opposing aspects of the Civil Constitution, an act denounced as "treason" by the departmental officials.[59] In nearby Sarthe, authorities were said to have enforced the oath legislation more strictly than required by the National Assembly itself. As early as January 1791, the district directory of Sablé accused local refractories of actions which might soon lead to a new Saint-Bartholomew's Day Massacre—an accusation for which the leading historian of the question claims to have found no evidence.[60] The efforts of officials in Angers (Maine-et-Loire) forcibly to impose juring priests on the population and repress popular pilgrimages has often been recounted. On occasion, the directors would force the closing of a church rather than leave it in the hands of a non-juror—and, in the process, would order the confiscation of parish sacred ornaments and bells. Alison Patrick has argued that the leaders of Maine-et-Loire were constantly abrasive in their implementation of the Civil Constitution and that their very style of administration, in its lack of sensitivity, would ultimately be a major element in the origins of the Vendée uprising.[61] In many instances, the

[57] Donald Sutherland, *The Chowans: The Social Origins of Popular Counterrevolution in Upper Brittany, 1770-1796* (Oxford, 1982), 229-31.

[58] Ibid., 249-50.

[59] See especially A. Lallié, *Le diocèse de Nantes pendant la Révolution*, 2 vols. (Nantes, 1893), 1:52-53; and the report of the department directory, Oct. 17, 1790: A.N., F[19] 440.

[60] Maurice Giraud, *Essai sur l'histoire religieuse de la Sarthe de 1789 à l'an IV* (Paris, 1920), 387-92.

[61] Alison Patrick, "How to Make a Counter-Revolution: Departmental Policy in the Maine-et-Loire, 1790-1793," paper delivered at the Society for French Historical Studies, Pittsburgh, March 1979. My thanks to Professor Patrick for allowing me to refer to her research.

irritation and impatience with priests on the part of the local officials in these departments of the west took on an openly anticlerical tone. The *procureur-général-syndic* of Maine-et-Loire, according to Patrick, found "all priests tiresome." The directors of Morbihan counseled the district officials in late 1790 to do everything possible to "stop the sacerdotal influence," and to "inspire defiance against the speeches of anything calling itself a priest." In Josselin there were references to "our aristo-calottinocrates." Later in 1791, the administrators of Ille-et-Vilaine would confess that they had welcomed the Civil Constitution, not as a plan for regenerating the Church, but as the means of "relegating priests to their proper place."[62]

A few case examples such as these are hardly sufficient to warrant general conclusions about the various regions of the kingdom. And, unfortunately, anything approaching a systematic typology of the departmental application of oath legislation is impossible at present. Nevertheless, the parallels between the departments examined here and the cahiers of 1789 are intriguing. The cautious and moderate reactions of the directories of the eastern departments of Bas-Rhin, Doubs, and Haute-Saône seemed already to be prefigured in the cahiers of the notables of the Third Estate in these same provinces. The markedly progressive, if not radical, cahiers of the western departments like Ille-et-Vilaine, Loire-Inférieure, Maine-et-Loire, and Sarthe might seem linked in continuity with the brash, anticlerical policies followed by the administrations of these regions. But if it is not feasible to gauge all French departments on the implementation of the oath, their reactions to another piece of religious legislation, the so-called "law of toleration" of May 7, 1791, can be assessed in a more systematic fashion.

The Implementation of the "Law of Toleration"

Such an assessment is possible because in late 1791 the law in question and its implementation in the departments became the subject of a major political struggle.[63] For the Constituent Assembly, the decree represented something of a reaction to the hard line taken at the beginning of the year. Impressed by the widespread opposition to the oath in some areas, the majority resolved to apply the principle of religious freedom to those supporting the refractory clergy, and to allow non-jurors to hold public

[62] Patrick, ibid.; J. Le Falher, *Le royaume de Bignan (1789-1805)* (Hennebont, 1913), 72, 104; Sutherland, 232.

[63] C. Constantin, "Constitution civile du Clergé," in *DTC*, vol. 3, pt. 2, cols. 1583-85.

religious services as long as no words were spoken against the Constitution. Clergymen who transgressed the law could be prosecuted, but only through normal criminal procedures. Yet almost from the beginning there were complaints that certain administrators were ignoring the official decree on toleration and ordering an assortment of illegal repressive measures against non-jurors. Six months later, the newly elected Legislative Assembly would further encourage such repression by voting to deny pensions to refractories and to force all non-jurors out of the parishes in which they had formerly served. The king, however, vetoed the bill and instructed his ministers to maintain the original law. In early 1792, the Minister of the Interior, Cahier de Gerville, conducted a survey to determine the fate of the law of May 7 in the departments.[64] The extent to which local administrators maintained or perverted the law of toleration can serve as a useful touchstone of their attitudes toward the religious reforms and toward the clergy in general.

The adjoining map (see Figure U) indicates the departments in which directives are known to have been issued prior to the French declaration of war (April 20, 1792), directives which forced all or part of the refractory clergy out of their parishes of residence.[65] Inevitably, the local alignments of forces which these directives represented were often complex and differed from department to department. District officials, municipal officials, political clubs, judicial magistrates, and private citizens all might come down on different sides of the issue in given instances. Positions might be modified when elections brought in new men to specific ad-

---

[64] Notes taken on the survey for the ministry are in A.N., F^{19} 311. These are not entirely complete, however, and have been complimented by documents in A.N., F^{19} 398-481, which contain many of the original departmental responses, and by various local studies: for Bouches-du-Rhône, Viviane Santini, "Le clergé et la vie religieuse à Marseille pendant la Révolution de 1789-95," D.E.S., Université de Marseille, 1965, 150-51; for Calvados, Winifred Edington, "An Administrative Study of the Implementation of the Civil Constitution of the Clergy in the Diocese of Lisieux," Ph.D. dissertation, University of London, 1958, 211; for Indre-et-Loire, F^{19} 433; for Lot (district Montauban), Daniel Ligou, *Montauban à la fin de l'Ancien régime et au début de la Révolution* (Paris, 1958), 334; for Morbihan, Le Falher, 99, 107; for Puy-de-Dôme, Yvon-Georges Paillard, "Fanatiques et patriotes dans le Puy-de-Dôme: histoire religieuse d'un département de 1792 à Thermidor," *AHRF*, 42 (1970), 302-304; for Basses-Pyrénées, A.N., F^{19} 461; for Bas-Rhin, Rodolphe Reuss, 1:287-95; for Sarthe, A.N., F^{19} 469; for Seine-Inférieure A.N., D XIX 22, dos. 364.

[65] After April 20, when war was declared, the repression became much more general. Not included here are departments giving orders against only one or a few individual priests. Thus, Cantal apparently ordered only specific priests to leave their parishes; Lot, Lot-et-Garonne, and Tarn each acted against only one or two priests. The interest is in blanket orders covering whole groups of refractories and bypassing the criminal court system, the legal mode of recourse against refractories. Note that in both Manche and Haute-Loire the orders involved only one district—the districts of Avranches and of Monistrol, respectively.

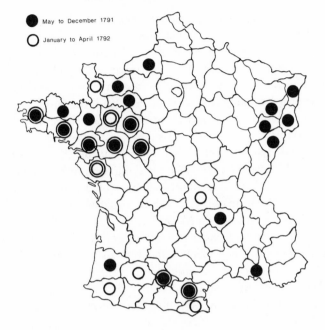

FIGURE U

Departments Forcing Residence Changes among the Refractory
Clergy, 1791-92. (Double circles indicate that refractories were
required to reside in a particular town or institution.)

ministrative bodies. The principal goal here will be to identify *regional*
trends, representing the position of dominant elites across several individual departments.

It is evident from the map that most of the French departments were
able to avoid major repressive actions and ultimately succeeded in maintaining a balance of tolerance through the spring of 1792. Not surprisingly,
none of the departments with strong majorities of constitutional clergymen seems to have taken illegal measures. Officials in Haute-Marne
noted proudly that they had never expelled priests from their parishes
except on a case-by-case basis through the court system. Loiret claimed
to have "religiously" followed the line traced by the Constitution. Cher
was attempting to smooth over the passions engendered by the oath,
while scrupulously following the law.[66] In many of these departments

[66] Report from the directory of Haute-Marne, Apr. 21, 1792: A.N., F[19] 448; from directory
of Loiret, Mar. 28, 1792: A.N., F[19] 441; M. Bruneau, *Les débuts de la Révolution dans les*

the greatest problem was not with the non-jurors themselves, but with the intolerance of the constitutionals and the population in general against the non-jurors. Ariège found itself in a lengthy battle with the town leaders of Pamiers and Saint-Lizier to preserve the right of refractories to hold religious services. Saône-et-Loire was even forced to call in the national guard to protect the refractories and guarantee their rights. Somme maintained that it was doing all in its power to convince certain groups that citizens were not "aristocrats" just because they attended another mass; but, unfortunately, it was "difficult indeed to persuade men that political and civil laws have nothing to do with religious laws."[67]

Yet there was also a substantial number of departments where refractories were in the majority and which managed, nevertheless, to avoid extralegal policies: most of the Massif-Central, Lorraine, the Basque country, and the northern frontier departments of Nord and Pas-de-Calais. The leaders of Gard and Hérault and Jura all had to struggle, but still succeeded in maintaining a semblance of religious liberty through the end of 1791.[68] By April of 1792 Pas-de-Calais had done nothing more than order all municipalities to inform the directory if any refractories were raising difficulties.[69] In Nord, the administration did, on occasion, transgress the law in minor ways, ordering the priests in a single parish to move at least six leagues away, and forbidding refractories to say mass in a parish church without the permission of the juring curé. But a general ruling forcing all refractories to leave their parishes came only after war had been declared. In a careful study of the application of the Civil Constitution in this department, one historian concluded that the local leaders generally tried to maintain a moderate and tolerant stance during the first year after the oath, though, buffeted by various external influences and beset by internal divisions, they did oscillate, at times, in their policies. On several occasions they also encouraged the prosecution of juring clergymen who refused to show due toleration.[70]

départements du Cher et de l'Indre (Paris, 1902), 400-401. See also the procureur-général-syndic of Meuse, Mar. 2, 1792: A.N., F19 451.

[67] G. Arnaud, Histoire de la Révolution dans le département de l'Ariège (Toulouse, 1904), 218-19, 226-27, 233; arrêté by the directory of Saône-et-Loire, June 4, 1791: A.N., F19 468; report by the directory of Somme, Apr. 21, 1792: F19 476.

[68] François Rouvière, Histoire de la Révolution française dans le département du Gard, 2 vols. (Nîmes, 1887-89), 2:43-44; F. Saurel, Histoire religieuse du département de l'Hérault pendant la Révolution, 4 vols. (Paris, 1894-96), 2:192-93; letter from the directory of Jura to the minister of the interior, April 26, 1792: A.N., F19 435.

[69] A.N., F19 311.

[70] C. Richard, "L'application de la Constitution civile du clergé dans le département du

In all, twenty-eight departmental administrations are known to have issued one or more blanket repressive directives prior to the war, requiring all or a substantial number of refractory clergymen to leave their former parishes.[71] The earliest such directives seem to have been signed in the west: on May 24, 1791, in Maine-et-Loire; in June in the departments of Morbihan, Ille-et-Vilaine, Calvados, and Côtes-du-Nord, as well as in the Provençal department of Bouches-du-Rhône; in July in Seine-Inférieure, Loire-Inférieur, and in the two Alsatian departments. The others were spread out through the autumn, winter, and spring, including seven issued in the first months of 1792. Most commonly, the orders were directed against all refractories who had been replaced, though sometimes they were aimed only at those judged to be "perturbateurs du repos public." The majority compelled the priests in question to reside a minimum distance—often 3 leagues—from their former parishes, but a few, as we shall see, imposed a specific place of residence and established a situation that was tantamount to imprisonment.

All but three of the twenty-eight departments were clustered together in three groups: along the northeastern frontier, in the southwestern Midi, and in the west. Given our earlier observations about the eastern provinces of Lorraine, Alsace, and Franche-Comté, the presence of five departments near the Rhine and the Jura is somewhat surprising. The key to this turnabout was probably the intense pressure exercised in the area by the National Assembly itself, particularly fearful of the threat from the emigrants just across the Rhine and of the possibility of "counterrevolution" within the provinces themselves. When a special commission from the Constituent concluded that the directory of Bas-Rhin was dragging its feet in implementing the Civil Constitution, the entire departmental executive was suspended and replaced by patriots of the

---

Nord," *RHMC*, 12 (1909), 230-44. Note also that on June 25, 1791 the directory had ordered all convent churches closed to anyone other than the regular clergy. In July 1791, the department apparently asked the National Assembly to be allowed to order all refractories away from their parishes; but the National Assembly refused and the department immediately backed off: Philippe Sagnac, "Le serment à la Constitution civile du clergé en 1791 dans la région du Nord," *Annales de l'Est*, 3 (1907), 183-84.

[71] This is substantially less than the figure of 42 departments indicated by some authors: *e.g.*, Pierre de La Gorce, *Histoire religieuse de la Révolution*, 5 vols. (Paris, 1909-24), 2:79; and, *Constantin*, col. 1585. The figures used by La Gorce were apparently taken from the speech given by Roland, the new interior minister, on April 23, 1792: *AP*, 42:307-310. Roland actually says 42 *arrêtés* had been issued. But several *arrêtés* are known to have been issued by the same departments. Also, as noted above, we are not including here those departments issuing illegal acts against only one or a few individual priests.

commission's own choosing—an unprecedented step at that point in the Revolution. It was actually the replacement directors who initiated repressive measures against the refractory clergy in the summer of 1791, and it was probably their example, coupled with the near panic occasioned by the king's flight to Varennes, which incited the actions of the neighboring departments. In any case, both Doubs and Haute-Saône seem quickly to have rescinded these initial measures.[72]

In the southwest, exceptional measures against the clergy were organized somewhat later: only in early 1792 for Gers, Basses-Pyrénées, and Pyrénées-Orientales, and in August and September 1791 elsewhere. Apparently, the actions first taken by the patriots of the Protestant stronghold of Montauban were of key importance in influencing repressive measures in Haute-Garonne—measures which were accepted several weeks later by the department directory in Toulouse and, on the same day, in neighboring Aude. But, despite the vigor of the *arrêts*, the directives were strongly opposed by many citizens in the towns and were applied only cautiously against the obvious troublemakers among the clergy.[73] In Landes, the *arrêt* in question was instigated in early September with the strong support of the local Jacobins, but two and perhaps three of the four districts openly refused to enforce it.[74]

It was in the west that the repressive measures were not only the earliest and the most numerous but also the most stringent and energetic. With the flight to Varennes, if not earlier, several of the departments began setting up veritable prisons in which large numbers of refractories were forcibly concentrated. In Angers they were sent to the *petit séminaire*, in Nantes to the main seminary and then to the chateau, in Morbihan to the citadel of Port-Louis, in Côtes-du-Nord to the seminary of Saint-Brieuc. Though the amnesty of September 1791 and pressure from the royal government succeeded in temporarily liberating the clergymen in question, the internment tactics were pursued even more vigorously in late 1791 and early 1792, to be implemented in a total of nine western departments by the time the war broke out.[75] In the entire kingdom

[72] Reuss, 1:99-116, 275-97; A.N., F19 311; and Tallett, 229-30, 234, 235-36.

[73] Jean-Claude Meyer, *La vie religieuse en Haute-Garonne sous la Révolution (1789-1801)* (Toulouse, 1982), 144-47, 153; Ligou, 334 and A.N., F19 427.

[74] A.N., F19 436 and Joseph Légé, *Les diocèses d'Aire et de Dax ou le département des Landes sous la Révolution française, 1789-1803*, 2 vols. (Aire, 1875), 1:148-49.

[75] On Maine-et-Loire: Serge Chassagne "L'église abolie? (1789-1802)," in *Le diocèse d'Angers*, François Lebrun, ed. (Paris, 1981), 164; on Loire-Inférieure: A.N., F19 440, and Lallié, 1:122-23, 153, 163-64; on Morbihan: Le Falher, 99, 121; on Côtes-du-Nord: Pommeret, 134-35, 138, 157-58 and Léon Dubreuil, *La vente des biens nationaux dans le département des Côtes-du-Nord* (Paris, 1912), xxxi; on Finistère: A.N., F19 425.

outside the west only five other departments went this far in the extralegal repression of refractories.

Though most of these policies in the west seem to have been initiated by the administrative elites, often influenced by the club patriots, one should not underestimate the support lent by the urban masses in certain of the towns. In Nantes, for example, popular rioting broke out when the department first attempted to release the imprisoned refractories, and crowds of anticlerical "sans-culottes"—as one historian has called them—helped pressure a whole range of additional measures against the refractory cult.[76] It was probably the urban support for repression which helped encourage the directors to bring the refractories into the towns under the watchful eyes of the citizenry, rather than to exile them a fixed distance from their former parishes.[77] The previously noted suspicion and impatience of the western administrators was only intensified in the eleven months from May 1791 to April 1792. Those in Ille-et-Vilaine were convinced that the priests of the department were perpetrating a well-organized plot to subvert the entire Revolution. In Nantes, where the clubs had become rapidly anticlerical, the leaders felt certain that the clergy was at the root of all the Revolution's problems: emigrants and priests leagued together, "those are our only enemies." In Vannes, the directors were bitter and enraged when the government tried to stop their anticlerical activities: "we should solve the whole problem [of priests] as the Spanish solved the problem of the Jesuits."[78]

That some refractories were actually encouraging broad opposition to the Revolution can scarcely be doubted. But a great many clergymen and their rural parishioners vigorously defended themselves from all wrongdoing. In a veritable flood of letters to the king and his ministers they maintained that they were innocent of any form of treason or attacks on the Revolution and that the directors were imagining everything—affirmations that were supported, in several instances, by letters from rural magistrates. It was the department officials themselves who were the most "intolerant" and "unconstitutional" in their actions, resurrecting a

[76] *Arrêt* of directory of Loire-Inférieure, July 22, 1791: A.N., F¹⁹ 440; and Lallié, 1:58-59, 140-43, 153.

[77] Note the contrast with Toulouse where the strong opposition of the majority of the town population to repression of the refractories forced the directors to reverse their decision and cease encouraging a concentration of non-jurors in Toulouse itself: Meyer, 146-47; *arrêts* of Aug. 2 and of Aug. 19-22, 1791: A.N., F¹⁹ 427.

[78] *Mémoire* from the directory of Ille-et-Vilaine, Oct. 1, 1791: A.N., F¹⁹ 431; letter to the king from the directory of Loire-Inférieure, Dec. 22, 1791: F¹⁹ 440; Paul Bois, "La Révolution et l'Empire," in *Histoire de Nantes*, Paul Bois, ed. (Toulouse, 1977), 257-59; Le Falher, 99.

new form of "lettres de cachet" to imprison French citizens illegally without trial.[79] Whatever the stance taken by their priests, it is clear that many of the countrypeople in the west felt fully as oppressed and persecuted in their religious beliefs as the Catholics of Gard or the other Protestant areas of the Midi. Indeed, their appeals were often couched in strikingly similar language. Though Protestants would now be allowed their pastors and Jews their rabbis and Moslems their mullahs, they, the Catholics of France, were to be denied the priests necessary for their salvation. They held to a religion for which priests were absolutely essential, and it was impossible for them to have confidence in those not in communion with the Church of Rome. Who would now baptize their children and care for the souls of the dead and dying? And what had happened to popular sovereignty?[80]

In the overall assessment of the oath of 1791, the actions and reactions of the urban elites were far from constituting a critical factor. The development of the previous chapters should be persuasive of the intricate set of structural, cultural, and individual elements which conditioned clerical options from one region to another. In virtually every case where extralegal repression was organized, administrations were operating in a context of real or potential riots and violence over the oath and the Civil Constitution. And, nevertheless, as we have also seen, many administrations confronted with equally dangerous threats—notably, in the Massif-Central and along the northern frontier—still managed to adopt alternate policies of appeasement or moderation.

But if the analysis here is perhaps ultimately inconclusive for many regions of the kingdom, the results do seem particularly revealing for the problem of the west. For no other region have we been able to identify so clear a continuity from Old Regime to Revolution: from the low clerical recruitment among urban notables and the concentration of literary societies and *chambres de lectures* during the eighteenth century; through the particularly vociferous stance for ecclesiastical transformation as evi-

[79] See the numerous petitions from communities in Loire-Inférieure; notably those from Saint-André-des-Eaux and Pontchâteau: A.N., F^{19} 440; likewise, from communities in Mayenne: A.N., F^{19} 449. Also, the letters from the mayor of Missillac, Jan. 28, 1792; from Divineau, "citoyen sans titre" in Nantes, Dec. 14, 1791; from Jeffreds, commissaire du roi in Blain, Jan. 8, 1792: ibid.; and by an unknown citizen, probably of Saint-Malo, Dec. 14, 1791: A.N., F^{19} 431.

[80] See, especially, the letters from the communities of Missillac (Jan. 28, 1792), Prinqueau (Feb. 16, 1792), Saint-André-des-Eaux (Nov. 26, 1791), and Laigné (late 1791): A.N., F^{19} 440 and 449.

denced in the cahiers of 1789; through the distinctly aggressive and confrontational positions of the Revolutionary officials in the implementation of the religious legislation and the oath. It is evident that most of the officials in question were not about to make things easy for the local clergymen faced with the option of 1791. And it is not implausible that many of these same clergymen found, in the actions and attitudes of the townsmen, confirmation of long-held suspicions about the irreligion and anticlericalism of the towns. The peculiar secularizing bent of the urban notability in the west—juxtaposed, as it was, with an intensely clerical countryside—measurably contributed to the confrontational atmosphere dominant in this region throughout much of the Revolution. The cultural clash between town and country in the west, closely paralleling the oft-described socioeconomic clash in the region, may also have contributed to the origins of the Vendée and the Chouan rebellions.[81]

[81] For a more elaborate development of this theme, see the author's article, "The West in France in 1789," cited above.

PART FOUR

CONCLUSIONS

TWELVE

The Meaning of the Oath

Patterns

ASSESSING the origins of collective opinion, the wellsprings of social behavior, is a delicate undertaking even in a contemporary setting and even under the most favorable of circumstances. For a historical period such as the French Revolution, a period when many of the norms and stays of authority and allegiance were regularly being put into question, the task is particularly complex. Our efforts to follow and understand one key event in that Revolution, the ecclesiastical oath of 1791, has led us down a surprisingly circuitous and at times frustrating route. Several of the seemingly promising approaches to oath options—the influence of the bishops, the stamp of seminary training, the factors of age or of social origin—ultimately proved to explain very little. Other potentially important elements—like land-tenure patterns, seigneurial structures, or demographic variables—have been largely neglected or only touched upon for lack of sufficient regional information. And, nevertheless, despite its inevitable limitations, our inquiry has uncovered a number of interlocking patterns which, when taken together, would seem to go far in explaining the overall picture of oath-taking.

It is now evident that there was a dialectic constantly at work between the perspectives and attitudes of the clergymen confronting the oath and the opinions of the laity with whom those clergymen lived and worked. Any interpretation which does not take into account the ripples and vibrations of this symbiotic interaction can never be fully successful. But, beyond this general proposition, various facets of explanation are revealed, depending on the magnification of one's lens and the aperture of one's field of vision. From a microscopic perspective, we have found that the particular benefits or disadvantages entailed in a specific position on the oath almost certainly influenced the decisions of some clergymen and some parishioners. There was a certain tendency to accept the oath among those curés gaining the greatest material benefits from the Civil Constitution—particularly those formerly receiving the *portion congrue*—though the *congruistes* now appear to have been much less numerous than was once believed, and though there was no corresponding tendency to refuse the oath among those whose incomes were most reduced. A juring position was also more common among those for whom the loss of a post would have been most economically and psychologically devastating: the elderly priests, the migrant priests living far from their home parishes, and the clerics from the lowest socioeconomic backgrounds—most notably, the sons of artisan families. To these categories, one must add that group of new curés who, having only recently obtained their first permanent status, found it particularly difficult to reject the oath and thus find themselves cast adrift once again. On the side of the laity, we have encountered instances in which the loss of political authority or the threat of economic discomfort occasioned by the new regime may have alienated significant elements of a town or parish, stimulating them to oppose the oath as a demonstration of their opposition to the whole Revolution. Among cases such as these, the disappointment registered by communities dominated by tenant farmers was particularly significant. Finally, we have explored the ongoing political and social dynamics of individual villages as they may have affected local positions: the extent to which the episode of the oath was merely a new installment in a long-term power struggle between clergymen and local notables.

Ultimately, however, local and personal factors such as these do not seem to take us very far toward a general explanation of the oath throughout the country. On closer examination, the hypothesis of the oath as a local referendum on the secular policies of the Revolution appears to be of relatively limited utility. As for the comparison between oath options and the collective biographies of clergymen, percentage variations are often rather marginal, measurable only within samples of several hundred priests. It now appears evident that throughout most of *rural* France, clerical options were related less to individual career experiences than to the broader cultural assumptions and opinions of fellow citizens and fellow clergymen across whole *pays* or provinces.

In order to comprehend the striking and remarkable regional patterns of oath-taking, it has been necessary to put aside the microscope and examine certain factors affecting larger territorial clusters of French men and women. The reception of the oath in a given region was influenced, in part, by the cultural and political distance between that region and the traditional—and now Revolutionary—core of the country. A whole range of factors combined potentially to increase this distance, factors which included the institutional structures for local political initiative (provincial parlements and estates, most notably), the independence from the Gallican Church, the local traditions of ultramontanism (more powerful in some areas for political and institutional reasons), the use of the *concours*, and, perhaps most essential, the presence of a significant non-French culture and language. But more important, in all likelihood, were those factors which directly impinged on the *religious* perspectives of a region. Thus, reception of the oath was strongly affected in a negative sense by the regional proximity of Calvinist or Lutheran populations, particularly insofar as those populations had a reputation for aggressive confrontations with their Catholic neighbors. It was also affected by the extent to which certain clerical corps had successfully evolved a *modus vivendi* between the "clericalized" Catholicism prescribed by the Tridentine reforms—and which had implicitly come under attack from the National Assembly—and their own popular religious cultures. Though the reasons for the regional success or failure of clericalization remain something of a mystery, it seems commonly to have been associated with the relative density of the rural clergy. A more numerous parish clergy, it has been argued, helped establish in the minds of the laity a sharper sense of a clerical *society*, of a clergy distinct and apart from the secular world. For the priests themselves, faced with the dilemma of the oath, the presence of other clerics in the community created a context of support and emulation, reinforcing their sense of hierarchy and strengthening their resolve to act in uniformity against the oath. By contrast, the regional penetration of Jansenism among the parish clergy had a *positive* influence on the acceptance of the Civil Constitution. In fostering clerical intolerance toward local "superstition," Jansenism hindered the development of a *modus vivendi* with popular religion. More concretely, it tended to create an irreducible kernel of curé opposition toward the episcopal corps, facilitating the break with the established hierarchy at the time of the oath. But other sources of clerical politicization were probably even more important than Jansenism. In the two or three zones of the kingdom where a longstanding tradition of clerical unrest was based in the regional economic structures of the Church and in local ecclesiastical institutions, a highly unified parish clergy had declared its independence from its prelates even before the Revolution. In regions such as these, politics might take precedence over everything else.

Yet the complex of forces affecting oath sentiments in the countryside might be strikingly different from those operating in the towns and cities of the kingdom. The urban milieu was a separate universe, with patterns of behavior and relations all its own. If in rural France clergy and laity tended to move in the same general direction on the oath, the two were probably more frequently at odds in the towns. The strong inverse correlation between urban oath-taking and the size of the local population (and to which Paris is the major exception) is remarkable and in need of explanation. In part, no doubt, the correlation was a function of the more dense ecclesiastical presence normally found in the larger towns—and in this sense there was a certain continuity with the situation in the hinterlands. Moreover, the cathedral town—which was usually, though not exclusively, a larger town—was the one site in which the bishop and his assistants seem to have had some measure of success in influencing lower clergy. But, at the same time, many clergymen living in the towns, especially the largest towns, stood to receive distinctly different impressions of the goals of the Revolutionaries in their implementation of the Civil Constitution. There can be little doubt that the large and medium-sized towns of the kingdom had been the principal fields of operation for the manifold forms of eighteenth-century anticlericalism—whether originating in the Parlements or the Jansenist movement or the writings of the *philosophes*, or generated from longstanding rivalries between Church and town fathers. We have seen the growing fears among clerical deputies in the National Assembly that the patriot Left was attacking the clergy, if not religion itself. Similar fears were reflected in the oath explanations of a whole segment of the refractories who announced their conviction that the Civil Constitution had been dictated by godless philosophy. The reality of such clerical perceptions could be debated at length. Yet the openly aggressive and unsympathetic attitude of the patriot administrators in certain towns easily aroused clerical suspicions about the true intentions of the urban Revolutionaries.

In both town and country, contrasting perspectives on the oath have frequently been associated with two different role models of the parish clergyman—which, for want of better terms, we have come to characterize as the "Tridentine priest" and the "citizen priest." To judge by their oath explanations, many non-jurors had decidedly different conceptions of the nature of their office and their position in society than did their constitutional colleagues. The first saw themselves as bound primarily to spiritual and supernatural functions and as tightly integrated into an ecclesiastical hierarchy of authority, whose opinions they had no choice but to follow; the second viewed themselves rather as the servants of humanity whose identity was shaped primarily by their toils in behalf of the secular society and state. To a certain extent, the image chosen seems related to the personality traits of individual clergymen—though the evidence for this conclusion remains rather thin. But the regional prevalence of one image or another depended most likely on a combination of the factors alluded to above: to the strength of the ultramontane tradition, to the rural clerical density—reinforcing a sense of hierarchy—to the relative success of clericalization, and to the strength and objectives of curé political activities. In the clash of conflicting loyalties which the oath represented, the relative force of one of the two models might well determine whether clergy and laity would heed the local bishop or the local patriots, would be more receptive to the demands of Rome or to those of the National Assembly.

A Tour de France

Obviously, then, in any explanation of oath reactions, it is essential to take note of the specific geographic settings in which the crisis was confronted, of the particular constellation of forces at play in the various regions of the country. The number and definition of such regions could be debated at length. As certain historians have noted, every village, every hamlet, in the traditional society of the Old Regime was a unique world in itself.[1] In the present context, we can make only a rapid journey through the France of 1791, through a series of seven zones defined pragmatically and very approximately around similar clusters of oath tendencies. We must confine ourselves here to the major attractions, the principal landmarks. Detailed accounts of the backroads and lesser-known sites will have to be left to local explorers.

The first and the largest single zone was centered on the "Parisian Basin," in the broadest sense of the term. But it included extensive projections north and east toward Picardy and Champagne, and south and west toward Berry, Bourbonnais, Upper Poitou, and perhaps even Bordelais: a sweep of provinces entirely dominated by the constitutional clergy, cutting diagonally across the historic core of the country from the border of the Austrian Lowlands to the mouth of the Gironde. Throughout most of the region, it has been suggested, the seventeenth-century efforts toward clericalization may have achieved a rather mediocre success. Local clerical recruitment was meager, especially from the rural areas, and for this reason a significant proportion—sometimes over half—of the parish clergy were "outsiders" arriving from the towns or from other provinces. But, despite such importations, the clerical presence remained sparse, and most parishes were manned by a single curé, without

[1] See, for example, Pierre de Saint-Jacob, *Les paysans de la Bourgogne du nord au dernier siècle de l'Ancien régime* (Paris, 1960), introduction.

the assistance of vicaires or chaplains or other priests. The regions closer to Paris had also been marked by a strong Jansenist tradition among the rural clergy, a tradition which contributed both in alienating the curés from their bishops and in alienating the lay parishioners from their clergy. As for the urban populations, the longstanding legacy of anticlericalism, mediated in the eighteenth century by Parlementarians, Jansenists, and the men of the Enlightenment, had undoubtedly had an effect. Entries into the clergy fell more rapidly in Paris than in any other urban area. In their cahier demands concerning religion and the clergy, the notables in the greater Parisian Basin were among the more progressive, even radical, in the country. Those in bailliages from Picardy to Bourbonnais and in the region near Bordeaux were among the few in the kingdom proposing the reorganization of popular religious festivities for the sake of economic efficiency. Later, in the Year II, much of the zone would be fertile ground for vigorous de-Christianizing activities.[2] Not surprisingly, the image of the citizen priest was dominant in a great many of the oath explanations of this region. One suspects that many priests, finding themselves only marginally appreciated as dominant sacral figures and necessary intermediaries to the supernatural, opted for a more viable role model, adopting the alternative pushed with such fervor by the philosophers and converting themselves into *social* intermediaries, the educated servants and tutors of the community. In this role—at least for the time being—they seem to have been generally accepted by the population, a population which would subsequently remain relatively indifferent to the loss of that small number of priests who chose to refuse the oath.

Traveling north from the capital, crossing Picardy into the small frontier provinces of Artois, Boulonnais, Flanders, Hainaut, and Cambrésis, one entered into a starkly different cultural milieu, a milieu in which both clergy and laity massively rejected the Civil Constitution. Outside the institutional structures of the Gallican Church, strongly marked by a heritage of Spanish dominance and by the Jesuit control of the local university of Douai, the clergy harbored strong ultramontane ties and looked askance at the importation of Jansenism. Indeed, a certain number of priests reacted against the Civil Constitution specifically because they

---

[2] Maurice Dommanget, *La déchristianisation à Beauvais et dans l'Oise* (Besançon, 1918); Gustave Bonneau, *Notes pour servir à l'histoire du clergé de l'Yonne pendant la Révolution, 1790-1800* (Sens, 1900); Michel Vovelle, *Religion et Révolution: la déchristianisation de l'an II* (Paris, 1977), 33 and *passim*. Unfortunately, the geography of de-Christianization for France as a whole is still poorly known.

found it "tainted" with Jansenism.[3] To a far greater extent, the priests in question were home-grown products. Substantial local entries into the secular clergy were supplemented, moreover, by a strong tradition of recruitment to various of the regular orders, present in great strength throughout the zone. Perhaps these recruitment patterns, coupled with the Jesuit influence, facilitated the development of a successful working relationship between popular culture and a clericalized religion. Significantly, this northern zone was one of the few regions in France in which a portion of the population took the defense of the regulars and their landholdings in 1790[4] The clergy's attachment to the ecclesiastical hierarchy had been reinforced by the widespread use of the *concours*, and was revealed in the oath explanations of parish clergymen and in the readiness with which they responded to the bishops' appeals for joint petitions opposing the oath. As for the laity, the urban notables revealed themselves particularly conservative in their cahier statements regarding the Church and the clergy. The relatively late entrance of the zone into the kingdom, the maintenance of local estates and a *conseil souverain*, and, in the case of Flanders, the barrier of language: all helped to promote a sense of distance and separation from the Paris Revolution and its religious legislation.

Skirting the border farther to the east, beyond the Ardennes, one entered into another frontier zone, a zone which stretched from Lorraine and Alsace southward to Franche-Comté and which perhaps included portions of Burgundy (a transition province cut into several different zones). This eastern periphery shared many characteristics with its northern counterpart, including a propensity on the part of most of the clergy to refuse the oath. Here, too, there was a strong historical and institutional basis for separatist sentiments toward the Parisian core. Here too, a vigorous ultramontane legacy—especially in Alsace and Franche-Comté[5]—and the use of the *concours* contributed in fixing a hierarchical sentiment among the clergy, a clergy which was generally quite numerous and recruited locally. In addition, perhaps one half of the population of Lorraine and the vast majority of the Alsatians had little or no facility with the French language. But, unlike the northern frontier, this zone

[3] C. Richard, "L'application de la Constitution civile du clergé dans le département du Nord," *RHMC*, 12 (1909), 233.

[4] Louis Trénard, "Eglise et état: le clergé face à la Révolution dans les diocèses du Nord de la France, 1788-1792," in *Christianisme et Pouvoirs politiques* (Lille, 1973), 74-76.

[5] Frank Tallett, "Religion and Revolution: the Rural Clergy and Parishioners of the Doubs, 1780-1797," Ph.D. thesis, University of Reading, 1981, 214.

also contained the catalyst of a large non-Catholic presence—Jews and Calvinists, but above all the active and highly organized Lutherans—which sharpened and heightened the sense of Catholic identity among the masses. Even the urban notables revealed themselves particularly conservative toward religion: both in their *cahiers de doléances* and in their initially lenient and conciliatory approach to the implementation of the oath. In Alsace, the combination of the linguistic barrier and the immediate presence of so many "heretics" produced a profound popular suspicion and incomprehension of the Civil Constitution, and laid the basis, according to Rodolphe Reuss, for a religious struggle as rude and potentially dangerous as in any region outside the Vendée.[6] If the religious issue never led to the same kind of civil war as in the west, it was probably because the National Assembly kept this border province under much closer surveillance and control. Of the three eastern provinces, Lorraine was clearly the most heterogeneous. The French-speaking southern sector was generally more constitutional than the northern "Germanic" sector. This was due, in part, to its separation by language and by the crest of the Vosges mountains from the Protestants of Alsace and northern Lorraine.[7] But more importantly, the juring zones revealed the outlines of the defunct diocese of Toul, where institutional and ideological peculiarities had rendered the parish clergy exceptionally politicized and suspicious of the hierarchy. Several cantons of this former diocese would have among the highest oath rates in the entire northeastern quadrant of the country.

Southward from the Jura another border zone could be traced between the left banks of the Saône and the Rhône and the crest of the Alps, a zone which included Bresse and Bugey in the north—and perhaps Mâconnais and Lyonnais—and Dauphiné and Provence farther south. Along with central France, this was the most strongly constitutional sector in the kingdom. While some Calvinist communities were present, nowhere were they as numerous or as organized as in Alsace. In fact, most of the Protestants resided in isolated rural valleys—in Diois, Queyras, the Baronnies, etc.—and were seldom encountered by the Catholics. Though clerical recruitment and clerical density were high in some areas, such as Champsaur or Briançonnais, the overall picture was inconsistent, and in Lower Provence and Lower Dauphiné there was often a chronic

---

[6] Rodolphe Reuss, *La Constitution civile du clergé et la crise religieuse en Alsace (1790-1795)*, 2 vols. (Strasbourg, 1922), 168-69.

[7] Félix Bouvier, *Les Vosges pendant la Révolution* (Paris, 1885), 5-6.

shortage of priests. In the Mediterranean sectors, a dense implantation of Penitent confraternities and a vital and independent popular religious tradition may have somewhat limited the clergy's power in the realm of the supernatural. Indeed, the evidence of sacerdotal recruitment and the clauses in wills would suggest an unusually dramatic shift in popular attitudes in Provence after 1750, away from a clericalized, "baroque" religion. Already, by late 1790, anticlericalism and even antireligion were very much in evidence in Marseille.[8] But the single most characteristic feature of this zone was the extraordinarily powerful and long-lived heritage of curé opposition to the ecclesiastical hierarchy. Although Jansenism had not been absent among the clergy of Provence and Lyonnais, the protest originated above all in the local economic structures of the Church, which left 60 to 90 percent of the curés with fixed salaries paid in money. Certain movements of this kind, directed against bishops and "priors," dated back at least to the early seventeenth century. The writings of Henri Reymond, widely distributed and read in Dauphiné and Provence after 1770, helped establish a sentiment of curé independence from the hierarchy well before the passage of the Civil Constitution. Reymond succeeded in encompassing the core of economic grievances in a general proposal for the rejuvenation and purification of the Church, a proposal which soon caught the imagination of both the clergy and the laity.

By contrast, on the opposite bank of the Rhône and through most of the regions of the Massif-Central and Languedoc, the refusal of the oath was widespread and general. Though numerous parish priests received a *portion congrue* here, as in Dauphiné and Provence, the salaries were frequently paid in kind rather than in money, making the curés largely immune to the effects of inflation which so traumatized their colleagues in the Alps. Much of the zone, particularly the upland regions of Rouergue and Auvergne, was characterized by a stronger than average clerical recruitment rate and by a dense ecclesiastical infrastructure that included numerous non-beneficed clergymen and societies of priests. But the unifying factor in regards to the oath was the presence of a large, self-confident Calvinist contingent. Since the time of the Camisards, if not earlier, this presence had served to put into relief the regional Catholic identity, selecting out the most defensive and combative elements of the faith and—partly in opposition to the Huguenot beliefs—placing particular emphasis on the essential role of the clergy in religion. With the imple-

[8] Viviane Santini, "Le clergé et la vie religieuse à Marseille pendant la Révolution de 1789-95," D.E.S., Université de Marseille, 1965, 106.

mentation of the Civil Constitution, large numbers of Catholics became totally convinced that the National Assembly was controlled by the Protestants and aimed at nothing less than the destruction of Catholicism. By 1791 a veritable siege mentality had taken hold of much of the population, both in the countryside and in many towns like Toulouse, Montauban, and Nîmes. The extreme case was the *pays* of Gévaudan in the department of Lozère. Inhabiting the heart of the Massif-Central, directly confronting the Cévenol Huguenots, virtually the entire population of this region vetoed the oath and offered its absolute loyalty to the local clergy (with the exception, of course, of the handful of constitutionals who might soon find themselves in danger of their lives). The great majority of the refractories apparently remained in their parishes, in and out of hiding, for the duration of the Revolution and the Terror, protected by all but the isolated band of local patriots.

The remainder of the Midi, the Pyrenees, and the southwest, present a far more complex image, with strongly constitutional areas alternating with strongly refractory ones. In this zone too, the Calvinist dynamic might come into play in certain sectors—as in portions of the Pays de Foix—but it was far from being an overriding factor. On either end of the Pyrenees two regions with evident particularist and ultramontane traditions and major linguistic barriers would massively reject the oath: Roussillon and the Basque country. Here, as in the northern frontier provinces, a form of Catholicism imported from Spain—reinforced in the case of Roussillon by a long-powerful Jesuit University—exercised considerable influence. In a few areas, like Cerdagne, that influence could be direct and immediate, with Spanish monks actually crossing the frontier and preaching a veritable crusade against the Civil Constitution among their Catalonian brothers.[9] In the central Pyrenees, by contrast—in regions like Comminges, Bigorre, and Couserans—economic structures in the Church similar to those in the Alps created an ecclesiastical mentality not unlike that found in Dauphiné and Provence. Congruist curés, entirely dependent on fixed moneyed salaries, had been highly politicized throughout most of the eighteenth century. Like the associates of Henry Reymond, the Pyrenean priests accepted the Revolutionary reforms with little conflict or crisis of conscience.

Finally, traveling northward along the Atlantic coast, one came to the

[9] Pierre Vidal, *Histoire de la Révolution française dans le département des Pyrénées-Orientales*, 3 vols. (Perpignan, 1885-89), 1:194-97. There was also a strong tradition in Roussillon of legal and institutional particularism: see A. Marcet, "Le Roussillon, une province à la fin de l'Ancien régime," in *Régions et régionalisme en France du XVIIIe siècle à nos jours* (Paris, 1977), 87-101.

the great triangle of the "west"—the provinces of Lower Poitou, Anjou, Maine, Brittany, and Normandy. The sweeping refusal of the oath in this zone by laity and clergy alike has been frequently described, though perhaps never fully understood. We have examined in some detail the peculiar nature of ecclesiastical structures and religious culture in the west. The rural clergy, preeminently local and agricultural in its origins, was in a particularly good position to understand and sympathize with popular religious values and to establish a *modus vivendi* between such values and the Catholic Reformation efforts to clericalize religion. A portion of the west was one of the few areas in the kingdom which actually witnessed an increase in clerical recruitment during the last decades of the Old Regime, a recruitment which easily provided candidates for the dense network of rural clerical posts—and which included numerous vicaires, *habitués*, and chaplains along with the curés and rectors. The fact that the western curés were also among the wealthiest of the kingdom could only have added to the clergy's stature in what was surely one of the most highly clericalized zones in France. If the clergy had not been untouched by Jansenism earlier in the century, the movement seems to have been rapidly repressed, surviving primarily in a few of the larger towns. This presence of a Jansenist legacy, however, was only one of the elements which sharply differentiated the towns of the west from the rural areas. While entries into the clergy had been stable or even rising in the countryside, they were dropping precipitously in the western cities. By 1789 the urban notables of the region would reveal themselves quite as progressive in their cahier demands concerning the Church as their counterparts in the Parisian Basin. Confronted with problems of implementing the new ecclesiastical policies, these same western notables would appear conspicuously impatient, even harsh and vindictive towards the local clergy, confirming suspicions in the minds of the latter that the Revolution was secretly attacking the Church and the Catholic faith. Yet, as all of the zones described in the present section, the west was by no means a monolith. If the department of Manche was markedly more constitutional than other sections of Lower Normandy, it was perhaps, in part, because of the near absence of important towns throughout the Cotentin Peninsula. If portions of the western Côtes-du-Nord were also notably less refractory, it is possibly because this region had the highest proportion of curés on the *portion congrue* of any section of the west. It also seems likely that certain "structural" problems in the west helped influence popular perspectives on the oath in certain regions. Rivalries and conflicts—of which those engendered by the substantial numbers of western tenant farmers may have been the most serious—gave rise to socio-economic divisions between town and country which closely paralleled, in many respects, the cultural-religious dichotomy.

A Cultural Revolution?

It would seem obvious that any attempt to generalize about the long-term impact of the oath in France must likewise take into account regional distinctions. In many sectors of the country—in the Parisian Basin and in the Alpine southeast, for example—the vast majority of the clergy and laity accepted the Civil Constitution and the oath as an altogether natural logical course of events: at times without emotion, at times with real enthusiasm. Numerous priests were convinced that the new provisions would bring about the regeneration and purification of religion, that the Constitution was a gift of God himself, working through the National Assembly. Both laymen and ecclesiastics could be largely content with an arrangement which solidly instated the citizen priest, which regularized and consecrated a social relationship already well developed under the Old Regime. But, elsewhere, the same set of laws might be profoundly upsetting, even traumatic. For large numbers of Frenchmen—and perhaps, especially, for large numbers of French women—near the northern frontier, in the west, in the northeast, in the Massif-Central, and in portions of Languedoc and Aquitaine, the events transpiring in the second winter of the Revolution were probably as disturbing and culturally destabilizing as anything experienced since the Protestant Reformation of the sixteenth century. The endless refrain that the National Assembly was attempting to "change religion" was much more than rhetorical hyperbole. It expressed rather the heartfelt conviction on the part of a great many that the actions of the Revolutionaries had placed the fate of their eternal souls in jeopardy. Issues of such dimensions had in the past and still could take precedence over everything else—even over such earthy problems as taxes and land and social class.

Whatever the specific regional reaction, the oath crisis served to crystallize and bring to the fore local cultural assumptions and patterns of behavior which distinctly predated the Revolution. With the advantages of historical hindsight, it is possible to explore the archeology of many of these mental structures and trace their continuity through 1791 and beyond. And nevertheless—and this is one of the important themes of the present study—it was not necessarily the *same* mental structures which were brought to light by the oath from one region to another. The notable differences in the context of oath reactions in the refractory zones of Languedoc, on the one hand, and of the west, on the other, are particularly revealing in this regard. The Antichrist of the Revolution might take on remarkably different forms from one province to the next: for some clergymen the Civil Constitution was the work of the Huguenots grasping for power; for others it was a plot of anticlericals and philosophers; and for still others it was the hand of the Jansenists which appeared most clearly. Though research in this area is still far from complete, it seems unlikely that any single variable or cluster of variables can "explain" oath reactions in all sectors of the kingdom. No single map of the Old Regime yet encountered matches the geography of the oath—neither the map of Jansenism, nor of Protestantism, nor of clerical recruitment, nor of settlement patterns, nor of popular peasant uprisings, nor of any obvious patterns of economic and social structures. The suggestive thesis of Edward Fox on the two Frances of an internal agricultural nexus versus a mercantile nexus of port cities seems of little value for understanding the oath.[10] Perhaps the closest parallel yet discovered involves the regional rural density of the clergy—as best as it can be estimated for 1790. But here, too, whole sectors of the country, the Alpine southeast in particular, ran sharply counter to the pattern. In sum, nothing from the past seems to have correlated with the oath as well as the oath would correlate with the future patterns of religious practice in the nineteenth and twentieth centuries.

For the crisis of the Civil Constitution and the oath was more than a catalyst and a precipitant. It was a seminal event in its own right. Substantially different regional reactions and trains of logic had come together in forming the oath geography. But, thereafter, the oath itself would rapidly set in motion a complex concatenation of action and reaction and would greatly intensify the polarization of clerical and anticlerical factions throughout the country. It served to unify, to "nationalize," the diverse forces of religious confrontation and thus contributed to the political realignment of French society. Patterns first engraved into the countryside in 1791 would thus be perpetuated into the nineteenth century and, beyond the Industrial Revolution and the economic modernization of the French countryside, well into the twentieth century. The exploration of this later history of the oath and its consequences is outside the scope of

[10] Edward Whiting Fox, *History in Geographic Perspective. The Other France* (New York, 1971).

the present study. It might easily be the subject of another book.[11] But, whether or not one chooses to describe these events as a "cultural revolution," it does seem clear that the ecclesiastical and religious crisis of 1791 represented for a great many men and women in a great many regions a veritable "événement structurant"; that it played a major role in recasting the gestalt of provincial France. Because of the oath, the mental topography of French society would never again be quite the same.

[11] See especially the suggestions of Claude Langlois, "Le serment de 1791 et la pratique religieuse des Catholiques aux dix-neuvième et vingtième siècles," in *Proceedings of the Eleventh Annual Meeting of the Western Society for French History*, John F. Sweet, ed. (Lawrence, Kansas, 1984), 166-75.

APPENDICES

Note on Method and Sources

Much of the analysis of the present work is based on statistics compiled over a period of years concerning the numbers of clergymen who accepted or rejected the oath required by the law of December 26, 1790. (See Appendix II.) The original law required the oath of all "ecclesiastical public functionaries," defined as bishops, curés, vicaires, and ecclesiastical teachers in secondary schools, universities, and seminaries. In February and March 1791 a few additional categories were added, including special preachers (*prédicateurs*) and certain kinds of chaplains (e.g., *aumôniers*). In general, the definition of *fonctionnaire public* followed the newly established juridical distinction between clergymen performing "useful" public functions and receiving a salary (*traitement*) and those such as regulars, canons, and simple benefice holders whose positions and benefices had been abolished and who were henceforth to receive only lifetime, non-transferable "pensions." In practice, however, the data available are far more complete for the parish clergy and especially the curés than for any other category of clergymen. The circular letter, by which the Ecclesiastical Committee initiated the survey, was somewhat ambiguous and at one point seemed specifically to request information only on bishops, curés and vicaires. Even where local administrations took the initiative in volunteering information on teachers or chaplains, the figures offered were usually incomplete and the category of "preacher" was mentioned only in a few rare instances. It is even more difficult to locate the non-parish "functionaries"in the other sources used here—parish registers, payment records, etc. Fortunately, the research of Marie-Madeleine Compère and Dominique Julia has revealed the position on the Civil Constitution of the majority of the ecclesiastical secondary schoolteachers.[1] But even partial information on the other categories of oathtakers has been reported whenever it has been discovered. On the other hand, no attempt has been made to determine the options of these clergymen not submitted to the oath in 1791. Without a doubt, there were a few areas—Paris, for example, as Bernard Plongeron has demonstrated[2]—in which *all* clergymen were pressured by the population

[1] *Les collèges français, 16e-18e siècles. Répertoire 1. France du Midi* (Paris, 1984).
[2] *Les religieux à Paris pendant la Révolution française* (Paris, 1964).

to participate in the oath-taking ceremony. Elsewhere, many former canons, monks and simple benefice holders voluntarily swore the oath—whether by conviction or in the hope of being elected to vacant cures. But, for the most part, the ecclesiastical "pensioners" were not held to such an act before August 1792, and their position prior to that date—and even after that date—is usually difficult to ascertain.

Insofar as possible, I have taken into account only those clergymen holding positions as of January 1791. Invariably, this group includes a few former regulars or cathedral clergymen who had just left their convents to fill recently vacated positions of curés or vicaires. But the major influx of former non-parish clergymen would come only after the oath decisions had taken place and after the decree of January 7 had been published and implemented. This decree temporarily waived the requirement in the Civil Constitution which required five years of parish experience before qualifying to direct a parish. While the law did not require an oath from clergymen whose parishes had been suppressed, local administrations seem commonly to have required it nevertheless, and an attempt has been made to include them here. In general, the goal has been to take into consideration the entire corps of parish clergymen of the end of the Old Regime as they faced the dilemma of the Revolution.

Of necessity, the basic geographical unit for the statistics has been the department, the obvious division chosen by the Ecclesiastical Committee itself in requesting its survey. But in order to obtain a finer degree of resolution for the distribution of the oath, I have also attempted to give figures by district, and, whenever possible, by Old-Regime diocese.

The single greatest difficulty in classifying the oaths concerned those clergymen who added various forms of restrictions. The variety of strategies in wording used by individual priests and the problem of oath interpretations on the part of administrators have been explored at length in the text. In the ideal case, the distinction used by Emile Sévestre has been used: anyone taking a restrictive oath in 1791 and remaining in his parish after August 1792 has been accepted as juror; anyone ultimately leaving to emigrate or go into hiding is a non-juror.[3] In those cases in which clergymen's later positions are unknown, we have had to extrapolate from the general pattern elsewhere in the department. In general, the great majority of initially restrictive oaths were ultimately viewed by the administrators and by the clergymen themselves as refusals. Thus in

---

[3] *Liste critique des ecclésiastiques fonctionnaires publics insermentés et assermentés en Normandie* (Paris, 1922), 15.

fifteen departments for which our sources allow the distinction to be made with some certainty, 86 percent of the priests (1,891 of 2,195) taking oaths with restrictions ultimately became refractories.

The time frame of the oath also posed certain problems, given the tendency of priests in some regions to modify their positions—primarily from juror to refractory, but sometimes in the opposite direction. Ultimately, it was decided to examine the situation at three periods in time: first, in the spring of 1791; second, in the summer of 1791 (with July 1 used as the cut-off date, whenever such precision was feasible); and, third, in the autumn of 1792, following the deportation decree.

A considerable range of source materials has been tapped to construct the statistics. First and foremost are the official lists drawn up in the spring of 1791, following the decree of March 12 and the circular letter sent to the departmental administrations on March 17 by the correspondent of the Ecclesiastical Committee, Durand de Maillane. Some forty-three of these lists have been located to date in the National Archives, where they were first exploited by Philippe Sagnac in 1906, and another dozen or so have been discovered as copies or in rough-draft form in departmental archives. It seems certain, however, that a number of local administrations, for various reasons, never completed or attempted to complete such surveys. Thus, the directors of Sarthe openly admitted defeat in their efforts to assemble rosters, pleading the "changements progressifs qui ont eu lieu dans diverses paroisses."[4] Many historians have been critical of the Sagnac study and of the source which he exploited. For present purposes, I have attempted to assess critically each of the departmental surveys, one by one, and compare them with at least one other independent source or independently conceived study. In the end, the majority seem to have been carried out with considerable accuracy.

In addition to this central series of documents, a number of other potential sources exist for the study of the oath, although experience proves that they are of unequal value from department to department. Whenever they are well kept, the ecclesiastical payment registers can reveal which priests were drawing full constitutional salaries in given districts at three-month intervals. The comparative study of a series of such registers is especially useful for determining the period of oath retractions. Parish registers have also been employed to follow the presence or sudden departure of individual curés. Unfortunately, the parish registers do not usually specify the reason for the disappearance of in-

---

[4] Maurice Giraud, *Essai sur l'histoire religieuse de la Sarthe* (Paris, 1920).

dividual clergymen and commonly give no information at all on the vicaires. On occasion, emigration rolls have proved helpful for determining which priests left the country as refractories in 1792 or 1793, although many of the rolls examined were disappointingly incomplete. Finally, various official retrospective inquiries into the Revolutionary clergy have sometimes been preserved. Particularly useful are those of the early Concordat period, at a time when the Napoleonic bishops were taking stock of local clergymen before they made new appointments. But a few surveys dating from the early Republican period have also been studied—surveys organized as officials struggled to enforce the deportation laws. In practice, however, the use of any such supplementary sources requires the possession of systematic lists of clergymen holding office in the various departments in 1790. In some cases, lists of this kind are almost impossible to find.

A final source, and frequently the most valuable of all, consists of the printed and manuscript catalogs of the clergy in individual departments during the Revolution prepared by local scholars. Experience has demonstrated that there is scarcely a department in France that has not had its local erudite devoting his life to a "dictionary" of the clergy of the Revolution. Indeed, in several departments, a succession of priests has taken up the task, sometimes helping to refine earlier *fichiers*, sometimes working repetitively in ignorance of one another. The best such studies— those by Sévestre on Normandy, Guillaume on Hautes-Alpes, Lesprand on Moselle, Laugardière on Cher and Indre, Destombes on Somme, Lecoq on Mayenne[5]—have been executed with consummate care and are based on a collation of all or most of the sources described above. But here too, considerable labor was often required on my part to standardize the lists according to the previously established criteria.

Despite a fairly extensive hunt through libraries and archives, the data on the oath in several departments remain incomplete and uncertain as to their accuracy. For this reason a designation of "reliability" has been introduced in the lists of Appendix II. In certain of these departments future research will undoubtedly serve to improve the statistics. Elsewhere, however—in Aisne, Pyrénées-Atlantiques, Lozère, Deux-Sèvres, for example—the destruction from war or fire may have rendered the task impossible. If statistics of this kind can never be definitive, future supplemental articles will hopefully be able to take into account the corrections and new research offered by scholars.

[5] See bibliography.

Oath Statistics by Department and District
(1791-1792)

N.B. Secondary works are indicated by the author's last name only. See the bibliography for complete references. In most cases, statistics on *professeurs de collège* are from the work by Marie-Madeleine Compère and Dominique Julia, *Les collèges français, 16e-18e siècles* (Paris, 1984).

AIN

District	Jan.-Feb. 1791		June 1791[1]	Total	Unknown
Bourg-en-Bresse	71	76%		94	3
Châtillon	44	94%		47	
Montluel	42	82%		51	
Pont-de-Vaux	45	92%		49	1
Trévoux	66	89%		74	
Belley	97	97%		100	
St.-Rambert	60	98%		61	
Nantua	72	97%		74	1
Gex	15	42%		36	≧ 4[2]
Total Par. clergy	512	87%	442 to 492 75-84%	586	9
Curés	336	88%		382	9
Vicaires	170	86%		197	
Desservants	6	86%		7	
Col. prof.	8			8	
Aum.	3			3	
Régents	1			3	

SOURCE: A.N., D XIX 21 (June 7, 1791).

RELIABILITY: Good.

COMMENTS: Alloing, 419-20, estimates 88% jurors in department; E. Dubois, II, 162, estimates 86%.

[1] The department estimated about 20 retractions at this time, and noted 40 to 50 others refusing to recognize the new bishop: A.N., D XIX 21.

[2] Four municipalities not listed; the number of vicaires in these is unknown.

AISNE

District (Curés only)	Spring 1791		Sept. 1792	Total
Laon[1]	170	81%	145-154[4] 69-73%	210[5]
Château-Thierry[1]	105	69%		153
Soissons[1]	138	78%		178
Vervins[2]	89	67%		132[5]
Chauny[3]	90	93%		97[5]
St.-Quentin	?			?
Total Curés 5 districts	592	77%		770

SOURCE: Fleury, I, 188-89; and Pécheur, 350-444.

RELIABILITY: Uncertain. Fleury's figures taken from departmental reports. Pécheur's are from records of election of new curés: both sources are somewhat doubtful. But much of the departmental archives were destroyed during World War I so that better figures will be difficult or impossible to obtain.

COMMENTS: There may have been a substantial number of retractions by September 1792 (note figures by Pécheur for district of Laon).

[1] Figures from Fleury, I, 188-89.
[2] Figures from Pécheur, 437-39.
[3] Figures from Pécheur, 417-22.
[4] Figures from Pécheur, 399-416.
[5] Total municipalities in district. No figures located for total parishes in district.

ALLIER

District	Jan.-Feb. 1791		Total	Unknown
Montluçon	78	98%	80	
Moulins	54	79%	68	
Le Donjon	34	71%	48	
Cusset	55	76%	72	7
Gannat	71	89%	80	1
Montmarault	59	95%	62	
Cérilly	39	95%	41	
Total Par. clergy	390	86%	451	8
Curés	312	89%	351	6
Vicaires	76	79%	96	1

ALLIER

District	Jan.-Feb. 1791		Total	Unknown
Desservants	2	50%	4	
Col. prof.	9		11	
Aum.	2		3	

Source: A.N., D XIX 21 (Mar. 2, 1791).
Reliability: Good.
Comments: Clément, 57-101, publishes comments on clergy of Allier made by the ecclesiastical authorities about 1802. There is no evidence of a significant number of retractions before the late 1790's.

BASSES-ALPES

District[1]	Jan.-Feb. 1791		June 1791		Sept. 1792		Total	Unknown
Digne	110	94%	110	94%	107	91%	117	9
Sisteron	66	97%	66	97%	64	94%	68	1
Forcalquier	69	77%	59	66%	57	63%	90	1
Castellane	79	90%	77	88%	69	78%	88	
Barcelonnette	63	98%	60	94%	50	78%	64	
Total Par. clergy	387	91%	372	87%	347	81%	427	11
Curés	228	91%	221	88%	207	82%	251	9
Vicaires	108	89%	101	83%	93	76%	122	
Desservants	51	94%	50	93%	47	87%	54	2
Col. prof.	8		8		8		8	
Sem. prof.	0		0		0		2	1
Régents	5		5		3		6	
Aum.	1		1		1		1	

Source: Maurel, 329-454.
Reliability: Good for Jan.-Feb.; somewhat less certain for later dates.
Comments: Date of retractions is not always indicated. I have estimated these as best as possible.
[1] Actually Maurel uses the 19th-century arrondissements, but these were very nearly the same as the districts.

HAUTES-ALPES

District	Mar.-June 1791		Sept. 1792		Total	Unknown
Gap	81	98%	80	96%	83	2
Serres	64	91%	61	87%	70	6
Embrun	59	81%	?		73	5
Briançon	41	82%	?		50	8
Total Par. clergy	ˊ245	89%			276	21
Curés	157	89%			177	10
Vicaires	82	88%			93	11
Desservants	6	100%			6	
Col. prof.[1]	1				9	
Sem. prof.[1]	0				4	

SOURCE: Author's ms. card file based on notes of Abbé P. Guillaume in A.D. Hautes-Alpes, ms. 399, and on numerous other sources.

RELIABILITY: Very good.

[1] From A.N., D XIX 21, certainly incomplete for professeurs.

ARDÈCHE

Old-Regime Diocese	1791(?)[1]		Total	Unknown
Viviers[2]	151	43%	353	14
Valence	35	88%	40	4
Vienne	51	57%	90	14
Total Par. clergy	237	49%	483	32
Curés	160	58%	278	28
Vicaires[3]	77	38%	205	4
Col. prof.	1		4	

SOURCE: "Le serment de 1791 dans l'Ardèche."

RELIABILITY: Good for curés. Some professors included with vicaires.

COMMENTS: Date somewhat uncertain. Probably less complete for Valence and Vienne.

ARDÈCHE

District	Oct. 1791		Total	Unknown
Le Mézenc	113	61%	185	
Le Coiron	108	63%	172	
Le Tanargue	27	16%	169	
Total *fonct. pub.*	248	47%	526	20 to 25

SOURCE: Jolivet, 270-79.

RELIABILITY: Uncertain, but compare above.

COMMENTS: Figures are those given by department administrators as corrected by Jolivet (271-73.) Jolivet seems to think great majority of unknowns were refractory, although his analyses is somewhat unclear. There may have been substantial retractions. Based on lists of emigrant clergy and other information, Jolivet, 279, estimates an oath rate of 30-35% after 1792.

[1] Data on Viviers taken largely from notes of refractory vicaire general in 1795. Data for Valence and Vienne seems to be for spring 1791.

[2] Includes professors for this diocese.

[3] Figures also include some professors.

ARDENNES

19th-Century Arrondissement	Mar. 1791		Total	Unknown
Vouziers	69	69%	100	4
Sedan	53	65%	82	
Rocroi	42	67%	63	2
Mézières	57	72%	79	1
Rethel	59	57%	103	
Total Par. clergy	280	66%	427	7
Curés	223	66%	339	
Vicaires	57	66%	87	7
Desservants	0	0%	1	
Prof.	7		19	

SOURCE: Ms. notes by Chanoine Ladame, A.D. Ardennes, 13 J 15. For profs., Leflon (1952), 9.

RELIABILITY: Apparently very good.

COMMENTS: Based on archives largely destroyed in 1914 and 1940. Leflon, 5, says that movement of retractions after April 1791 "n'a pas gagné notre département; celles-ci se limitent à quelques unités." Those taking oath with restrictions almost all removed their restrictions: Leflon, 11.

ARIÈGE

District	May 1791		Total	Unknown
Tarascon	78	60%	130	3
Mirepoix	71	56%	127	
St.-Girons	89	83%	107	
Total Par. clergy	238	65%	364	
Curés	152	66%	230	
Vicaires	86	64%	134	

SOURCE: A.N., F^{IC} III Ariège 9 (May 16, 1791).

RELIABILITY: Good for St.-Girons (see below). Probably good for Mirepoix and Tarascon.

COMMENTS: Comparison of above with A.D. Ariège, L 56, would suggest that a few parishes with refractory clergymen may have been suppressed and thus not recorded on list. Additional research will be difficult since the archives of Ariège were decimated by fire in the early 19th century.

Former Diocese of Couserans[1]	Jan.-Feb. 1791		June 1791		Sept. 1792		Total	Unknown
Total Par. clergy	75	81%	70	75%	54	58%	93	13
Curés	54	81%	49	73%	35	52%	67	7
Vicaires	16	80%	16	80%	16	80%	20	3
Desservants	5	83%	5	83%	3	50%	6	3

SOURCE: Cau-Durbon, *passim*.

RELIABILITY: Good for initial oath, but date of retraction not always clear.

[1] Approximately, district of St.-Girons.

AUBE

District	Mar. 1791		June 1791		Total	Unknown
Troyes	52	53%	50	51%	98	
Arcis-sur-Aube	57	70%	55	67%	82	
Bar-sur-Aube	61	66%	59	63%	93	
Bar-sur-Seine	44	60%	42	58%	73	
Ervy	49	69%	47	66%	71	1
Nogent	60	86%	58	83%	70	
Total Par. clergy	323	66%	311	64%	487	

AUBE

District	Mar. 1791		June 1791		Total	Unknown
Curés	250	68%	241	66%	366	
Vicaires	46	58%	44	56%	79	
Desservants	27	64%	26	62%	42	
Col. prof.	12				12	
Sem. prof.	0				8	
Régents	1				2	
Aum.	4				7	

SOURCE: Prévost, *Histoire du diocèse de Troyes*, I, 433-547.
RELIABILITY: Very good. Based on detailed *répertoire*.

AUDE

District	April 1791		ca. June 1791[1]		ca. Sept. 1792[1]		Total
Carcassonne	133	86%					154
Castelnaudary	41	42%					97
Lagrasse	64	90%					71
Limoux	75	68%					111
Narbonne	80	83%					96
Quillan	27	39%					69
Total Par. clergy	420	70%	348	58%	325	54%	598
Curés	318	71%					448
Vicaires	102	68%					150
Col. prof.	30						38
Sem. prof.	0						6
Aum.	1						1

SOURCE: A.N., D XIX 21 (April 15, 1791) and Sabarthès, *Histoire du clergé, passim*.

RELIABILITY: Very good: verified in detailed study by Sabarthès (see "La constitution civile dans l'Aude," 141).

[1] Sabarthès, "La Constitution civile dans l'Aude," 148. Data is actually given for retractions in "1791" and "1792," but, in the case of 1791, he says that most took place soon after the papal condemnation.

AVEYRON

District	Spring 1791		After Aug. 1792		Total	Unknown
St.-Affrique	9	7%	≈9	7%	137	22
Millau	6	6%	≈5	5%	94	
Rodez	24	16%	21	14%	146	
Sauveterre	12	13%	≈12	13%	94	
Sévérac-le-Château	33	39%	15	18%	84	
St.-Geniez-d'Olt	≈50	51%	26	26%	99	
Mur-de-Barrez	42	46%	25	27%	91	
Villefranche	54	36%	≈52	35%	150	30
Aubin	≈15	13%	15	13%	116	3
Total Par. clergy	245	24%	180	18%	1,011	55
Curés	137	23%	102	17%	587	
Vicaires	108	25%	78	18%	424	
Col. prof.	13				32	
Sem. prof.	0				6	
Aum.	2				3	

SOURCE: A.D. Aveyron, L 1937, L 1841, 7 L 136, 10 L 104, 107 and 109, Q 266, 4 L 91, L 1860.

RELIABILITY: Good.

COMMENTS: The basic lists drawn up in the districts in the spring of 1791 (L 1937) are vastly incomplete for the districts of Mur-de-Barrez, Saint-Geniez, Villefranche, and Aubin, and have been complemented by other sources. The number of retractions have been determined or estimated by means of lists of clerical salaries and of emigrants. I was unable to make use of the rough-draft card file of the clergy of the department during the Revolution made by the Abbé Verlaguet: A.D. Aveyron, 29 J 10-62. Though difficult to use, this mass of notes (on slips of paper of all sizes) may allow future researchers to complement, complete, and correct the above figures.

BOUCHES-DU-RHÔNE

District	Spring 1791		Summer 1791		Total
Aix	102	83%	65	53%	123
Arles	21	55%			38
Apt	50	55%			91
Marseille	64	55%	36	31%	117
Salon	41	89%	34	74%	46
Orange	15	68%			22

BOUCHES-DU-RHÔNE

District	Spring 1791		Summer 1791		Total
Tarascon[3]	50	93%			54
Total Par. clergy	343	70%	≈240 ≈49%[1]		491
Curés[2]	108	69%	83	53%	157
Vicaires[2]	140	66%	96	45%	213
Desservants[2]	34	69%	27	55%	49
Col. prof.	6				7
Sem. prof.	0				6
Petit Sem. prof.	0				3
Aum.	5				18

SOURCE: A.N., D XIX 21 (Dist. Arles and Orange, March 26, 1791); A.D. Bouches-du-Rhône L 490 (Dist. Apt., Apr. 28, 1791); L 490 and L 1469-1470 (Dist. Salon, March 26, 1791); L 822 (Dist. Aix, no date); Santini, p. 112 (city of Marseille) and estimates of Michel Vovelle (rural dist. Marseille); *Les Bouches-du-Rhône, Encyclopédie,* 16 vols. (Paris, 1913-1930), X, 603 (basis of estimate for district Tarascon).

RELIABILITY: Good for districts Aix, Arles, Apt, Salon, and Marseille-ville; uncertain for dist. Marseille, Orange, Tarascon.

[1] Estimate only, based on extrapolation from known districts.

[2] Excludes districts of Orange and Tarascon, for which no distinctions of different elements of parish clergy can be made.

[3] Figures given are the number of refractories in "twenty parishes." The total number of parish clergy has been estimated by extrapolation from neighboring districts.

CALVADOS

District	April 1791		June 1791		Sept. 1792		Total
Bayeux	150	52%					287
Caen	79	22%					361
Falaise	59	27%					217
Lisieux	97	40%					240
Pont-l'Evêque	82	34%					244
Vire	99	49%					203
Total *fonct. pub.*	566	36%					1,552
Curés	402	41%	388	40%	382	39%	973
Vicaires	144	33%	136	31%	135	31%	434
Total Par. clergy	546	39%	524	37%	517	37%	1,407

(continued)

CALVADOS

District	April 1791	June 1791	Sept. 1792	Total
Col. prof.	7			33
Univ. prof.	3			10
Sem. prof.	0			21
Maîtres d'école	2			2
Aum.	2			23

SOURCE: Sévestre, *Liste critique* and *L'acceptation*, 192-93.
RELIABILITY: Very good.
COMMENTS: Sévestre includes all *fonctionnaires publics*, including bishops and vicars-general.

CANTAL

District	Spring 1791		Summer 1791		Autumn 1792		Total
Mauriac	55	54%	49	49%	40	40%	101
Aurillac	104	60%	103	59%	95	55%	174
Murat	41	72%	40	70%	38	67%	57
St.-Flour	52	42%	52	42%	49	40%	123
Total Par. clergy	252	55%	244	54%	222	49%	455
Curés	143	55%	138	53%	125	48%	258
Vicaires	109	55%	106	54%	97	49%	197
Col. prof.			11				25
Sem. prof.			0				8
Aum.			0				5

SOURCE: A.N., D XIX 21 (May 28, 1791) and ms. work by Jean Delmas in A.D. Cantal: Fonds Delmas, dossier 226 and uncatalogued card file of refractory and retracting clergy.
RELIABILITY: Good.

COMMENTS: D XIX 21 has been partially corrected and complemented for retractions by means of departmental archives and the Delmas manuscripts. Some estimations had to be made in establishing the precise period of retractions. Future research can refine the above figures, but the contention of the Abbé Serres, VI, 93-98, that only a small number took the oath is certainly unfounded.

CHARENTE

District	May 1791		Total	Unknown
Ruffec	72	82%	88	
Cognac	61	76%	80	
La Rochefoucauld	79	87%	91	
Confolens	76	88%	86	
Barbezieux	58	63%	92	
Angoulême	68	67%	101	1
Total Par. clergy	414	77%	538	1
Curés	354	78%	453	1
Vicaires	55	71%	78	
Desservants	5	71%	7	
Prof.	0		3	
Aum.	0		2	

SOURCE: A.N., D XIX 21 (May 24, 1791).

RELIABILITY: Good. Approximately corroborated below.

Old-Regime Diocese	Mar. 1791		June 1791		Sept. 1792		Total	Unknown
Angoulême	173	83%	160	77%	147	71%	208	22
Périgueux	19	54%	18	51%	15	43%	35	1
Limoges	42	75%	40	71%	36	64%	56	10
Saintes	89	70%	84	66%	71	55%	128	13
Poitiers	45	70%	43	67%	40	63%	64	11
Total Par. clergy	368	75%	345	70%	309	63%	491	57
Curés	329	75%	308	70%	273	62%	441	12
Vicaires	39	81%	37	77%	36	75%	48	44
Desservants	0		0		0		2	1

SOURCE: Nanglard, II, 14-430; III, 3-463.

RELIABILITY: Good for curés, mediocre for vicaires because of large number of unknowns. Mediocre for data on retractions.

COMMENTS: For many parishes, Nanglard gives only the date at which priest ceased signing parish register. If this date was prior to September 1792, I have assumed priest refused or retracted oath. Some of these may have died or retired for health or old age. Parish register signatures are very little reliable for status of vicaires.

CHARENTE-INFÉRIEURE

District	Spring 1791 (?)		Total
Saintes	63	52%	122
La Rochelle	37	40%	93
Rochefort	46	74%	62
Marennes	46	82%	56
St.-Jean-d'Angély	112	91%	123
Montlieu	36	67%	54
Pons	35	38%	91
Total Par. clergy	375	62%	601
Curés	322	65%	498
Vicaires	49	51%	96
Desservants	4	57%	7
Prof.	4		12
Aum.	11		13

SOURCE: A.N., D XIX 21 (no date).

RELIABILITY: Good. See below.

COMMENTS: Lemonnier, 116-17, calculated that 387 of 696 priests in the department took and maintained the oath (56%); but this included the regular clergy and the chapter clergy as well, the exclusion of which would probably raise the percentage slightly.

CHER

District	June 1791		Sept. 1792		Total	Unknown
Bourges	41	53%	33	42%	78	4
Aubigny	24	75%	24	75%	32	
Châteaumeillant	34	89%	33	87%	38	
St.-Amand	42	86%	40	82%	49	2
Sancerre	29	66%	27	61%	44	
Sancoins	47	92%	44	86%	51	2
Vierzon	39	100%	39	100%	39	
Total Par. clergy	256	77%	240	73%	331	8
Curés	213	76%	200	72%	279	6
Vicaires	41	82%	38	76%	50	2

CHER

District	June 1791		Sept. 1792		Total	Unknown
Desservants	2	100%	2	100%	2	
Col. prof.[1]	12				15	
Univ. prof. [1]	"nearly all"					

SOURCE: Ms. notes by Chanoine Laugardière, A.D. Cher, J 828.
RELIABILITY: Very good.
COMMENTS: Based on careful, case by case study, using salary records and a wide variety of other sources. Supplants the partial statistics given in Bruneau, 367-69.

[1] From Bruneau, 369-70.

CORRÈZE

District	April 1791		Total
Tulle	54	36%	150
Brive	58	45%	128
Uzerche	56	59%	95
Ussel	52	55%	94
Total Par. clergy	220	47%	467
Curés	158	51%	308
Vicaires	62	39%	159
Col. prof.	6		17
Sem. prof.	0		5
Aum.	2		4

SOURCE: A.N., D XIX 21 (April 28, 1791).
RELIABILITY: Uncertain.
COMMENTS: Fage, 44-45, gives the account of an unknown constitutional priest writing to Grégoire in 1796, stating that of 320 parishes there were only about 40 "prêtres assermentés" and by 1792 only about half of the parishes in the diocese had curés or desservants. This is probably an exaggeration, but it is possible that a proportion of those listed as jurors in D XIX actually took restricted oaths. Pérouas, "Le clergé creusois," 565, argues that the above figures "call up serious reservations."

CORSE

	Jan. 1791		Total
Total Curés	479	92%	518

SOURCE: Casta, "La réorganisation," 71.

RELIABILITY: Uncertain.

COMMENTS: In "Le clergé corse et les serments," 16, 21-23, Casta says that about 10% retracted with the pope's condemnation and that retractions continued through 1793 with the greatest number in 1792. In "La réorganisation," 71, he says, "la plupart" retracted, but no figures are given, nor sources cited. A.N., D XIX 21 is vastly incomplete.

CÔTE D'OR

District	Spring 1791		Autumn 1792		Total
Dijon[1]	76	51%	73	49%	149
Beaune	41	45%	38	42%	91
Châtillon-sur-Seine	75	83%	70	78%	90
Is-sur-Tille	49	75%	46	71%	65
Semur-en-Auxois	104	70%	95	64%	149
St.-Jean-de-Losne	27	50%	26	48%	54
Arnay-le-Duc	49	59%	47	57%	83
Total Par. clergy	421	62%	395	58%	681
Curés	311	63%	290	59%	491
Vicaires	90	61%	86	59%	147
Desservants	20	47%	19	44%	43
Col. prof.	23				28
Sem. prof.	1				2
Aum.	4				11

SOURCE: A.N., D XIX 21, revised and corrected by the manuscript studies of the Abbés Eugène Reinert (B.M. Dijon, ms. non-coté) and Emmanuel Debrie (B.M. Dijon, ms. 2186).

RELIABILITY: Good.

COMMENTS: Neither the ms. Reinert nor the ms. Debrie covers all of the parishes of the department. Since many oaths with restrictions were counted as simple oaths in A.N., D XIX 21, a complete case-by-case study would possibly lower the proportion of jurors a few more percentage points.

CÔTES-DU-NORD

District	Spring 1791		Aug. 1791		Total
Lamballe	13	18%	13	18%	71
Lannion	25	27%	25	27%	92
Rostrenen	6	10%	4	6%	62
Broons	5	10%	5	10%	52
Dinan	21	22%	10	11%	95
St.-Brieuc	11	13%	11	13%	83
Loudéac	10	16%	2	3%	62
Pontrieux	56	60%	51	55%	93
Guingamp	28	60%	28	60%	47
Total Par. clergy	175	27%	149	23%	657
Curés	84	27%	68	22%	313
Vicaires	89	26%	79	23%	341
Desservants	2	67%	2	67%	3
Col. prof.	8				40
Sem. prof.	0				4
Aum.	2				3

Source: A.N., D XIX 21 (August 1791) and, for district of Guincamp, Lemasson, I, 87-88 and 92.

Reliability: Good.

CREUSE

District	Aug. 1791		End of 1791		Total Aug. 1791	Total End of 1791
Guéret	47	75%	45	73%	63	62
Aubusson	64	100%	50	79%	64	63
Felletin	33	55%	32	52%	60	62
Bourganeuf	45	71%	44	69%	63	64
Boussac	45	100%	45	98%	45	46
Evaux	41	76%	40	73%	54	55
La Souterraine	27	51%	27	51%	53	53
Total Par. clergy	302	75%	283	70%	402	405

(continued)

CREUSE

District	Aug. *1791*		End of *1791*	Total Aug. *1791*	Total End of *1791*
Curés	223	76%		295	
Vicaires	79	74%		107	
Col. prof.	5			5	

SOURCE: A.N., D XIX 21 (Aug. 25, 1791); Pérouas, "Le clergé creusois," map opposite p. 562, rectified with data provided by the author for the end of 1791.

RELIABILITY: Very good.

COMMENTS: Pérouas, 568, implies that the number of clergymen retracting in 1792 was very minimal. His study confirms the approximate accuracy of A.N., D XIX 21.

DORDOGNE

District	Spring-Summer *1791*		Sept. *1792*		Total	Unknown
Périgueux	40	56%	33	46%	71	10
Sarlat	41	65%	40	63%	63	7
Bergerac	76	66%	66	57%	115	10
Excideuil	49	75%	38	58%	65	2
Nontron	35	66%	29	55%	53	8
Montignac	43	75%	31	54%	57	1
Belvès	49	69%	48	68%	71	11
Mussidan	32	57%	28	50%	56	5
Ribérac	51	84%	49	80%	61	5
Total, Curés only	416	68%	362	59%	612	59

SOURCE: A.D. Dordogne, I L 621-629, 5 L 142, 6 L 68, 8 L 141-142, 9 L 106: registres de traitements et paiements ecclésiastiques; complemented by parish registers.

RELIABILITY: Good, though probably better for September 1792. It is sometimes impossible to distinguish between refusals to take the oath and later retractions.

COMMENTS: A.N., D XIX 21 is entirely incomplete and biased in favor of the jurors. Brugière has been found little useful for present purposes.

DOUBS

District	Spring 1791		Summer 1791	Total	Unknown
Besançon	37	36%		102	2
Baume-les-Dames	47	65%		72	3
Ornans	7	11%		66	
Pontarlier	17	18%		94	1
Quingey	3	11%		28	38
St.-Hippolyte	7	15%		47	31
Total Par. clergy	118	29%	Ca. 98[1] 24%	409	75
Curés	88	40%		218	24
Vicaires	18	17%		104	17
Vicaires en chef	12	14%		87	34
Col. prof.	2			17	
Univ. prof.	0			10	
Sem. prof.	1			2	
Aum.	2			8	

Source: Tallett, chart after p. 194, and information provided by Tallett for the parishes of Besançon. For non-parish clergy: Sauzey, I, 315-68, 721-45.

Reliability: Very good, except for the substantial number of unknowns. Based on initial reports of municipalities and assessments by district and departmental authorities.

Comments: A.N., D XIX 21 is seemingly incomplete and is some what confused as to how many oaths had restrictions.

[1] Tallett, 187: "At least" 20 had retracted.

DRÔME

District	Spring 1791		Summer 1791		Autumn 1792		Total	Unknown
Crest	58	97%	58	97%	58	97%	60	
Montélimar	64	68%	63	67%	57	61%	94	
Die	86	100%	86	100%	78	91%	86	
Nyons	57	69%	56	67%	54	65%	83	
Valence	80	93%	80	93%	79	92%	86	2
Romans	89	86%	88	85%	65	63%	103	1
Total Par. clergy	434	85%	431	84%	391	76%	512	3

(continued)

DRÔME

District	Spring 1791		Summer 1791		Autumn 1792		Total	Unknown
Curés	312	84%	309	83%	272	73%	372	3
Vicaires	114	86%	114	86%	111	84%	132	
Desservants	8	100%	8	100%	8	100%	8	
Col. prof.	1						8	
Sem. prof.	1						1	
Sem. prof.	2						3	
Aum.	0						6	

SOURCE: A.N., D XIX at (September 2, 1971), corrected from Loche, 1-179.
RELIABILITY: Very good.
COMMENTS: The study by Loche, a careful case-by-case study based on virtually every available departmental source, complements the list of the A.N.

EURE

District	April 1791		June 1791		Sept. 1792		Total
Evreux	170	63%					268
Les Andelys	146	68%					215
Bernay	154	58%					265
Louviers	118	58%					203
Pont-Audemer	126[1]	43%					292
Verneuil	118	70%					168
Total fonct. pub.	832	59%					1,411
Curés	573	63%	550	60%	531	58%	912
Vicaires	241	62%	234	60%	229	59%	391
Total Par. clergy	814	62%	784	60%	760	58%	1,303
Col. prof.	14						21
Sem. prof.	0						5
Aum.	1						7

SOURCE: Sévestre, Liste critique and L'acceptation, 192.
RELIABILITY: Very good.
COMMENT: See Calvados.

[1] Sévestre, Liste critique, 299 gives the figure 186 for the number of jurors in the district of Pont-Audemer, but this is a typographical error.

EURE-ET-LOIRE

District	May *1791*		Autumn *1792*[1]		Total	Unknown
Chartres	140	85%			164	
Dreux	121	98%			124	
Châteauneuf	83	82%			101	
Nogent-le-Rotrou	75	79%			95	
Châteaudun	92	84%			110	
Janville	60	78%			77	2
Total Par. clergy	571	85%	547	82%	671	2
Curés	403	84%			479	2
Vicaires	160	88%			182	
Desservants	8	80%			10	
Col. prof.	16				20	
Sem. prof.	4				7	
Aum.	1				7	

SOURCE: A.N., D XIX 21 (May 31, 1791).

RELIABILITY: Probably good. Accepted as generally accurate by Caillaut, opening remarks without pagination and 42-44.

[1] Caillaut, 137-39, has found 24 refractories in 1791 and 1792 among 101 for which date of retraction is known. There were another 77 for which the date of retraction is unknown, but the great majority were most likely much later than 1792.

FINISTÈRE

District	May *1791*		Total
Quimper	27	41%	66
Châteaulin	24	45%	53
Morlaix	5	8%	65
Pont-Croix	17	33%	51
Quimperlé	16	35%	46
Brest	9	10%	91
Landerneau	9	13%	70
Lesneven	4	5%	82
Carhaix	12	24%	51
Total Par. clergy	123	21%	575

(continued)

FINISTÈRE

District	May 1791		Total
Curés	58	24%	239
Vicaires	64	19%	330
Succursaliers	1	17%	6

Source: A.N., D XIX 21 (May 23, 1791).
Reliability: Good. Approximately confirmed below.

Old-Regime Diocese	Spring 1791 (?)		Summer 1792 (?)		Total
Léon	24	11%	16	7%	227
Tréguier	5	15%	4	12%	34
Dol	0	0%	0	0%	4
Cornouaille	78	27%	70	24%	286
Vannes	1	17%	1	17%	6
Total Par. clergy	108	19%	91	16%	557
Curés	48	21%	38	16%	233
Vicaires	60	19%	53	16%	324
Col. prof.			8		15
Sem. prof.			0		13
Aum.			31		55

Source: Bernard, 83 (1957), 74-75.
Reliability: Very good. Careful case-by-case study.
Comments: Bernard does not indicate the precise dates for which his figures are valid, mentioning only the initial oath and then "retractions."

GARD

District	May 1791		June 1791	Total
Beaucaire	14	33%		42
Uzès	16	16%		100
Nîmes	15	26%		57
Sommières	26	43%		61
St.-Hyppolyte	26	68%		38
Alais	24	29%		82

GARD

District	May 1791		June 1791		Total
Le Pont-St.-Esprit	26	54%			48
Le Vigan	20	38%			53
Total Par. clergy	167	35%(34%)[1]	≈137	28%[2]	481(491)[1]
Curés	128	36%(35%)			360(369)
Vicaires	39	32%(32%)			121(122)
Col. prof.	9				21
Aum.	2				5

SOURCE: A.N., D XIX 21 (May 7, 1791) and Durand (1918), 421-31.
RELIABILITY: Good.
[1] According to Durand, 431, the official figures left out 9 curés and 1 vicaire, all refractory.
[2] Durand, 208, estimates about 30 retractions after the pronouncement of the pope.

HAUTE-GARONNE

District	Spring 1791		November 1791		Total
Castelsarrasin			16	26%	61
Grenade			50	40%	125
Muret			32	27%	118
Revel			15	17%	86
Rieux			57	56%	102
St.-Gaudens			203	61%	331
Toulouse			58	29%	198
Villefranche			10	13%	80
Total Par. clergy	474	43%	441	40%	1101
Curés			223	40%	558
Vicaires			218	40%	543
Col. prof.			21		24

SOURCE: Meyer (1982), 86 and 107.
RELIABILITY: Very good. Based on case-by-case study.

GERS

District	Spring-Summer 1791[1]		Total	Unknown
Auch	59	35%	170	
Lectoure	82	64%	129	
Condom	48	48%	99	
L'Isle-Jourdain[2]	14	10%	135	
Mirande	54	47%	116	6
Nogaro[3]	26	18%	141	
Total Par. clergy	283	36%	790	
Curés	205	40%	507	
Vicaires	78	28%	283	
Col. prof.	17		31	
Sem. prof.	1		5	
Aum.	0		1	

SOURCE: A.D. Gers, L 419.

RELIABILITY: Uncertain.

COMMENTS: Brégail, 108, is incomplete and inexact in his publication of data from L 419. A substantial number of the priests listed are described as having taken restrictive oaths or as not having handed in the *procès-verbaux* of their decisions on the oath (in some cases, as late as August 1791). These have been counted as refractories, but a case-by-case study, based on multiple sources, needs to be carried out. Rives, 175, arrives at an oath-taking rate of 33%, but this is only for curés who collected the tithes.

[1] District of Auch: Aug. 6; Lectoure: May 13; Condom: Aug. 11; L'Isle-Jourdain: Aug. 4; Mirande: May 11; Nogaro: no date.

[2] Included as refractories are 13 curés and 14 vicaires for which there were no *procès-verbaux* as of Aug. 1791.

[3] An undated list of refractories has been compared with the list of April 1791 listing all the priests of the district.

GIRONDE

District	May 1791		June 1791	Total
Bordeaux	73	37%		197
Bazas	45	67%		67
La Réole	75	80%		94
Cadillac	45	48%		94
Libourne	98	59%		166

GIRONDE

District	May 1791		June 1791		Total
Bourg	54	64%			84
Lesparre	41	72%			57
Total *fonct. pub.*	431	57%	418	55%	759

SOURCE: Guitraud, 127-29, based on *fichiers* of Abbé Gaillard (A.M. Bordeaux, ms. 411) and Abbé Pelette.

RELIABILITY: Very good. Corrected, case-by-case, from the official departmental list.

Department	May 1791		Total
Curés	343	63%	544
Vicaires	62	44%	140
Desservants	2	40%	5
Total Par. clergy	407	59%	689
Col. prof.	14		19
Univ. prof.	3		7
Sem. prof.	0		8
Aum.	0		6

SOURCE: A.N., D XIX 21 (May 14, 1791).

RELIABILITY: Good overall, but incomplete. Compare above.

HÉRAULT

District	April 1791		Total
Montpellier	32	20%	161
Bézier	63	38%	167
Lodève	74	61%	121
St.-Pons	62	79%	78
Total Par. clergy	231	44%	527
Curés	182	46%	393
Vicaires	49	37%	133
Desservants	0	0%	1

(continued)

HÉRAULT

District	April 1791	Total
Col. prof.	15	33
Univ. prof.	0	4
Régents	4	10
Aum.	0	7

SOURCE: A.N., D XIX 21 (April 12, 1791).
RELIABILITY: Good. Compare below.

Old-Regime Diocese	April 1791		Total
Montpellier	37	21%	178
Bézier	63	35%	178
Agde	15	37%	41
Lodève	50	66%	76
St.-Pons	63	80%	79
Alès	3	100%	3
Nîmes	5	100%	5
Narbonne	6	55%	11
Total fonct. pub.	242	42%	571

SOURCE: Cholvy, I, 73-74.
RELIABILITY: Very good. Case-by-case correction of above.
COMMENTS: Cholvy gives a total for the *fonctionnaires publics* of 556, but this seems to be an error.

ILLE-ET-VILAINE

District	May 1791		Total
Rennes	29	22%	131
Bain	7	10%	69
Dol	16	17%	93
Fougères	30	30%	100
La Guerche	18	26%	70
Montfort	10	11%	89
Redon	0	0%	57
St.-Malo	14	17%	84
Vitré	8	9%	87
Total Par. clergy	132	17%	780
Curés	65	18%	359
Vicaires	67	16%	421

SOURCE: Bricaud, 371, based on A.D. Ille-et-Vilaine, L 1007.
RELIABILITY: Good. Only slightly different than Calan, 1-2.

INDRE

District	Feb. 1791		June 1791		Sept. 1792		Total	Unknown
Châteauroux	54	78%	53	77%	49	71%	69	
Argenton	53	82%	49	75%	46	71%	65	
Châtillon	34	83%	32	78%	30	73%	41	2
Issoudun	59	97%	59	97%	58	95%	61	
La Châtre	45	85%	45	85%	42	79%	53	
Le Blanc	49	100%	47	96%	43	88%	49	
Total Par. clergy	294	87%	285	84%	268	79%	338	2
Curés	237	89%	231	87%	219	82%	267	2
Vicaires	54	79%	51	75%	46	68%	68	
Desservants	3	100%	3	100%	3	100%	3	
Col. prof.			1				9	
Aum.			1				1	

SOURCE: Ms. notes by Chanoine Lagaudière: A.D. Cher, J 828.
RELIABILITY: Very good: a case-by-case study, based on a wide variety of sources.

INDRE-ET-LOIRE

District	April 1791		Total
Tours	43	39%	110
Amboise	42	86%	49
Château-Renault	29	64%	45
Loches	41	63%	65
Chinon	49	41%	119
Preuilly	29	69%	42
Langeais	42	72%	58
Total Par. clergy	275	56%	488
Curés	176	54%	328
Vicaires	93	62%	150
Desservants	6	60%	10
Col. prof.	7		13
Aum.	2		4

SOURCE: A.N., D XIX 21 (April 8, 1791).
RELIABILITY: Good. Compare below.

(continued)

INDRE-ET-LOIRE

COMMENTS: There is some doubt for the districts of Chinon and Preuilly, in which some 45 are said neither to have taken nor refused the oath. They are counted here and by the administrators as refractories.

Total Department	1791		1792		Total
Par. clergy	259	58%	243	54%	449
Col. prof.	13		13		22
Sem. prof.	0		0		4

SOURCE: Plongeron, "Autopsie," 196-200, corrected version of card file by Abbé Audard.
RELIABILITY: Very good.

ISÈRE

District	ca. March 1791		June 1791		Sept. 1792[1]		Total
La Tour-du-Pin	152	85%	151	84%	151	84%	179
St.-Marcellin	99	88%	97	86%	85	75%	113
Grenoble	195	87%	182	81%	157	70%	224
Vienne	152	80%	151	79%	144	75%	191
Total Par. clergy	598	85%	581	82%	537	76%	707
Curés	460	84%	443	81%	402	74%	545
Vicaires	122	84%	122	84%	119	82%	145
Desservants	16	94%	16	94%	16	94%	17
Col. prof.	32		32		30		34
Sem. prof.	0		0		0		2
Aum.	6		6		6		17

SOURCE: Martenelli, *annexe* XIX.
RELIABILITY: Very good.

[1] Decline in jurors through September 1792 entirely based on whether or not they accepted the constitutional bishop.

JURA

Old-Regime Doyenné within Diocese Besançon	ca. June 1791		Total
Montagne	36	45%	80
Lons-le-Saunier	18	19%	95
Salins	30	57%	53
Dole	23	34%	67
Neublans	7	35%	20
Total Par. clergy (former diocese of Besançon only)	114	36%	315
Curés	101	45%	222
Vicaires	3	4%	75
Desservants	10	56%	18

SOURCE: Sauzay, I, 724-31.

RELIABILITY: Uncertain. Vastly incomplete for vicaires.

COMMENTS: According to A.N., D XIX 21, there were 332 jurors (202 curés and 130 vicaires) out of a total of 453 (273 curés and 179 vicaires); thus 73% jurors. These figures most likely did not take note of numerous oaths with restrictions.

District of St.-Claude[1]	1791 (?)		Total
Parish Clergy	22	35%	62

SOURCE: Chamouton, 23.

RELIABILITY: Uncertain.

[1] Approximately equal to the Old-Regime diocese of St.-Claude within the department.

LANDES

District	May 1791		Total
Mont-de-Marsan	31	32%	98
Dax	57	52 to 54%	106 to 109
Tartas	28	39 to 47%	59 to 71
St.-Sever	16	15%	105
Total Par. clergy	132	34 to 36%	368 to 383
Curés	114	36 to 38%	299 to 314

(continued)

LANDES

District	May 1791		Total
Vicaires	18	26%	68
Desservants	0		1
Col. prof.	4		5

Source: A.N., D XIX 21 (May 23, 1791).
Reliability: Good. See below.
Comments: For 15 parishes in two districts, A.N., D XIX 21 lists no curés or vicaires. One can presume either that these parishes had no curés or, more likely, that no priests presented themselves to take the oath: Hence the uncertainty as to exact totals.

Total Department	ca. Sept. 1792		Total
Par. clergy	115	31%	374
Curés	83	30%	278
Vicaires	32	33%	96

Source: Légé, I, 181-88.
Reliability: Seemingly good: lists name by name.

LOIR-ET-CHER

District	May 1791		ca. Aug. 1792		Total 1791	Total 1792
Blois			49	48%		102
Vendôme			56	54%		103
Romorantin			57	81%		70
Mer			42	68%		62
St.-Aignan			37	76%		49
Mondoubleau			28	62%		45
Total *fonct. pub.*	277	65%	269	62%	425	431
Col. prof.			10		19	
Old-Regime Diocese[1]						
Blois			137	54%		252
Orléans			63	84%		75

334

LOIR-ET-CHER

District	May 1791	ca. Aug. 1792	Total 1791	Total 1792
Le Mans		38 84%		45
Bourges		27 82%		33
Tours		13 65%		20
Chartres		11 92%		12

SOURCE: Gallerand, "Le serment du clergé," 36-37; and *Les cultes sous la Terreur*, 5-7.
RELIABILITY: Good.
[1] Totals here (289 jurors out of 437 = 66%) as indicated by Gallerand, are not the same as above. Gallerand does not explain the difference.

HAUTE-LOIRE

District	November 1791	1792[1]	Total
Le Puy (curés only)[2]	23 19%	18 15%	118
Monistrol (curés only)[2]	14 40%		35
Brioude	102 59%		172
Total	139 43%		325
Curés[3]	67 58%		116
Vicaires[3]	32 60%		53
Desservants[3]	3 100%		3
Col. prof.[3]	9		9
Aum.[3]	1		1

SOURCE: Gonnet, 121-25, for the districts of Le Puy and Monistrol; Tavernier, "Le clergé constitutionnel," 54-58, for the district of Brioude.
RELIABILITY: Good for Brioude. Uncertain and incomplete for Le Puy and Monistrol.

Old-Regime Diocese of Le Puy	ca. Feb. 1791	ca. July 1791	Total
Curés	39 29%	31 23%	136

SOURCE: Tavernier, *Le diocèse du Puy*, 63-65.
RELIABILITY: Good.
[1] Gonnet, 122-23. note.
[2] Only for parishes with the Old-Regime diocese of Le Puy but excluding the town of Le Puy itself for which Gonnet is ambiguous.
[3] District of Brioude only.

LOIRE-INFÉRIEURE

District	May 1791		Total	Unknown
Ancenis	12	20%	60	
Blain	3	9%	33	
Châteaubriant	8	17%	48	
Clisson	7	12%	59	
Guérande	24	38%	63	
Machecoul	5	10%	50	
Paimboeuf	18	45%	40	
Savenay	8	22%	36	
Nantes	21	23%	92	1
Total Par. clergy	106	22%	481	1
Curés	47	22%	214	
Vicaires	59	22%	267	
Col. prof.	11		12	3
Sem. prof.	0		5	2
Other *fonct. pub.*[1]	10		32	
Aum.	2		5	

SOURCE: A.N., D XIX 22 (May 20, 1791) and, for the district of Nantes, P. Grégoire, *passim*, and, Lallié, vol. 2, *passim*. Lallié, 1: 128 publishes a table for all *fonctionnaires publics* by district.
RELIABILITY: Good.

[1] Some of these are schoolmasters, others may have been desservants.

LOIRET

District	Spring 1791		Total	Unknown
Orléans	110	92%	120	2
Beaugency	29	73%	40	
Neuville	44	83%	53	
Boiscommun	32	84%	38	
Montargis	117	98%	120	
Gien	59	98%	60	
Pithiviers	62	95%	65	
Total Par. clergy	453	91%	496	
Curés	331	91%	364	

LOIRET

District	Spring 1791		Total	Unknown
Vicaires	100	94%	106	
Desservants	22	85%	26	
Prof.	4		10	

SOURCE: A.N., D XIX 22, corrected by Guillaume, *Essai sur la vie religieuse dans l'Orléanais*, 39.

RELIABILITY: Very good.

LOT

District	Spring 1791		Autumn 1792		Total	Unknown
Cahors	104	60%	82	47%	173	43
Figeac	38	32%	34	29%	119	12
Gourdon	36	39%	34	37%	92	7
Lauzerte	40	40%	37	37%	99	28
Montauban	46	40%	41	36%	115	17
St.-Céré	29	30%	23	23%	98	27
Total Par. clergy	293	42%	251	36%	696	134
Curés	191	40%	157	33%	477	62
Vicaires	78	48%	72	45%	161	42
Desservants	24	41%	22	38%	58	30
Col. prof.	7				27	
Sem. prof.	0				6	
Aum.	0				1	1

SOURCE: A.E. Cahors, ms. monographs on the parishes of Lot by Chanoine E. Albe (a microfilm of this is held in A.D. Lot, but is incomplete); Sol, *Le clergé du Lot et le serment*, 152-234. District divisions established from A.D. Lot, L 299, and ms. map kindly furnished by the archivist of Lot.

RELIABILITY: Relatively good.

COMMENTS: Due to the high number of unknowns, the percentages for the vicaires and desservants are possibly too high. With more complete data, the proportion of jurors among the total parish clergy would probably be a few percentage points lower. Albe is not entirely complete for all parishes of Lot. Sol contains numerous obvious errors, repetitions of names under more than one parish, etc. He also includes many parishes of the Old-Regime diocese of Cahors which were not part of Lot in 1791 (Dordogne, Lot-et-Garonne, Aveyron, even Tarn). His list must thus be carefully edited. Future research which establishes a repertory by individual (Albe and Sol establish lists by parish and annex only) and uses parish registers can certainly improve upon these statistics.

LOT-ET-GARONNE

District	May-June 1791		Total	Unknown
Casteljaloux	32	68%	47	1
Monflanquin	75	84%	89	
Nérac	55	69%	80	
Tonneins	54	68%	79	1
Villeneuve	99	86%	115	2
Agen	75	65%	115	8
Marmande	No Data			
Valence	"			
Lauzun	"			
Total Par. clergy (6 districts)	390	74%	525	12
Curés	299	77%	387	
Vicaires	88	65%	135	
Desservants	3	100%	3	
Col. prof.	12		16	
Sem. prof.	0		2	
Aum.	3		3	

SOURCE: A.D. Lot-et-Garonne, L 593, L 630, L 718, L 753, L 763, L 816 (lists made to be sent to Paris, May-June 1791).

RELIABILITY: Good. Compare below.

	Spring 1791		Autumn 1792		Total	Un-known
Curés of former diocese of Agen	251	77%	198	61%	327	54

SOURCE: Durengues, *Pouillé, passim*.

RELIABILITY: Good for Spring 1791, uncertain for Autumn 1792.

COMMENTS: Durengues is not always careful with the dates of the retractions of oaths. It is clear that in many instances, the retractions mentioned occurred after the Year II and sometimes as late as the Concordat. Counted as retractions by autumn 1792 are only those specified as "rétractent tôt" or those said to have been deported after having retracted.

LOZÈRE

19th-Century Arrondissement	Spring 1791		Autumn 1792		Total
Mende	16	16%	11	11%	102
Marvejols	17	12%	11	8%	137
Florac	18	23%	18	23%	79
Total Par. clergy	51	16%	40	13%	318
Curés	31	17%	21	11%	185
Vicaires	16	14%	15	13%	118
Desservants	4	27%	4	27%	15
Col. prof.	7				7

SOURCE: Pourcher, I, 193-688 and II, entirety.

RELIABILITY: Uncertain.

COMMENTS: Included as oath-takers are only those specifically designated as such by Pourcher. For many parishes, he does not say what the priests' position on the oath was, indicating only that they were imprisoned, deported, or in hiding in 1792-94. It can be assumed that the vast majority of these were refractories. The percentages here are of the same order of magnitude as the estimate of Delon, 68-69 (20 to 30 jurors of about 400 priests = 5 to 8%). Lozère is a particularly difficult case, since a great many refractories remained in or near their parishes throughout the Revolution, never emigrating and even continuing to sign their parish registers.

MAINE-ET-LOIRE

District	Jan.-Feb. 1791		ca. June 1791		Sept. 1792		Total
Angers	56	36%					156
Saumur	106	85%					124
Baugé	77	65%					118
Châteauneuf	24	38%					63
Segré	46	47%					97
St.-Florent	12	21%					57
Cholet	5	5%					94
Vihiers	24	32%					74
Total Par. clergy	350	45%	302	39%	291	37%	783
Curés	189	47%	171	42%	163	40%	405
Vicaires	161	43%	131	35%	128	34%	378

(continued)

MAINE-ET-LOIRE

District	Jan.-Feb. 1791	ca. June 1791	Sept. 1792	Total
Col. prof.		21		39
Sem. prof.		0		15
Aum.		5		32

Source: Chassagne, 161, for Jan.-Feb. 1791: based on M. Perrin du Rouvray, "Dictionnaire biographique du clergé angevin en 1789 et sous la Révolution," typed ms. in A.E. Angers; estimates from Quéruau-Lamerie, *passim*, for June 1792 and Sept. 1792 and for aum. and sem. prof.

Reliability: Good.

MANCHE

District	April 1791		June 1791		Sept. 1792		Total
Coutances	142	53%					268
Avranches	107	37%					290
Carentan	114	59%					192
Cherbourg	85	59%					143
Mortain	83	41%					202
Valognes	100	43%					230
St.-Lô	131	60%[1]					220
Total *fonct. pub.*	762	49%[2]					1545
Curés	383	53%	362	50%	341	47%	721
Vicaires	358	50%	338	47%	310	43%	716
Total Par. clergy	741	52%	700	49%	651	45%	1437
Col. prof.	7						33
Sem. prof.	3						25
Aum.	6						13
Maîtres d'école	3						10

Source: Sévestre, *Liste critique* and *L'application*, 192-93.

Reliability: Very good. See Calvados.

[1] Rather than 59% as indicated by Sévestre.

[2] Rather than 50% as indicated by Sévestre.

MARNE

District	ca. March 1791		ca. June 1791		Total
Reims[1]	?		92	53%	172
Epernay[1]	55	83%	53	80%	66
Châlons-sur-Marne	75	65%	70	60%	116
Ste.-Menehould	60	81%	52	70%	74
Sézanne	105	86%	104	85%	122
Vitry-le-François	96	77%	92	74%	124
Total Par. clergy			463	69%	674
Curés[2]	339	79%	322	75%	429
Vicaires[2]	52	71%	49	67%	73
Col. prof.			14		42
Sem. prof.[3]			3		6

SOURCE: Bouchez, 375; Millard, *passim.*

RELIABILITY: Very good. Case-by-case studies based on virtually all the available information.

[1] In fact, this is the 19th-century *arrondissement* of Reims and the district of Epernay *minus* the cantons of Ay, Châtillon, Hautvelliers and Louvois which became part of the *arrondissement* of Reims. These divisions are necessitated by the divisions used by Millard and Bouchez.

[2] Excluding the district of Reims.

[3] Châlons only.

HAUTE-MARNE

District	May 1791		Total
Joinville	71	90%	79
St.-Dizier	64	90%	71
Langres	34	25%	138
Bourmont	62	89%	70
Bourbonne	26	43%	60
Chaumont	70	60%	117
Total Par. clergy	327	61%	535
Curés	252	65%	390
Vicaires	71	51%	138
Desservants	4	57%	7
Col. prof.	12		12
Aum.	1		1

SOURCE: A.N., D XIX 22 (May 17, 1791) with minor corrections from Mettrier, 36n.
RELIABILITY: Good. Verified approximately by Bresson, 3n.

MAYENNE

District	Spring 1791		Summer 1791		Autumn 1792		Total	Un-known
Laval	18	17%	15	14%	15	14%	109	
Evron	26	36%	26	36%	25	35%	72	2
Ernée	24	28%	23	27%	15	18%	85	2
Mayenne	42	36%	39	33%	38	32%	118	
Craon	20	30%	20	30%	19	29%	66	
Château-Gontier	25	29%	17	20%	13	15%	87	3
Villaines	24	28%	23	27%	18	21%	86	
Total Par. clergy	179	29%	163	26%	143	23%	623	7
Curés	84	30%	77	27%	67	24%	283	1
Vicaires	95	28%	86	25%	76	22%	340	6
Col. prof.	11						20	
Aum.	1						9	

SOURCE: Le Coq, *passim*.
RELIABILITY: Very good.
COMMENTS: Numerous priests took oaths with restrictions on preambles. Le Coq followed each case to determine the ultimate decision.

MEURTHE

District	ca. June 1791		Total
Nancy	20	21%	94
Lunéville	47	54%	87
Toul	45	64%	70
Vézelise	52	68%	77
Château-Salins	33	38%	86
Dieuze	10	14%	69
Sarrebourg	28	44%	63
Blâmont	28	48%	58
Pont-à-Mousson	45	56%	81
Total Par. clergy	308	45%	685
Curés	223	46%	488
Vicaires	29	29%	99
Desservants[1]	56	57%	98

MEURTHE

District	ca. June 1791	Total
Col. prof.	29	53
Univ. prof.	0	2
Sem. prof.	0	2
Aum.	3	11

SOURCE: Constantin, vol. I, 713-89.
RELIABILITY: Very good.
[1] Called "administrateurs."

MEUSE

District	ca. April 1791		Total
Verdun	56	76%	74
Etain	46	80%	61
Clermont	34	56%	61
St.-Mihiel	72	89%	81
Bar-le-Duc	103	90%	115
Commercy	50	94%	53
Gondrecourt	49	94%	52
Montmédy	40	57%	70
Total Par. clergy	453	80%	567
Curés[1]	273	83%	330
Vicaires[1]	81	87%	93
Col. prof.	14		19
Aum.	10		11

SOURCE: Aimond, 105-137, and A.N., D XIX 22 (April 14, 1791).
RELIABILITY: Good.
[1] Excluding districts of Verdun and Montmédy for which distinction not made by Aimond.

MORBIHAN

District	February 1791		June 1791		Summer 1792(?)[1]		Total
Vannes	1	1%	1	1%	1	1%	67
Auray	2	4%	2	4%	2	4%	51
Hennebont	11	20%	11	20%	11	20%	54
Le Faouët	16	48%	16	48%	15	45%	33
Pontivy	6	11%	3	5%	2	4%	56
Josselin	5	8%	4	7%	3	5%	59
Ploërmel	5	9%	3	5%	3	5%	56
Rochefort	1	2%	1	2%	1	2%	53
La Roche-Bernard	3	9%	2	6%	2	6%	35
Total Par. clergy	50	11%	43	9%	40	9%	464
Curés	26	13%	23	12%	21	11%	194
Vicaires[2]	24	9%	20	7%	19	7%	270
Col. prof.	0						9
Sem. prof.	0						2

SOURCE: Cariou, 77-79, 82-83.
RELIABILITY: Very good.
COMMENTS: A.N., D XIX 22 is slightly incomplete, but generally rather accurate.
[1] Carion specifies simply "during the following months."
[2] Includes 10 professors and aumôniers.

MOSELLE

District	Spring 1791		Summer 1791		Autumn 1792		Total	Unknown
Metz	55	42%	54	42%	52	40%	130	1
Briey	41	71%	39	67%	38	66%	58	2
Longwy	55	62%	53	60%	48	54%	89	1
Thionville	28	31%	25	28%	22	25%	89	
Boulay	8	15%	6	11%	5	9%	54	
Morhange	23	40%	19	33%	15	26%	57	
Sarreguemines	6	7%	6	7%	6	7%	88	2
Bitche	1	2%	1	2%	1	2%	50	
Sarrelouis	21	27%	19	24%	17	22%	79	
Total Par. clergy	238	34%	222	32%	204	29%	694	6

MOSELLE

District	Spring 1791		Summer 1791		Autumn 1792		Total	Unknown
Curés	172	39%	163	37%	147	34%	436	5
Vicaires	26	22%	23	19%	22	18%	120	1
Desservants[1]	40	29%	36	26%	35	25%	138	
Col. prof.	12						16	
Sem. prof.	0						12	
Aum.	2						8	

SOURCE: Lesprand, III and IV, *passim*.

RELIABILITY: Very good.

COMMENTS: Eich's figures, 179-80, are based on Lesprand's summary, IV, 461. The above is a recount to distinguish parish clergy from other *fonctionnaires publics* and to note the dates of retractions.

[1] Called "vicaires d'annexe" or "administrateurs" locally.

NIÈVRE

District	ca. Spring 1791		Summer 1791	Total
Nevers	40	43%		93
Moulins-Engilbert	33	85%		39
Decize	33	85%		39
Cosne	35	92%		38
Château-Chinon	20	67%		30
Corbigny	24	75%		32
Clamecy	51	89%		57
St.-Pierre-le-Moûtier	?	?		?
La Charité	?	?		?
Total *fonct. pub.* (7 districts)	236	72%	≥66%	328

SOURCE: Charrier, I, 91-94; and A.D. Nièvre, L, "cultes" (district Clamecy).

RELIABILITY: Apparently good for districts in question.

COMMENTS: Lists for districts of La Charité and St.-Pierre may be in Series L, district archives, but these are as yet unclassed. On page 92 Charrier speculates that the proportions of jurors in these two districts are similar to that in the other districts outside Nevers. One can thus suppose that the total departmental percentage of jurors was somewhat higher. On page 94 Charrier estimates that even after the condemnation by the pope of the Civil Constitution, at least two-thirds of the clergé remained jurors.

NORD

District	ca. June 1791		Total
Avesnes	47	40%	117
Bergues	35	28%	125
Cambrai	30	15%	206
Douai	6	4%	138
Hazebrouck	7	5%	139
Le Quesnoy	23	18%	125
Lille	36	14%	250
Valenciennes	6	4%	147
Total *fonct. pub.*	190	15%	1,247
Col. prof.[1]	11		27
All "prof."	18		158

SOURCE: Peter and Poulet, I, 134-36.

RELIABILITY: Very good. Wide range of documents used.

COMMENTS: It is not clear which categories of priests in addition to the parish clergy are included above, or if the 158 professors are included.

[1] Based on A.N., D XIX 22 and excludes districts of Avesnes, Cambrai, and Douai.

OISE

District	March 1791		Total
Beauvais	121	90%	135
Breteuil	62	78%	80
Chaumont	67	68%	99
Clermont	101	94%	108
Compiègne	69	83%	83
Crépy	81	81%	100
Grandvilliers	68	81%	84
Noyon	68	58%	117
Senlis	78	78%	100
Total Par. clergy	715	79%	906
Curés	554	79%	702
Vicaires	141	79%	178
Desservants	20	77%	26
Col. prof.	7		10

OISE

Source: A.N., D XIX 22 (March 12, 1791).
Reliability: Uncertain. The careful study by Gruart, below, of the diocese of Senlis (districts of Senlis and Crepy) suggests that the administrators counted a number of restrictive oaths as simple oaths.

Old-Regime Diocese of Senlis	June 1791		Total
Total Par. clergy	54	69%	78
Curés	45	71%	63
Vicaires	7	64%	11
Desservants	2	50%	4
Col. prof.	2		2
Aum.	1		2

Source: Gruart, 87-126.
Reliability: Very good. Case-by-case study.

ORNE

District	April 1791		June 1791		Sept. 1792		Total
Alençon	86	40%					217
Argentan	95	36%					267
Bellême	68	58%					117
Domfront	64	35%					183
L'Aigle	103	60%					173
Mortagne	69	58%					119
Total *fonct. pub.*	485	45%					1,076
Curés	302	46%	287	44%	268	41%	653
Vicaires	166	45%	164	45%	147	40%	366
Total Par. clergy	468	46%	451	44%	415	41%	1,019
Col. prof.	10						24
Sem. prof.	0						5
Aum.	5						15

Source: Sévestre, *Liste critique* and *L'acceptation*, 192-93.
Reliability: Very good. See Calvados.

347

PAS-DE-CALAIS

District[1]	April 1791		Total
St.-Omer	24	18%	132
Boulogne	29	25%	117
Béthune	23	26%	89
Bapaume	8	8%	95
Montreuil	27	22%	124
Arras	15	12%	121
Calais	13	29%	45
St.-Pol	3	3%	100
Total, curés only	142	17%	823
Vicaires	50	20%	256
Col. prof.	35		46
Sem. prof.	0		4
Aum.	4		7

SOURCE: A.N., D XIX 22 (April 30, 1791).

RELIABILITY: Probably good for curés, very poor for vicaires. For numerous parishes, it is stated simply "ne se sont pas présentés." In these cases, I have assumed that the curé is refractory, but it is unclear how many vicaires are involved. Future research in the departmental archives could much improve the accuracy.

[1] Curés only.

PUY-DE-DÔME

District	ca. March 1791		Late 1791		Total
Besse	17	33%			52
Clermont-Ferrand	51	32%			161
Ambert	45	40%			112
Billom	29	34%			86
Thiers	36	40%			90
Riom	93	60%			156
Issoire	87	67%			130
Montaigut	47	73%			64
Total fonct. pub.	405	48%	ca. 345	41%	851

SOURCE: Paillard, 299-300.

RELIABILITY: Very good. Corrects A.N., D XIX 22.

PUY-DE-DÔME

Total Department	July 1791		Total	Unknown
Curés	218	48%	454	5
Vicaires	116	49%	239	
Desservants	11	58%	19	
Total Par. clergy	345	48%	712	5
Col. prof.	21		49	
Sem. prof.	0		6	
Aum.	1		5	

SOURCE: A.N., D XIX 22 (July 21, 1791).
RELIABILITY: Good. See above.

BASSES-PYRÉNÉES

Old-Regime Diocese of Lescar	ca. March 1791		After Retractions		Total
Total Par. clergy	157	63%	140	56%	250
Col. prof.	12				19

SOURCE: "Notes sur le clergé béarnais pendant la Révolution," ms., A.D. Pyrénées-Atlantiques, I J 200/13.
RELIABILITY: Seemingly good.

Old-Regime Diocese of Bayonne	Mid-1791		Total
Curés	9	13%	69
Vicaires	3	5%	64
Total Par. clergy	12	9%	133
Col. prof.	0		10

SOURCE: "Tableau du diocèse de Bayonne," unsigned document in papers of Jean Annat, A.D. Pyrénées-Atlantiques. 1 J 232/2.

RELIABILITY: Probably good. Haristoy, I, 123, suggests that there were approximately 12% jurors among the curés and vicaires of the district of Ustaritz—which constituted about two-thirds of the diocese of Bayonne.

COMMENTS: Thus for the approximately two-thirds of the department included here, there were 152/383 = 40% jurors toward the middle of 1791. Most of the departmental archives were destroyed by fire in the early 20th century, so more complete data will be difficult to obtain.

HAUTES-PYRÉNÉES

District	July 1791		Total
Tarbes	128	89%	144
Argelès	110	99%	111
Bagnères	57	93%	61
Vic	46	85%	54
La Barthe	52	38%	138
Total Par. clergy	393	77%	508
Curés	264	80%	329
Vicaires	129	72%	179
Col. prof.	12		12

SOURCE: A.N., D XIX 22 (July 4, 1791).
RELIABILITY: Good. Accepted by Abbé Ricaud, 60, as reliable.

PYRÉNÉES-ORIENTALES

District	May 1791		Total
Perpignan	22	23%	95
Prades	37	28%	131
Céret	27	38%	71
Total Par. clergy	86	29%	297
Curés	57	28%	207
Vicaires	26	32%	82
Desservants	3	38%	8
Col. prof.	5		≈12
Univ. prof.	2		6
Sem. prof.	0		4

SOURCE: For district Perpignan: Torreilles, 217-19; for districts Prades and Céret: A.N., D XIX 22, annotated by lists of emigrants, A.D. Pyrénées-Orientales, L 1151.

RELIABILITY: Relatively good. Note that a list drawn up in about 1801 shows that 31% (27 of 88) of the parish clergy of the former diocese of Elne, still able to serve at that date, were considered "constitutionals": A.D. Pyrénées-Orientales, I V 3.

COMMENTS: The lists in A.N., D XIX 22 are entirely unreliable. According to Torreilles, 16, they include numerous clergymen as jurors who actually took restrictive oaths. Thus, in fact, by June of 1791 the administration recognized only 20 juring curés in the district of Perpignan

PYRÉNÉES-ORIENTALES

(in D XIX 22, it recognized 45): A.D. Pyrénées-Orientales, L 1150. For the district of Prades, the official list omits several parishes. Torreilles, 220-21, maintains that only 8 clergymen in the district of Céret remained jurors, but we have been unable to confirm this via the emigrant rolls. The latter, however are possibly incomplete Already on July 15, 1791, the directory complained that the entire portion of the department bordering Spain was "totally infested" with non-juring and retracting clergymen: A.N., D XXIX 85.

BAS-RHIN

District	June 1791		Total
Strasbourg	9	14%	66
Benfeld	8	7%	119
Haguenau	8	8%	105
Wissembourg	8	8%	95
Total Par. clergy	33	9%	385
Curés	28	10%	288
Vicaires	5	5%	93
Desservants	0	0%	4
Col. prof.	0		17
Univ. prof.	1		5
Sem. prof.	0		4
Régents	0		3
Aum.	0		1

SOURCE: A.N., D XIX 22 (June 18, 1791).
RELIABILITY: Apparently good.

HAUT-RHIN

District	Spring 1971		Summer 1791		Autumn 1792		Total
Colmar	36	25%	36	25%	36	25%	146
Altkirch	73	41%	70	40%	66	38%	176
Belfort	71	58%	70	57%	68	55%	123
Total Par. clergy	180	40%	176	40%	170	38%	445
Curés	119	39%	115	37%	110	36%	307
Vicaires	57	43%	57	43%	56	42%	133
Desservants	4	80%	4	80%	4	80%	5

(continued)

HAUT-RHIN

SOURCE: Notes by Jules Joachim in 12 vols.: B.M. Colmar, ms. 972. A.N., D XIX 22 used for district boundaries.

RELIABILITY: Very good. Detailed study by individuals, based on a wide range of sources.

COMMENTS: Both Frayhier, 185-256, and A.N., D XIX 22 are entirely incomplete and unreliable.

RHÔNE-ET-LOIRE

District	Spring 1791		March 1792		Total	Unknown
Roanne	137	81%	126	75%	169	
Montbrison	170	82%	140	67%	208	
St.-Etienne	106	88%	74	61%	121	4
Total Par. clergy (3 districts)	413	83%	340	68%	498	
Curés	256	89%	220	76%	289	
Vicaires	140	76%	106	57%	185	
Desservants	17	71%	14	58%	24	
Col. prof.	8				21	

SOURCE: Research by Colin Lucas, kindly communicated to the author.

RELIABILITY: Very good. Case-by-case study.

COMMENTS: For Lyon itself, only 5 of 14 curés seem to have taken the oath: Cattin, *passim*, and Camelin, *passim*. There is no easily accessible source for reactions to the oath in the districts of Lyon-Campagne, and Villefranche—i.e., in the future department of Rhône—but it would appear that these two districts had oath-taking rates roughly similar to those in the rest of the department. Camelin gives information only on the jurors and would appear to be incomplete even for these. The above more or less confirm Brossard, I, 227, 376-78, 91.

HAUTE-SAÔNE

District	November 1791		Total	Unknown
Vesoul	53	42%	126	
Gray	30	35%	86	
Jussey	17	24%	71	2
Luxeuil	20	29%	68	
Lure	18	30%	60	1
Champlitte	23	42%	55	3
Total Par. clergy	161	35%	466	

HAUTE-SAÔNE

District	November *1791*		Total	Unknown
Curés	118	40%	294	6
Vicaires	37	24%	152	
Vicaires en chef	6	30%	20	
Col. prof.	18		24	
Aum.	4		6	

SOURCE: Ms. "Répertoire biographique du clergé séculier et régulier de la Haute-Saône pendant la Révolution" by Jean Girardot: A.D. Haute-Saône, 2 J 330: 2:86-107 and *passim*. District distribution determined by comparison with A.N., D XIX 22.

RELIABILITY: Very good. Case-by-case study using all available sources.

COMMENTS: Oath options difficult to determine earlier since department often initially counted restrictive oaths as pure and simple oaths. A.N., D XIX 22 is totally unreliable for oath options.

SAÔNE-ET-LOIRE

19th-Century Arrondissement	*ca. June 1791*		Total	Unknown
Autun	46	55%	83	4
Chalon-sur-Saône	72	45%	159	8
Mâcon	130	78%	166	5
Charolles	102	59%	172	
Louhans[1]	58	63%	92	
Total Par. clergy	408	61%	672	17
Curés	354	63%	559	15
Vicaires	54	48%	113	2
Col. prof.	18		32	
Sem. prof.	1		11	
Aum.	4		12	

SOURCE: Bauzon, Muguet, and Chaumont, *passim*; for the region of Louhans, Guillemaut, 294, and Ravenet, *passim*.

RELIABILITY: Good to mediocre. Very likely incomplete for vicaires in some arrondissements. Montarlot, 137, published the proportion of curés jurors in the department as 345 of 658 (52%), but he gives no indication of his source or of the date for which such figures might have been valid.

[1] Actually the *district* of Louhans, though very nearly the same as the 19th-century *arrondissement*.

SARTHE

District (Curés only)	Sept. 1792[1]
Le Mans	37%
Sillé-le-Guillaume	46%
Sablé	35%
La Flèche	34%
Fresnay	59%
Mamers	49%
La Ferté-Bernard	60%
St.-Calais	53%
Château-du-Loir	78%
Total, curés only	48%

SOURCE: Giraud, 245-46.

RELIABILITY: Good. All verified via parish registers. See also below.

COMMENT: Giraud, 225-26, argues that between mid-1791 and September 1792 there may have been even more refractories becoming jurors than original jurors retracting. The overall percentage would probably be somewhat lower if vicaires were included (see below). It will be difficult to obtain more precise figures for 1791. The department seems to have made no lists and to have allowed many priests with restrictive oaths to remain at their posts until August 1792.

	Summer 1792		Total
Curés	209	46%	450
Vicaires, prof., aum.	154	40%	386
Total *fonct. pub.*	363	43%	836
Col. prof.	5		12

SOURCE: Girault, 12 and 34. Girault's *fichier* is in A.D. Sarthe, 2 J 40-41.

RELIABILITY: Very good. Case-by-case study based on most available documents.

[1] No figures are given, only percentages for most districts.

SEINE

	Mid-1791		Total
Paris, city	57	48%	119
Paris, suburbs	107	84%	128
Total Par. clergy	164	66%	247
Curés	86	67%	128
Vicaires	78	66%	119

SEINE

	Mid-*1791*	Total
Col. and Univ. prof.	41	83
Sem. prof.	2	55
Aum.	35	69
Other *fonct. pub.*[1] (habitués, etc.)	173	389

SOURCE: Pisani, *L'Eglise de Paris*, I, 191-99.

RELIABILITY: Good. When all clergymen held to the oath are taken into account, the proportion for the city of Paris drops to 43%. Pisani says that the statistics given by Abbé Delarc are based in part on erroneous information.

[1] Many of these were not technically required to take the oath, but were generally considered parish clergy by the Parisians and were virtually forced to make a decision.

SEINE-INFÉRIEURE

District	April *1791*		June *1791*		Sept. *1792*		Total
Rouen	139	44%					317
Caudebec	88	39%					226
Montivilliers	113	46%					244
Cany	99	43%					230
Dieppe	170	47%					362
Neufchâtel	165	67%					245
Gournay	100	70%					142
Total *fonct. pub.*	874	49%					1,766
Curés	542	50%	526	49%	509	47%	1,077
Vicaires	298	50%	294	49%	290	49%	594
Total Par. clergy	840	50%	820	49%	799	48%	1,671
Col. prof.	17						38
Sem. prof.	1						19
Aum.	11						19

SOURCE: Sévestre, *Liste critique* and *L'acceptation*, 192-93.

RELIABILITY: Very good. See Calvados.

SEINE-ET-MARNE

Old-Regime Diocese	ca. Mar. 1791		ca. Mid-1791[1]		Total
Meaux	170	61%	163	58%	279
Paris	70	71%	62	63%	99
Sens	305	84%	289	80%	363
Troyes	6	60%	5	50%	10
Soissons	1	11%	2	22%	9
Senlis	1		1		1
Total *fonct. pub.*	553	73%	522	69%	761

Source: Bridoux, I, 58-59.
Reliability: Very good.

District	Spring 1791			Total	Unknown
Meaux	146	68%		216	8
Nemours	111	98%		113	2
Rozay	72	69%		105	2
Melun	98	68%		145	
Provins	?	?		?	
Total Par. clergy (4 districts)	427	74%	ca. 398 (69%)	579	
Curés	346	74%		468	
Vicaires	71	72%		98	
Desservants	10	77%		13	

Source: A.D. Seine-et-Marne, L 281-82, L 285-88.
Reliability: Good. Cf. above.
[1] Precise date unclear. Author describes second period as "après les rétractations."

SEINE-ET-OISE

District	March 1791		November 1791	Total	Unknown
Corbeil	101	83%		122	1
Dourdan	64	84%		76	2
Etampes	94	96%		98	1
Gonesse	80	74%		108	3
Mantes	103	90%		115	2
Montfort-L'Amaury	78	80%		98	

SEINE-ET-OISE

District	March 1791		November 1791		Total	Unknown
Pontoise	94	78%			120	5
St.-Germain-en-Laye	94	82%			115	
Versailles	97	76%			127	
Total Par. clergy	805	82%	797	81%	979	14
Curés	552	83%	547	82%	668	10
Vicaires	223	80%	220	79%	278	3
Desservants	30	91%	30	91%	33	1
Col. prof.	4				4	
Aum.	3				7	
Prédicateurs	2				2	

SOURCES: A.D. Yvelines, 1 LV 758, for initial oaths (Feb. 4 through Mar. 31); and 1 LV 759 on *traitements* for indication of retractions through late 1791.

RELIABILITY: Good. Alliot, 25-26, corroborates these statistics for the district of Versailles.

COMMENTS: The "Fichier Staes" held by the A.D. Yvelines may ultimately allow a more accurate statistic. But the untimely death of its author left it in an unfinished state and a substantial amount of editing would be required. Lemoine, 93, argues that "about two-thirds" took the oath, but no figures are given or sources cited.

DEUX-SÈVRES

Old-Regime Archiprêtré (Diocese Poitiers Only)	Spring 1791		Autumn 1792(?)		Total	Unknown
Niort	8	57%	6-8		14	
St.-Maixent	26	58%	21-26		45	1
Melle	70	95%	61-70		74	
Exoudun	15	60%	14-15		25	
Parthenay	42	75%	25-42		56	1
Thouars	54	78%	44-54		69	
Rom	8	100%	7-8		8	
Chaunay	13	87%	10-13		15	
Total Par. clergy	236	77%	188-236	61-77%	306	
Curés	223	80%	178-223	64-80%	278	
Vicaires	13	50%	10-13	38-50%	26	
Desservants	0		0		2	
Col. prof.	11				14	

(continued)

DEUX-SÈVRES

Source: Lastic-Saint-Jal., 294-306, based on a list established in 1800 by a representative of the refractory clergy of the former diocese of Poitiers.

Reliability: Uncertain.

Comments: Figures include only parishes in eastern portion of department, within former diocese of Poitiers. Numerous jurors are mentioned as retracting and/or emigrating, but without any specific date given: hence the uncertainty about their status in Autumn 1792. Much of the archives were destroyed by a fire in 1805, so a complete statistic will be difficult.

District of Bressuire	Autumn 1792		Total
Curés	19	34%	56

Source: A.N., AA 42 (1231^A): list of refractory *fonctionnaires publics* as of Nov. 11, 1792 as declared by the District of Bressuire to the central government; and A.N., NN*14 for the number of parishes in the district.

Reliability: Uncertain.

Comments: List notes only refractory clergy: 37 curés, 18 vicaires, and 1 aumônier. Thus, for the curés of the department as a whole, one can estimate that 242 of 334 (72%) were jurors.

SOMME

District	ca. March 1791		June 1791		Sept. 1792		Total	Unknown
Amiens	216	63%	208	61%	194	57%	341	3
Abbeville	187	68%	183	67%	163	59%	275	10
Doullens	39	47%	38	46%	35	42%	83	1
Montdidier	87	50%	85	49%	73	42%	173	5
Péronne	123	60%	117	57%	94	46%	204	6
Total Par. clergy	652	61%	631	59%	559	52%	1076	25
Curés	485	60%	467	58%	419	52%	802	19
Vicaires	114	60%	112	59%	99	52%	191	4
Desservants	53	64%	52	63%	41	49%	83	2
Col. prof.	9		9		9		20	
Sem. prof.	0		0		0		5	
Aum.	4		4		4		17	

Source: Destombes, *passim*.

Reliability: Very good. Detailed, case-by-case study based on a wide range of sources.

TARN

District	Spring 1791		Total	Unknown
Castres	23	17%	134	3
Gaillac	39	21%	190	3
Lacaune	3	6%	53	2
Lavaur	11	10%	106	
Albi	No Data			172[1]
Total Par. clergy (4 districts)	76	16%	483	180
Curés	49	18%	280	101
Vicaires	27	13%	203	79
Col. prof.	9		15	

SOURCE: A.D. Tarn, L 833, L 905, L 943, L 1056.
RELIABILITY: Good, compare below.

Total Par. clergy	112	14%	786	

SOURCE: Lagger, 31.
RELIABILITY: Apparently good.
COMMENTS: Lagger does not break figures down by district.
[1] The number of the parish clergy in the district of Albi is taken from the salary rolls of January 1791, A.D. Tarn, L 758.

VAR

District	March 1791		June 1791		Sept. 1792		Total
Toulon	51	96%	48	91%	44	83%	53
Grasse	68	84%	67	83%	65	80%	81
Hyères	34	89%	33	87%	32	84%	38
Draguignan	86	99%	84	97%	81	93%	87
Brignoles	49	100%	49	100%	40	82%	49
St.-Maximin	42	100%	40	95%	37	88%	42
Fréjus	39	91%	36	84%	32	74%	43
St.-Paul	28	85%	28	85%	24	73%	33
Barjols	56	97%	53	91%	48	83%	58
Total Par. clergy	453	94%	438	90%	403	83%	484

(continued)

VAR

District	March 1791		June 1791		Sept. 1792		Total
Curés	188	91%	180	87%	153	74%	206
Vicaires	259	95%	252	93%	244	90%	272
Desservants	6	100%	6	100%	6	100%	6
Prof.	40						40
Aum.	18						21

SOURCE: A.N., D XIX 22 (April 6, 1791), completed and corrected in some instances by Laugier, 224-303.

RELIABILITY: Good.

VENDÉE

District	March 1791		Sept. 1792		Total	Unknown
Fontenay-le-Comte	51	46%	48	44%	110	
La Châtaigneraie	29	35%	28	34%	82	
Montaigu	11	13%	8	10%	82	
Challans	19	32%	14	23%	60	
Les Sables-d'Olonne	25	37%	23	34%	68	
La Roche-sur-Yon	22	33%	19	28%	67	
Total Par. clergy	157	33%	140	30%	469	
Curés	112	35%	106	33%	320	
Vicaires	45	30%	34	23%	149	
Col. prof.	1				12	
Sem. prof.	0				4	
Aum.	1				7	3

SOURCE: Chaille (1960), *passim* (apparently based on Bourloton).

RELIABILITY: Good.

COMMENTS: No date is given for many retractions of oaths, thus the status for the summer of 1791 is not entirely clear. Not a single priest is mentioned as having taken a restrictive oath: all are described as outright refusals.

VIENNE

District	Feb. 1791		June 1791		Sept. 1792		Total
Poitiers	67	50%	66	50%	62	47%	133
Civray	43	78%	38	69%	36	65%	55
Lusignan	24	67%	23	64%	22	61%	36
Montmorillon	70	74%	68	72%	66	70%	94
Châtellerault	72	77%	69	73%	66	70%	94
Loudun	65	72%	63	70%	59	66%	90
Total Par. clergy	341	68%	327	65%	311	62%	502
Curés	257	69%	247	66%	235	63%	375
Vicaires	84	66%	80	63%	76	60%	127

SOURCE: Roux (1911), 384-85 and 411-20.
RELIABILITY: Very good. Based on case-by-case study of clerical payment registers.

HAUTE-VIENNE

District	Jan.-Feb. 1791		July 1792		Total
Limoges	44	55%	31	39%	80
St.-Junien	52	85%	39	64%	61
St.-Léonard	25	38%	22	34%	65
St.-Yrieix	27	44%	21	34%	61
Le Dorat	54	90%	46	77%	60
Bellac	55	82%	53	79%	67
Total Par. clergy	257	65%	212	54%	394
Curés	166	65%			255
Vicaires	91	65%			139
Col. prof.	0				12

SOURCE: Research of Paul d'Hollander toward a Doctorat de 3ᵉ Cycle, kindly communicated to the author.
RELIABILITY: Very good.
COMMENTS: Corrects A.N., D XIX 22 (April 15, 1791). Leclerc's claim (I, 147) that 180 priests had retracted by February 1792 is clearly an exaggeration.

VOSGES

District	Spring 1791		Summer 1791		Autumn 1792		Total
Epinal	24	55%	23	52%	23	52%	44
Bruyères	23	66%	22	63%	21	60%	35
Darney	30	64%	29	62%	28	60%	47
Lamarche	35	80%	33	75%	33	75%	44
Mirecourt	69	75%	66	72%	62	67%	92
Neufchâteau	70	78%	65	72%	62	69%	90
Rambervillers	9	20%	9	20%	9	20%	45
Remiremont	35	69%	35	69%	34	67%	51
St.-Dié	39	65%	39	65%	37	62%	60
Total Par. clergy	334	66%	321	63%	309	61%	508
Curés	199	68%	192	66%	183	63%	291
Vicaires	135	62%	129	59%	126	58%	217
Col. prof.	9						9
Sem. prof.	0						4
Aum.	1						1

SOURCE: A.N., D XIX 22 (April 15, 1791), complemented and corrected by A.D. Vosges L 559 and by Lahache, *passim*.

RELIABILITY: Good. I have corrected D XIX 22 case-by-case by means of Lahache. Unfortunately, the latter is not entirely complete.

YONNE

District	ca. Feb. 1791		June 1791		Sept. 1792		Total	Unknown
Auxerre	76	82%	74	80%	73	78%	93	12
Sens	114	98%	112	97%	106	91%	116	4
Joigny	56	95%	54	92%	48	81%	59	24
St.-Fargeau	45	100%	45	100%	43	96%	45	
Avallon	50	79%	45	71%	45	71%	63	3
Tonnerre	49	79%	45	73%	41	66%	62	12
St.-Florentin	42	86%	38	78%	36	73%	49	14
Total Par. clergy	432	89%	413	85%	392	80%	487	69

YONNE

District	ca. Feb. *1791*		June *1791*		Sept. *1792*		Total	Unknown
Curés	370	89%	354	85%	336	81%	416	61
Vicaires	57	92%	55	89%	52	84%	62	7
Desservants	5	56%	4	44%	4	44%	9	1
Col. prof.	7		7		4		7	
Sem. prof.	6		6		6		6	
Aum.	4		4		4		4	

SOURCE: Bonneau, *passim*; and Galley, *passim*.
RELIABILITY: Good.

Oath Statistics (Summary)

Department	Type of Data	Total Clergy	Spring 91 Oath	%	Summer 91 Oath	%	Autumn 92 Oath	%	Reliability
Ain	PC (1)	586	512	87	492	84			G(2)
Aisne	C	770	595	77					U
Allier	PC	451	390	86					G
Alpes, Basses-	PC	427	387	91	372	87	347	81	G
Alpes, Hautes-	PC	276	245	89					VG
Ardèche	FP	483	237	49					G/U
Ardennes	PC	427	280	66					VG
Ariège	PC	364	238	65					G
Aube	PC	487	323	66	311	64			VG
Aude	PC	598	420	70	348	58	325	54	VG
Aveyron	PC	1,011	245	24			180	18	G
Bouches-du-Rhône	PC	491	343	70	240	49			G/U
Calvados	PC	1,407	546	39	524	37	517	37	VG
Cantal	PC	455	252	55	244	54	222	49	G
Charente	PC	491	368	75	345	70	309	63	G
Charente-Inférieure	PC	601	375	62					G
Cher	PC	331			256	77	240	73	VG
Corrèze	PC	467	220	47					U
Corse	C	518	479	92					U
Côte-d'Or	PC	681	421	62			395	58	G
Côtes-du-Nord	PC	657	175	27	149	23			G
Creuse	PC	402			302	75			G
Dordogne	C	612			416	68	362	59	G
Doubs	PC	409	118	29	98	24			VG
Drôme	PC	512	434	85	431	84	391	76	VG
Eure	PC	1,303	814	62	784	60	760	58	VG
Eure-et-Loir	PC	671	571	85			547	82	G
Finistère	PC	557	108	19			91	16	VG
Gard	PC	491	167	34	137	28			G
Garonne, Haute-	PC	1,101	474	43	441	40			VG
Gers	PC	790			283	36			U

Oath Statistics (Summary) (cont.)

Department	Type of Data	Total Clergy	Spring 91 Oath	%	Summer 91 Oath	%	Autumn 92 Oath	%	Reliability
Gironde	FP	759	431	57	418	55			VG
Hérault	PC	527	231	44					G
Ille-et-Vilaine	PC	780	132	17					G
Indre	PC	338	294	87	285	84	268	79	VG
Indre-et-Loire	PC	449			259	58	243	54	VG
Isère	PC	707	598	85	581	82	537	76	VG
Jura	C	222			101	45			U/I
Landes	PC	374	132	35			115	31	G
Loir-et-Cher	FP	431	277	64			269	62	G
Loire, Haute-	C	325			139	43			G/I
Loire-Inférieure	PC	481	106	22					G
Loiret	PC	496	453	91					VG
Lot	PC	696	293	42			251	36	G
Lot-et-Garonne	C	327	251	77			198	61	G/I
Lozère	PC	318	51	16			40	13	U
Maine-et-Loire	PC	783	350	45	302	39	291	37	G
Manche	PC	1,437	741	52	700	49	651	45	VG
Marne	PC	674			463	69			VG
Marne, Haute-	PC	535	327	61					G
Mayenne	PC	623	179	29	163	26	143	23	VG
Meurthe	PC	685			308	45			VG
Meuse	PC	567	453	80					G
Morbihan	PC	464	50	11	43	9	40	9	VG
Moselle	PC	694	238	34	222	32	204	29	VG
Nièvre	FP	328	236	72	216	66			G/I
Nord	FP	1,247			190	15			VG
Oise	PC	906	715	79					U
Orne	PC	1,019	468	46	451	44	415	41	VG
Pas-de-Calais	C	823	142	17					G
Puy-de-Dôme	FP	851	405	48	345	41			G
Pyrénées, Basses-	PC	383			152	40			G/I
Pyrénées, Hautes-	PC	508			393	77			G
Pyrénées-Orientales	PC	297	86	29					G
Rhin, Bas-	PC	385			33	9			G
Rhin, Haut-	PC	445	180	40	176	40	170	38	VG
Rhône-et-Loire	PC	498	413	83			340	68	VG/I
Saône, Haute-	PC	466			161	35			VG
Saône-et-Loire	PC	672			408	61			G
Sarthe	FP	836					363	43	VG

Oath Statistics (Summary) (cont.)

Seine	PC	247			164	66			G
Seine-Inférieure	PC	1,671	840	50	820	49	799	48	VG
Seine-et-Marne	PC	579	427	74	398	69			G/I
Seine-et-Oise	PC	979	805	82	797	81			G
Sèvres, Deux-	PC	306	236	77			188	61	U/I
Somme	PC	1,076	652	61	631	59	559	52	VG
Tarn	PC	483	76	16					G/I
Var	PC	484	453	94	438	90	403	83	G
Vendée	PC	469	157	33			140	30	G
Vienne	PC	502	341	68	327	65	311	62	VG
Vienne, Haute-	PC	394	257	65			212	54	VG
Vosges	PC	508	334	66	321	63	309	61	G
Yonne	PC	487	432	89	413	85	392	80	G

[1] PC = parish clergy; C = curés only; FP = "fonctionnaires publics."

[2] VG = very good; G = good; U = uncertain; I = incomplete data for certain parts of the department.

Estimated Oath-taking for
Old-Regime Dioceses[1]

Agde	37%	Châlons/Marne	72
Agen	76	Chalon/Saône	45
Aire	23	Chartres	84
Aix	64	Clermont	50
Albi	21	Comminges	56
Alès	40	Condom	69
Alet	?	Couserans	81
Amiens	60	Coutances	54
Angers	47	Dax	47
Angoulême	77	Die	95
Apt	53	Digne	?
Arles	55	Dijon	58
Arras	7	Dol	17
Auch	33	Embrun	80
Autun	63	Evreux	64
Auxerre	88	Fréjus	92
Avranches	44	Gap	88
Basel	38	Geneva	42
Bayeux	39	Glandèves	?
Bayonne	9	Grasse	83
Bazas	75	Grenoble	81
Beauvais	88%	Langres	55
Belley	93	Laon	77
Besançon	40	La Rochelle	36
Beziers	35	Lavaur	?
Blois	54	Lectoure	64
Bordeaux	52	Le Mans	39
Boulogne	26	Le Puy	23
Bourges	84	Lescar	56
Cahors	43	Limoges	65
Cambrai	22	Lisieux	37
Carcassonne	86	Lodève	66
Carpentras	?	Lombez	10
Castres	14	Luçon	30
Cavaillon	?	Lyon	85

Estimated Oath-taking for Old-Regime Dioceses[1] (cont.)

Mâcon	78	St.-Malo	10
Marseille	31	St.-Omer	18
Meaux	58	St.-Papoul	?
Mende	16	St.-Paul-Trois-Châteaux	44
Metz	27	St.-Pol-de-Léon	11
Mirepoix	?	St.-Pons	80
Montauban	31	Sarlat	68
Montpellier	21	Sées	38
Nancy	40	Senez	88
Nantes	22	Senlis	69
Narbonne	86	Sens	87
Nevers	55	Sisteron	66
Nîmes	35	Soissons	73
Noyon	58	Strasbourg	9
Oloron	?	Tarbes	92
Orange	68	Toul	83
Orléans	88	Toulon	89
Pamiers	?	Toulouse	25
Paris	74	Tournai	14
Périgueux	68	Tours	57
Perpignan	29	Tréguier	28
Poitiers	69	Troyes	72
Quimper	27	Tulle	36
Reims	62	Uzès	28
Rennes	17	Vabres	7
Rieux	57	Vaison	83
Riez	?	Valence	93
Rodez	29	Vannes	8
Rouen	54	Vence	83
St.-Brieuc	15	Verdun	76
St.-Claude	35	Vienne	78
St.-Dié	63	Viviers	43
Saintes	66	Ypres	?
St.-Flour	58		

[1] See chp. 5, note 5, for explanation of method and sources.

Incidence of Curé Collective Action, 1730-1786

Date	Diocese	Objective
ca. 1735-37	Comminges (1)	1) Raise pc; 2) Reform *décimes*
1740's	Sens (2)	Cs rights in hierarchy
1746-49	Metz (3)	1) *Décime* distribution; 2) Cs rights in hierarchy
1746-47	Tarbes (4)	1) Elect cs to bd; 2) Cs rights in hierarchy
1747-48	Dax (4)	Elect cs to bd
1752	Toulon (5)	Tithers pay pc and furnishings
1755	Nîmes (6)	1) Raise pc; 2) Return tithes to cs
ca. 1755(?)	Lyon (7)	Raise pc
ca. 1755(?)	Meaux (7)	Raise pc
ca. 1755(?)	"Montagnes du Cantal" (7)	Raise pc
1756	Avranches (8)	Elect cs to bd
1756-60	Coutances (9)	1) Elect cs to bd; 2) Open tax rolls
1759-60	Sées (10)	Oppose new *rituel* and *cas réservés*
ca. 1760-63	Chartres (11)	Raise pc
ca. 1760-63	Montpellier (11)	Raise pc
ca. 1760-63	Bayeux (11)	Raise pc
1762	Grenoble (11)	Raise pc
1763	"Artois" (12)	1) Return part of tithes from monks to cs; 2) Tithers provide furnishings for the mass
1763	Noyon (12)	Raise pc
1764	Grenoble (13)	Elect cs to bd
1765	Lyon (14)	Raise pc
1765	Riez (14)	Raise pc
1765	Beauvais (14)	Raise pc
1765	Coutances (15)	Reform *décimes*
1765	Grenoble (16)	Raise pc
1765	Gap (16)	Raise pc
1765	Valence (16)	Raise pc

Incidence of Curé Collective Action, 1730-1786 (cont.)

Date	Diocese	Objective
1765	Die (16)	Raise pc
1766	Rodez (17)	Reform bd
1767	Vienne (16)	Raise pc
1767	Luçon (18)	1) Reform bd; 2) Expand cs voice in diocesan affairs
1768	Vannes (19)	Elect cs to bd
ca. 1767	Troyes (20)	Elect cs to bd
ca. 1770's	Saint-Brieuc (21)	Elect cs to bd
1770's	Châlons-sur-Marne (22)	Elect cs to bd
1770's	Riez (22)	Elect cs to bd
1770-71	Troyes (23)	1) Cease new *rituel*; 2) Give cs voice in diocesan affairs; 3) Cs can confess in all parishes
1770	Gap (24)	Elect cs to bd
1772	Auch (19)	Elect cs to bd
ca. 1772	Le Mans (25)	End bishop's yearly control of vicaires
1773	Toul (26)	Reestablish rural synods
1773	Vienne (27)	Elect cs to bd
ca. 1773-78	Lisieux (28)	1) End seminary retreats and eccles. conferences; 2) Cs rights in diocesan government
1775	Chartres (29)	Raise pc
1775	Orléans (29)	Raise pc
1775	"Béarn" (29)	Return *novales* tithes to cs
1775	"Bas-Languedoc" (30)	1) Oppose edict of 1768; 2) Return *novales*; 3) Tithers must pay furnishings
ca. 1775	Lyon (31)	Raise pc
ca. 1775	Cahors (31)	Raise pc
ca. 1775	Embrun (31)	Raise pc
1775	Bayeux (32)	Raise pc
1775	Bazas (32)	Raise pc
1775	Agen (32)	Raise pc
1777	Périgueux (33)	Elect cs to bd and reform it
1777	Langres (19)	Elect cs to bd
1777-78	Bordeaux (34)	Affirm cs right to form "corporation"
1778	Nancy (19)	Return cs right to hold rural synods

Incidence of Curé Collective Action, 1730-1786 (cont.)

Date	Diocese	Objective
1778	Saint-Dié (19)	Return cs right to hold rural synods
1778	Oloron (17)	Allow cs independent assemblies
1779	Poitiers (35)	End oligarchy on bd
1779	Apt (36)	End oligarchy on bd
1779-80	Aix (37)	1) Raise pc; 2) Tithers provide furnishings
1779-80	Marseille (38)	Same
1779-80	Toulon (37)	Same
1779-80	Sisteron (37)	Same
1779-80	Riez (32)	Same
1779-80	Vienne (39)	Same
1779-80	Gap (39)	Same
1779-80	Grenoble (39)	Same
1779-80	Embrun (39)	Same
1779-80	Valence (39)	Same
1779-80	Die (39)	Same
1780	Tréguier (19)	Elect cs to bd
1780	"Normandy" (40)	Raise pc
1780	Tarbes (41)	Raise pc
1781	Nancy (42)	Return cs right to hold independent synods
1781	Aire (43)	1) Change Edict of 1768; 2) Raise pc
1782	Bazas (19)	Elect cs to bd
1785	Angers (44)	Give cs just representation on bd

Abbreviations: pc = portion congrue; cs = curés; bd = bureau diocésain

[1] *Rapport de l'Agence, 1735-40* (Paris, 1742) *Procès-verbaux de l'Assemblée générale du Clergé de France, 1780* (Paris, 1782), 103-106.

[2] Edmond Préclin, *Les Jansénistes du XVIIIe siècle et la Constitution civile du clergé* (Paris, 1928), 143-49.

[3] René Tavenaux, *Le Jansénisme en Lorraine* (Paris, 1960), 694.

[4] Préclin, 390.

[5] A.N., G⁸* 2687; and *Précis des rapports de l'Agence du Clergé de France* (Paris, 1786), 148.

[6] A.N., G⁸ 642.

[7] Pierre de Vaissière, *Curés de campagne de l'ancienne France* (Paris, 1932), 244-48.

[8] Jean Bindet, "Contestataires au diocèse d'Avranches," *Revue de l'Avranchin*, 47 (1970), 271-83.

[9] Préclin, 391.

[10] *Précis*, 143-44.

[11] Préclin, 387.

[12] A.N., G⁸ 185.

[13] Henri Reymond, *Droits des curés* (Paris, 1776), 283.

[14] A.N., G⁸* 2629, ff. 29 and 32.

[15] *Précis*, 103-106.

[16] A.N., G⁸* 2524.

[17] Préclin, 397-98.

[18] Préclin, 315-20.

[19] Préclin, 397.

[20] Préclin, 395.

[21] P. Lemarchand, "Journal d'un curé de campagne," *Bulletin de la Société d'émulation des Côtes-du-Nord*, 88 (1960), 66-68.

[22] *Collection des procès-verbaux des Assemblées générales du Clergé de France*, 8 vols. (Paris, 1767-80), 8: part 2, 1858.

[23] Préclin, 295.

[24] A.N., G⁸ 632 (Gap) and G⁸* 2598, no. 610.

[25] Préclin, 313-15.

[26] Taveneaux, 704.

[27] A.N., G⁸ 661 (Vienne).

[28] Préclin, 324-30.

[29] Henri Marion, *La dîme ecclésiastique en France au XVIIIe siècle* (Bordeaux, 1912), 27.

[30] A.A.E., 1375, ff. 187-88.

[31] A.N., G⁸* 2518, ff. 134-37.

[32] A.N., G⁸* 2630, ff. 550.

[33] A.N., G⁸* 2631, ff. 142.

[34] A.D. Gironde, C 98.

[35] *Procès-verbaux ... 1780*, 361.

[36] *Procès-verbaux ... 1780*, 363.

[37] A.A.E., 1741; and *Procès-verbaux ... 1780*, 102-103.

[38] A.A.E., 1386, ff. 228.

[39] A.A.E., 1388; A.N., G⁸* 2544, no. 323; *Mémoires à consulter pour les curés de la province de Dauphiné* (Paris, 1780), 100-108.

[40] A.A.E., 1388, ff. 64.

[41] A.A.E., 1488.

[42] *Rapports de l'Agence, 1780-1785* (Paris, 1788), 306.

[43] A.N., G⁸* 2631, ff. 374, 378; Préclin, 397.

[44] Préclin, 410-11.

SOURCES AND BIBLIOGRAPHY

I. Manuscript Sources

ARCHIVES NATIONALES

Numerous series dealing with the early Revolution were sampled. The following were of particular importance:

AA 42, no. 1321ᵃ, documents from the Ministry of Justice on the oath in Deux-Sèvres.

BB³ 31, dossier from the Ministry of Justice concerning those amnestied in Sept. 1791, by district.

C 114-119, addresses and adherences received by the National Assembly, April to July 1790.

D IV 14-69, miscellaneous papers from the Committee on the Constitution dealing with religious affairs, 1790-91.

D IV bis 37-38, Committee on Divisions, lists of active citizens and electors in 1790, by district.

D XIX 21-22, replies from the departments to the survey by the Ecclesiastical Committee concerning the numbers of jurors and non-jurors, Mar. to Sept. 1791 (includes about one half of the departments).

D XIX 45, *réclamations* to the Ecclesiastical Committee concerning the oath and other matters, 1790-91.

D XIX 80-88, correspondence received by the Ecclesiastical Committee during the period of the oath, late 1790 to 1791 (D XIX 102 was used as an index).

D XXIX, series with papers from the Committee for Reports (awkward to use, since filed by place; sampled via inventory).

D XXIX bis 5-13, isolated documents from the Committee for Research, sampled via inventory.

D XXIX bis 20-23 and 25, Committee for Research, papers dealing with the problems of implementing the oath, Nov. 1790 to June 1791. The single most important source on the oath in the A.N.

Fˡᶜ III, series with correspondence addressed to the Ministry of the Interior concerning the *esprit public*, sampled for certain departments of interest.

F¹⁹ 311, report on the reactions of the departments to the "Law of Toleration" of May 1791.

F¹⁹ 398-481, papers from the Ministry of the Interior regarding religious questions under the Revolution and the Empire, by department (most with dossiers for the period 1790-92).

F^{19} 865-66, inquiry by the prefects of each department on the local ecclesiastical personnel, Year IX.

F^{19} 1255-56, circulars and correspondence concerning the salaries of ecclesiastical personnel in the departments and districts, 1790-91.

G^8 30, papers on the composition of the *bureaux diocésains*, eighteenth
century.

G^{8*} 2467, 2555, 2622-26, 2632 (end), 2832, and 2834, tables and indices
to the papers of the Agents-General of the Clergy of France, eighteenth
century.

DEPARTMENTAL ARCHIVES

The departmental archives were visited above all in order to assemble
statistics on oath-taking. For this, I relied primarily on documents in
series L, V, Q, and J. See Appendix II for details. A few departments
were targeted for more careful research among non-quantifiable materials. The following archives were used:

Aisne	Jura
Allier	Loiret
Alpes-de-Haute-Provence	Lot
Hautes-Alpes	Lot-et-Garonne
Ardennes	Lozère
Ariège	Maine-et-Loire
Aveyron	Mayenne
Bouches-du-Rhône	Moselle
Calvados	Nièvre
Cantal	Oise
Charente-Maritime	Pas-de-Calais
Cher	Pyrénées-Atlantiques
Corrèze	Pyrénées-Orientales
Côte-d'Or	Rhône
Dordogne	Haute-Saône
Doubs	Saône-et-Loire
Drôme	Sarthe
Eure-et-Loir	Seine-et-Marne
Gard	Yvelines
Haute-Garonne	Deux-Sèvres
Gers	Tarn
Gironde	Vendée
Ille-et-Vilaine	Haute-Vienne
Isère	Vosges

MUNICIPAL ARCHIVES

Colmar, ms. 972, notes by Jules Joachim on the clergy of Haut-Rhin during the Revolution.

Dijon, *fichier* Reinert (unclassed) and ms. 2186 (*fichier* Debrie) on the clergy of Côte-d'Or during the Revolution.

II. Printed Sources

Not listed here are the various printed editions of the *cahiers de doléances*. See the works of Beatrice Hyslop, cited below in section III, for a complete list. Many of the books and articles in section III also contain collections of documents.

Archives parlementaires de 1787 à 1860. Recueil complet des débats législatifs et politiques des chambres françaises. Première série (1787-1799), Jérôme Mavidal, Emile Laurent *et al.*, eds., 82 vols. Paris, 1867-1913.

André, Ferdinand, ed. *Délibérations de l'administration départementale de la Lozère et de son directoire de 1790 à 1800*, 4 vols. Mende, 1882-84.

Barruel, Abbé. *Collection ecclésiastique ou recueil complet des ouvrages faits depuis l'ouverture des Etats-Généraux relativement au clergé et sa Constitution civile, décrétée par l'Assemblée nationale, sanctionnée par le roi*, 14 vols. Paris, 1791-93.

Brette, Armand, ed. *Recueil de documents relatifs à la convocation des Etats-Généraux de 1789*, 4 vols. Paris, 1894-1915.

Camus, Armand-Gaston. *Développement de l'opinion de Monsieur Camus, député de l'Assemblée nationale, dans la séance du 27 novembre*. Paris, 1790.

Collection des procès-verbaux des Assemblées générales du Clergé de France, 9 vols. Paris, 1767-80.

Combes de Patris, Bernard. *Procès-verbaux des séances de la société populaire de Rodez*. Carrère, 1912.

Déclaration d'une partie de l'Assemblée nationale sur le décret rendu le 13 avril 1790 concernant la religion. Paris, 1790.

Durand de Maillane, Pierre-Toussaint. *Dictionnaire de droit canonique et de pratique bénéficiale*, 5 vols. Lyon, 1776.

———. *Histoire apologétique du Comité ecclésiastique de l'Assemblée nationale*. Paris, 1791.

Exposition des principes sur la Constitution civile du Clergé. Paris, 1790.

Ferrière, Claude-Joseph de. *Dictionnaire de droit et de pratique contenant*

l'explication des termes de droit, d'ordonnances, de coutumes et de pratique,
2 vols. Toulouse, 1779.

Grégoire, Henri. *La légitimité du serment civique exigé des fonctionnaires ecclésiastiques.* Paris, 1791.

———. *Mémoires,* H. Carnot, ed., 2 vols. Paris, 1840.

Liste de MM. les archevêques, évêques, curés et autres membres ecclésiastiques de l'Assemblée nationale, qui croyant ne pouvoir, par devoir de conscience, prêter le serment dans la formule qu'exigeait l'Assemblée, ont adopté le 4 janvier celle qui avait été proposée par M. l'évêque de Clermont. Paris, 1791.

Martineau, Louis. *Rapport imprimé par ordre de l'Assemblée nationale.* Paris, 1790.

Précis des rapports de l'Agence du Clergé de France par ordre de matières. Paris, 1786.

Procès-verbaux de l'Assemblée générale du Clergé de France, 1780. Paris, 1782.

Procès-verbaux de l'Assemblée générale du Clergé de France, 1782. Paris, 1783.

Procès-verbaux de l'Assemblée générale du Clergé de France, 1785. Paris, 1789.

Rapport de l'Agence . . . du Clergé depuis 1780 jusqu'en 1785. Paris, 1788.

La République française en 84 départements. Paris, 1793.

Treilhard, Jean-Baptiste. *Discours imprimé par ordre de l'Assemblée nationale.* Paris, 1790.

III. Studies

Anonymous. "Le serment de 1791 dans l'Ardèche," *Semaine religieuse du diocèse de Viviers,* 83-84 (1964-65), *passim.*

Ado, A. V. (*The Peasant Movement in France during the Great Bourgeois Revolution*) [untranslated from the Russian]. Moscow, 1971.

Agulhon, Maurice. *Pénitents et Francs-Maçons de l'ancienne Provence.* Paris, 1968.

———. *La vie sociale en Provence au lendemain de la Révolution.* Paris, 1970.

Aimond, Charles. *Histoire religieuse de la Révolution dans le département de la Meuse et le diocèse de Verdun (1789-1802).* Paris, 1949.

Allain, Ernest. "Un grand diocèse d'autrefois [Bordeaux]. Organisation administrative et financière," *Revue des questions historiques,* 56 (Oct. 1894), 493-534.

Alliot, J.-M. *Le clergé de Versailles pendant la Révolution.* Versailles, 1913.

Alloing, Louis. *Le Diocèse de Belley. Histoire religieuse des pays de l'Ain.* Belley, 1938.

Ampoulange, Lucien. *Le clergé et la convocation aux Etats-généraux de 1789 dans la sénéchaussée de Périgord.* Montpellier, 1912.

Angeville, Adolphe d'. *Essai sur la statistique de la population française,* new ed. Paris, 1969.

Annat, Jean. *Le clergé du diocèse de Lescar pendant la Révolution.* Pau, 1954.

Appolis, Emile. *Le Jansénisme dans le diocèse de Lodève au XVIIIe siècle.* Albi, 1952.

———. *Le Tiers-Parti catholique au XVIIIe siècle: entre Jansénistes et Zélanti.* Paris, 1960.

Armogathe, Jean-Robert. "Le diocèse de Mende au XVIIe siècle: perspectives d'histoire religieuse," *Revue du Gévaudan,* n. sér., no. 17 (1971), 91-109.

Arnaud, G. *Histoire de la Révolution dans le département de l'Ariège.* Toulouse, 1904.

Aulard, Alphonse. *La Révolution française et le régime féodal.* Paris, 1919.

———. *Christianity and the French Revolution* (trans. by Lady Frazer). New York, 1966.

Baboin, F. "L'application de la Constitution civile du clergé dans la Drôme," *La Révolution française,* 37 (1899), 223-51, 344-65.

Bachelier, Alcime. *Le jansénisme à Nantes.* Angers, 1934.

Bardou, Paul. "Le clergé angevin et la reconstruction concordataire du diocèse d'Angers," Thèse de 3e cycle, Université de Paris-Sorbonne, 1981.

Barnedès, Jeanne. Le clergé paroissial du diocèse d'Elne à la fin du XVIIIe siècle. Mémoire de maîtrise, Université de Montpellier III, 1977.

Barran, Hippolyte, Eugène and Fernand de. *L'Epoque révolutionnaire en Rouergue.* Rodez, n.d.

Barranguet, P. "Les confréries dans le diocèse de Toulouse au milieu et à la fin du XVIII siècle," *Actes du Xe Congrès fédéral de la société Languedoc-Pyrénées-Gascogne, 1954.* Montauban, 1956, 293-302.

Barruel, Abbé. *Collection ecclésiastique ou recueil complet des ouvrages faits depuis l'ouverture des Etats-généraux relativement au clergé, et sa Constitution civile, décrétée par l'Assemblée nationale, sanctionnée par le roi,* 14 vols. Paris, 1791-93.

Baumont, H. "Le département de l'Oise pendant la Révolution, l'année

1791," *Bulletin de la Société historique et scientifique de l'Oise*, 3 (1907), 1-99.

Bauzon, Louis; Paul Muguet; and Louis Chaumont. *Recherches historiques sur la persécution religieuse dans le département de Saône-et-Loire pendant la Révolution*, 4 vols. Chalon-sur-Saône, 1889-1903.

Beauhaire, Joseph. *Chronologie des évêques, des curés, des vicaires et des autres prêtres de ce diocèse [de Chartres]*. Paris, 1892.

Bée, Michel. "Les confréries de charité: mutuelles funéraires et confréries de bienfaisance," *Cahiers Léopold Delisle*, 21, fasc. 3-4 (1972), 5-22.

Bénac, J. "Le séminaire d'Auch," *Revue de Gascogne* (1906-1907).

Bercé, Yves-Marie. *Fête et révolte. Des mentalités populaires du XVIe au XVIIIe siècle*. Paris, 1976.

Bernard, Daniel. "Le clergé régulier du diocèse de Cornouaille en 1790," *Bulletin de la Société d'archéologie du Finistère*, 80 (1954), 83-109.

———. "Le clergé séculier du diocèse de Cornouaille en 1790," *Bulletin de la Société d'archéologie du Finistère*, 81 (1955), 7-46; 82 (1956), 160-85; 83 (1957), 60-79.

Berthe, Léon-Noël. "Le Boulonnais Louis-Léonard Lefèvre (1750-1796), curé constitutionnel et arithméticien politique," *Bulletin de la Commission départementale des monuments historiques du Pas-de-Calais*, 9 (1971-73), 175-86.

Berthelot du Chesnay, Charles. "Les missions de Saint Jean Eudes," *XVIIe siècle*, no. 41 (1958), 328-48.

———. "Le clergé séculier en Normandie au XVIIIe siècle," *Cahiers Léopold Delisle*, 17, fasc. 3-4 (1968), 20-21.

———. "Les prêtres séculiers en Haute-Bretagne au XVIIIe siècle," Thèse de doctorat d'état, Université de Rennes II, 1974.

———. "Etudes ecclésiastiques et formation du clergé de Bretagne au XVIIIe siècle," *Annales de Bretagne*, 83 (1976), 657-63.

———. *Les prêtres séculiers en Haute-Bretagne au XVIIIe siècle*. Rennes, 1984.

Besnard, Yves-François. *Souvenirs d'un nonagénaire*, 2 vols. Paris, 1880.

Besse, Guy. "La représentation du peuple chez un prédicateur: François-Léon Réguis, 1725-1789," in *Images du peuple au XVIIIe siècle*. Paris, 1973, 159-76.

Bianchi, Constant. "L'application de la Constitution civile du clergé dans l'ancien diocèse de Grasse," *Annales de la Société scientifique et littéraire de Cannes*, 13 (1951-54), 97-108.

Bien, David. *The Calas Affair: Persecution, Toleration and Heresy in Eighteenth-Century Toulouse*. Princeton, 1960.

Biernawski, L. *Un département sous la Révolution française (l'Allier de 1789 à l'An III)*. Moulins, 1909.

Bindet, Jean. "Le diocèse d'Avranches sous l'épiscopat de Mgr. Godart de Belboeuf, dernier évêque d'Avranches," *Revue de l'Avranchin*, 87 (1969), 1-96.

————. "Contestataires au diocèse d'Avranches pendant le XVIIe et le XVIIIe siècles," *Revue de l' Avranchin*, 88 (1970), 255-83.

————. *François Bécherel, 1732-1815*, 2nd ed. Coutances, 1971.

Blanchet, J.P.G. *Le clergé charentais pendant la Révolution*. Angoulême, 1898.

Bois, Paul. *Paysans de l'Ouest*, abr. ed. Paris, 1971.

————. "Révolution et contre-révolution, 1787-1815," in *Histoire des Pays de la Loire*, François Lebrun, ed. Toulouse, 1970, 311-61.

————. "La Révolution et l'Empire," in *Histoire de Nantes*, Paul Bois, ed. Toulouse, 1977.

Boivin-Champeaux, L. *Notices historiques sur la Révolution dans le département de l'Eure*, 2nd ed., 2 vols. Evreux, 1893-94.

Bonneau, Gustave. *Notes pour servir à l'histoire du clergé de l'Yonne pendant la Révolution, 1790-1800*. Sens, 1900.

Bonnenfant, G. *Les séminaires normands du XVIe au XVIIIe siècle*. Paris, 1915.

Bouchard, Gérard. *Le village immobile*. Paris, 1972.

Bouchez, Emile. *Le clergé du pays rémois pendant la Révolution et la suppression de l'archevêché de Reims (1789-1821)*. Reims, 1913.

Bourloton, Edgar. *Le clergé de la Vendée pendant la Révolution*. Vannes, 1908.

Boutier, J. "Jacqueries en pays croquant. Les révoltes paysannes en Aquitaine (décembre 1789-mars 1790)," *Annales E.S.C.*, 34 (1979), 760-86.

Bouvier, Henri. *Histoire de l'Eglise et de l'ancien archidiocèse de Sens*, 3 vols. Paris, 1906-1911.

Boysson, R. de. *Le clergé périgourdin pendant la persécution révolutionnaire*. Paris, 1907.

Brégail, G. *Le Gers pendant la Révolution (1789-1804)*. Auch, 1934.

Brelot, Jean. "Les familiarités en Franche-Comté et spécialement dans le département du Jura," *Mémoires de la Société pour l'histoire de droit et des institutions des anciens pays bourguignons, comtois et romands*, fasc. 24 (1963), 22-23.

Bresson, A. *Les prêtres de la Haute-Marne déportés sous la Convention et le Directoire*. Langres, 1913.

Bricaud, Jean. *L'administration du département d'Ille-et-Vilaine au début de la Révolution (1790-91)*. Rennes, 1965.

Bridoux, Fernand. *Histoire religieuse du département de Seine-et-Marne pendant la Révolution*, 2 vols. Melun, 1953.

Brossard, E. *Histoire du département de la Loire pendant la Révolution*, 2 vols. Paris, 1904-1907.

Brugière, Hippolyte. *Le livre d'or des diocèses de Périgueux et de Sarlat ou le clergé de Périgord pendant la période révolutionnaire*. Montreuil-sur-Mer, 1893.

Bruneau, M. *Les débuts de la Révolution dans les départements du Cher et de l'Indre*. Paris, 1902.

Caillault, Claudine. "Clergé constitutionnel et réfractaire en Eure-et-Loire de 1790 à 1795," D.E.S., Faculté des Lettres, Université de Tours, 1969.

Calan, Charles de. *Le clergé séculier et les congrégations religieuses en Ille-et-Vilaine de 1790 à 1792*. Rennes, 1923.

Camelin, Joseph. *Deux prêtres de Lamourette*. Lyon, 1929.

————. "Pourquoi et comment dresser par diocèse une liste exacte et quasi officielle du clergé constitutionnel," *RHEF*, 23 (1937), 326-32.

————. *Les prêtres de la Révolution. Répertoire officiel du clergé schismatique du Rhône-et-Loire*. Lyon, 1944.

Cardenal, Louis de. "Le 'citoyen' de 1791 payait-il plus ou moins d'impôts que le 'sujet' de 1790?" *Comité des travaux historiques et scientifiques, section d'histoire moderne et d'histoire contemporaine. Notices, inventaires et documents*, 22 (1936), 61-110.

Cariou, Augustin. "La Constitution civile du Clergé dans le département du Morbihan," *Mémoires de la Société d'histoire et d'archéologie de la Bretagne*, 45 (1965), 59-88.

Casta, François J. "Le clergé corse et les serments constitutionnels pendant la Révolution française," *Corse historique*, 9 (1969), 5-36.

————. "La réorganisation religieuse en Corse au lendemain de la Révolution française," in *Mélanges offerts au Professeur Paul Arrighi*. Gap, 1971, 51-126.

Cattin, M. *Mémoires pour servir à l'histoire ecclésiastique des diocèses de Lyon et de Belley, depuis la Constitution civile du clergé jusqu'au Concordat*. Lyon, 1867.

Cau-Durban. "Le clergé du diocèse de Couserans pendant la Révolution," *Revue de Comminges*, 16 (1901), 218-29; 17 (1902), 13-28, 101-118, 182-93, 201-210.

Censer, Jack Richard. *Prelude to Power. The Parisian Radical Press, 1789-1791*. Baltimore, 1976.

Certeau, Michel de. "L'histoire religieuse du XVIIe siècle, problèmes de méthode," *Recherches de science religieuse*, 57 (1969), 231-50.

Certeau, Michel de, Dominique Julia, and Jacques Revel. *La politique de la langue*. Paris, 1975.

Chaille, Yves. "Livre d'or du clergé vendéen," *Archives du diocèse de Luçon*, n.s., 32-36 (1960-64).

————. "Les divisions ecclésiastiques de la Vendée en 1789. Les conférences," *Revue du Bas-Poitou*, 78 (1967), 235-43.

Chamouton, E. *Histoire de la persécution révolutionnaire dans le département du Jura, 1789-1800*. Lons-le-Saunier, 1893.

Champion, Edme. *La France d'après les cahiers de 1789*. Paris, 1904.

Charrier, Jules. *Histoire religieuse du département de la Nièvre pendant la Révolution*, 2 vols. Paris, 1926.

Chartier, Roger. "Cultures, lumières, doléances: les cahiers de 1789," *RHMC*, 28 (1981), 68-93.

Chassagne, Serge. "L'église abolie? (1789-1802)," in *Le diocèse d'Angers*, François Lebrun, ed. Paris, 1981, 149-72.

Chassin, Charles-Louis. *Les cahiers des curés*. Paris, 1882.

Chaunu, Pierre. "Jansénisme et frontière de catholicité," *RH*, 127 (1962), 115-38.

————. "Une histoire religieuse sérielle. A propos du diocèse de La Rochelle (1648-1724) et sur quelques exemples normands," *RHMC*, 12 (1965), 5-34.

————. *La mort à Paris*. Paris, 1978.

Chaussinand-Nogaret, Guy. *La noblesse au XVIIIe siècle*. Paris, 1976.

Chevalier, Jules. *L'Eglise constitutionnelle et la persécution religieuse dans le département de la Drôme pendant la Révolution*. Valence, 1919.

Cholvy, Gérard. "Une chrétienté au XIXe siècle: la Lozère," *Bulletin de la Société des Lettres, Sciences et Arts de la Lozère*, n.s., no. 18-19 (1972-73), 365-82.

————. *Religion et société au XIXe siècle. Le diocèse de Montpellier*, 2 vols. Lille, 1973.

Clément, Joseph-M.-H. *Le personnel concordataire dans le département de l'Allier*. Moulins, 1904.

Colfavru, J. C. "Le serment. De son importance politique pendant la Révolution," *Révolution française*, 2 (1882), 970-82.

Colombet, A. "Le curé, homme de confiance du seigneur (1770)," *Annales de Bourgogne*, 17 (1945), 274-80.

SOURCES AND BIBLIOGRAPHY

Compère, Marie-Madeleine, Roger Chartier, and Dominique Julia. *L'éducation en France du XVIe au XVIIIe siècle*. Paris, 1976.

Compère, Marie-Madeleine and Dominique Julia. *Les collèges français. 16e-18e siècles. Répertoire I: France du Midi*. Paris, 1984.

Constantin, C. *L'évêché du département de la Meurthe de 1791 à 1801. Tome 1. La fin de l'Eglise d'Ancien régime et l'établissement de l'Eglise constitutionnelle*. Nancy, 1935.

————. "Constitution civile du Clergé," in *DTC*, vol. 3, pt. 2, cols. 1537-1604.

Crégut, Régis. *Le diocèse de Clermont pendant la Révolution*. Clermont, 1914.

Croix, Alain. *La Bretagne aux 16e et 17e siècles. La vie, la mort, la foi*, 2 vols. Paris, 1981.

Dansette, Adrien. *Histoire religieuse de la France contemporaine, l'Eglise catholique dans la mêlée politique et sociale*, 2nd ed. Paris, 1965.

Darnton, Robert. *The Literary Underground of the Old Regime*. Cambridge, Mass., 1982.

————. *The Great Cat Massacre and Other Episodes in French Cultural History*. New York, 1984.

Darsy, F. I. *Le clergé de l'Eglise d'Amiens en 1789*. Amiens, 1892.

Davis, Natalie Zemon. *Society and Culture in Early-Modern France*. Stanford, 1975.

Dawson, Philip and Gilbert Shapiro, "Social Mobility and Political Radicalism: The Case of the French Revolution of 1789," in *The Dimensions of Quantitative Research in History*. Princeton, 1972.

Debard, Jean-Marc. "Piété populaire et Réforme dans la principauté de Montbéliard du XVIe au XVIIIe siècle," *ACSS*, 99 (1974), 1:7-34.

Debuc, André. "Les charités du diocèse de Rouen au XVIIIe siècle," *ACSS*, 99 (1976), 1:211-36.

Dégert, Antoine. *L'ancien diocèse d'Aire*. Auch, 1907.

————. *Histoire des séminaires français jusqu'à la Révolution*, 2 vols. Paris, 1912.

Delarc, O. *L'église de Paris pendant la Révolution française*, 3 vols. Paris, 1895-98.

Delon, Pierre-Jean-Baptiste. *La Révolution en Lozère*. Mende, 1922.

Delumeau, Jean. *Le catholicisme entre Luther et Voltaire*. Paris, 1971.

————. "Déchristianisation ou nouveau modèle de christianisme?" 40 (1975), 3-20.

————. *La mort des pays de Cocagne*. Paris, 1976.

384

————, ed. *Le diocèse de Rennes*. Paris, 1979.

Denys-Buirette, A. *Les questions religieuses dans les cahiers de 1789*. Paris, 1919.

Deramecourt, A. *Le clergé du diocèse d'Arras, Boulogne et Saint-Omer pendant la Révolution (1789-1802)*, 4 vols. Arras, 1884-86.

Deschuytter, G. *L'esprit public et son évolution dans le Nord de 1791 au lendemain de Thermidor An II*, 2 vols. Gap, 1957-59.

Destombes, Michel. *Le clergé du diocèse d'Amiens et le serment à la Constitution civile, 1790-91*. Amiens, 1971.

Dion-Knockaert, Micheline. "Histoire religieuse d'Armentières sous la Révolution," *Bulletin du Comité Flamand de France*, fasc. 2 (1958), 187-237.

Dommanget, Maurice. *La déchristianisation à Beauvais et dans l'Oise*. Besançon, 1918.

Dubois, Eugène. *Histoire de la Révolution dans le département de l'Ain*, 6 vols. Bourg, 1931-35.

Dubois, Jacques. "La carte des diocèses de France avant la Révolution," *Annales. E.S.C.*, 20 (1965), 680-91.

Dubreuil, Léon. *La vente des biens nationaux dans le département des Côtes-du-Nord*. Paris, 1912.

————. "Le clergé de Bretagne aux Etats-Généraux," *Révolution française*, 70 (1917), 481-503.

Dumoulin, Chrétien. "La Révolution," in *Le diocèse de Bourges*, ed. Guy Devailly. Paris, 1973, 144-65.

Dupuy, André. "La réforme pastorale dans les diocèses d'Aire et de Dax aux XVIIe et XVIIIe siècles," *Bulletin de la Société Borda*, 98 (1974), 151-72, 309-403.

Dupuy, Roger. *La garde nationale et les débuts de la Révolution en Ille-et-Vilaine (1789-mars 1793)*. Paris, 1972.

Durand, Albert. *Etat religieux des trois diocèses de Nîmes, d'Uzès, et d'Alès à la fin de l'Ancien régime*. Nîmes, 1909.

————. *Histoire religieuse du département du Gard pendant la Révolution française, Tome I (1788-92)*. Nîmes, 1918.

Durengues, Antoine. *Pouillé historique du diocèse d'Agen pour l'année 1789*. Agen, 1894.

————. *L'église d'Agen pendant la Révolution, le diocèse de Lot-et-Garonne*. Agen, 1903.

Edington, Winifred. "An Administrative Study of the Implementation of the Civil Constitution of the Clergy in the Diocese of Lisieux," Ph.D. dissertation, University of London, 1958.

Egret, Jean. *Les derniers Etats de Dauphiné*. Grenoble, 1942.

———. "La dernière assemblée du Clergé de France," *RH*, 219 (1958), 1-15.

———. *Louis XV et l'opposition parlementaire*. Paris, 1970.

Ehrard, Jean and Paul Viallaneix, eds. *Les fêtes de la Révolution. Colloque de Clermont-Ferrand. Juin 1974*. Paris, 1977.

Eich, Jean. "La situation matérielle de l'Eglise de Metz à la fin de l'Ancien régime," *Annuaire de la Société d'histoire et d'archéologie de la Lorraine*, 58 (1958), 45-65.

———. *Les prêtres mosellans pendant la Révolution. Répertoire biographique*. Metz, 1959.

———. *Histoire religieuse du département de la Moselle pendant la Révolution*. Metz, 1964.

Endrès, André. "Les conférences du diocèse de Meaux aux XVIIe et XVIIIe siècles," *ACSS*, 88 (1963), 9-16.

Fage, René. *Le diocèse de Corrèze pendant la Révolution*. Tulle, 1889.

Faucheux, Marcel. *L'insurrection vendéenne de 1793*. Paris, 1964.

Favreau, Robert. *Atlas historique français. Anjou*. Paris, 1973.

Ferté, Jeanne. *La vie religieuse dans les campagnes parisiennes*. Paris, 1962.

Flament, Pierre. "Recherches sur le diocèse de Sées sous la Révolution et l'Empire," *Société historique et archéologique de l'Orne*, 85 (1967), 61-81.

Flandrin, Jean-Louis. *Familles, parenté, maison, sexualité dans l'ancienne société*. Paris, 1976.

Fleury, Edouard. *Le clergé du département de l'Aisne pendant la Révolution*, 2 vols. Paris, 1853.

Font-Réaulx, Jacques de. *Pouillés de la province de Bourges*, 2 vols. Paris, 1961-62.

Fournier, Paul. "Un curé au XVIIIe siècle. Jean-François Couquot, curé de Maron, 1747-74," *Mémoires de l'Académie de Stanislas*, 6e sér., 1 (1903-04), 41-128.

Fournoux, Bernard de. "Les revenus des curés dans l'Allier en 1790 et à la veille de la Révolution," *Bulletin de la Société d'Emulation du Bourbonnais*, 52 (1963), 413-17.

Fox, Edward Whiting. *History in Geographic Perspective. The Other France*. New York, 1971.

Frayhier, C. A. *Histoire du clergé catholique d'Alsace avant, pendant et après la grande Révolution*. Colmar, 1877.

Frêche, Georges. *Toulouse et la région Midi-Pyrénées au siècle des Lumières.* Toulouse, 1974.

Froeschlé-Chopard, Marie-Hélène. *La religion populaire en Provence orientale au XVIIIe siècle.* Paris, 1980.

Furet, François, ed. *Livre et société dans la France du XVIIIe siècle.* Paris, 1965-70.

———. *Penser la Révolution.* Paris, 1978.

Furet, François and Jacques Ozouf. *Lire et écrire: l'alphabétisation des Français de Calvin à Jules Ferry,* 2 vols. Paris, 1977.

Furet, François and Denis Richet. *La Révolution française.* Paris, 1973.

Gagnol, Pierre. *La dîme ecclésiastique en France au XVIIIe siècle.* Paris, 1910.

Gaillard, A. *A travers le schisme constitutionnel en Gironde.* Bordeaux, 1912.

Gaillemin, André. "Bar ecclésiastique et le clergé de la Révolution," *Bulletin des Sociétés d'histoire et d'archéologie de la Meuse,* 12 (1975), 59-82.

Gallard, Louis. "Le clergé saumurois de 1789 à 1795," D.E.S., Université de Poitiers, 1960.

———. "Le clergé saumurois sous la Révolution (1789-91)," *Bulletin de la Société des lettres et sciences du Saumurois,* 54 (1963), 39-50.

Gallerand, J. "Le serment du clergé de Loir-et-Cher en 1791," *Mémoires de la Société des sciences et lettres du Loir-et-Cher,* 24 (1922), 36-37.

———. *Les cultes sous la Terreur en Loir-et-Cher (1792-95).* Blois, 1928.

Gally, M. *Notice sur les prêtres et religieuses de l'ancien archidiaconé d'Avallon insermentés et persécutés pendant la Révolution.* Tours, 1898.

Gane, Robert. "La querelle des dîmes dans la France rurale de 1750 à 1789," *Mémoires de l'Académie nationale de Metz,* 5e sér., vol. 15 (1971-72), 13-27.

Gard, Michel. *Le clergé du diocèse d'Orléans face à la persécution révolutionnaire de l'Orléanais.* Orléans, 1978.

Gaugain, Ferdinand. *Histoire de la Révolution dans la Mayenne,* 4 vols. Laval, 1919-21.

Gildea, Robert and Michel Lagrée. "The Historical Geography of the West of France: the Evidence of Ille-et-Vilaine," *English Historical Review,* 94 (1979), 830-47.

Gillet, Pierre. "Le drame des prêtres jureurs: Jacques-Martin Dupuis (1757-1838)," *Mémoires de la Société d'agriculture, commerce, sciences et arts du département de la Marne,* 92 (1977), 231-32.

Girardot, Jean. "La Constitution civile du clergé et son application en

Haute-Saône," *Bulletin de la Société d'agriculture, lettres, sciences, et arts du département de la Haute-Saône* (1933), 27-28.

————. "Clergé réfractaire et clergé constitutionnel en Haute-Saône pendant la Révolution," *Mémoires de la Société pour l'histoire du droit et des institutions des anciens pays bourguignons, comtois et romands*, 24 (1963), 123-32.

————. "Conseils pratiques pour l'étude de la Révolution en Haute-Saône," *Bulletin de l'histoire économique et sociale de la Révolution française* (1964), 3e partie, 97-107.

————. *Le département de la Haute-Saône pendant la Révolution*, 3 vols. Vesoul, 1973.

Giraud, Maurice. *Essai sur l'histoire religieuse de la Sarthe de 1789 à l'an IV*. Paris, 1920.

Girault, Charles. *Les biens d'Eglise dans la Sarthe à la fin du XVIIIe siècle*. Laval, 1953.

————. *Le clergé sarthois face au serment constitutionnel de 1790*. Laval, 1959.

Godechot, Jacques. *Les institutions de la France sous la Révolution et l'Empire*, 2nd ed. Paris, 1968.

Godel, Jean. *La reconstruction concordataire dans le diocèse de Grenoble après la Révolution*. Grenoble, 1968.

Golden, Richard. "The Mentality of Opposition: the Jansenism of the Parisian Curés during the Religious Fronde," *CHR*, 64 (1978), 565-80.

————. *The Godly Rebellion: Parisian Curés and the Religious Fronde, 1652-1662*. Chapel Hill, 1981.

Gonnet, Ernest. *Essai sur l'histoire du diocèse du Puy-en-Velay (1789-1802)*. Paris, 1907.

Gouesse, Jean-Marie. "Assemblées et associations cléricales, synodes et conférences ecclésiastiques dans le diocèse de Coutances aux XVIIe et XVIIIe siècles," *Annales de Normandie*, 24 (1974), 37-71.

Greenbaum, Louis. *Talleyrand, Statesman Priest. The Agent-General of the Clergy and the Church of France at the End of the Old Regime*. Washington, 1970.

Greer, Donald. *The Incidence of the Terror during the French Revolution. A Statistical Interpretation*. Cambridge, Mass., 1935.

Grégoire, Henri, *Mémoires*, 2 vols. H. Carnot, ed. Paris, 1840.

Grégoire, P. *Etat du diocèse de Nantes en 1790*. Nantes, 1882.

Greyerz, Kaspar von, ed. *Religion and Society in Early Modern Europe, 1500-1800*. London, 1984.

Gros, L. *Le clergé de Maurienne pendant la Révolution (1792-1802)*. Chambéry, 1965.

Gruart, Léon. *Le diocèse de Senlis et son clergé pendant la Révolution*. Senlis, 1979.

Guillaume, P. *Essai sur la vie religieuse dans l'Orléanais de 1789 à 1801*, n.p., n.d.

Guillemaut, Lucien. *Histoire de la Révolution dans le Louhannais (1789-1792)*. Louhans, 1899.

Guilliot, O. "Les curés-maires des districts de Grandpré et de Vouziers pendant la Révolution," *Nouvelle revue de Champagne et de Brie*, 8 (1930), 31-45.

Guitraud, Roger. "L'attitude du clergé girondin devant le serment constitutionnel," *Revue historique de Bordeaux et du département de la Gironde*, n.s., 14 (1965), 117-30.

Guyot, Charles. "La communauté des enfants-prêtres de la paroisse de Mirecourt," *Mémoires de la Société d'archéologie lorraine*, 42 (1982), 154-87.

Hardy, G. "L'anticléricalisme paysan dans une province française avant 1789: le Berry," *Annales révolutionnaires*, 5 (1912), 605-24.

Haristoy, Abbé. *Les paroisses du pays basque pendant la période révolutionnaire*, 2 vols. Pau, 1895-99.

Hayden, J. Michael. *France and the Estates General of 1614*. Cambridge, 1974.

Heinrichs, K. *Die politische Ideologie des französischen Klerus bei Beginn der grossen Revolution*. Berlin, 1934.

Hoffman, Philip T. *Church and Community in the diocese of Lyon, 1500-1789*. New Haven, 1984.

——. "The Church and the Rural Community in the 16th and 17th Centuries," *Proceedings of the 6th Meeting of the Western Society for French History. San Diego 1978*. Santa Barbara, 1979, 46-54.

Hood, James N. "The Riots in Nîmes in 1790." Ph.D. dissertation, Princeton University, 1968.

——. "Protestant-Catholic Relations and the Roots of the First Popular Counterrevolutionary Movement in France," *JMH*, 43 (1971), 245-75.

Houdailles, Jacques. "La célébration saisonnière des mariages avant, pendant et après la Révolution française," *Population*, 33 (1978), 367-80.

Hufton, Olwen. "Women in Revolution, 1789-1796," *Past and Present*, 53 (1971), 90-108.

Hunt, Lynn Avery. *Revolution and Urban Politics in Provincial France*. Stanford, 1978.

———. "The Rhetoric of Revolution in France," *History Workshop*, 15 (1983), 78-94.

———. "The Political Geography of Revolutionary France," *Journal of Interdisciplinary History*, 14 (1984), 535-59.

———. *Politics, Culture, and Class in the French Revolution*. Berkeley, 1984.

Hutt, Maurice G. "The Role of the Curés in the Estates General of 1789," *Journal of Ecclesiastical History*, 6 (1955), 190-220.

———. "The Curés and the Third Estate: the Ideas of Reform in the Pamphlets of the French Lower Clergy in the Period, 1787-1789," *Journal of Ecclesiastical History*, 8 (1957), 74-92.

Hyslop, Beatrice. *French Nationalism in 1789 According to the General Cahiers*. New York, 1934.

———. *A Guide to the General Cahiers of 1789*. New York, 1936.

Izard, Frédéric. "Le clergé paroissial gévaudanais à la fin du XVIIIe siècle." Mémoire de maîtrise, Université de Montpellier III, 1978.

Jarnoux, Adolphe. *La Loire leur servit de linceul*. Quimper, 1972.

Jérôme, Louis. *Les élections et les cahiers du clergé lorrain aux Etats-Généraux de 1789*. Paris, 1899.

Jolivet, Charles. *La Révolution en Ardèche*. Largentière, 1930.

Jones, Peter M. "*La République au village* in the southern Massif-Central," *The Historical Journal*, 23 (1980), 793-812.

———. "Parish, Seigneurie and the Community of Inhabitants in Southern Central France during the Eighteenth and Nineteenth Centuries," *Past and Present*, 91 (1981), 74-108.

Joutard, Philippe. *La légende des Camisards*. Paris, 1977.

Julia, Dominique. "La réforme posttridentine en France d'après les procès-verbaux de visites pastorales: ordre et résistances" in *La società religiosa nell'età moderna. Atti del convegno studi di storia sociale e religiosa. Cupaccio-Paestum, 18-21 maggio 1972*. Naples, 1973, 311-97.

Kaminski-Parisot de Bernecourt, Anne-Marie. "Les curés de campagne en Franche-Comté au XVIIIe siècle." Thèse, Ecole des chartes, 1975.

Kaplan, Steven L. *The Famine Plot Persuasion in Eighteenth-Century France*. Philadelphia, 1982.

Kastener, Jean. "Nicolas Halanzeir, curé assermenté de Plombières, 1790-An II," *Révolution dans les Vosges*, 21 (1932), 13-30.

Kennedy, Michael L. *The Jacobin Club in the French Revolution. The First Years*. Princeton, 1982.

Kerviler, René. *Recherches et notices sur les députés de la Bretagne aux Etats-Généraux*, 2 vols. Rennes, 1889.

Kreiser, B. Robert. *Miracles, Convulsions, and Ecclesiastical Politics in Eighteenth-Century Paris*. Princeton, 1978.

Lacouture, Joseph. "La Constitution civile du clergé dans les Landes," *Bulletin de la Société de Borda*, 52 (1928), 89-94, 171-74, 239-45; 53 (1929), 21-24, 91-97, 161-69, 221-27; 56 (1932), 75-84; 57 (1933), 140-51.

―――. *La politique religieuse de la Révolution*. Paris, 1940.

Laffon, Jean-Baptiste. *Le diocèse de Tarbes et de Lourdes*. Paris, 1971.

Laffont, A. "Notes sur le clergé de Lombez pendant la Révolution," *Revue de Gascogne*, n.s., 15 (1920), 278-82.

―――. "Assermentés et insermentés du diocèse de Lombez," *Revue de Gascogne*, n.s., 17 (1922), 84-87.

Lafforgue, Edmond. *Le clergé du diocèse de Tarbes sous l'Ancien régime*. Tarbes, 1929.

Lagger, Louis de. *L'état administratif des anciens diocèses d'Albi, de Castres, et de Lavaur*. Paris, 1921.

―――. "La crise religieuse de la Révolution dans le Tarn," *Bulletin de la littérature ecclésiastique*, 58 (1957), 25-51.

―――. "L'église dans le Tarn: l'Ancien régime à son déclin," *Revue du Tarn*, 3e sér., 7 (1957), 217-41.

La Gorce, Pierre de. *Histoire religieuse de la Révolution*, 5 vols. Paris, 1909-24.

Lagrée, Michel. *Mentalités, religion et histoire en Haute-Bretagne au XIXe siècle. Le diocèse de Rennes, 1815-1848*. Paris, 1977.

Lahache, Abbé. "Notes d'histoire diocésaine," *Semaine religieuse du diocèse de Saint-Dié*, 34 to 38 (1910-14), *passim*.

Lajusan, Alfrèd. "La carte des opinions françaises," *Annales. E.S.C.*, 4 (1949), 406-414.

Lallié, A. *Le diocèse de Nantes pendant la Révolution*, 2 vols. Nantes, 1893.

Lançon, Pierre. "Les confréries du Rosaire en Rouergue aux XVIe et XVIIe siècles," *Annales du Midi*, 96 (1984), 121-33.

Langlois, Claude. *Le diocèse de Vannes, 1800-1830*. Paris, 1974.

―――. "Les effectifs des congrégations féminines au XIXe siècle," *RHEF*, 60 (1974), 39-64.

―――. *Le catholicisme au féminin: les congrégations françaises à supérieure générale au XIXe siècle*. Paris, 1984

―――. "Le serment de 1791 et la pratique religieuse des Catholiques aux dix-neuvième et vingtième siècles," in *Procèedings of the Eleventh*

Annual Meeting of the Western Society for French History, John F. Sweet, ed. Lawrence, Kansas, 1984, 166-75.

Lastic-Saint-Jal, Vicomte. *L'église et la Révolution à Niort et dans les Deux-Sèvres*. Niort, 1870.

Latreille, André. *L'Eglise catholique et la Révolution française*, 2 vols. Paris, 1946-50.

Laugier, François. *Le schisme constitutionnel et la persécution dans le Var*. Draguignan, 1897.

Le Bras, Gabriel. "Les confréries chrétiennes, problèmes et propositions," *Revue historique de droit français et étranger*, 4e sér., 19-20 (1940-41), 310-63.

————. *Introduction à l'histoire de la pratique religieuse*, 2 vols. Paris, 1942-45.

————. *Etudes de sociologie religieuse*, 2 vols. Paris, 1955-56.

Lebrun, François, ed. *L'histoire des Catholiques en France*. Toulouse, 1980.

————, ed. *Le diocèse d'Angers*. Paris, 1981.

Lecestre, L. *Abbayes, prieurés et couvents d'hommes en France. Liste générale d'après les papiers de la Commission des réguliers en 1768*. Paris, 1902.

Lecler, A. *Martyrs et confesseurs de la foi du diocèse de Limoges pendant la Révolution française*, 4 vols. Limoges, 1897-1904.

Leclercq, Henri. *L'Eglise constitutionnelle (juillet 1790-avril 1791)*. Paris, 1934.

Leclère, Adhémard. *La Révolution à Alençon*, 2 vols. Alençon and Paris, 1912-14.

Lecoq, Frédéric. *Documents authentiques pour servir à l'histoire de la Constitution civile du clergé dans le département de la Mayenne*. Laval, 1890.

Le Cornec, Yvonnick. "Les débuts de la contre-révolution dans les districts de Saint-Brieuc et de Lamballe, 1789-1793," Mémoire de maîtrise, Université de Rennes II, 1976.

Ledré, Charles. *L'église de France sous la Révolution*. Paris, 1949.

Le Falher, J. *Le royaume de Bignan (1789-1805)*. Hennebont, 1913.

Lefebvre, Georges. *Les paysans du Nord pendant la Révolution française*. Paris, 1924.

Leflon, Jean. *La crise révolutionnaire, 1789-1846*. Paris, 1949.

————. "Le clergé des Ardennes et la Constitution civile," *Présence ardennaise*, 13 (1952), 4-12.

————. "Armand-Jules Seraine, curé constitutionnel de Saint-Remi (Reims)," *Etudes champenoises*, 2 (1976), 55-66.

Le Gac, Jean-Luc, "Les confréries de dévotion dans le diocèse de Vannes aux XVIIe et XVIIIe siècles," Mémoire de maîtrise, Université de Rennes II, 1980.

Légé, Joseph. *Les diocèses d'Aire et de Dax ou le département des Landes sous la Révolution française, 1789-1803*, 2 vols. Aire, 1875.

Le Goff, T.J.A. *Vannes and Its Region: A Study of Town and Country in Eighteenth-Century France*. Oxford, 1981.

Le Goff, T.J.A. and D.M.G. Sutherland. "Religion and Rural Revolt in the French Revolution: An Overview," in *Religion and Rural Revolt*, Janos M. Bak and Gerhard Benecke, eds. Manchester, 1984.

Le Goué, Pierre. "Aspects sociaux du problème religieux en Ille-et-Vilaine, 1789-1793," D.E.S., Université de Rennes II, 1970.

Le Grand, Léon. *Les sources de l'histoire religieuse de la Révolution aux Archives nationales*. Paris, 1914.

Lemaire, Suzanne. *La Commission des réguliers*. Paris, 1926.

Lemaître, Nicole. "La communauté des prêtres-filleuls d'Ussel à la fin de l'Ancien régime," *ACSS*, 102 (1977), 1:295-309.

―――. "Pour l'indépendance des curés au XVIIIe siècle: le curé de la cathédrale contre son évêque," *Actes du colloque du VIIe centenaire de la cathédrale de Rodez. Rodez, 20 mai 1977* (Rodez, 1979).

Lemarchand, G. "Le féodalisme dans la France rurale des temps modernes: essai de caractérisation," *AHRF*, 41 (1969), 77-108.

Lemarchand, P., ed. "Journal d'un curé de campagne du XVIIIe siècle (Georges-Pierre-Félicité de Lamarre)," *Bulletin et mémoires de la Société d'émulation des Côtes-du-Nord*, 88 (1960), 56-97.

Lemasson, Auguste. *Les paroisses et le clergé du diocèse actuel de Saint-Brieuc de 1789 à 1815*, 2 vols. Rennes, 1926-28.

Le Mée, René. "Population agglomérée, population éparse au début du XIXe siècle," *Annales de démographie historique, 1971*. Paris, 1972, 467-93.

Le Mené, Joseph-Marie. *Histoire du diocèse de Vannes*, 2 vols. Vannes, 1888-89.

Lemoine, Henri. "Le clergé rural en Seine-et-Oise pendant la Révolution," *Revue de l'histoire de Versailles*, 55 (1965), 91-102.

Lemonnier, P. *Le clergé de la Charente-Inférieure pendant la Révolution*. La Rochelle, 1905.

Lempereur, L. *Etat du diocèse de Rodez en 1771*. Rodez, 1906.

Le Roy Ladurie, Emmanuel and André Zysberg. "Géographie des hagiotoponymes en France," *Annales. E.S.C.*, 38 (1983), 1304-35.

Lesprand, P. *Le clergé de la Moselle pendant la Révolution. Les débuts de la Révolution et la suppression des ordres religieux*, 4 vols. Montguy-lès-Metz, 1934-39.

Le Sueur, F. *Le clergé picard et la Révolution*, 2 vols. Amiens, 1904-1905.

Levy, Joseph. "Les prêtres assermentés et insermentés du district de Colmar au commencement de la grande Révolution," *Bulletin ecclésiastique du diocèse de Strasbourg*, 49 (1930), 543-47.

Lévy-Schneider, Léon. *Le conventionnel Jeanbon Saint-André*, 2 vols. Paris, 1901.

Lewis, Gwynne, *The Second Vendée: The Continuity of Counter-revolution in the Department of Gard, 1789-1815*. Oxford, 1978.

Lhuillier, Thomas. "Un curé de campagne à l'époque de la Révolution: Romain Pichonnier," *Revolution française*, 34 (1898), 490-502.

Ligou, Daniel. *Documents sur le Protestantisme montalbanais au XVIIIe siècle*. Toulouse, 1955.

————. *Montauban à la fin de l'Ancien régime et au début de la Révolution*. Paris, 1958.

Loche, Adrien. *Les prêtres de la Drôme devant la Révolution*. Saint-Vallier, n.d.

Loupès, Philippe. "Le casuel dans le diocèse de Bordeaux aux XVIIe et XVIIIe siècles," *RHEF*, 57 (1972), 19-52.

Lucas, Colin. "The Problem of the Midi in the French Revolution," *Transactions of the Royal Historical Society*, 28 (1978), 1-25.

Luria, Keith. "Territories of Grace: Seventeenth-Century Religious Change in the Diocese of Grenoble," Ph.D. dissertation, University of California, Berkeley, 1982.

Mahaus, Joseph. "Le concours pour l'obtention des curés dans le diocèse de Vannes au XVIIIe siècle," *Mémoires de la Société d'histoire et d'archéologie de Bretagne*, 45 (1965), 41-52.

Maier, Hans. *Revolution und Kirche. Studien zur Frühgeschichte der christlichen Demokratie, 1789-1850*. Freiburg, 1959.

Mandon, Guy. "Les curés en Périgord au XVIIIe siècle," Thèse de 3e cycle, Université de Bordeaux III, 1979.

Mandrou, Robert. "Clergé tridentin et piété populaire: Thèses et hypothèses," *ACSS*, 99 (1974), 1:107-117.

———— et al. *Histoire des Protestants en France*. Toulouse, 1977.

Marcade, Jacques. "Curés congruistes et curés à portion congrue (le diocèse de Poitiers au XVIIIe siècle)," *Bulletin de la Société des antiquaires de l'Ouest*, sér. 4, 13 (1976), 613-31.

Marion, Henri. *La dîme ecclésiastique en France au XVIIIe siècle et sa suppression*. Bordeaux, 1912.

Marion Marcel. "Le recouvrement des impôts en 1790," *RH*, 121 (1916), 1-47.

————. *Dictionnaire des institutions de la France aux XVIIe et XVIIIe siècles*. Paris, 1923.

Markoff, John. "Who Wants Bureaucracy? French Public Opinion in 1789," Ph.D. dissertation, Johns Hopkins University, 1972.

Markoff, John and Gilbert Shapiro. "The Linkage of Data Describing Overlapping Geographical Units," *Historical Methods Newsletter*, 7 (1973), 34-46.

Martin, Eugène. *Histoire des diocèses de Toul, de Nancy et de Saint-Dié*, 3 vols. Nancy, 1903.

Martinelli, J. "Les serments de 1790 à 1792 dans l'Isère," D.E.S., Université de Grenoble II, 1971.

Marx, Roland. *Recherches sur la vie politique de l'Alsace pré-révolutionnaire et révolutionnaire*. Strasbourg, 1966.

————. *La Révolution et les classes sociales en Basse-Alsace*. Paris, 1974.

Mathiez, Albert. *Contributions à l'histoire religieuse de la Révolution française*. Paris, 1907.

————. *Rome et le clergé français sous la Constituante. La Constitution civile du clergé. L'affaire d'Avignon*. Paris, 1911.

Matter, José-Léon. "L'abbé Spol, ancien curé de Sailly (Moselle) en 1791, peint par lui-même," *Revue ecclésiastique du diocèse de Metz*, 46 (1939), 59-72, 87-98, 168-78.

Maurel, Joseph-Marie. *Histoire religieuse du département des Basses-Alpes pendant la Révolution*. Marseille, 1902.

Maury, André. "Sylvestre Agussol, curé de la Cavalerie, prêtre constitutionnel," *Revue du Rouergue*, 24 (1970), 27-54.

Mayeur, Jean-Marie. "Religion et politique. Une carte de la résistance aux inventaires, février-mars 1906," *Annales. E.S.C.*, 21 (1966), 1259-72.

Mazoyer, Louis. "L'application de l'Edit de 1787 dans le Midi de la France," *Bulletin de la Société de l'histoire du Protestantisme français*, 74 (1925), 149-76.

————. "La question protestante dans les cahiers des Etats-Généraux," *Bulletin de la Société de l'histoire du Protestantisme français*, 80 (1931), 41-73.

McManners, John. *French Ecclesiastical Society under the Ancien Régime. A Study of Angers in the Eighteenth Century*. Manchester, 1960.

————. *The French Revolution and the Church*. London, 1969.

McManners, John. "Aristocratic Vocations: the Bishops of France in the Eighteenth Century," *Religious Motivation, XVIth Meeting of the Ecclesiastical History Society.* Oxford, 1978, 305-25.

————. "Jansenism and Politics in the 18th Century," *Church, Society, and Politics. 13th and 14th Meetings of the Ecclesiastical Historical Society.* Oxford, 1975, 253-73.

Mellor, Alec. *Histoire de l'anticléricalisme français.* Paris, 1978.

Merley, Jean. *La Haute-Loire de la fin de l'Ancien régime aux débuts de la Troisième République*, 2 vols. Le Puy, 1974.

Mettrier, Henri. "Etat du clergé constitutionnel de la Haute-Marne d'après un document aux Archives nationales," *Mémoires de la Société des lettres, des sciences et des arts de Saint-Dizier*, 9 (1899-1903), 1-40.

Meuvret, Jean. "La situation matérielle des membres du clergé séculier dans la France du XVIIe siècle," *RHEF*, 54 (1968), 47-68.

Meyer, Jean-Claude. *La vie religieuse en Haute-Garonne sous la Révolution (1789-1801).* Toulouse, 1982.

Michel, Louis. "La dîme et les revenus du clergé d'Anjou à la fin de l'Ancien régime," *Annales de Bretagne*, 86 (1979), 565-605.

Millard, A. D. *Le clergé du diocèse de Châlons-sur-Marne. Première partie. Le serment.* Châlons-sur-Marne, 1903.

Minois, Georges. "Le problème de la portion congrue dans le Trégor au XVIIIe siècle," *Mémoires de la Société d'histoire et d'archéologie de Bretagne*, 56 (1979), 179-96.

————. "Les vocations sacerdotales dans le diocèse de Tréguier au XVIIIe siècle," *Annales de Bretagne*, 86 (1979), 45-57.

————. "Le rôle politique des recteurs de campagne en Basse-Bretagne (1750-1790)," *Annales de Bretagne*, 89 (1982), 153-65.

Moizo, Yves. "La contre-révolution dans le district de la Roche-Bernard (1789-1793)," Mémoire de maîtrise, Université de Rennes II, 1978.

Molinier, Alain. "Le Vivarais sous l'Ancien régime." Thèse de 3e cycle, Ecole des hautes études en sciences sociales, 1976.

Morembert, Henri de, ed. *Le diocèse de Metz.* Paris, 1970.

Mornet, Daniel. *Les origines intellectuelles de la Révolution française, 1715-1787.* Paris, 1933.

Mours, Samuel. *Le protestantisme en Vivarais et en Velay des origines à nos jours.* Valence, 1949.

————. *Les églises réformées en France: tableaux et cartes.* Paris, 1958.

————. *Le protestantisme en France au XVIIe siècle.* Paris, 1967.

Muchembled, Robert. *Culture populaire et culture des élites dans la France moderne.* Paris, 1978.

Nanglard, Jean. *Pouillé historique du diocèse d'Angoulême*, 3 vols. Angoulême, 1894-1900.

Necheles, Ruth. "The Curés in the Estates General of 1789," *JMH*, 46 (1974), 425-44.

Nivelle. *La constitution "Unigenitus" déférée à l'Eglise universelle ou Recueil général des actes d'appel*, 4 vols. Cologne, 1757.

Norberg, Kathryn. "Rich and Poor in Old-Regime Grenoble, 1600-1804," Ph.D. dissertation, Yale University, 1978.

———. "Women, the Family, and the Counter Reformation," *Proceedings of the 6th Annual Meeting of the Western Society for French History 1978*. Santa Barbara, 1979, 55-63.

Normand, Jean-Luc. "Un essai d'utilisation des registres des insinuations ecclésiastiques: étude sur les bénéfices ecclésiastiques du diocèse de Bayeux (1740-1790)," *Annales de Normandie*, 27 (1977), 295-319.

Obelkevich, James, ed. *Religion and the People, 800-1700*. Chapel Hill, North Carolina, 1979.

Orcibal, Jean. *Etat présent des recherches sur la répartition géographique des 'Nouveaux Catholiques' à la fin du XVIIe siècle*. Paris, 1948.

Ory, Jean-Marie. "Cahiers de doléances vosgiennes et mentalités prérévolutionnaires." D.E.S., Université de Paris, 1966.

———. "Les curés du diocèse de Toul en 1773 d'après les notes de l'abbé Chatrian," *Annales de l'Est*, 5e sér., 29 (1977), 29-70.

———. "Attitudes laïques devant le monde ecclésiastique en France au XVIIIe siècle," *Revue d'histoire et de philosophie religieuse*, 58 (1978), 399-424.

Paillard, Yvon-Georges. "Fanatiques et patriotes dans le Puy-de-Dôme: histoire religieuse d'un département de 1792 à Thermidor," *AHRF*, 42 (1970), 294-328.

Payrard, Charles. "Notes pour servir à l'histoire du Grand séminaire de Nevers (1653-1793)," *Bulletin de la Société nivernaise des lettres, des sciences et des arts*, 21 (1906), 1-86.

Pécheur, Louis-Victor. *Annales du diocèse de Soissons. Vol. VIII. La Révolution*. Soissons, 1891.

Perceveaux, Paul. "La portion congrue. Notes sur les conditions de vie du bas-clergé en Valromey au XVIIe et XVIIIe siècles," *Bulletin historique et archéologique du diocèse de Belley*, 22 (1967), 83-95.

Pernot, Michel. "Etude sur la vie religieuse de la campagne lorraine à la fin du XVIIe siècle. Le visage religieux du Xaintois, d'après la visite canonique de 1687," *Annales de l'Est, Mémoire no. 39*. Nancy, 1971.

Peronnet, Michel. "Les problèmes du clergé dans la société de l'Ancien régime de 1700 à 1789," in Roland Mousnier, *Société française de 1700 à 1789*, 2 vols. Paris, 1970, 1:17-58.

————. *Les évêques de l'ancienne France*. Lille, 1977.

Pérouas, Louis. "Saint Louis Grignion de Montfort," *XVIIe siècle*, no. 41 (1958), 375-95.

————. "Le nombre des vocations sacerdotales, est-il un critère valable en sociologie religieuse historique aux XVIIe et XVIIIe siècles," *ACSS*, 87 (1962), 35-40.

————. *Le diocèse de La Rochelle de 1648 à 1724*. Paris, 1964.

————. *Pierre-François Hacquet. Mémoires des missions des Montfortains dans l'Ouest (1740-1779)*. Fontenay-le-Comte, 1964.

————. *Grignion de Montfort*. Paris, 1966.

————. *Ce que croyait Grignion de Montfort*. Paris, 1973.

————. "La diffusion de la confrérie du Rosaire au XVIIe siècle dans les pays creusois," *Mémoires de la Société des sciences naturelles et archéologiques de la Creuse*, 38 (1975), 431-48.

————. "Le clergé creusois durant la période révolutionnaire," *Mémoires de la Société des sciences naturelles et archéologiques de la Creuse*, 39 (1976), 552-94.

Perrot, Jean-Claude. "La vie religieuse en Normandie sous l'Ancien régime et à l'époque révolutionnaire," *Annales de Normandie*, 10 (1960), 403-14.

Peter, J. and Charles Poulet. *Histoire religieuse du département du Nord pendant la Révolution*, 2 vols. Lille, 1930.

Petitfrère, Claude. "Les causes de la Vendée et de la Chouannerie: essai d'historiographie," *Annales de Bretagne*, 84 (1977), 75-101.

————. *Les Vendéens d'Anjou (1793). Analyse des structures militaires, sociales et mentales*. Paris, 1981.

————. "Paysannerie et militantisme politique en Anjou au début de la Révolution (1789-1793)," *Annales de Bretagne*, 89 (1982), 173-83.

Pierrard, Pierre, ed. *Le diocèse de Cambrai et de Lille*. Paris, 1978.

Pila, Claire. "Piété populaire en Beaujolais et Lyonnais au XVIIe et XVIIIe siècles," *Bulletin du Centre d'histoire économique et sociale de la région lyonnaise*, 4 (1977), 43-55.

Piolin, Paul. *L'église du Mans durant la Révolution*, 4 vols. Le Mans, 1868-71.

Pisani, Paul. *Répertoire biographique de l'épiscopat constitutionnel (1791-1802)*. Paris, 1907.

————. "Les derniers évêques de l'Ancien régime," *Correspondant*, 24 (1908), 490-515.

——. *L'église de Paris et la Révolution*, 4 vols. Paris, 1908-1911.

——. "Le serment de 1791," *Revue du clergé français*, 91 (1917), 481-94.

Playoust, Arlette. *La vie religieuse dans le diocèse de Boulogne au XVIIIe siècle (1725-1790)*. Arras, 1976.

Plongeron, Bernard. *Les réguliers de Paris devant le serment constitutionnel*. Paris, 1964.

——. "Une image de l'Eglise d'après les 'Nouvelles ecclésiastiques' (1728-1790)," *RHEF*, 53 (1967), 248-68.

——. "Autopsie d'une Eglise constitutionnelle: Tours de 1794 à 1802," *ACSS*, 93 (1968), 2:147-201.

——. *Conscience religieuse en révolution. Regards sur l'historiographie religieuse de la Révolution française*. Paris, 1969.

——. "Recherches sur l'Aufklärung catholique en Europe occidentale (1770-1830)," *RHMC*, 16 (1969), 555-605.

——. "Historiographie religieuse de l'époque révolutionnaire," *Recherches de science religieuse*, 58 (1970), 589-97.

——. *Théologie et politique au siècle des Lumières, 1770-1820*. Geneva, 1973.

——. "Théologie et politique au siècle des Lumières (1770-1820)," *AHRF*, 45 (1973), 437-53.

——. *La vie quotidienne du clergé français au XVIIIe siècle*. Paris, 1974.

——. "Le fait religieux dans l'histoire de la Révolution française," *AHRF* 47 (1975), 95-133.

——. "Le procès de la fête à la fin de l'Ancien régime," in *Le christianisme populaire*. Paris, 1976, 171-98.

Plongeron, Bernard and Robert Panet. *Le christianisme populaire*. Paris, 1976.

Plumet, Jules. *L'évêché de Tournai pendant la Révolution française*. Louvain, 1963.

Pocquet, Barthélémy. *Les origines de la Révolution en Bretagne*, 2 vols. Paris, 1885.

Poitrineau, Abel. *La vie rurale en Basse-Auvergne au XVIIIe siècle (1726-1789)*, 2 vols. Paris, 1965.

Poland, Burdette. *French Protestantism and the French Revolution*. Princeton, 1957.

Pommeret, Hervé. *L'esprit public dans le département des Côtes-du-Nord pendant la Révolution*. Saint-Brieuc, 1921.

Poole, Stafford. *A History of the Congregation of the Mission*. N.p., 1973.

Porée, Charles. *Cahiers des curés et des communautés ecclésiastiques du bailliage d'Auxerre pour les Etats-Généraux de 1789*. Auxerre, 1927.

Pourcher, Pierre. *L'épiscopat français et constitutionnel et le clergé de la Lozère durant la Révolution*, 3 vols. St. Martin de Bourbaux, 1896-1900.

Poyer, Alex. "Les curés de la Quinte du Mans au XVIIIe siècle (de 1723 au début de la Révolution)," *La Province de Maine*, 76 (1974), fasc. 12, 405-15, fasc. 13, 45-62.

Préclin, Edmond. *Les Jansénistes du XVIIIe siècle et la Constitution civile du clergé*. Paris, 1929.

Prévost, Arthur. *Histoire du diocèse de Troyes pendant la Révolution*, 3 vols. Troyes, 1908-1909.

————. *Répertoire biographique du clergé du diocèse de Troyes à l'époque de la Révolution*. Dijon, 1914.

Quéniart, Jean. *Les hommes, l'église, et Dieu dans la France du XVIIIe siècle*. Paris, 1978.

————. *Culture et société dans la France de l'Ouest au XVIIIe siècle*. Paris, 1978.

Quéruau-Lamerie, E. *Le clergé du département de Maine-et-Loire pendant la Révolution*. Angers, 1899.

Rameau, Barthélémy. *La Révolution dans l'ancien diocèse de Mâcon*. Mâcon, 1900.

Raulet, Jacques. "Les confréries de dévotion dans l'ancien diocèse de Saint-Brieuc, du concile de Trente à la Révolution," Mémoire de maîtrise, Université de Rennes II, 1981.

Ravenet, Chanoine. *Histoire religieuse du Louhannais au cours des années 1789-1802*. N.p., 1938.

Ravitch, Norman. "The Taxing of the Clergy in Eighteenth-Century France," *Church History*, 33 (1964), 157-74.

Rébillon, Armand. *La situation économique du clergé à la veille de la Révolution*. Rennes, 1913.

————. "La situation économique du clergé français à la fin de l'Ancien régime," *La Révolution française*, 82 (1929), 328-50.

Rebouillat, Marguerite. "La vie religieuse au XVIIIe siècle dans l'archiprêtré de Carlieu," *ACSS*, 96 (1971), 2:135-56.

Reinhard, Marcel. *Religion, Révolution et Contre-Révolution*. Paris, 1960.

La Religion populaire. Paris, 17-19 octobre 1977. (Colloques internationaux du Centre national de la recherche scientifique, no. 576.) Paris, 1979.

Renouvin, Pierre. *Les assemblées provinciales de 1787: origines, développement, résultats*. Paris, 1921.

Reuss, Rodolphe. *L'Alsace pendant la Révolution française*, 2 vols. Paris, 1881-84.

———. *L'église Luthérienne de Strasbourg au XVIIIe siècle*. Paris, 1892.

———. *Les églises Protestantes en Alsace pendant la Révolution (1789-1802)*. Paris, 1906.

———. *La Constitution civile du clergé et la crise religieuse en Alsace (1790-1795)*, 2 vols. Strasbourg, 1922.

Rey, Maurice, ed. *Les diocèses de Besançon et de Saint-Claude*. Paris, 1977.

Ricaud, Louis. *Un régime qui commence. Etudes sur les dix années de la Révolution dans les Hautes-Pyrénées*. Tarbes, 1911.

Richard, Antoine. "Les troubles agraires des Landes en 1791 et 1792," *AHRF*, 4 (1927), 564-77.

Richard, C. "L'application de la Constitution civile du clergé dans le département du Nord," *RHMC*, 12 (1909), 229-56.

Riollet, Marius. "Le journal d'un curé de compagne, 1768-1790," *Revue d'histoire de Lyon*, 10 (1911), 281-312.

Rives, Jean. *Dîme et société dans l'archevêché d'Auch au XVIIIe siècle*. Paris, 1976.

Robert, Daniel. *Les Eglises réformées en France (1800-1830)*. Paris, 1961.

Roche, Daniel. *Le siècle des Lumières en province*, 2 vols. Paris, 1978.

Roman, Joseph. *Le clergé des Hautes-Alpes pendant la Révolution*. Paris, 1899.

Roquet, H. *Observation de Me. Beucher, curé de Brûlon*. Le Mans, 1929.

Rose, R. B. "Tax Revolt and Popular Organization in Picardy, 1789-1791," *Past and Present*, no. 43 (1969), 92-108.

Rossignol, E. A. *Histoire de l'arrondissement de Gaillac pendant la Révolution*. Albi, 1895.

Roudaut, François. "Les cahiers de doléances de la sénéchaussée de Lesneven (1789)," *Annales de Bretagne*, 87 (1980), 493-531.

Rouvière, François. *Histoire de la Révolution française dans le département du Gard*, 2 vols. Nîmes, 1887-89.

———. *Les religionnaires des diocèses de Nîmes, Alais, et Uzès et la Révolution française*. Paris, 1889.

Roux, Marquis Marie de. *La Révolution à Poitiers et dans la Vienne*. Paris, 1911.

———. *Histoire religieuse de la Révolution à Poitiers et dans la Vienne*. Lyon, 1952.

Roy, Jean. "Le prêtre paroissial dans deux diocèses provençaux: Aix et Arles au XVIIIe siècle," Thèse de 3e cycle, Université d'Aix-Marseille, 1975.

Rudé, George. *The Crowd in the French Revolution*. Oxford, 1959.

Sabarthès, A. *Histoire du clergé de l'Aude de 1789 à 1803. Répertoire onomastique*. Carcassonne, 1939.

—. "La Constitution civile du clergé dans le département de l'Aude," *Bulletin de littérature ecclésiastique*, 60 (1959), 38-56, 135-49.

—. "L'organisation de l'Eglise constitutionnelle de l'Aude," *Bulletin de littérature ecclésiastique*, 62 (1961), 245-74.

Sage, Pierre. *Le "bon prêtre" dans la littérature française d'Amadis de Gaule au Génie du Christianisme*. Geneva, 1951.

Sagnac, Philippe. *La législation civile de la Révolution française (1789-1804)*. Paris, 1898.

—. "Etude statistique sur le clergé constitutionnel et le clergé réfractaire en 1791," *RHMC*, 8 (1906), 97-115.

—. "L'Eglise de France et le serment à la Constitution civile du clergé (1790-1791)," *Révolution française*, 53 (1907), 289-302.

— and C. Richard. "Le serment à la Constitution civile en 1791 dans la région du Nord," *Annales de l'Est et du Nord*, 3 (1907), 176-93.

Salvini, Joseph. "Clergé rural en Haut-Poitou à la veille de la Révolution," *Bulletin de la Société des antiquaires de l'Ouest*, 4e série, 4 (1957), 237-51.

Santini, Viviane. "Le clergé et la vie religieuse à Marseille pendant la Révolution de 1789-95." D.E.S., Université de Marseille, 1965.

Sarramon, Armand. *Les paroisses du diocèse de Comminges en 1786*. Paris, 1968.

Saurel, F. *Histoire religieuse du département de l'Hérault pendant la Révolution*, 4 vols. Paris, 1894-96.

Sauzay, Jules. *Histoire de la persécution révolutionnaire dans le département du Doubs de 1789 à 1801*, 10 vols. Besançon, 1867.

Sauzet, Robert. "Prédications et missions dans le diocèse de Chartres au début du XVIIIe siècle," *Annales de Bretagne*, 81 (1974), 491-500.

—. *Les visites pastorales dans le diocèse de Chartres pendant la première moitié du XVIIe siècle*. Rome, 1975.

—. *Contre-Réforme et Réforme catholique en Bas-Languedoc. Le diocèse de Nîmes au XVIIe siècle*. Louvain, 1979.

Savina, J. *Le clergé de Cornouaille à la fin de l'Ancien régime et sa convocation aux Etats-Généraux*. Quimper, 1926.

Schaer, André. "La francisation du clergé alsacien après la Guerre de Trente Ans (1675-1756)," *Bulletin ecclésiastique du diocèse de Strasbourg*, 84 (1965), 470-83.

————. *La vie paroissiale dans un doyenné alsacien d'Ancien régime (Colmar), 1648-1789.* Haguenau, 1971.

Schafer, B. C. "Quelques jugements de pamphlétaires sur le clergé à la veille de la Révolution," *AHRF*, 16 (1939), 110-22.

Scheidhauer, M. *Les églises luthériennes en France, 1800-1815, Alsace-Montbéliard-Paris.* Strasbourg, 1975.

Schmitt, Thérèse-Jeanne. *L'organisation ecclésiastique et la pratique religieuse dans l'archidiaconé d'Autun de 1650 à 1750.* Autun, 1957.

Schnerb, R. *Les contributions directes à l'époque de la Révolution dans le Puy-de-Dôme.* Paris, 1933.

Sciout, Ludovic. *Histoire de la Constitution civile du clergé (1790-1801)*, 4 vols. Paris, 1872-81.

Scott, Samuel. "The Problem of Law and Order during 1790, the 'Peaceful' Year of the French Revolution," *American Historical Review*, 80 (1975), 859-88.

Sée, Henri. "Les troubles agraires en Haute-Bretagne (1790-91)," *Bulletin d'histoire économique de la Révolution* (1920-21), 231-370.

Serres, Jean-Baptiste. *Histoire de la Révolution en Auvergne*, 10 vols. Paris, 1895-99.

Sévestre, Emile. *Organisation du clergé à la veille de la Révolution.* Paris, 1911.

————. *L'enquête gouvernementale et l'enquête ecclésiastique sur le clergé en Normandie et du Maine de l'an IX à l'an XIII*, 2 vols. Paris, 1913-18.

————. *L'acceptation de la Constitution civile du clergé en Normandie.* Paris, 1922.

————. *Liste critique des ecclésiastiques fonctionnaires publics insermentés et assermentés en Normandie (Janvier-Mai 1791).* Paris, 1922.

————. *Les problèmes religieux de la Révolution et de l'Empire en Normandie, 1787-1815*, 2 vols. Paris, 1924.

————. *Le personnel de l'Eglise constitutionnelle en Normandie, 1791-1795.* Paris, 1925.

————. *La vie religieuse dans les principales villes normandes pendant la Révolution (1787-1801). Troisième série. Manche.* Paris, 1943.

Shapiro, Gilbert, John Markoff, and Sasha Weitman. "Quantitative Studies of the French Revolution," *History and Theory*, 12 (1973), 163-91.

Sicard, Augustin. *L'ancien clergé de France. Tome II. Les évêques avant la Révolution.* Paris, 1899.

————. *Le clergé de France pendant la Révolution*, 3 vols. Paris, 1912-27.

Soboul, Albert. "Survivances 'féodales' dans la société rurale française au XIXe siècle," *Annales. E.S.C.*, 23 (1968), 965-86.

———. "A propos d'une thèse récente sur le mouvement paysan dans la Révolution française," *AHRF*, 45 (1973), 85-101.

———. "De l'Ancien régime à la Révolution: problème régional et réalités sociales," in *Régions et régionalisme dans la France du XVIIIe siècle à nos jours*. Paris, 1977, 25-54.

———. *Le clergé du Lot et le serment exigé des fonctionnaires publics ecclésiastiques*. Paris, 1927.

———. *La Révolution en Quercy*, 4 vols. Paris, 1932.

———. *L'Eglise de Cahors à l'époque moderne*. Paris, 1947.

———. *L'Eglise de Cahors au XVIIIe siècle*. Aurillac, 1948.

Soreau, Edmond. "La Révolution française et le prolétariat rural," *AHRF*, 9 (1932), 28-36, 116-27, 325-35.

Soulet, J. F. "Recherches récentes sur la vie religieuse dans la région gasco-pyrénéenne à l'époque moderne," *Revue de Pau et de Béarn*, 2 (1974), 97-109.

Staes, Jacques. "La vie religieuse dans l'archidiaconé de Josas à la fin de l'Ancien régime," Thèse, Ecole des chartes, 1969.

Starobinski, Jean. *1789. Les emblèmes de la raison*. Paris, 1979.

Strohl, Henri. *Le protestantisme en Alsace*. Strasbourg, 1950.

Sutherland, Donald. *The Chouans: the Social Origins of Popular Counter-revolution in Upper Brittany*. Oxford, 1982.

Tackett, Timothy. *Priest and Parish in Eighteenth-Century France*. Princeton, 1977.

———. "The Citizen Priests: Politics and Ideology among the Parish Clergy of Eighteenth-Century Dauphiné," *Studies in Eighteenth-Century Culture*, 7 (1978), 307-328.

———. "L'histoire sociale du clergé diocésain dans la France du XVIIIe siècle," *RHMC*, 26 (1979), 198-234.

———. "The West in France in 1789: The Religious Factor in the Origins of the Counterrevolution," *JMH*, 54 (1982), 715-45.

———. "Les revenus des curés à la fin de l'Ancien régime: esquisse d'une géographie," in *La France d'Ancien régime. Etudes réunies en l'honneur de Pierre Goubert*, Alain Croix, Jean Jaquart, and François Lebrun, eds. Toulouse, 1984.

———. "French Clericalism under the Old Regime and the Ecclesiastical Oath of 1791," in *Proceedings of the Eleventh Annual Meeting of the Western Society for French History*, John F. Sweet, ed. Lawrence, Kansas, 1984, 156-65.

Tackett, Timothy and Claude Langlois. "Ecclesiastical Structures and Clerical Geography on the Eve of the French Revolution," *FHS*, 11 (1980), 715-45.

Tallett, Frank. "Religion and Revolution: the Rural Clergy and Parishioners of the Doubs, 1780-1797," Ph.D. thesis, University of Reading, 1981.

Taveneaux, René. *Le Jansénisme en Lorraine*. Paris, 1960.

Tavernier, Claude. *Le diocèse du Puy pendant la Révolution*. Le Puy, 1938.

―――. "Le clergé du district de Brioude devant la Constitution civile du clergé," *Almanach de Brioude*, 38 (1958), 31-51.

―――. "Le clergé réfractaire dans le Brivadois," *Almanach de Brioude*, 46 (1966), 91-110.

―――. "Le clergé constitutionnel dans le Brivadois de 1791 à 1794," *Almanach de Brioude*, 47 (1967), 29-59.

Taylor, George V. "Revolutionary and Non-Revolutionary Content in the *Cahiers* of 1789," *FHS*, 7 (1972), 479-502.

Thédenat, H. *Journal d'un prêtre lorrain pendant la Révolution (1791-99)*. Paris, 1912.

Thiriet, H. J. *L'abbé Chatrian, 1732-1814, sa vie et ses écrits*. Nancy, 1890.

Tilly, Charles. "Civil Constitution and Counter-Revolution in Southern Anjou," *FHS*, 1 (1959), 172-99.

―――. *The Vendée: A Sociological Analysis of the Counterrevolution of 1793*. Cambridge, Mass., 1964.

―――. *From Mobilization to Revolution*. Reading, Mass., 1978.

Todd, Emmanuel and Hervé Le Bras. *L'invention de la France*. Paris, 1981.

Torreilles, Philippe. *Histoire du clergé dans le département des Pyrénées-Orientales pendant la Révolution française*. Perpignan, 1890.

Toussaint, Joseph. "Le recrutement des prêtres dans le diocèse de Coutances au XVIII siècle," *Semaine religieuse de Coutances et d'Avranches*, 107 (1971), 212-15.

Trénard, Louis. "Eglise et état: le clergé face à la Révolution dans les diocèses du Nord de la France, 1788-1792," in *Christianisme et Pouvoirs politiques*. Lille, 1973, 57-90.

―――. "Les Lumières dans les Pays-Bas français," *Dix-huitième siècle*, 10 (1978), 123-45.

Trésal, J. "Le débat sur la Constitution civile du clergé," *Revue du clergé français*, 36 (1903), 472-88.

Tribout, Henri. *La Révolution dans l'Eure. Le journal d'un curé d'Evreux, 1788-1792*. Evreux, 1934.

Turner, Victor. *The Ritual Process. Structure and Anti-Structure*. Chicago, 1969.

Ultée, Maarten. "The Suppression of *Fêtes* in France, 1666," *CHR*, 62 (1976), 181-99.

Vaissière, Pierre de. *Curés de campagne de l'ancienne France*. Paris, 1932.

Van Kley, Dale. *The Jansenists and the Expulsion of the Jesuits, 1757-65*. New Haven, 1975.

————. "Church, State, and the Ideological Origins of the French Revolution: The Debate over the General Assembly of the Gallican Clergy in 1765," *JMH*, 51 (1979), 629-66.

————. *The Damiens Affair and the Unraveling of the Ancien Regime, 1750-1770*. Princeton, 1984.

Vasseur, Gaston. "Le curé de Vron de l'Ancien régime à la Révolution," *Bulletin de la Société d'émulation historique et littéraire d'Abbeville*, 20 (1957), 59-74.

Vaussard, Maurice. "Eclaircissements sur la Constitution civile du clergé," *AHRF*, 42 (1970), 287-93.

Venard, Marc. *L'Eglise d'Avignon au XVIe siècle*, 5 vols. Lille, 1980.

Verlaguet, P.-A. *Notices sur les prêtres du Rouergue déportés pendant la période révolutionnaire*, 4 vols. Rodez, 1927-32.

Vernus, Michel. "Le clergé du doyenné de Lons-le-Saunier, diocèse de Besançon (1662-1790)." Thèse de 3e cycle, Université de Nancy, 1975.

Vidal, Pierre. *Histoire de la Révolution française dans le département des Pyrénées-Orientales*, 3 vols. Perpignan, 1885-89.

Viguerie, Jean de. *Une oeuvre d'éducation sous l'Ancien régime. Les pères de la Doctrine chrétienne en France et en Italie*. Paris, 1976.

————. "Les fondations et la foi du peuple chrétien. Les fondations de messes en Anjou aux XVIIe et XVIIIe siècles," *RH* 256 (1976), 289-320.

Vivier, M. E. "La condition du clergé séculier dans le diocèse de Coutances au XVIIIe siècle," *Annales de Normandie*, 2 (1952), 3-2.

Vovelle, Michel. "Les troubles sociaux en Provence, 1750-1792," *ACSS*, 93 (1968), 2:325-72.

————. *La chute de la monarchie*. Paris, 1972.

————. *Piété baroque et déchristianisation. Attitudes provençales devant la mort au siècle des Lumières d'après les clauses des testaments*. Paris, 1973.

————. "L'élite ou le mensonge des mots," *Annales. E.S.C.*, 29 (1974), 49-72.

————. *Religion et Révolution: la déchristianisation de l'an II*. Paris, 1977.

————. "Formes de politisation de la société rurale en Provence sous la Révolution française," *Annales de Bretagne*, 89 (1982), 185-204.

————. "Géographie des confréries à l'époque moderne," *RHEF*, 69 (1983), 259-68.

Wahl, Maurice. *Les premières années de la Révolution à Lyon (1788-1792)*. Paris, 1894.

Weber, Eugen. *Peasants into Frenchmen: The Modernization of Rural France, 1870-1914*. Stanford, 1976.

Weitman, Sasha. "Bureaucracy, Democracy, and the French Revolution," Ph.D. dissertation, Washington University, 1968.

Welter, Louise. "Les communautés de prêtres dans le diocèse de Clermont du XIIIe au XVIIIe siècle," *RHEF*, 35 (1949), 5-35.

————. *La réforme ecclésiastique du diocèse de Clermont au XVIIe siècle*. Paris, 1956.

Wemyss, Alice. "Les Protestants du Midi pendant la Révolution," *Annales du Midi*, 69 (1957), 307-22.

————. *Les Protestants du Mas-d'Azil, histoire d'une résistance, 1680-1830*. Toulouse, 1961.

Williams, William H. "Voltaire and the Utility of the Lower Clergy," *Studies on Voltaire and the Eighteenth Century*, 58 (1967), 1869-74.

Index

The following index does not include Appendices II, III, IV, and V. Anyone interested in the local history of the oath should also consult these appendices. Insofar as possible, the spelling of place names has been modernized. Present-day departments are indicated in parentheses. Abbreviations: c. = curé; bs. = bishop or archbishop; dp. = deputy to National Assembly; prt. = priest; vc. = vicaire.

LIBRARY OF CONGRESS CATALOGING IN PUBLICATION DATA

Tackett, Timothy, 1945-
Religion, revolution, and regional culture in eighteenth-century France.

Bibliography: p.   Includes index.
1. Catholic Church—France—History—18th century.   2. Catholic
Church—France—Clergy—History—18th century.   3. France—History—Revolution, 1789-1799—Religious history.   4. France—Church history—18th century.   I. Title.

BX1530.T3   1986   944.04′1   85-43317
ISBN 0-691-05470-3 (alk. paper)